standard catalog of®
THUNDERBIRD
1955-2004

MW00843519

Jerry Heasley photo

John Gunnell

Published by

700 East State Street • Iola, WI 54990-0001
715-445-2214 • 888-457-2873
www.krause.com

Please call or write for our free catalog of publications. Our toll-free number to place an order or obtain a free catalog is (800) 258-0929.

Library of Congress Catalog Number: 2003115034

ISBN: 0-87349-756-2

Edited by Brian Earnest

Designed by Jamie Griffin

Front cover photography by Mike Mueller and Daniel B. Lyons
Back cover photography by Daniel B. Lyons

Foreword

The concept behind Krause Publications' Standard Catalogs of American Cars is to compile massive amounts of information about motor vehicles and present it in a standard format that the hobbyist, collector, or professional dealer can use to answer some commonly asked questions.

Those questions include: What year, make and model is my vehicle? What did it sell for when it was new? How rare is it? What is special about it? In our general automotive catalogs, some answers are provided by photos and others are provided by the fact-filled text. In our special one-marque catalogs, such as *The Standard Catalog of Thunderbird 1955-2004*, additional information, such as paint color charts and specific facts about Thunderbird history, are included throughout the book.

Chester L. Krause, the founder of Krause Publications, is responsible for the basic concept behind the Standard Catalog of American Cars series. Automotive historian David V. Brownell undertook preliminary work on the concept while editing *Old Cars Weekly* in the 1970s. John A. Gunnell edited the first of the *Standard Catalogs of American Cars* in 1978. Krause books department publisher Bill Krause (no relation to "Chet") originated the series of single-model color catalogs that first appeared in 2000. Since then, catalogs on Corvettes, Mustangs, Firebirds, Camaros, Chevelles and Pontiac Tempest/LeMans/GTO-based models have evolved. These catalogs are not the work of one person and many well-known historians and car collectors have contributed to them over the past 25 years.

No claims are made that these catalogs are infallible. They are not repair manuals or "bibles" for motor vehicle enthusiasts. They are meant as a contribution to the pursuit of greater knowledge about many wonderful vehicles. They are much larger in size, broader in scope, and more deluxe in format than most other collector guides, buyer's guides, or price guides.

The long-range goal of Krause Publications is to make all of our Standard Catalogs of American Cars (and trucks) as accurate as possible. At the same time, we expect they will always raise new questions and bring forth new facts that were not previously unearthed. We maintain an ongoing file of new research, corrections, and additional photos that are used regularly to update, refine, and expand our standard catalogs.

This first edition of *The Standard Catalog of Thunderbird 1955-2004* was compiled by the experienced editorial team at Krause Publications' books division. In this first edition we have put particular emphasis on refining the Thunderbird-related vehicle identification number (VIN) information, on better organizing Thunderbird engine options, and on reducing the number of codes and abbreviations used so that the overall book is more "reader friendly." Readers will find full-color photos of Thunderbird models from the classic two-seaters of 1955-1957 to today's popular "retro" 'Bird.

Should you have knowledge or photos of cars that you wish to see in future editions of this book, please don't hesitate to contact the editors at *The Standard Catalog of Thunderbird 1955 2004*, editorial department, 700 East State Street, Iola, WI 54990.

This first edition of the Standard Catalog of Thunderbird *1955-2004 is dedicated to the late Dr. Richard L. Schatz, who made invaluable contributions to Krause Publications' book* T-Bird: 40 Years of Thunder, *published in 1995. The following thoughts are edited from a memoriam written by his daughter, Amy.*

—John Gunnell

Dr. Richard L. Schatz
January 9, 1941 - January 23, 2003

My father died suddenly January 23, 2003. Dad was a founding member of the International Thunderbird Club and the editor-in-chief of the club magazine, *The Script*. Besides being a doctor for about 60 hours a week, he spent at least 20 hours working on *The Script* and helping ITC grow.

Dad loved Thunderbirds, but more importantly, he loved people. Winning an award was not as important to him as reuniting with old friends—laughing and having a good time. Many of the people he considered very dear friends were not those he knew all his life, but those he met through the hobby.

My father had a good and happy life and I know that he was glad—as I am—that Thunderbirds were a part of it.

— Amy Schatz

Acknowledgments

The following individuals made direct or indirect contributions to the Thunderbird facts contained in this catalog: Dean Batchelor, Gil Baumgartner, Jerry Capizzi (Cappy Collection), Bill Coombe, Dick Dance, Chad Elmore, International Thunderbird Club, Ron Kowalke, James T. Lenzke, Chuck Mill (Cappy Collection), James F. Petrik, Bill Randel (Collector's Den), Sandra L. Schatz, Dr. Richard L. Schatz, Alan H. Tast (senior editor *Thunderbird Scoop*), Bob Welsch (Cappy Collection). Photo credits are given inside. Photos of the Cappy Collection cars are by the author.

Contents

Introduction

THUNDERBIRD: PAST, PRESENT AND FUTURE

Thunderbird history started in Paris, France, nearly a half-century ago. Since then, the flight of the Thunderbird has included classic two-seaters, cherished roadsters, convertibles and four-door models, as well as exciting hardtops and sedans — more than 4 million T-Birds in all. There has been the "square" look, the "projectile" look, the "jet aircraft" look, and the "luxury" look. Yet, through the years, through the many changes and near extinction, Thunderbird's uniqueness, individuality, and engineering innovations have survived.

As one writer put it: "The Thunderbird was brought to life by men who knew what good cars were at a time Ford Motor Company needed an exciting car — fast." Two men, Louis D. Crusoe and George Walker, were primarily responsible for the birth of the Thunderbird. Both were devoted to the automobile and its constant development and refinement. Crusoe, a millionaire lured out of retirement by Henry Ford II, was a businessman with a solid "feel" for the automobile market. As a Ford vice president and Ford Division general manager, it was his responsibility to strengthen a young Ford Division; to give it a car that breathed excitement; to create a car that would add prestige to the Ford name. Walker, later a Ford vice president and chief stylist, is described by contemporaries as a "stylist with the soul of an artist burning in his heart."

It was October 1951 when the two men were walking along the aisles of the Grand Palais in Paris that Crusoe gestured toward one of the sportier automobiles on display and turned to Walker. "Why can't we have something like that?" Crusoe asked. "We have a job just like that in the works right now," was Walker's quick response. It was not quite so, until Walker got to a telephone and told his aides back in Dearborn to go to work. By the time he and Crusoe returned to the United States, there was indeed a "job just like that" in the works.

In the months that followed, there was a lot of talk about a "true Ford sports car." Some preparations were made. "Paper sports cars" took shape in the design studios. All hands had been instructed to go to work on a completely new Ford car for the 1955 model year. Official approval of a crash program to develop the Ford sports car came in a product letter dated February 9, 1953. It set May 1, 1953, as the target date for a full-size clay model. The letter also authorized parallel work by the engineers on a suitable chassis. The initial guidelines called for a two-passenger, canvas-topped open car that "would make maximum use of standard production components." Design objectives included a weight of 2,525 lbs. an Interceptor V-8 engine, a balanced weight distribution, better acceleration than the competition, and a top speed of more than 100 mph.

The new Ford sports car also was "to retain Ford product

characteristics and identification to the extent necessary for a ready association with the standard production car." The Ford Design Studio was given basic styling responsibilities. With no time for scale-model studies and the like, the first sports car styling suggestions were full-profile, full-sized air-brush renderings on paper of five different cars, cut out and mounted so they could be viewed like automobiles on the highway. It was an effective, if unorthodox, technique. None of these proposals led directly to a final car, but each provided ideas for the full-size clay model that was taking shape.

While the clay model was being developed, other decisions were being made. The grille design would be a combination of the Ford's trademark arched upper shape and a Ferrari-style egg-crate mesh. For cost reasons, the new car would use the same taillights and headlight bezels as the 1955 Ford. A handsome hood scoop was executed to cover a bulge required to house the air cleaner. "Bullet-shaped" insets at the end of the bumpers carried twin exhaust tips, then the latest craze. On May 18, 1953, 17 days after his deadline, Crusoe saw a complete, painted clay model for the first time. It closely corresponded to the shape of the original production Thunderbird. Meanwhile, Chief Engineer Bill Burnett had cut up a Ford two-door sedan. He made it fit the 102-in. wheelbase of the sports car in order to test handling and brake balance.

By the summer of 1953, the car was far enough along for a decision to be made about building it. The decision came in September when Crusoe, in Paris to view the renowned sports cars of the world and measure them against the clay models back in Dearborn, decided the Ford car was right. Although production wouldn't begin until the fall of 1954, making the new car a 1955 model, Ford was anxious to tell the world about it. Only one small detail remained — a name for the car.

There were 5,000 names considered. Hep Cat, Beaver, and Detroiter were early, yet undistinguished frontrunners. Also suggested were Runabout, Arcturus, Savile, El Tigre, and Coronado. Crusoe was unimpressed and offered a $250 suit to anyone who could do better. A young Ford stylist, Alden "Gib" Giberson, submitted the name that would quickly earn approval and eventually acclaim: Thunderbird. He thought of the name because he had once lived in the Southwest, where the legend of the Thunderbird was well known. According to that legend, the Thunderbird ruled the sky and was a divine helper of man. The great wings — invisible to mortal man — created the winds and the thunder and provided rains in the arid desert, where fate had brought the Native Americans. The name was fitting for a car that has become an American icon.

Chief Stylist Frank Hersey, also a Southwesterner and an

enthusiast, spotted the name on Giberson's list and picked it for the new car. When it came time for Giberson to claim his prize, the modest young designer passed on what would have been the equivalent of a $800-$1,000 suit today and settled for $95 and an extra pair of trousers from Saks Fifth Avenue.

With the name selected and a couple of last-minute appearance changes made, the Ford Thunderbird was ready to go to market. Its initial public appearance took place on February 20, 1954, at Detroit's first postwar auto show. Thunderbird No. 1 came off the line at Ford Motor Company's Dearborn, Michigan, assembly plant on September 9, 1954. The press announcement of the new Ford sports car was September 23. It went on sale October 22, 1954, starting a legend that would grow with each new generation of Thunderbird cars.

The 1955 Thunderbird was more of a personal car concept than a sports car because of a decision that Crusoe made during the winter of 1953-1954. The car's more luxurious character created the personal-luxury car segment of the automotive market where the Thunderbird would enjoy almost uninterrupted leadership for decades.

The car was immediately a smash hit. Buyers of all ages and all walks of life described the car in terms such as "wonderful," a "masterpiece," "advanced automobile" and a "morale builder that is real fun and sport to drive."

The magic of the name and the impact of the car made it a natural merchandising tie-in for manufacturers of a wide range of goods — coats, jackets, shirts, shoes, rugs, furniture, and toys, to name a few. Magazines also featured the Thunderbird in promotional campaigns. The Powercar Company of Mystik, Connecticut, offered the Thunderbird Jr., a child's car powered by a 6-volt car battery and a Ford starter motor. *Mechanix Illustrated* offered a full-size Thunderbird as first prize in its 1955 Build Words Contest. Cluett-Peabody used the Thunderbird to promote and sell Arrow shirts. Worsted-Tex marketed Thunderbird-inspired coats, and many other clothiers used the car in promotions.

The public went for the Thunderbird in a big way, placing more than 3,500 orders in the first 10-day selling period. The planning volume for the entire model year was only 10,000 units. Ford had explored an uncharted market for unique transportation and came up with a winner.

However, with all of its popularity, the two-seat Thunderbird would have a short flight. There were changes almost immediately. The original design presented some problems. The cockpit needed better ventilation. Rear-quarter vision had to be improved. More trunk space was a necessity. Design changes on 1956 models corrected these deficiencies. Flip-out side vents provided improved ventilation, porthole windows enhanced rear vision, and an outside tire carrier added trunk space. In addition, the 1956 Thunderbird featured Ford's new safety concept of "packaging the passengers."

The 1957 Thunderbird was the first to have a fully padded dash surface. It featured optional Dial-O-Matic power seats and a radio that automatically adjusted the volume in proportion to the speed of the engine. It would be the last of the two-seaters. With production of 1958 models delayed, 1957 Thunderbird production continued for three extra months. The last one rolled off the assembly line December 13, 1957. An era had ended. Absolute evidence of the two-seat Thunderbird's impact on the motoring world came just four years after the last one was built when "Today Show" host Dave Garroway referred to it as "an American classic." Vic Take of Clayton, Missouri, heard the Garroway comment and took the first steps toward establishing the Thunderbird Club International. He was the club's first president. Today, Thunderbird clubs worldwide boast memberships in the tens of thousands.

The two-seat Thunderbird had given Ford Division the prestigious car it needed and sales exceeded planning volumes, but the economic realities of the time, the public's motoring needs and Ford's market share inhibited the potential of the car. Even as the two-seater was being designed, plans for a four-passenger car were on Ford's drawing board. Marketing research showed two-seaters were not being purchased by families with children. Seating capacity and price also restricted Thunderbird ownership to multi-car, upper-income families. Significant numbers of two-seater owners were interested in a four-passenger model so long as Thunderbird styling was maintained. Additionally, five percent of all car buyers said they'd purchase a Thunderbird if seating capacity were increased. Armed with this rationale, Ford ushered in 1958 by unveiling a four-passenger Thunderbird to a group of prominent Americans at a New Year's Eve Party at the exclusive Thunderbird Golf Club in Palm Springs, California. The public introduction was held later in January.

The 1958 Thunderbird retained the classic lines of the original Thunderbird, adding some classic styling touches of its own. The improvements included a one-piece grille and bumper, and clean contemporary rooflines that would set new styling standards for the industry. It had a low-slung, relaxed, reverse-wedge stance. Another leading feature was unit-body construction. The car boasted more room per passenger than any luxury car. Horsepower also was close to that of significantly bigger luxury cars. Styling features included: an anodized aluminum honeycomb-pattern grille, twin deeply browed headlights, a flat roofline, and twin taillights set over a honeycomb-pattern design. Inside, there were four individual bucket seats and a console that housed controls for the heater, air conditioner, power windows, radio speaker, and front and rear ashtrays.

Classified as a "semi-luxury" car, the 1958 Thunderbird was square in design, with few concessions to rounded corners, front or aft. It solidly established Ford Division in the luxury car market and was a sensation from the time it was introduced. The car lived up to all of its pre-introduction plaudits and was named *Motor Trend's* "Car of the Year." Sales totaled 48,482, almost matching two-seater deliveries for three years. Ford management's decision to drop the smaller car was almost immediately vindicated.

Thunderbird production was moved to Ford's Wixom (Michigan) assembly plant, where Lincoln luxury cars were built. As with the two-seaters, the bodies were built by the Budd Company in Philadelphia and shipped to Michigan for assembly. Two models, a hardtop and a convertible, were offered in 1958. The "little Bird's" tachometer and adjustable steering wheel were among the deleted items. Gone, too, was the semi-sports car ride of the two-seater. The unitized construction of the 1958 Thunderbird was a forerunner of this type construction in the industry. The 1960 Thunderbird was the first postwar American-built car to offer an optional sunroof.

In keeping with a three-year planning cycle, Thunderbird styling was again changed in 1961. This time, the now-established Ford Division flagship introduced the "projectile" design, featuring full-length body sculpturing and an even thinner roof than previous models. Standard equipment included automatic transmission, power steering and power brakes. A unique swing-away steering wheel — ordered by nearly 77 percent of all Thunderbird buyers — was optional.

The projectile styling introduced in 1961 continued through 1963, with the 1962 model offering more than 100 improvements and two exciting new models: a two-seater sports roadster, and a vinyl-covered Landau hardtop coupe. The swing-away steering wheel was made standard equipment. A new 30,000-mile disposable fuel filter was among 15 improvements, and oil change intervals were extended from 4,000 to 6,000 miles. A new factory-installed coolant needed changing only once every two years or 6,000 miles, eliminating the need for regular fall and spring cooling system changes.

The 1962 sports roadster was a grand experiment and the cult of "roadster" collectors quickly grew. It was an unusual car with a molded fiberglass tonneau and padded headrests that transformed the four-seat convertible into a two-seat car. Special features included wire wheels with chrome-plated spokes and rims, simulated knock-off hubcaps, and an assist bar for passenger comfort during cornering. Interestingly, the roadster had a special emblem — a gull-like bird, not a Thunderbird — superimposed over a red-white-and-blue crest that was mounted on the front fenders below the Thunderbird script.

The 1964 Thunderbird reverted partially to the square design theme. It was more angular than the 1961-1963 models, yet not as square as the 1958-1960 models. The new styling featured a longer hood, a shorter roofline and sculptured side panels. With the bumper and grille designed to provide a faster, more aerodynamic look, the overall styling continued the traditional image of "swift-lined sleekness." Interior design also reflected the space-age styling of the early and mid-1960s. Featured were

Daniel B. Lyons photo

luxuriously-padded, high, thin-shell contoured bucket seats, "pistol grip" door handles and a full-width safety-padded instrument panel. New options included individual reclining seats and trailer towing equipment. The 1966 edition offered Town Hardtop and Town Landau models. Windshield washers and vacuum door locks were added to the standard equipment list. Power six-way seats and a power antenna were new options. Ford discontinued the Thunderbird convertible after 1966, but a total of 70,234 four-seat convertibles were produced.

The Thunderbird grew a little more in 1967. Passenger capacity was increased to six. Jet aircraft-like design features included a long, thrusting hood and a short rear deck. The front end had a crisp lattice-work grille deeply inset and outlined with thin, bright metal moldings on the top and sides. The grille was framed at the bottom by a new deep-sectioned bumper that blended into the sheet metal. The headlights were concealed by doors at the outboard edges of the grille. Inside were newly sculptured twin bucket seats, a full-length console, all-vinyl door panels with full-length armrests trimmed in bright metal, and the all-new Tilt-Away steering wheel — an exceptionally popular Thunderbird comfort and convenience feature. A four-door model was added, but it didn't help sales very much and only 70,988 were built during the two years it was on the market. Today they rapidly gaining in value as collector cars.

The 1970 Thunderbird introduced new styling, featuring a long hood treatment and a unique bumper-and-grille treatment that made the bumper almost invisible. Other exterior design features included a new extruded-aluminum grille (the "poke-thru nose") flanked by dual headlights. A concealed radio antenna promoted a non-cluttered look and eliminated antenna noise. Concealed windshield wipers and cowl air vents provided a clean and "sweeping" line from the hood to the roof, and back-up lights were concealed in the center rear panel. Ultra-luxurious appointments on the inside included a standard full-width front bench seat with attractive, re-designed head restraints, individual bucket-style seatbacks, and a fold-down center armrest. Thick, padded armrests extended the full length of the front door panels. Safety innovations included a "Uni-Lock" three-point safety belt and shoulder harness system.

By 1971, the Thunderbird name and the car that wore it were so popular that the famed Nieman-Marcus department store offered "His and Her" Thunderbirds in their catalog as "gifts for the person who has everything" The twin Thunderbirds were equipped with telephones, tape recorders and other special equipment. They carried a price tag of $25,000 for the pair.

A new generation of even more luxurious Thunderbirds started with the 1972 model. Only a two-door hardtop was offered. The emphasis was on styling and comfort. Strikingly handsome and formal in appearance, it achieved new levels of luxury and comfort. Michelin steel-belted radial-ply tires and body-side protection moldings were standard. The standard power front disc brakes were designed to provide more positive braking and longer brake life than previous systems. The number of parts in the all-new braking system was reduced from 26 to 12 for even greater reliability and quicker service. The Sure-Track brake control system was added as optional equipment.

The Thunderbird reached its pinnacle as a personal luxury car with the 1975 model. Skipping the traditional three-year styling change, the 1975 design was basically the same as the previous model, except that the car was longer and heavier. The added length was there to accommodate a 460-cid V-8. Other standard refinements included: concealed windshield wipers, a distinctive opera window, a dense-grain vinyl roof, solid-state ignition, power side windows, an automatic seatback release, a spare tire lock, and white-sidewall steel-belted-radial tires. Available for the first time were power four-wheel disc brakes. Other options included power mini-vent windows, a Quick-Defrost windshield and rear window and a moonroof. The 1976 Thunderbird marked the end of another era. After this, the flight of the Thunderbird would change directions.

The 1977 T-Bird leaped into the high-volume, mid-size specialty-car market. The 1977 model was a slimmer and sleeker automobile, but retained many of the traditional Thunderbird styling touches. Appearance features were highlighted by a unique wrap-over roof treatment featuring beveled glass opera windows in the center pillars. Other distinctive features included a chrome-plated grille, hidden headlights and "wall-to-wall" taillights. The early 1980s saw a completely different direction for the Thunderbird, which became smaller and more angular. Targeted to a more conservative, economy-conscious customer, this car was not popular and lasted only two years.

Ford took the Thunderbird into a new design phase in the mid 1980s, introducing an "aero-style" coupe. The restyled Thunderbird burst onto the NASCAR circuit in 1982 and went on to win more than 150 races in NASCAR's top division, including four victories in the Daytona 500. For 1989, the Thunderbird was new from the ground up. It featured an exterior design that further reshaped aero-styling trends and was a leader in technology transfer from racing to production. The Thunderbird was among the first vehicles outfitted with Ford's next-generation electronic engine control module developed through Formula One racing.

Very few changes were made to the model during the early 1990s, as customer's tastes again shifted. The LX and Super Coupe models got a major restyling in 1994, with new rounded front and rear ends, but model-year production actually declined. Continuing sales drops led Ford to announce that the 1997 model would be the last Thunderbird — at least for a time. Jac Nasser, president of Ford's automotive operations at the time, declared that, although the old platform was going away, the Thunderbird nameplate would see a bright future in a very familiar form.

On January 3, 1999, Nasser lived up to his promise by unveiling a new two-seat concept car at the 1999 North American International Auto Show in Detroit. Featuring modern interpretations of the original 1955 Thunderbird's styling characteristics, the all-new "retro" T-Bird created a sensation among automotive buffs and industry observers. This new car brought Ford accolades and showroom traffic and was destined to carry on the Thunderbird namepate for three or four more years. The future of the model beyond 2005 or 2006 is a little hazy at present, but there have been hints that the Thunderbird will rise from the ashes again when the time is right.

(Based on a 1999 Ford Thunderbird press release)

The beautiful inaugural 'Bird was one of the best-looking cars on the market, according to *Motor Trend*. Collectors and car buffs over the years have agreed.

1955 *Thunderbird*

The original Ford Thunderbird had many outstanding selling features. Its styling was less radical than that of the other American sports cars. L.D. Crusoe, Ford Motor Company vice president and general manager of Ford Division, insisted that the new car be based on a full-sized Ford for "family" identity and to ensure that major parts would be interchangeable with other 1955 Fords. Parts sharing cut development time, too.

BODY COLOR INFORMATION

Color Name	Code	Color Name	Code
Raven Black	A	Torch Red	R
Snowshoe White	E	Special Color	S
Primer	P	Thunderbird Blue	T
		Goldenrod Yellow	V

Note: Goldenrod Yellow and Snowshoe White were added in March 1955.

TOP COLOR INFORMATION

Convertible tops of Black canvas with all body colors.
Standard finish for the glass-fibre hardtop was painted to match body color.

INTERIOR TRIM INFORMATION

Seat Type	Material	Black/White	Red/White	Turquoise/White	Black/Yellow
Bench Seat	All-Vinyl	XA or A	XB or B	XC or C	XD or D

THUNDERBIRD PRODUCTION

Model Number	Body/Style Number	Body Type & Seating	Factory Price	Shipping Weight	Production Total
H	40	2d Convertible-2P	$2,944	2,980 lbs.	16,155

Designers were able to skip the time-consuming job of making mock-ups or models, going straight to the creation of full-sized drawings of the T-Bird's profile instead. The car's dimensions were based on those of the Corvette and the Jaguar XK-120. To save even more time, a used Ford sedan was obtained to serve as a designers' "mule." It was cut down with a torch and re-welded to fashion a small Ford with a 102-inch wheelbase.

Ford's chief engineer, William Burnett, decided to go at the project this way. Those involved with it called the car the "Burnetti" after him. They thought this name had an Italian sports car ring to it. The first plan was to call the production version the Fairlane (after Henry Ford's estate in Michigan). Crusoe was said to prefer "Savile," but he proposed a contest in which FoMoCo employees could suggest names. The winner was offered a prize of $250, but actually won a suit worth $75-$100. Designer Alden "Gib" Giberson, a native of the Southwest, suggested the name "Thunderbird." In Indian mythology, the Thunderbird helped humans by flapping its wings, bringing thunder, lightning, and rain to alleviate a drought. On February 15, 1954, the name was made official. The T-Bird nickname may well have stemmed from Ford ads referring to the car's introductory date as "T-day."

Although the car-buying public got a few peeks at the T-Bird early in 1954, it wasn't until October 22 that the production version was officially unveiled. Its introductory retail price was $2,695, less federal taxes and delivery and handling charges. This compared to $2,700 for a 1955 Corvette. Later, the price was increased when a fiberglass hardtop became standard equipment. Looking very much like a scaled-down Ford, the Thunderbird was trim, though not sub-compact.

The standard telescoping steering wheel allowed large T-Bird drivers to get comfortable inside the car. The styling of the car was quite pleasing. Its "frenched" headlights gave

Mike Mueller photo

The first Thunderbird was similar in size to the Corvette and Jaguar XK-120, and rested on a 102-inch wheelbase.

it a forward-thrusting look at the front, while the crisp tail fins seemed to "flip-off" a little message to every slower car passed on the highway. They seemed to be saying, "I'm the latest and the greatest thing for the young and the young at heart."

In its September 1955 issue, *Motor Trend* selected the Thunderbird as one of the six best-looking cars of 1955. "Overall consistency of design. Width, height, length ratios show excellent proportion," noted *Motor Trend*. "Its small hardtop version has a very classic look." The low, square Ford look emphasized the car's width and the production version featured only minimal use of chrome. "Pretty well de-chromed and clean-looking," *Motor Trend* said. "First and foremost a car for comfort and looks."

For a 1955 American car, the Thunderbird offered excellent driving characteristics. Vision over the hood was exceptionally good, as the cowl stood just 37.2 inches above the surface of the road. The wraparound windshield created some distortion at the corners. Inside, the operator was greeted with a modern-looking dashboard featuring a tachometer, "idiot lights" (to monitor oil pressure and electrical output) and a clock with a sweep second hand that was great for rallying. A firm ride made the first Thunderbird feel like a sports car. Still, it was somewhat prone to understeering and would break loose in a tight turn, before drifting around it like a competition racer. However, it hung in the corners well enough to take them at 10 to 15 mph faster than most contemporary, full-size American cars.

STANDARD EQUIPMENT

292-cid Y-block V-8 engine, four-barrel carburetor, dual exhausts, 6-volt electrical system, 40-amp generator, 90 amp-hr 6-volt battery, three-speed manual transmission with all-helical gears and floor-mounted shift lever Hotchkiss drive, ball-joint front suspension, five-leaf spring rear suspension, five 6.70 x 15 tubeless tires, vinyl upholstery, Astra-Dial control panel with illuminated control knobs, 150-mph Astra-Dial speedometer, parcel compartment with locking-type push-button latch, inside

hood release, tachometer, Telechron (GE) electric clock with sweep second hand, power seat, left-hand outside rearview mirror, full-width seat with foam rubber padding, adjustable steering wheel, built-in armrests, floor carpet, ashtray, four-way illuminated starter-ignition switch, cigar lighter, panel courtesy light with integral switch and automatic door switches, rearview mirror on windshield upper molding, dual horns, half-circle steering wheel horn ring, and (as a running addition) glass-fiber hardtop. Some Thunderbirds shipped to Europe had metric speedometers that read from 0 to 240 km/hr, which was basically the same as 0 to 150 mph

I.D. NUMBERS

Located on plate on left door pillar. First symbol denotes engine: P=292 cid/193 hp four-barrel Thunderbird Special V-8 (manual transmission). P=292 cid/193 hp four-barrel Thunderbird Special V-8 (overdrive transmission). P=292 cid/198 hp four-barrel Thunderbird Special V-8 (automatic transmission). Second symbol denotes model-year: 5=1955. Third symbol denotes the assembly plant: F=Dearborn, Michigan. Fourth symbol denotes body type: H=Thunderbird convertible. Fifth thru 10th symbols denote sequential production number of specific vehicle starting at 100001. Body number plate located on firewall. Serial number: Same as number on left door pillar tag. Symbols below "BODY" are body symbol code: 40A=Thunderbird. Symbols below "COLOR" are paint color code. See the table below. Symbols below "TRIM" are trim combination code. See table below. Symbols below "PRODUCTION DATE" are the production date code. The numerical prefix indicates the date of the month the car was made. The letters indicate month of manufacture: A=January, B=February, C=March, D=April, E=May, F=June, G=July, H=August, J=September, K=October, L=November, M=December. The numerical suffix indicates the production sequence.

ENGINES

BASE V-8 (WITH SYNCHROMESH OR OVERDRIVE): 90-degree V-8. Overhead valves. Cast-iron block. Bore and stroke: 3.75 x 3.30 in. Displacement: 292 cid. Compression

Snowshoe White was one of eight colors for the first-year 1955 T-Bird.

Daniel B. Lyons photo

Goldenrod Yellow was one of two colors added during the 1955 model year. A 'Bird in this condition is worth upwards of $60,000 on today's collector's market.

ratio: 8.1:1. Brake hp: 193 at 4400 rpm. Taxable hp: 45. Torque: 280 lbs.-ft. at 2600 rpm. Five main bearings. Solid valve lifters. Crankcase capacity: 5 qt. (add 1 qt. with new oil filter). Cooling system capacity: 19 qt. Carburetor: Holley four-barrel. Code P. (Early reports gave the horsepower rating of this engine as 190.)

BASE V-8 (WITH FORD-O-MATIC): Overhead valve. Cast-iron block. Bore and stroke: 3.75 x 3.30 in. Displacement: 292 cid. Compression ratio: 8.50:1. Brake hp: 198 at 4400 rpm. Taxable hp: 45. Torque: 286 lbs.-ft. at 2500 rpm. Five main bearings. Solid valve lifters. Crankcase capacity: 5 qt. (add 1 qt. with new oil filter). Cooling system capacity: 19 qt. Carburetor: Holley four-barrel. Code P.

CHASSIS

Wheelbase: 102 in. Overall length: 175.3 in. Overall width: 70.3 in. Overall height: 50.2 in. Ground clearance: 5.5 in. Front tread: 56 in. Rear tread: 56 in. Front headroom: (with hardtop) 32.2 in. Front hip room: 58.8 in. Front shoulder room: 53.3 in. Front legroom: 45.4 in. Top of door height: 34.2 in. Tires: 6.70 x 15 four-ply. Brake swept area: 175 sq. in. Turning diameter: 36 ft. Turns lock-to-lock: 3.5. Steering ratio: 20.0:1. Steering wheel: 17 in. diameter. Weight distribution: 50/50. Chassis type: X-frame. Front suspension: Ball-joints, coil springs, tube shocks and stabilizer. Rear suspension: Composite axle, 5-leaf springs, double-acting shock absorbers. Steering: Symetrical linkage type. Steering wheel: Three-inch in-and-out adjustable. Front brakes: 11-in. diameter double-sealed. Rear brakes: 11-in. diameter double-sealed. Standard transmission: Three-speed synchromesh with helical gears, ratios: (first) 2.32:1, (second) 1.48:1, (third) 1:1 and (reverse) 2.82:1. Optional transmission: Planetary overdrive with planetary gears, 27-mph cut-in speed and 0.70:1 ratio. Optional transmission: Ford-O-Matic torque converter transmission with planetary gears, ratios: (drive) 1.48:1 and 1.00 x torque converter with a 2.1:1 maximum ratio at stall, (low) 2.44:1 x torque converter, (reverse) 2.0:1 x torque converter.

Standard rear axle with synchromesh transmission: 3.73:1, optional 4.10:1 axle was optional. Standard rear axle with overdrive: 3.92:1. Standard rear axle with Ford-o-matic transmission: 3.31:1.

OPTIONS

Full-flow oil filter. Oil bath air cleaner. Four-way power seat. Swift-Sure power brakes ($40). Master-Guide power steering.($92). Power-Lift windows ($70). I-Rest tinted safety glass ($25). Ford-O-Matic Drive ($215). Overdrive ($110). White-sidewall tires ($30). Tachometer. Electric clock. Cigarette lighter. Convertible fabric top in lieu of hardtop ($75). Convertible fabric top in addition to hardtop was originally $290 until glass-fiber hardtop became standard equipment. Special fuel and vacuum pump unit. MagicAire Heater ($85). Radio ($100). Rear fender shields. Full wheel covers. Simulated wire wheels. Engine dress-up kit ($25). Windshield washers ($10).

HISTORICAL FOOTNOTES

At the beginning of the 1955 model year, Ford Motor Company projected that it would sell 10,000 Thunderbirds—a conservative estimate. Dealers reportedly took 4,000 orders on October 22, 1954, the first day it was available. The *1956 Ward's Automotive Yearbook* listed September 7, 1954, as the day that Thunderbird production began, but the Classic Thunderbird Club International reports that the earliest production unit had serial number P5FH100005 and was made on September 9, 1954. This car was referred to in the October 4, 1954, issue of *Sports Illustrated*, which carried three pages of Thunderbird coverage entitled "America's newest Sports Car." The writer documented that the car was "not a pilot model Thunderbird, but the Number 1 production model."

In the summer of 1965, a Thunderbird owner named George Watts found the remains of serial number P5FH100005 sitting outside a small, Southern California body shop. It had only 78,000 miles on its odometer, but had deteriorated from obvious neglect and improper storage. The car's upholstery was bad, both tops were missing and it had been repainted several times. Originally black, the car showed evidence of being refinished twice, once in white and a second time in blue. The man who owned the car had an unsatisfied loan with a finance company. He also owed the body shop owner for some work he had commissioned. The bills on the car totaled $500. This situation helped Watts purchase the remains for a price he considered fair. After towing the T-Bird home, Watts checked the serial number. He found it was very low.

Cappy collection

This 1955 has had a continental kit installed. Technically, this option was not available until 1956, but dealers could retrofit the 1955s if the buyers were so inclined.

A total of 16,155 T-Birds left the factory in the first year. This model was painted Raven Black.

He thought it was the fifth 1955 T-Bird made. A restoration was carried out while his research into the car's background continued. In February 1966, a letter from Ford Motor Company's General Counsel arrived at Watts' home. It revealed that he had the first production Thunderbird. Watts put 10,000 additional miles on the car, driving it until 1973. He then did a restoration and repainted P5FH100005 in its original Raven Black color. Automotive historian James F. Petrik researched Thunderbird factory records and reported that a Thunderbird with serial number P5FH100004 had been discovered, but the Classic Thunderbird Club International agrees that P5FH100005 is considered the first *production* vehicle. According to *Ward's*, Thunderbird production ended August 26, 1955. However, James F. Petrik discovered that a Thunderbird with serial number P5FH260557 was the last 1955 Ford product built. He found that the invoice for this car was typed on September 14, 1955, and that it was constructed on September 16, 1955.

In a variety of contemporary magazine road tests, the Thunderbird with the 198-hp version of the 292-cid V-8 did 0 to 60 mph in 8.8 seconds, 9.5 seconds, 10.75 seconds and 11 seconds. Typical quarter-mile times were given as 16.9 seconds, 17.1 seconds and 17.75 seconds (at 83 mph). Top speed was recorded as 120 mph. Thunderbirds were being raced before the year ended. They became fairly popular in the "A" Sports Cars class at drag races across the country. The T-Birds got noticeably faster after firms such as Edelbrock Equipment Company began offering dual four-barrel and triple two-barrel carburetor intake manifolds and high-speed distributors designed specifically for Thunderbirds.

The lone Thunderbird exterior name plate on the 1955 models was located on the rear fender.

15

Daniel B. Lyons photo

The 1956 T-Bird had a few exterior updates, including the continental kit and optional hardtops with "porthole" windows.

1956 *Thunderbird*

Most exterior alterations to the 1956 Thunderbird were not very obvious ones. The emblem on the front of the car, above the grille, was changed from crossed checkered racing flags to a stylized rendition of the American Indian thunderbird symbol. The headlight doors now had a rib under the hooded area. The badges behind the simulated louver trim on the front fenders were revised from V-8 insignias to Ford crests. Door-like air vents were added to the sides of the Thunderbird's cowl to improve interior cooling. Also added were wind-wings on the car's chrome windshield frame.

The standard continental tire kit on the rear of the car was the most obvious update. "The Thunderbird's brand-new, rear spare-tire mounting folds back handily, as quick as a wink," advertisements boasted. "It adds greatly to your luggage space as it does to the overall beauty of the car." Cars built before November 14, 1955 had their continental spare tires raised for added ground clearance. Later, Ford dealers had to recall these cars to change the height of the continental kits by 1 3/8 inches. The 1956 frame had to be modified for this feature, since the original 1955 frame couldn't tolerate the "cantilever" effect of the heavy continental kit at the extreme rear of the vehicle.

A new, vented gas cap was used on the center-fill gas tank's neck. The door that the gas filler hid behind was devoid of the checkered flag emblem used to dress it up in 1955. Slight modifications were made to the Thunderbird's taillights. Though still large and circular, the rear red lenses had a wider center protrusion with more elaborate chrome trim. The arch-shaped area above the round red lens was also restyled. A small, circular reflector was added to the chrome molding right at the top of the arch. Back-up lamps could again be ordered in place of the metal filler plate. Offered again was the same fiberglass hardtop used in 1955. A new version with "port" windows in its side panels was also available for 1956.

The hardtop in matching body color (with or without port windows) was optional at no extra cost. Having the top finished in a contrasting color did cost extra, though. Some Ford dealers added the porthole windows to the standard-style hardtop when buyers found their Thunderbirds claustrophobic or complained about blind spots.

The 1956 Thunderbird's interior door panels had new "stitching" embossments molded into the seams in the vinyl. The patterning on the seats, supplied by McInerney Spring & Wire Company, was also changed. In 1955, the

BODY COLOR INFORMATION

Color Name	Code	Color Name	Code
Raven Black	A	Goldenglow Yellow	M
Colonial White	E	Thunderbird Gray	P
Buckskin Tan	J	Sunset Coral	Y
Fiesta Red	K	Thunderbird Green	Z
Peacock Blue	L		

Sunset Coral and Goldenglow Yellow were deleted at midyear.
Thunderbird Gray was added at midyear.

TWO-TONE COLORS (EARLY)

Color A (Body)	Color B (Hardtop)	Code	Color A (Body)	Color B (Hardtop)	Code
Thunderbird Gray	Colonial White	18	Goldenglow Yellow	Colonial White	31
Thunderbird Gray	Raven Black	19	Goldenglow Yellow	Raven Black	32
Raven Black	Colonial White	21	Peacock Blue	Colonial White	33
Colonial White	Raven Black	21 (I)	Colonial White	Peacock Blue	33 (I)
Raven Black	Fiesta Red	23	Sunset Coral	Raven Black	35 (I)
Buckskin Tan	Colonial White	28	Sunset Coral	Colonial White	36
Colonial White	Buckskin Tan	28 (I)	Thunderbird Green	Colonial White	37
Fiesta Red	Colonial White	30	Colonial White	T-bird Green	37 (I)
Colonial White	Fiesta Red	30 (I)			

(I) Indicates inverted arrangement of same colors.

TWO-TONE COLORS (LATE)

Color A (Body)	Color B (Hardtop)	Code	Color A (Body)	Color B (Hardtop)	Code
Raven Black	Colonial White	21	Peacock Blue	Colonial White	33
Colonial White	Raven Black	21 (I)	Colonial White	Peacock Blue	33 (I)
Raven Black	Fiesta Red	23	Sunset Coral	Raven Black	35 (I)
Buckskin Tan	Colonial White	28	Sunset Coral	Colonial White	36
Colonial White	Buckskin Tan	28 (I)	Thunderbird Green	Colonial White	37
Fiesta Red	Colonial White	30	Colonial White	T-bird Green	37 (I)
Colonial White	Fiesta Red	30 (I)			

(I) Indicates inverted arrangement of same colors.

TOP COLOR INFORMATION

Convertible tops of black canvas or white vinyl available with all body colors.

INTERIOR TRIM INFORMATION

Seat Type	Material	Black/White	Red/White	Peacock/White	Tan/White	Green/White	Brown/White
Bench Seat	Vinyl	XA	XB	XC	XD	XF	XG

THUNDERBIRD PRODUCTION

Model Number	Body/Style Number	Body Type & Seating	Factory Price	Shipping Weight	Production Total
H	40B	2d Hardtop-2P	$3,158	3,297 lbs.	Note 1
H	40A	2d Convertible-2P	$3,233	3,159 lbs.	Note 1

NOTE 1: Combined production of both models was 15,631.
NOTE 2: *Ward's 1956 Automotive Yearbook* showed an introductory price of $2,842 for the Thunderbird, but most 1956 models were sold for about $300 more than that. The base price in June 1956 was $3,147.60. This included the suggested retail price at the main factory, federal tax and delivery and handling (but not freight).

vertically ribbed insert sections of the seats were separate from each other. The 1956 design brought the ribs across the center of the backrest. They ran nearly the full width of the seat back and gave the visual impression that the seat had been widened.

A three-spoke Lifeguard deep-dish steering wheel was standard equipment in the Thunderbird. It replaced the flat, two-spoke steering wheel used the previous year. This steering wheel required alterations to the signal lamp stalk and the steering column adjusting collar. Also standard were Lifeguard door latches that were not supposed to open in a serious accident. Other Ford Lifeguard features, such as seat belts, a ribbed padded dash, and padded sun visors were optional.

Ford's Lifeguard safety program was a reaction to Cornell University Medical College's assertion that 1955 automobiles were no safer than those built between 1940-1949. Ford spent months researching auto safety. Auto accident statistics and data were gathered from safety research centers including the Cornell Medical College. As a result, Ford isolated injury-causing components of cars and set up a test lab to redesign such components. As an extra-cost item, the safety features were a flop, but *Motor Trend* magazine presented Ford with its "1st annual *Motor Trend* Award," for making the most significant advancement on a United States production car. "Rising high in stature, above all other (advances), however, is the progress toward automotive safety made by the Ford Motor Co.," wrote editor Walt Woron and engineering editor John Booth. "This company, and each of its divisions, is not alone in its pursuit of those elusive qualities we'd like to see built into all cars. What this company has initiated is without a doubt the biggest step forward in 1956."

There were a few additional "running" production changes in 1956 Thunderbirds. With the spare tire out of the trunk, changes were made in the way that the luggage compartment was trimmed. A curtain made of material similar to the ribbed rubber trunk mat was added at first.

Later, the rubber trim was replaced with trim made of a composition material called Burtex and the curtain was no longer used. At mid-model year, a dual four-barrel carburetor "competition kit" was released for Thunderbirds with manual transmissions. Engines fitted with the kit, which was intended for serious racing, were rated at 260 hp.

STANDARD EQUIPMENT

292-cid Y-block V-8 engine, automatic choke, 12-volt electrical system, dual exhausts, three-speed manual transmission, Hotchkiss drive, ball-joint front suspension, five-leaf spring rear suspension, five 6.70 x 15 tubeless tires, all-vinyl interiors with harmonizing looped-rayon carpeting, 17-in. diameter deep-center Lifeguard steering wheel with 2-in. adjustment, Lifeguard double-grip door latches, Lifeguard rearview mirror, Astra-Dial control panel with illuminated control knobs, parcel compartment with locking-type push-button latch, four-way illuminated starter-ignition switch, panel courtesy light with integral switch and automatic door switches, dual horns, half-circle steering wheel horn ring, and glass-fiber hardtop.

I.D. NUMBERS

Located on plate on left door pillar. First symbol denotes engine: M=292-cid/202-hp four-barrel Thunderbird V-8 (manual transmission), P=312-cid/215-hp four-barrel Thunderbird Special V-8 (overdrive transmission), P=312-cid/225-hp four-barrel Thunderbird Special V-8 (automatic transmission), P=312-cid/260-hp dual four-barrel Thunderbird Special V-8 (overdrive transmission). Second symbol denotes model-year: 6=1956 Third symbol denotes the assembly plant: F=Dearborn, Michigan. Fourth symbol denotes body type: H=Thunderbird convertible/hardtop. Fifth thru tenth symbols denote sequential production number of specific vehicle starting at 100001. Body number plate located on firewall. Serial number: Same as number on left door pillar tag. Symbols below "BODY" are body symbol code: 40A=Thunderbird. "COLOR" are paint color code. "TRIM" are trim combination code. "PRODUCTION CODE"

Daniel B. Lyons photo

Buckskin Tan was a new color option on the '56 T-Birds.

are the production date code. The numerical prefix indicates the date of the month the car was made. The letters indicate month of manufacture: A=January, B=February, C=March, D=April, E=May, F=June, G=July, H=August, J=September, K=October, L=November, M=December. The numerical suffix is the sequence the car was built in.

ENGINES

THUNDERBIRD BASE V-8 (WITH MANUAL TRANSMISSION): Overhead valve. Cast-iron block. Bore and stroke: 3.75 x 3.30 in. Displacement: 292 cid. Compression ratio: 8.40:1. Brake hp: 202 at 4600 rpm. Taxable hp: 45. Torque: 289 lbs.-ft. at 2600 rpm. Five main bearings. Solid valve lifters. Crankcase capacity: 5 qt. (add 1 qt. with new oil filter). Cooling system capacity: 19 qt. Carburetor: Holley 4000 four-barrel. Code M.

THUNDERBIRD SPECIAL V-8 (WITH OVERDRIVE): Overhead valve. Cast-iron block. Bore and stroke: 3.80 x 3.44 in. Displacement: 312 cid. Compression ratio: 8.4:1. Brake hp: 215 at 4600 rpm. Taxable hp: 45. Torque: 317 lbs.-ft. at 2600 rpm. Five main bearings. Crankcase capacity: 5 qt. (add 1 qt. with new oil filter). Cooling system capacity: 19 qt. Carburetor: Holley 4000 four-barrel. Code P.

THUNDERBIRD SPECIAL V-8 (WITH FORD-O-MATIC OR OVERDRIVE): Overhead valve. Cast-iron block. Bore and stroke: 3.80 x 3.44 inches. Displacement: 312 cid. Compression ratio: 9.0:1. Brake hp: 225 at 4600 rpm. Taxable hp: 45. Torque: 324 lbs.-ft. at 2600 rpm. Five main

bearings. Crankcase capacity: 5 qt. (add 1 qt. with new oil filter). Cooling system capacity: 19 qt. Carburetor: Holley 4000 four-barrel. Code L.

THUNDERBIRD SPECIAL DUAL FOUR-BARREL V-8 (WITH MANUAL TRANSMISSION): Overhead valve. Cast-iron block. Bore and stroke: 3.80 x 3.44 in. Displacement: 312 cid. Compression ratio: 9.5:1. Brake hp: 260 at unknown rpm. Taxable hp: 45. Five main bearings. Crankcase capacity: 5 qt. (add 1 qt. with new oil filter). Cooling system capacity: 19 qt. Carburetor: Two Holley four-barrel. Code P.

CHASSIS

Wheelbase: 102 in. Overall length: 185.1 in. Overall width: 70.3 in. Overall height (top of fiberglass hardtop to ground): 50.2 in. Road clearance: 5.9 in. Front tread: 56 in. Rear tread: 56 in. Front headroom: (with hardtop) 33.1 or 33.6 in. Hip room: 58.8 in. Front shoulder room: 53.3 in. Front legroom: 45.1 in. Top of door height: 34.2 in. Standard hypoid axle: (manual transmission) 3.73:1, (overdrive transmission) 3.92:1, (Ford-O-Matic) 3.31:1. Tires: 6.70 x 15 four-ply. Wheel studs: 5.5 in. Wheel stud circle: 4.5 in. diameter. Brake swept area: 175.5 sq. in. Turning diameter: 36 ft. Steering ratio: 23.0:1. Weight distribution: 49.4/50.6. Chassis type: X-frame. Front suspension: Ball-joints, coil springs, tube shocks and stabilizer. Rear suspension: Composite axle, four-leaf springs, double-acting shock absorbers. Steering: Parallel linkage type. Steering wheel: 3-in. in-and-out adjustable. Front brakes: 11-in. diameter double-sealed. Rear brakes: 11-in. diameter double-sealed. Standard transmission: Three-speed synchromesh with helical gears. Optional transmission: Planetary overdrive with planetary gears. Optional transmission: Ford-o-matic torque converter transmission with planetary gears. Standard rear axle ratio with manual transmission: 3.73. Standard rear axle with overdrive: 3.92. Standard rear axle with Ford-o-matic transmission: 3.31.

OPTIONS

Full-flow oil filter. Four-way power seat ($65). Swift Sure power brakes ($34). Master-Guide power steering ($64). Power-Lift windows ($70). I-Rest tinted safety glass. Ford-O-matic Drive ($215). Overdrive ($146). White-sidewall tires. Fuel and vacuum pump unit. MagicAire Heater ($84). Radio ($107). Rear fender shields (the type of fender skirts

The continental kits added to the trunk space on the early 'Birds. Kits on cars before Nov. 14, 1955, were raised slightly for better ground clearance, but these kits were later recalled.

The hood and front fender badging on the 1956 T-Birds was slightly different from the 1955 models—the '56s had the Ford emblem.

The "bullets" on the front grille returned on the 1956 models. They were gone by 1957.

Jerry Heasley photo

The 1956 convertible T-Bird came with an original sticker price of $3,233. Cars with "both tops" are more collectible today, as are the cars with the 312-cid engine.

with an edge molding and gravel shield, as used mostly from April 1955 on). Full wheel covers. Simulated wire wheel covers. Engine dress-up kit. Auto-Wipe windshield washers. Turn signals. Lifeguard seat belts (March 1956). Lifeguard padded sun visors and Lifeguard instrument panel padding (March 1956) ($22-$32). Thunderbird 312-cid four-barrel V-8. Thunderbird 312-cid dual four-barrel V-8. Convertible fabric top alone ($75). Convertible top and hardtop ($290). Tonneau cover.

HISTORICAL FOOTNOTES

Henry Ford II was President of Ford Motor Company in 1956. Earnest R. Breech was chairman of the board. Robert S. McNamara, who later went on to become United States secretary of defense, was a FoMoCo vice president and general manager of Ford Division. A man who would later become an automotive industry legend, Lee Iacocca, was Ford Division's truck marketing manager. The 1956 Thunderbird bowed on September 23, 1955. Ford announced that its target was to built 20,000 of the cars in 1956. They were often used to attract attention to other Fords. Thunderbirds appeared in many FoMoCo ads featuring Mainline, Customline, and Fairlane models. The 202-hp "Thunderbird Y-8" was mentioned in many advertisements. Ford ultimately produced 15,631 T-Birds, which was below its target, but only 524 less than in 1955, which was a record year for the auto industry.

Motor Trend did its second annual Thunderbird versus Corvette comparison road test in June 1956. The magazine noted that GM had added "more fuel to an old duel" by adding a hardtop, roll-up windows, and more power to the Corvette's equipment. "But don't get the idea that Ford has been lulled into a no-progress policy by their sales leadership with the Thunderbird," advised editor Walt Woron. "The No. 1 sales position is hard to come by and is jealously guarded." *Hot Rod* magazine did a "Rod Test" of the 1956 Thunderbird in July and expanded it to discuss Thunderbird modifications. According to editor Racer Brown, the car's popularity "was soon resolved into a matter of appearance." He believed that horsepower, performance, fuel economy, economics, and utilitarian value had little to do with the appeal of Ford's two-seater. "It was the bold

American lines that captivated the majority (of buyers)," he opined. "Yet, these lines have been restrained by good taste."

Under the test car's hood was the 312.7-cid V-8 in its 225-hp "power pack" format. It went from 0 to 60 mph in an average 9.1 seconds and hit 0 to 80 mph in an average 15.5 seconds with Brown "shifting" the automatic transmission. Keeping the gear-shifter in drive range only, the comparable times were 9.8 seconds and 16.6 seconds. The car averaged 77 mph for the standing-start quarter mile.

Jerry Heasley photo

This gorgeous 1956 T-Bird came in Peacock Blue. Its mint-condition interior is hard to miss with the top down.

Was there a snappier-looking car in 1957 than a yellow T-Bird with a white hardtop?

Jerry Heasley photo

1957 *Thunderbird*

There were big styling changes to the 1957 Thunderbird, but only minor mechanical alterations. New appearance features included a larger, stronger front bumper incorporating rectangular parking lamps. A larger front grille was said to improve engine cooling. The shape of the front wheel cut outs was modified. Chrome "Thunderbird" name scripts were added to the front fenders, ahead of the louver decorations. Tail fins were added to the T-Bird. A body-side feature line curved up and over the door handles, then swept to the rear atop the outward-canted fins. A higher deck lid had a reverse-angle shape at its rear.

The longer 1957 body provided more luggage space. After being externally mounted in 1956, the spare tire was moved back inside the 6-inch-longer trunk. This made getting into the trunk a lot easier. Ford said that it also helped enhance handling, due to improvements in weight distribution caused by the extra poundage at the rear. The spare tire sat at an upright angle in the trunk's tire well.

The Thunderbird's longer, larger, finned rear fenders ended with large round taillights. The rear bumper was also enlarged and had more curves than in the past. Built-in exhaust outlets were featured at either side. The license plate was mounted in the center of the rear bumper. A badge on the center of the rear deck lid, shaped like a stylized Thunderbird, identified the model.

The new Thunderbird had a firmer ride than big sedans of its era, due mainly to its shorter wheelbase. However, it was plush, comfortable, and soft riding in comparison to European sports cars. For 1957, the ride was improved through a lowered center of gravity and the use of recalibrated shock absorbers. Five-leaf rear springs were reintroduced after being dropped in favor of four-leaf springs in 1956. Despite the fact that smaller wheels were employed in 1957, the front brakes were enlarged. The smaller new 14-in. diameter safety rim wheels with 7.50 x 14 tires mounted brought the car closer to the ground. They were dressed up with handsome new louvered full-wheel disks.

The 1957 frame was virtually the same as before. However, the number four cross-member was changed to a box section (instead of channel section) design. This provided added strength to support the extra bulk of the bigger body.

The hardtop model was again really a convertible with a detachable fiberglass top. Ford literature still described it as a "glass-fibre standard hardtop." The standard top had port windows in 1957. Optional at no extra cost was the hardtop without port windows. Both were available in contrasting or matching colors. Some 75 percent of all 1957s had the porthole tops, which had no trim badges. The non-porthole tops featured round emblems with V-shaped Thunderbird insignias. Both hardtops used a revised clamping mechanism. The convertible came with a folding fabric top. Modifications were made to the top mechanism to make it easier to operate.

Two types of fabric tops were offered. The canvas convertible top was available in three colors, while an optional vinyl top came only in one color. Many owners preferred both hard and soft tops. In this case, the convertible model was purchased with the hardtop as a separate option. In October 1956, the Thunderbird was offered in 10 single colors. All 10 colors were also offered on the fiberglass hardtops with specific body and interior color

BODY COLOR INFORMATION (SEPTEMBER 1, 1956)

Color Name	Code	Color Name	Code
Raven Black	A	Gunmetal Gray	N
Dresden Blue	C	Thunderbird Bronze	Q
Colonial White	E	Flame Red	V
Starmist Blue	F	Dusk Rose	X
Cumberland Green	G	Inca Gold	Y
Willow Green	J	Coral Sand	Z

ADDED COLORS (SEPTEMBER, 1957)

Color Name	Code	Color Name	Code
Sun Gold	G	Seaspray Green	N
Gunmetal Gray	H	Torch Red	R
Azure Blue	L		

Sun Gold (G) replaced Inca Gold (Y); Seaspray Green (N) replaced Cumberland Green (G); Gunmetal Gray (H) replaced Gunmetal Gray (N); Torch Red (R) replaced Flame Red (V).

TU-TONE 1957 BODY COLORS (SEPTEMBER 1, 1956)

Color I (Body)	Color II (Hardtop)	Code	Color I (Body)	Color II (Hardtop)	Code
Raven Black	Colonial White	AE	Colonial White	Thunderbird Bronze	EQ
Raven Black	Flame Red	AV	Willow Green	Colonial White	JE
Raven Black	Inca Gold	AY	Willow Green	Raven Black	JA
Raven Black	Dusk Rose	AX	Gunmetal Gray	Colonial White	NE
Raven Black	Coral Sand	AZ	Gunmetal Gray	Raven Black	NA
Raven Black	Williow Green	AJ	Gunmetal Gray	Inca Gold	NY
Raven Black	Starmist Blue	AF	Flame Red	Raven Black	VA
Starmist Blue	Colonial White	FE	Flame Red	Colonial White	VE
Starmist Blue	Raven Black	FA	Inca Gold	Colonial White	YE
Colonial White	Raven Black	EA	Inca Gold	Raven Black	YA
Colonial White	Starmist Blue	EF	Inca Gold	Gunmetal Gray	YN
Colonial White	Willow Green	EU	Coral Sand	Colonial White	ZE
Colonial White	Gunmetal Gray	EN	Coral Sand	Raven Black	ZA
Colonial White	Flame Red	EV	Coral Sand	Gunmetal Gray	ZN
Colonial White	Coral Sand	EZ	Thunderbird Bronze	Colonial White	QE
Colonial White	Inca Gold	EY	Dusk Rose	Raven Black	XA
Colonial White	Dusk Rose	EX	Dusk Rose	Colonial White	XE

TOP COLOR INFORMATION

Convertible tops of Blue, Black, or Tan canvas or White vinyl available with all body colors.

INTERIOR TRIM INFORMATION

Seat Type	Material	Black/White	Blue/Blue	Green/Green	Red	White	Bronze
Bench Seat	All-Vinyl	XA	XL	XM	XH	XK	XJ

THUNDERBIRD PRODUCTION

Model Number	Body/Style Number	Body Type & Seating	Factory Price	Shipping Weight	Production Total
H	40A	2d Convertible-2P	$3,458	3,134 lbs.	Note 1
H	40B	2d Hardtop-2P	$3,383	3,299 lbs.	Note 1

NOTE 1: Combined production of both models was 21,380.

combinations.

Inside, the 1957 T-Bird had modest interior alterations. The dashboard was based on the one used in full-size 1957 Fords with a simulated engine-turned face panel added. The visor above the instrument panel no longer had a transparent "window." A tachometer was mounted low at the driver's left and was a bit hard to see. "Idiot" lights monitored oil pressure and the battery's state of charge.

The seats were redesigned. They had separate sections for the driver and passenger. New springs that gave better spine support and much improved lateral support were employed. The seats were the same basic size and shape as in 1956, but the new springs were said to reduce driver fatigue. The door panels were also changed. A "Dial-O-Matic" seat was optional. Dash-mounted buttons permitted adjusting the seat to the driver's favorite position. When the ignition was turned off, it automatically moved to its rearmost position. When the ignition was turned on, the seat moved automatically to the pre-selected driving position.

A new idea in radios was a speed-sensitive receiver. There was an electronic device built into the circuit between the radio volume control and the distributor. It automatically increased volume as the car speed got higher. As the engine speed increased, a capacitor wired in series with the distributor lead raised the volume. This maintained the listening level at a constant level at all times and kept the radio from blasting loudly when the car was idling at a traffic light. A safety feature added to the 1957 Thunderbird was a reflecting strip along the rear edge of the left door. When the door was opened at night, headlights from oncoming cars were reflected from the strip, warning drivers of another car's presence. The doors also had heavier hinges than those used in previous years.

STANDARD EQUIPMENT

292-cid Y-block V-8 engine, automatic choke, Super-Filter air cleaner with reusable paper element (effective Feb. 1957), 12-volt electrical system, dual exhausts, three-speed manual transmission, Hotchkiss drive, ball-joint front suspension, 5-leaf spring rear suspension, five 7.50 x 14 tubeless tires, Safety-Contoured 14-in. wheel rims, pleated all-vinyl Tu-Tone interiors or all-vinyl monochromatic interiors with harmonizing looped-rayon carpeting, standard fiberglass hardtop with port windows or optional fiberglass hardtop without port windows (in contrasting or matching colors), Lifeguard cushioned sun visors and Lifeguard instrument panel padding, deep-center Lifeguard steering wheel, Lifeguard double-grip door latches, Lifeguard rearview mirror, parcel compartment with locking-type push-button latch, 4-way illuminated starter-ignition switch, panel courtesy light with integral switch and automatic door switches, dual horns, and half-circle steering wheel horn ring.

I.D. NUMBERS

VIN located on plate on left door pillar. First symbol denotes engine: C=292-cid/206-hp V-8 (manual transmission) or 212-hp V-8 (Ford-O-Matic transmission) four-barrel Thunderbird V-8, D=312-cid/245-hp four-barrel Thunderbird Special V-8, E=312-cid/270-hp dual four-barrel Thunderbird Special V-8, F=312-cid/300-hp supercharged Thunderbird Special V-8. Second symbol denotes model-year: 7=1957 Third symbol denotes the assembly plant: F=Dearborn, Michigan. Fourth symbol denotes body type: H=Thunderbird convertible. Fifth thru tenth symbols denote sequential production number of specific vehicle starting at 100001. Body number plate located on firewall. Serial number: Same as number on left door pillar tag. Symbols below "BODY" are body symbol code: 40=Thunderbird. Symbols below "COLOR" are paint color code. Symbols below "TRIM" are trim combination code. Symbols below "PRODUCTION CODE" are the production date code. The numerical prefix indicates the date of the month the car was made. The letters indicate month of manufacture: A=January, B=February, C=March, D=April, E=May, F=June, G=July, H=August, J=September, K=October, L=November, M=December. The numerical suffix indicates production sequence.

The T-Bird was again merchanidised in convertible and hardtop models in 1957. It was still a small car with a less-than-plush ride, but it had plenty of amenities and compared very favorably in the comfort department to its European and U.S. competition.

Daniel B. Lyons photo

The profile of the T-Bird changed noticeably in 1957. This hardtop-equipped car is outfitted in Thunderbird Bronze.

The 1957 T-Bird came in 10 different colors, and all 10 were offered on the fiberglass tops, including Dusk Rose.

ENGINES

THUNDERBIRD BASE V-8 (MANUAL TRANSMISSION): Overhead valve. Cast-iron block. Bore and stroke: 3.75 x 3.30 in. Displacement: 292 cid. Compression ratio: 9.10:1. Brake hp: 212 at 4500 rpm. Torque: 297 lbs.-ft. at 2700 rpm. Taxable hp: 45.0. Five main bearings. Solid valve lifters. Crankcase capacity: 5 qt. (add 1 qt. with new oil filter). Cooling system capacity: 19 qt. Carburetor: Holley two-barrel. Code C.

THUNDERBIRD SPECIAL V-8 (OVERDRIVE OR FORD-O-MATIC TRANSMISSION): Overhead valve. Cast-iron block. Bore and stroke: 3.80 x 3.44 in. Displacement: 312 cid. Compression ratio: 9.70:1. Brake hp: 245 at 4500 rpm. Taxable hp: 45.0. Torque: 332 lbs.-ft. at 3200 rpm. Five main bearings. Crankcase capacity: 5 qt. (add 1 qt. with new oil filter). Cooling system capacity: 19 qt. Carburetor: Single Holley four-barrel. Code D.

THUNDERBIRD SUPER V-8 (WITH DUAL FOUR-BARREL CARBURETORS; ALL TRANSMISSIONS): Overhead valve. Cast-iron block. Bore and stroke: 3.80 x 3.44 inches. Displacement: 312 cid. Compression ratio: 9.70:1 (10.0:1 with racing kit installed). Brake hp: 270 at 4800 rpm. Taxable hp: 45.0. Torque: 336 at 3400 rpm. Five main bearings. Solid valve lifters. Crankcase capacity: 5 qt. (add 1 qt. with new oil filter). Cooling system capacity: 19 qt. Carburetor: Two Holley four-barrel. Code E.

THUNDERBIRD SUPER V-8 (RACING KIT VERSION; ALL TRANSMISSIONS): Overhead valve. Cast-iron block. Bore and stroke: 3.80 x 3.44 in. Displacement: 312 cid. Compression ratio: 9.70:1 (10.0:1 with racing kit installed). Brake hp: 285 at 5200 rpm. Taxable hp: 45.0. Torque: 343 lbs.-ft. at 3500 rpm. Five main bearings. Solid valve lifters. Crankcase capacity: 5 qt. (add 1 qt. with new oil filter). Cooling system capacity: 19 qt. Carburetor: Two Holley four-barrel. Code E.

THUNDERBIRD SPECIAL SUPERCHARGED V-8 (ALL TRANSMISSIONS): Overhead valve. Cast-iron block. Bore

Some testers were disappointed in the T-Bird's performance, but a 312-cid dual-four barrel model like this one still delivered a reported 270 hp.

and stroke: 3.80 x 3.44 in. Displacement: 312 cid. Compression ratio: 8.5:1. Brake hp: 300 at 4800 rpm. Taxable hp: 45.0. Torque: 340 at 5300 rpm. Five main bearings. Solid valve lifters. Crankcase capacity: 5 qt. (add 1 qt. with new oil filter). Cooling system capacity: 19 qt. Carburetor: Holley four-barrel with McCulloch/Paxton centrifugal supercharger. Code F.

CHASSIS

Wheelbase: 102 in. Overall length: 181.4 in. Overall width: 72.8 in. Overall height: 49.6 in. Front tread: 56 in. Rear tread: 56 in. Front headroom: (with hardtop) 33.1 in.; (with convertible top) 33.6 in. Front hip room: 58.8 in. Front shoulder room: 53.3 in. Front legroom: 44.9 in. Top of door height: 34.2 in. Top of soft top height: 51.8 in. Standard hypoid axle: (Manual transmission) 3.56:1, (Overdrive transmission) 3.70:1, (Ford-o-matic) 3.10:1. Wheels: 14-in. Safety Contour. Tires: 7.50 x 14 four-ply. Wheel studs: 5.5 in. Wheel stud circle: 4.5 in. diameter. Brake swept area: 175.5 sq. in. Turning diameter: 36 ft. Steering wheel: 17-in. Lifeguard type. Steering wheel adjustment: 2 in. Turns lock-to-lock: 4.5. Steering ratio: 23.0:1. Weight distribution: 50/50. Chassis type: X frame. Front suspension: Ball joints, coil springs, tube shocks and stabilizer. Rear suspension: Composite axle, five-leaf springs, double-acting shock absorbers. Steering: Parallel linkage type. Steering wheel: 3-in. in-and-out adjustable. Front brakes: 11-in. diameter double-sealed. Brake swept area: 176 sq. in. Rear brakes: 11-in. diameter double-sealed. Standard transmission: Three-speed synchromesh with helical gears. Optional transmission: Planetary overdrive with planetary gears. Optional transmission: Ford-o-matic torque converter transmission with planetary gears. Axle ratios: (manual transmission) 3.56:1, (overdrive transmission) 3.70:1 and (automatic transmission) 3.10:1. Gas tank: 20 gal.

Cappy collection

The Thunderbird got its first major makeover in 1957. The front and back ends were both redesigned, with the front receiving a different grille and heavier bumper.

Dusk Rose was a color befitting of this 1957 T-Bird.

OPTIONS

Dial-O-Matic four-way power seat. Swift Sure power brakes ($38). Master-Guide power steering ($68). Power-Lift windows ($70). I-Rest tinted safety glass. Ford-O-Matic drive ($215). Overdrive ($108). White sidewall tires. Special fuel and vacuum pump unit for positive-action windshield wipers. MagicAire Heater. Volumatic radio. Deluxe antenna. Rear fender shields. Back-up lights. Locking gas cap. Hooded mirror. Auto-Home electric shaver. Turbine wheel covers. Simulated wire wheel covers. Engine dress-up kit ($25). Aquamatic windshield wipers/washers. Thunderbird 312-cid four-barrel V-8. Thunderbird 312-cid Super V-8. Convertible fabric top. Tonneau cover. Seat belts. Full-flow oil filter (left off some early literature). Super Filter air cleaner (changed to standard equipment effective Feb. 1957).

HISTORICAL FOOTNOTES

Henry Ford II was president of Ford Motor Company in 1957, Earnest R. Breech was chairman of the board, and J. O. Wright was a vice president and general manager of Ford Division. Lee Iacocca was promoted to car marketing manager this year.

Production of 1957 Thunderbirds began on September 14, 1956 with car number D7FH100010. Model introductions took place on October 3, 1956. Ford continued building these cars after full-size Fords underwent the normal model changeover late in the summer of 1957. The company had set a production target of 20,000 units, but the '57s were popular and orders ran higher than expected. Model-year production eventually hit 21,380. The extended model run allowed Ford to "build out" the two-seat T-Bird and use up parts in inventory before switching to four-seat model production for the 1958 model year. The last 1957 model, reportedly owned by David Koto of Michigan, had serial number E7FH395813.

Ford boasted that the T-Bird had outsold all other sports-type personal cars combined. According to *Popular Mechanic's 1957 Car Facts Book*, during 1956 it outsold its principal domestic competitor, the Chevrolet Corvette, by more than 10 to 1. Even though the Corvette had whipped the T-Bird in sports car racing, the T-Bird was the big winner on the boulevards of America. By the time the extended 1957 season came to a close, the three-year total of T-Bird production stood at 53,166 units. That compared to just 14,446 Corvettes built in five years.

Most car magazines test drove early versions of the 1957 Thunderbird. The cars Ford loaned them for the tests seemed to have many convenience options like Ford-O-Matic transmission, an adjustable steering wheel, a four-way power seat and power windows. Usually the 245-hp Thunderbird Special engine was under the hood. *Motor Life's* Ken Fermoyle found this T-Bird's performance, "Frankly disappointing." He said he had trouble believing

Mike Mueller photo

The potent 312-cid supercharged Thunderbird Special V-8 for 1957.

Daniel B. Lyons photo

A stunning '57 outfitted in Gunmetal Gray.

Daniel B. Lyons photo

The tailfins were one of several additions that changed the look of the T-Bird in 1957.

that the car needed 11.5 seconds to go from 0 to 60 mph. In May 1957, *Speed Age* did an "Expert Test" comparing the Corvette, T-Bird, and Studebaker Golden Hawk. Of the three, the T-Bird was slowest. However, it registered an 8.49-second 0-to-60 time and a top speed of 119.3 mph.

Mike Mueller photo

The all-new Thunderbird had a deeper passenger compartment that was described as a "sunken living room."

1958 *Thunderbird*

The 1958 four-seat Thunderbird was one of the most totally changed cars in history. Much larger than the two-seat T-Bird, it also featured unit-body construction. A two-door hardtop was the only model offered at first. This was a true pillarless coupe, rather than a convertible with an add-on fiberglass top like the 1955-1957 "hardtop" model. A convertible was introduced in mid 1958. It had the first power-operated cloth top on a T-Bird, but the ragtop was not fully automatic in its operation.

The new car had a square "Ford" look that led to the nickname "Squarebird." Angular, sculptured feature lines characterized the hood scoop, the front fenders, the body side "projectiles" and the twin "jet-pod" rear end. There were two headlights on each side up front. Chrome decorations included Thunderbird scripts on the front fender sides with bombsight ornaments atop both fenders. The integral bumper-grille had twin guards mounted on the lower part of the grille frame. The insert was a piece of stamped sheet metal with round holes punched into it in diagonal rows. Five cast-metal ornaments with groups of chrome hash marks decorated the projectiles on the lower body sides. Each rear jet-pod held two large, round taillights set into small painted grilles with inserts matching the front grille. Back-up lights were optional. The rear license plate was in the center. Small tail fins graced the top of the rear fenders. They ran from ahead of the door handles, canting slightly outwards at the rear. The center area of the deck lid had a wide depression with a chrome Thunderbird emblem

in its center.

The formal-roof hardtop had a long and low appearance. The roof sail panels carried small round Thunderbird medallions. Bright metal strips with horizontal ribbing decorated the bottom of the roof pillars. The standard full wheel disks had turbine-fins with large flat centers. Vent windows were a new feature.

Approval to make the 1958 Thunderbird convertible was delayed until May 1957 and it bowed in June 1958. Its top disappeared completely into the trunk, leaving no fabric exposed and a smooth, unbroken trunk line. Top operation came from two hydraulic cylinders that derived pressure from an electrically operated rotor pump. To stack the top, the operator had to release the header clamps, unsnap eight fasteners in the quarter window area (above the side rails), and unlatch the luggage compartment door. When the latches were released by forward pressure on the cylinder of the luggage compartment door latch lock, the operator had to release the door safety catch and raise the door by hand. After the door had been raised upright, the upper back finish panel had to be raised in position to avoid damage when the lid was lowered with the top stacked. The panel had to be raised and locked. A release-knob plunger was provided. The top could then be lowered by means of a safety switch located in the luggage compartment. After the top was stacked, the luggage compartment door had to be lowered by hand and latched by putting pressure on the

BODY COLOR INFORMATION

Color Name	Code	Color Name	Code
Raven Black	A	Platinum+++	O
Winterset White	B	Primer++	P
Desert Beige ++	C	Special++++	S
Palomino Tan+	D	Casino Cream++	V
Colonial White	E	Cameo Rose	W
Grenadier Red ++	I	Cascade Green++	X
Everglade Green ++	K	Monarch Blue++	Y
Gulfstream Blue	M	Regatta Blue++	Z

+ In August 1958 Colonial White (E) Replaced Winterset White (B)
++ The 1958 T-Birds and 1958 Lincolns were built in the same plant and shared these colors.
+++ Cars delivered in primer were usually those that received special non-standard finishes.
++++ Code S indicated special-order finish with standard colors from other Ford car lines.

ADDITIONAL BODY COLOR INFORMATION (SPRING 1958)

Oriental Rose+++	W	Peach+++	X

+++ Oriental Rose and Peach do not appear in our factory references. They are listed in aftermarket Ditzler paint books and may be midyear replacements for Cameo Rose and Cascade Green.

TWO-TONE 1958 BODY COLORS

Color I (Lower)	Color II (Upper)	Code	Color I (Lower)	Color II (Upper)	Code
Winterset White	Raven Black	BA	Gulfstream Blue	Winterset White	MB
Desert Beige	Winterset White	CB	Platinum	Winterset White	OB
Winterset White	Gulfstream Blue	BM	Monarch Blue	Winterset White	YB
Winterset White	Platrinum	BO	Regatta Blue	Winterset White	ZB
Winterset White	Monarch Blue	BY	Everglade Green	Winterset White	KB
Winterset White	Regatta Blue	BZ	Cascade Green/Peach	Winterset White	XB
Winterset White	Everglade Green	BK	Casino Cream	Winterset White	VB
Winterset White	Cascade Gr/Peach	BX	Grenadier Red	Winterset White	IB
Winterset White	Casino Cream	BV	Cameo Rs./Orien Rs.	Winterset Wh	WB
Winterset White	Grenadier Red	BI	Platinum	Raven Black	OA
Winterset White	Cam. Rs./Orien.Rs	BW	Casino Cream	Raven Black	VA
Raven Black	Winterset White	AB	Grenadier Red	Raven Black	IA
Raven Black	Platinum	AO	Cam. Rs./Orien.Rs	Raven Black	WA
Raven Black	Casino Cream	AV	Monarch Blue	Regatta Blue	YZ
Raven Black	Grenadier Red	AI	Regatta Blue	Monarch Blue	ZY
Raven Black	Cam. Rs./Orien.Rs	AW	Everglade Green	Cascade Green	KX
Palomino Tan	Winterset White	DB	Cascade Green	Everglade Green	XK
Desert Beige	Winterset White	CB			

TOP COLOR INFORMATION

No. 1: Black top with Gray headlining and black frame
No. 2: Light Green top with Green headlining and Tan frame
No. 3: Light Blue top with Blue headlining and Black frame
No. 4: White top with Gray headlining and Black frame
No. 5: White top with Blue headlining and Black frame
No. 6: White top with Green headlining and Tan frame
No. 7: White top with Buff headlining and Tan frame.

INTERIOR TRIM INFORMATION

Soft-textured vinyl with horizontal pleats

Seat Type	Material	Blue/ White	Green/ White	Red/ White	Black/ White	Tan/ White	Turquoise/ White
Bucket Seats	All-Vinyl	XE	XF	XG	XH	XL	XM

Vinyl bolsters with Highland Tweed cloth inserts

Seat Type	Material	Blue/ Blue	Green/ Green	Black/ B & W	Turquoise/ Turquoise
Bucket Seats	Cloth & Vinyl	XA	XB	XC	XK

THUNDERBIRD PRODUCTION

Model Number	Body/Style Number	Body Type & Seating	Factory Price	Shipping Weight	Production Total
H	63A	2d Tudor-4P	$3,631	3,708 lbs.	35,758
J	76A	2d Convertible-4P	$3,914	3,733 lbs.	2,134

door, near the latches. This procedure was reversed to raise the top.

Inside, the T-Bird was also totally redesigned. It was the first American car to come standard with bucket seats and a center console. To keep overall height as low as possible, the passenger compartment had a deeper-than-usual well described as a "sunken living room." The transmission/drive shaft tunnel was high and the full-length console was used to make it functional. The console housed controls for a heater (and optional air conditioner), the power window switches, the radio speaker and front and rear ashtrays. Each of the four seats was virtually a separate "cubicle." The dashboard had "twin pods" for driver and passenger. There was a deep-dish steering wheel, safety-padded instrument panel, padded sun visors and a service-tray glove box door. Molded door and side panels were also new. Overall, the interior design was very attractive.

Powering 1958 T-Birds was a new 352-cid "Interceptor" V-8. A 430-cid/375-hp engine mentioned in some literature and ads did not materialize. Also new was an angle-poised ball-joint front suspension. The 1958 model was also the only Thunderbird to have a coil spring rear suspension prior to 1967.

STANDARD EQUIPMENT

[December 1957 for hardtop only] 300-hp/352-cid Thunderbird Special V-8, four-barrel carburetor, dual exhausts, full-flow oil filtration, automatic choke, three-speed manual transmission, Lifeguard padded instrument panel, cushioned sun visors, cigarette lighter, horn ring, dual horns, automatic dome light, and turn signals. [January 1958 for hardtop only] 300-hp/352-cid Thunderbird Special V-8, four-barrel carburetor, dual exhausts, full-flow oil filtration, automatic choke, three-speed manual transmission, Lifeguard padded instrument panel, cushioned sun visors, double-grip door locks, safety-swivel inside rearview mirror, deep-center steering wheel with horn ring, manually adjustable driver's seat, automatic dome light, cigarette lighter, coat hooks in rear compartment, dual horns, and turn signals. [May 1958 for hardtop and convertible] 300-hp/352-cid Thunderbird Special V-8, four-barrel carburetor, dual exhausts, full-flow oil filtration, automatic choke, Lifeguard padded instrument panel, cushioned sun visors, double-grip door locks, safety-swivel rearview mirror, deep-center steering wheel, manually adjustable front seats, electric clock, automatic dome light in hardtop and courtesy light in convertible, cigarette lighter, gunsight front fender ornaments, dual horns, and turn signals.

I.D. NUMBERS

VIN located on plate on left door pillar. First symbol denotes engine: H=352-cid/300-hp Thunderbird Special V-8. Second symbol denotes model-year: 8=1958. Third symbol denotes the assembly plant: Y=Wixom (Novi), Michigan. Fourth symbol denotes body type: H=Thunderbird two-door hardtop, J=Thunderbird two-door convertible. Fifth thru 10th symbols denote sequential production number of specific vehicle starting at 100001. Body number plate located on left front door hinge post. Serial number: Same as number on VIN tag. Symbols below "BODY" are body symbol code: 63A=Thunderbird hardtop, 76A=Thunderbird convertible. Symbols below "COLOR" are paint color code. First symbol indicates lower body color. Second symbol, if used, indicates upper body color on cars with two-tone paint. Symbols below "TRIM" are trim combination code. Symbols below "DATE" are the production date code. The number indicates the date of the month the car was made. The letters indicate month of manufacture: A=January, B=February, C=March, D=April, E=May, F=June, G=July, H=August, J=September, K=October, L=November, M=December. Symbols below "TRANS" are transmission code: 1-conventional three-speed manual transmission,

2=three-speed manual transmission with overdrive, 4=Cruise-O-Matic transmission. Symbols below "AXLE" are axle code: 1=3.10, 3=3.70.

ENGINES

THUNDERBIRD BASE V-8 (ALL TRANSMISSIONS): Overhead valve. Cast-iron block. Bore and stroke: 4.00 x 3.50 in. Displacement: 352 cid. Compression ratio: 10.2:1. Brake hp: 300 at 4600 rpm. Taxable hp: 51.2. Torque: 395 lbs.-ft. at 2800 rpm. Five main bearings. Valve lifters: (early) solid; (late) hydraulic. Crankcase capacity: 5 qt. (add 1 qt. with new oil filter). Cooling system capacity: 19.5 qt. Dual exhaust. Carburetor: Ford-Holley Model B8A-9510-E four-barrel or Carter numbers 2640S-SA-SC four-barrel. Code H.

CHASSIS

Wheelbase: 113.2 in. Overall length: 205.4 in. Overall width: 77 in. Overall height: (hardtop) 54.5 in., (convertible) 53.1 in. Front headroom (hardtop): 34.5 in. Rear headroom (hardtop): 33.3 in. Front seat cushion to floor height (hardtop): 11 in. Rear seat cushion to floor height (hardtop): 13.1 in. Front shoulder room (hardtop): 56.2 in. Rear shoulder room (hardtop): 54.1 in. Front hip room (hardtop): 59.6 in. Rear hip room (hardtop): 48.7 in. Front legroom (hardtop): 43.4 in. Rear legroom (hardtop): 38.1 in. Road clearance: 5.8 in. Front tread: 60 in. Rear tread: 57 in. Tires: 8.00 x 14 4-ply. Turning diameter: 39 ft. Steering ratio: 25.0:1. Chassis type: Welded, integral body and frame. Front suspension: Ball joints, coil springs, and tube shocks. Rear suspension: Trailing arm type with coil springs, rubber-mounted pivots and double-acting shock absorbers. Steering: Re-circulating ball type. Turning circle, curb-to-curb: 40.32 ft. Front brakes: 11-in. diameter double-sealed, ceramic linings. Rear brakes: 11-in. diameter double-sealed, ceramic linings. Brake swept area: (standard) 168.98 sq. in., (optional) 193.5 sq. in. Standard transmission: Three-speed synchromesh with helical gears. Optional transmission: Planetary overdrive with planetary gears. Optional transmission: Cruise-O-Matic torque converter transmission with planetary gears. Standard rear axle ratio: (manual and overdrive) 3.70, (Cruise-O-Matic): 3.10. Gas tank: 20 gal. (premium fuel required).

OPTIONS

Manually adjustable front passenger seat (Manually adjustable front seats became standard in May 1958). Power brakes ($37). Overdrive transmission ($108). Power windows ($101). Four-way power driver's seat ($64). Tube-type radio ($77). Signal-seeking radio ($99). Five 8.00 x 14 whitewall tires in place of black sidewall ($36). I-Rest Tinted glass ($20). Windshield washers/wipers ($12). Back-up lights ($10). Power steering ($69). MagicAire heater ($95). SelectAire conditioner (N/A). Leather interior ($106). Radio antennas. Seat belts. Positive windshield wipers. Electric clock (became standard after May 1958). Outside mirrors. Rear fender shields. Fashion-Ray wheel covers. Locking gas cap (first offered in January 1958). Gunsight front fender ornaments (became standard in May 1958). Cruise-O-Matic transmission (Sale literature says "optional, installed in production" after May 1958).

HISTORICAL FOOTNOTES

Henry Ford II remained president of Ford Motor Company in 1958 and Earnest R. Breech remained chairman of the board. Robert S. McNamara was a Ford Motor Company Group vice president and president of the Car and Truck Division. J. O. Wright was vice president and

The "Square Bird" of 1958 may not have looked quite as square with the top down, but it was definitely a radical departure from the cars of the first three model years.

Mike Mueller photo

The 1958 T-Bird had a back seat and could carry four adults, and Ford played up the four-passenger angle in its advertising.

general manager of Ford Division.

The new four-passenger Thunderbird entered production on Jan. 13, 1958. It was built in the brand new Wixom factory near Novi, Michigan, alongside the 1958 Lincoln and Continental Mark III. Since it was all-new, it arrived in showrooms later than other 1958 Ford products. Dealer introductions took place on Feb. 13, 1958. The convertible was added to the line on May 1, 1958. T-Bird product planner Tom Case had wanted to continue the two-passenger model (with a new power top) and add a four-passenger model. This was guaranteed to bring a sales increase, but there was no guarantee profits would go up. McNamara, the new general manager of Ford Division, told Case to drop the two-car idea. McNamara fought with the board of directors to get the four-passenger car he knew would bring higher profits. The T-Bird became one of only two U.S. cars to increase sales in 1958.

"Despite a late introduction and the fact that 1958 was a miserable flop as a year for selling cars, the '58 T-Bird sold 37,000 units and dealers ended up at changeover time with orders backlogged for 800 cars," is how *Hot Rod* magazine put it in July 1959. *Ward's Automotive Yearbook* reported that Thunderbird sales climbed from 1.3 percent to 3.8 percent of Ford's sales total.

Optional power plants had been considered for the 1958 Thunderbird, since the long list of engines offered in 1957 had helped to sell cars. One plan was to use the 361-cid Edsel V-8 with a choice of four horsepower ratings. However, the total budget for styling, engineering, and

tooling work was only $50 million. After tooling costs absorbed 90 percent of the money, the plan was changed to one offering only one engine. A 430-cid V-8 was mentioned in some T-Bird literature and advertisements. It is believed that this engine was not used in production cars. It was a Lincoln V-8 suitable only for use with Cruise-O-Matic (Lincoln called it Turbo-Drive) transmission.

Motor Trend tested a prototype Thunderbird with this engine and shaved about 2 seconds off normal 0-to-60 times. The 352-cid-powered 1958 T-Bird hardtop was tested at 12.9 seconds for 0 to 60 mph and 17.6 seconds for the quarter mile.

The 1958 Thunderbird was only 511 lbs. heavier than a Ford Custom Tudor V-8, but lacked the ladder frame and had a shorter wheelbase. Gutted of its console and other goodies, the T-Bird held promise as a stock car racer. This wasn't lost on NASCAR fans. Some car builders wanted to start constructing competition versions of the four-seat T-Bird right away. As things turned out, the "Square-Bird" would go stock car racing, but not in 1958.

A one-year-only coil spring rear suspension was introduced in anticipation of using the "Ford Aire" system —an early type of air suspension—in the T-Bird. When Ford Aire proved unreliable, the idea of using it on the T-Bird was dropped, but Ford was stuck with the coil springs for 1958. T-Birds went back to leaf springs in 1959. *Motor Trend* magazine picked the 1958 Thunderbird to win its "Car of the Year" award. Ford produced its 50 millionth vehicle of all time on March 17, 1958.

Daniel B. Lyons photo

The 1959 Thunderbird changed little from the previous year, but it did receive a few minor cosmetic changes. The grille had a more horizontal pattern, a chrome arrowhead badge appeared on the doors, and the nameplates moved to the doors.

1959 *Thunderbird*

The 1959 T-Bird was changed very little from 1958. A new horizontal louver pattern filled the "air scoop" grille and was repeated in the recessed taillight panels. Instead of hash marks, the body-side projectiles had a chrome arrowhead at the front of the bulge. Thunderbird nameplates were moved from the front fenders to the doors and decorated the projectiles. The round medallion seen on the rear window pillar of the 1958 hardtop was replaced by a sculptured Thunderbird medallion. The convertible's top was power operated and folded completely into the trunk.

The base 352-cid V-8 had ignition improvements and a new Holley model 9510 four-barrel carburetor. A 430-cid Thunderbird Special V-8 was optional, but only with SelectShift Cruise-O-Matic transmission. This V-8 did not have a conventional combustion chamber in the cylinder head. The valves seated on a flat head surface and the combustion chamber was formed between the tops of the pistons and the top of the block, which was milled 10 degrees from perpendicular to the cylinder bore. Dual exhausts were standard with both V-8s. Other technical revisions in T-Birds included a new radiator fan, a new auxiliary coolant tank, a relocated windshield washer system, an "Angle-Poised" ball-joint front suspension, 4-foot-wide doors, 20 cu. ft. of trunk space, and individually adjustable front seats. The T-Bird bucket seats had a kind of rounded and overstuffed look. The front passenger seat folded to permit entry into the rear from the curb side of the

car. The 1959 instruments and gauges had white faces, instead of the previous black ones. The T-Bird's unit-constructed body had the floor pan, frame, body side panels, front and rear fenders, roof panel and cross braces all welded together into one durable unit of double-walled sculptured steel. There was a new leaf-spring rear suspension with longitudinal springs on either side that gave a more evenly balanced ride with slightly less lean in the corners.

STANDARD EQUIPMENT

Built-in armrests, floor carpets, individually adjusted seats with deep-foam rubber seat cushions and backs, full folding front passenger seat, optional choice of deep-pleated all-vinyl interior or linen seat inserts with vinyl bolsters, padded dash and sun visors, front and rear ashtrays, cigarette lighter, electric clock, courtesy lights, dual exhausts, fuel filter, a deep-center "Lifeguard" steering wheel with a horn ring, turn signals, dual horns, spare tire, and bumper jack.

I.D. NUMBERS

VIN located on plate on left door pillar. First symbol denotes engine: H=352-cid/300-hp Thunderbird Special V-8, J=430-cid/350-hp Thunderbird Special V-8. Second symbol denotes model-year: 9=1959. Third symbol denotes the

BODY COLOR INFORMATION

Color Name	Code	Color Name	Code
Raven Black	A	Doeskin Beige ++	M
Baltic Blue ++	C	Starlight Blue ++	N
Indian Turquoise	D	Primer +++	P
Colonial White	E	Sea Reef Green ++	Q
Hickory Tan ++	F	Brandywine Red	R
Glacier Green	G	Special ++++	S
Tahitian Bronze	H	Flamingo Pink ++	T
Steel Blue ++	J	Cordovan	U
Sandstone ++	K	Casino Cream +	V
Diamond Blue ++	L	Tamarack Green	W
		Platinum+	Z

+ Color also used on Lincolns and Mercurys
++ Color also used on Lincolns
+++ Special order for dealer painted cars in standard colors used on other Fords
++++ Special order non-standard colors

TWO-TONE 1959 BODY COLORS

Color I (Lower)	Color II (Upper)	Code	Color I (Lower)	Color II Upper)	Code
Raven Black	Colonial White	AE	Diamond Blue	Baltic Blue*	LC
Colonial White	Raven Black	EA	Baltic Blue	Colonial White	CE
Platinum	Colonial White	ZE	Colonial White	Baltic Blue	EC
Colonial White	Platinum	EZ	Starlight Blue	Baltic Blue	NC
Raven Black	Platinum	AZ	Baltic Blue	Starlight Blue	CN
Colonial White	Sandstone	EK	Stool Blue	Colonial White	JE
Baltic Blue	Diamond Blue	CL	Colonial White	Steel Blue	EJ
Colonial White	Hickory Tan	EF	Diamond Blue	Steel Blue	LJ
Brandywine Red	Colonial White	RE	Steel Blue	Diamond Blue	JL
Colonial White	Brandywine Red	ER	Starlight Blue	Colonial White	NE
Doeskin Beige	Hickory Tan	MF	Colonial White	Starlight Blue	EN
Brandywine Red	Raven Black	RA	Glacier Green	Tamarack Green	GW
Raven Black	Brandywine Red	AR	Colonial White	Sea Reef Green	EQ
Indian Turquoise	Colonial White	DE	Glacier Green	Colonial White	GE
Colonial White	Indian Turquoise	ED	Sea Reef Green	Colonial White	QE
Flamingo Pink	Colonial White	TE	Tamarack Green	Colonial White*	WE
Colonial White	Flamingo Pink	ET	Colonial White	Tamarack Green	EW
Flamingo Pink	Raven Black	TA	Tamarack Grteen	Glacier Green	WG
Tahitian Bronze	Colonial White	HE	Glacier Green	Tamarack Green	GW
Sandstone	Colonial White	KE	Cordovan	Colonial White	UE
Casino Cream	Colonial White	VE	Cordovan	Doeskin Deige	UM
Casino Cream	Raven Black	VA	Hickory Tan	Colonial White	FE
Diamond Blue	Raven Black	LA	Hickory Tan	Doeskin Beige	FM
Tahitian Bronze	Raven Black	HA			

* Not listed in company literature, but documented vehicles exist with this combination

TOP COLOR INFORMATION

No. 1: Black rayon with Black headlining and Black frame
No. 4: Light Blue vinyl with Blue headlining and Blue frame
No. 5: Turquoise vinyl with Turquoise headlining and Turquoise frame
No. 6: White vinyl with Black headlining and Black frame
No. 7: White vinyl with Turquoise headlining and Turquoise frame
No. 8: White vinyl with Blue headlining and Blue frame
No. 9: White vinyl with Buff headlining and Buff frame

INTERIOR TRIM INFORMATION

Vinyl & Nylon Check Cloth Interiors

Seat Type	Material	Blue/ Blue	Green/ Green	Turquoise/ Turquoise	Black/ Black & White
Bucket Seats	Cloth & Vinyl	1X	2X	3X	4X

All-Vinyl With Horizontal Pleats Interiors

Seat Type	Material	Blue/ Blue	Green/ White	Turquoise/ White	Black/ White	Red/ White
Bucket Seats	Vinyl	5X	6X	7X	8X	9X

Leather Interiors

Seat Type	Material	Black/ Black	Tan/ Tan	Turquoise/ Turquoise	Red/ Red	Tan/ White
Bucket Seats	Leather	1Y	2Y	3Y	4Y	5Y

THUNDERBIRD PRODUCTION

Model Number	Body/Style Number	Body Type & Seating	Factory Price	Shipping Weight	Production Total
H	63A	2d Tudor-4P	$3,368	3,813 lbs.	57,195
J	76A	2d Convertible-4P	$3,631	3,903 lbs.	10,261

assembly plant: Y=Wixom (Novi), Michigan. Fourth symbol denotes body type: H=Thunderbird Tudor hardtop, J=Thunderbird two-door convertible. Fifth thru tenth symbols denote sequential production number of specific vehicle starting at 100001. Body number plate located on left front door hinge post. Serial number: Same as number on VIN tag. Symbols below "BODY" are body symbol code: 63A=Thunderbird hardtop, 76A=Thunderbird convertible. Symbols below "COLOR" are paint color code. First symbol indicates lower body color. Second symbol, if used, indicates upper body color on cars with two-tone paint. Symbols below "TRIM" are trim combination code. Symbols below "DATE" are the production date code. The number indicates the date of the month the car was made. The letters indicate month of manufacture: A=January, B=February, C=March, D=April, E=May, F=June, G=July, H=August, J=September, K=October, L=November, M=December. Symbols below "TRANS" are transmission code: 1-conventional three-speed manual transmission, 2=three-speed manual transmission with overdrive, 4=Cruise-O-Matic transmission. Symbols below "AXLE" are axle code: 1=3.10, 3=3.70 and 0=2.91:1.

ENGINES

352-CID V-8 (ALL TRANSMISSIONS): Overhead valve. Cast-iron block. Bore and stroke: 4.00 x 3.50 in. Displacement: 352 cid. Compression ratio: 9.6:1. Brake hp: 300 at 4600 rpm. Taxable hp: 51.2. Torque: 395 lbs.-ft. at 2800 rpm. Five main bearings. Hydraulic valve lifters. Crankcase capacity: 5 qt. (add 1 qt. with new oil filter). Cooling system capacity: 19.5 qt. Dual exhaust. Carburetor: Ford four-barrel Model 5752304 and 5752305, or Holley four-barrel. Code H.

430-CID SPECIAL V-8 (CRUISE-O-MATIC ONLY): Overhead valve. Cast-iron block. Bore and stroke: 4.30 x 3.70 in. Displacement: 430 cid. Compression ratio: 10.0:1. Brake hp: 350 at 4600 rpm. Taxable hp: 51.2. Torque: 490 lbs.-ft. at 2800 rpm. Five main bearings. Hydraulic valve lifters. Crankcase capacity: 5 qt. (add 1 qt. with new oil

There was no doubt that Ford targeted the female audience in its 1959 Thunderbird ads. It was promoted as a fun, versatile car that could take a woman from the golf course, to the shopping center, to a night on the town.

filter). Cooling system capacity: 19.5 qt. Dual exhaust. Carburetor: Holley four-barrel Model 4160-C. Code J.

CHASSIS

Wheelbase: 113 in. Overall length: 205.3 in. Overall width: 77.0 in. Overall height: (hardtop) 54.2 in., (convertible) 53.1 in. Front headroom (hardtop): 34.5 in. Rear headroom (hardtop): 33.3 in. Front seat cushion to floor height (hardtop): 11 in. Rear seat cushion to floor height (hardtop): 13.1 in. Front shoulder room (hardtop): 56.2 in. Rear shoulder room (hardtop): 54.1 in. Front hip room (hardtop): 59.6 in. Rear hip room (hardtop): 48.7 in. Front legroom (hardtop): 43.4 in. Rear legroom (hardtop): 38.1 in. Road clearance: 5.80 in. Front tread: 60 in. Rear tread: 57 in. Tires: 8.00 x 14 four-ply. Steering ratio: 25.0:1. Chassis type: Welded, integral body and frame. Front suspension: Ball-joints, coil springs and tube shocks. Rear suspension: Outboard-mounted rear leaf springs, shackles and wind-up control rubber bumpers over springs with double-acting shock absorbers. Steering: Re-circulating ball type. Turning circle, curb-to-curb: 40.32 ft. Front brakes: 11-in. diameter double-sealed, ceramic linings. Rear brakes: 11-in. diameter double-sealed, ceramic linings. Brake swept area: 194 sq. in. Standard transmission: Three-speed synchromesh with helical gears. Optional transmission: Planetary overdrive with planetary gears. Optional transmission: Cruise-O-Matic torque converter transmission with planetary gears.

Standard rear axle ratio with manual transmission: 3.70. Standard rear axle with overdrive: 3.70. Standard rear axle ratio with 352-cid V-8 and Cruise-O-Matic: 3.10. Standard rear axle ratio with 430-cid V-8 and Cruise-O-Matic: 2.91. Gas tank: 20 gal. (premium fuel required).

OPTIONS

Cruise-O-Matic ($242). Overdrive ($145). Radio ($105). Signal seeker radio ($92.60*). Rear seat speaker ($13.50*). Power brakes ($43). Fresh air heater and defroster ($83). Driver's side power seat ($86). Select Air Conditioner ($446). 350-hp engine ($177). Genuine leather interior ($106). Rear fender shields ($27). Two seat belts ($26). White-sidewall tires ($36). Full wheel disks ($17). Back up lights ($10). Tinted glass ($38). Power windows ($102). Windshield washers ($14). Left-hand OSRV mirror ($5) Tu-Tone paint ($26). Two-speed electric wipers ($7.10*). Pair of regular floor mats ($3.50*). Pair of contoured floor mats ($7.95*). Equa-Lock differential ($32.15*). Heavy-duty 70-amp battery ($8). Door-mounted side view mirror ($5.95*). Fender-mounted side view mirror ($8.95*). Visor-vanity mirror ($1.95*). Factory undercoating ($15*). Tu-Tone paint ($22*). Clear plastic seat covers ($29.95 *). Antifreeze ($6.95 *). Tissue dispenser ($6.75*) Note: (*) indicates dealer wholesale price, retail prices for these items are unknown.

Cappy collection

The "love-it-or-hate-it" style of the "Square Bird" T-Birds continued in 1959, with a heavier grille and twin headlights. The base engine was a 392-cid V-8, but a 430-cid Thunderbird Special V-8 with 350 hp was also available with the Cruise-O-Matic transmission.

HISTORICAL FOOTNOTES

The 1959 T-Bird was introduced on October 17, 1958, 10 days later than other Fords. Despite a 116-day steel workers strike, Ford continued operating the Thunderbird assembly lines with minimum downtime. Thunderbird production for the calendar year improved by 42 percent.

Hot Rod magazine did a test of the 430-cid Thunderbird in its July 1959 issue. With the 430-cid 350-hp V-8 the T-Bird hardtop did 0 to 60 mph in 9.0 seconds and covered the quarter mile in 17.0 seconds at 86.57 mph.

The offering of a larger V-8 had a big influence on the Thunderbird's role in professional motorsports. The unit-bodied T-Bird was shorter in wheelbase and lighter in weight than standard Fords with ladder-type frames, which enhanced its racing potential.

Ford formed an association with Holman & Moody, of Charlotte, North Carolina, for the construction of several very hot 1959 T-Bird stock cars that made their racing debut at the new 2.5-mile International Daytona International Speedway in February. After completion by Holman & Moody, these cars were sold to the public. In race-ready form, the cars went for $5,500. At least two of the Holman & Moody Thunderbird racecars survive. In 1989, Billy Cooper & Associates of Barnwell, South Carolina, obtained one of the cars in exchange for a complete restoration. This car was restored to like-new condition and displayed at the Klassics Auto Museum in Daytona Beach, Florida. A few years ago, a second car with the special racing equipment, but non-racing trim, showed up at the Barrett-Jackson Classic Car Auction in Scottsdale, Arizona.

Fins were a sign of the times in the late 1950s, and the T-Bird's were sharp and distinctive.

Ford produced more than 67,000 T-Birds for 1959, but only 10,261 were convertibles. Black was one of four convertible top colors available.

Cappy collection

Mike Mueller photo

The stylish 1960 T-Bird was similar to the two previous years' models and remained a good seller, with 81,555 cars leaving dealer showrooms during the calendar year.

1960 *Thunderbird*

The four-passenger "Squarebird" styling of 1958-1959 was carried forward for one more year in 1960. There was a new grille. It had a large, horizontal main bar that was intersected by three vertical bars. Behind the bars was a grid-pattern insert. There was a trio of chrome hash marks, each consisting of three vertical bars, decorating the rear fenders. They were positioned towards the rear, just ahead of new taillight clusters that had three round lenses on each side. The hardtop model's rear roof pillars had elongated Thunderbird emblems. There was also a winged badge on the trunk, just above the license plate. The lower body-side projectiles now carried chrome Thunderbird scripts.

A manually operated sliding sunroof was a new option

for hardtops. Cars with sunroofs were known as Golde Top models. Golde was the name of the German company that licensed the sunroof design to Ford. A large, circular chrome fixture inside the car locked the sliding panel in place. It was the first sunroof offered on postwar domestic production cars. Only 2,536 buyers ordered it.

Inside, the 1960 Thunderbird had the same kind of dual-pod dash, front bucket seats, and a panel console. There were several new upholstery options. One two-tone design had large squares stitched into the seat inserts and upper door panels. Another choice had lengthwise pleating on the seats, vertical pleats on the upper door panels, and monochromatic color schemes. The rear seats had built-in

BODY COLOR INFORMATION

Color Name	Code	Color Name	Code
Raven Black	A	Diamond Blue	N
Kingston Blue	B	Primer	P
Aquamarine	C	Moroccan Ivory	R
Sapphire	D	Briarcliffe Green	S
Acapulco Blue	E	Meadowvale Green	T
Skymist Blue	F	Springdale Rose	U
Tawny Beige	G	Palm Springs Rose	V
Beachwood Brown	H	Adriatic Green	W
Pale Turquoise	I	Royal Burgundy	X
Monte Carlo Red	J	Gunpowder Gray	Y
Sultana Turquoise	K	Platinum	Z
Gold Dust	L		
Corinthian White	M		

TWO-TONE BODY COLORS

Color Panel/Color Overlay	Code	Color Panel/Color Overlay	Code
Sultana Turquoise/Aquamarine	KC	Palm Springs Rose/Corinthian White	VM
Corinthian White/Raven Black	MA	Beachwood Brown/Corinthian White	HM
Corinthian White/Aquamarine	MC	Sultana Turquoise/Corinthian White	KM
Platinum/Raven Black	ZA	Kingston Blue/Corinthian White	BM
Acapulco Blue/Skymist Blue	EF	Acapulco Blue/Corinthian White	EM
Platinum/Corinthian White	ZM	Corinthian White/Skymist Blue	MF
Gunpowder Gray/Corinthian White	YM	Acapulco Blue/Diamond Blue	EN
Monte Carlo Red/Corinthian White	JM	Kingston Blue/Skymist Blue	BF
Kingston Blue/Diamond Blue	BN	Corinthian White/Meadowvale Green	MT
Monte Carlo Red/Raven Black	JA	Briarcliffe Green/Corinthian White	SM
Moroccan Ivory/Corinthian White	RM	Briarcliffe Green/Meadowvale Green	ST
Moroccan Ivory/Raven Black	RA	Corinthian White/Adriatic Green	MW
Royal Burgundy/Corinthian White	XM	Meadowvale Green/Adriatic Green	TW
Springdale Rose/Corinthian White	UM	Briarcliffe Green/Adriatic Green	SW

Any combination of exterior colors and interior trim would be furnished upon specific order.

TOP COLOR INFORMATION

No.1: Black Rayon (Available with all but two trims)
No. 2: White Vinyl (Available with all trims)
No. 3: Light Blue Vinyl (Available with trims No. 52 and 72)
All tops have black headlining.

INTERIOR TRIM INFORMATION

Button-Tufted All- Vinyl Interiors

Seat Type	Material	2-Tone Blue	2-Tone Green	2-Tone Beige	White/ Red	White/ Black	2-Tone Turquoise
Bucket Seats	Vinyl	52	53	54	55	56	57

Button-Tufted Cloth & Vinyl Interiors

Seat Type	Material	2-Tone Blue	2-Tone Green	2-Tone Beige	Black/ L. Gray	Black/ L. Gray	2-Tone Turquoise
Bucket Seats	Cloth & Vinyl	72	73	74	75	76	77

Leather Interiors

Seat Type	Material	2-Tone Tan	2-Tone Red	2-Tone Black	2-Tone Turquoise
Bucket Seats	Leather	84	85	86	87

THUNDERBIRD PRODUCTION

Model Number	Body/Style Number	Body Type & Seating	Factory Price	Shipping Weight	Production Total
73	63A	2d Tudor-4P	$3,426	3,799 lbs.	78,447
71	76A	2d Convertible-4P	$3,860	3,897 lbs.	11,860
73	63B	2d Golde Top-4P	$3,638	3,850 lbs.	2,536

NOTE 1: Model No. 63B appears on Ford documents, but not on vehicle data plate.

armrests. Also new was a polarized day/night inside rearview mirror.

There were two 1960 T-Bird engines: the 352-cid Thunderbird Special V-8, and the 350-hp Thunderbird 430 Special V-8 that won so many 1959 stock car races. A chrome dress-up kit was available to make the engine compartments shine. Ford cleverly advertised "Precision Fuel Induction" for the larger engine, which actually used a conventional Holley four-barrel carburetor with "precision fuel metering." Ford promoted that Cruise-O-Matic Drive

was optional with either engine, although it was actually *mandatory* with the 430-cid Lincoln motor. The 352-cid V-8 also came with a three-speed manual gearbox or three-speed manual with overdrive.

STANDARD EQUIPMENT

Built-in dual exhausts, fuel filter, oil filter, 352-cid four-barrel V-8 engine, padded instrument panel and sun visors, electric clock with sweep second hand, courtesy lights, turn signals, deep-center steering wheel, dual horns and horn rings, individually adjustable front seats, day-night tilt-type rearview mirror, double-grip door locks, wheel covers, built-in armrests, floor carpets, full-width foam rubber seat, all-vinyl upholstery, ashtray, cigar lighter, air cleaner, and five black 8.00 x 14 tubeless tires.

I.D. NUMBERS

Die-stamped on top of front fender crossbar to right of hood lock striker plate. First symbol denotes model-year: 0=1960. Second symbol denotes the assembly plant: Y=Wixom (Novi), Michigan. Third symbol denotes the carline: 7=Thunderbird. Fourth symbol denotes body type: 1=Thunderbird Tudor hardtop, 3=Thunderbird two-door convertible. Fifth symbol denotes engine: Y=352-cid/300-hp Interceptor V-8, J=430-cid/350-hp Thunderbird Special V-8. Sixth through 11th symbols denote sequential production number of specific vehicle starting at 100001. Body number plate located on left front body pillar. Serial number: Same as number on VIN tag. Symbols above "BDY" are body symbol code: 63A=Thunderbird hardtop, 76A=Thunderbird convertible. Symbols above "CLR" are paint color code. First symbol indicates lower body color. Second symbol, if used, indicates upper body color on cars with two-tone paint. Symbols above "TRM" are trim combination code. Symbols below "DT" are the production date code. The number indicates the date of the month the car was made. The letters indicate month of manufacture: A=January, B=February, C=March, D=April, E=May, F=June, G=July, H=August, J=September, K=October, L=November, M=December, N=January and P=February, etc. (Ford listed two-year codes in case the 1960 model run was extended). Symbols above DSO indicate information including the Ford Motor Co. Sales District Code. Symbols above AX indicate rear axle. Axles used on 1960 Thunderbirds were: 3=3.10:1, 9=3.70:1. Symbols above TR indicate type of transmission: 1=Three-speed manual; 2=Three-speed manual with overdrive and 4=SelectShift Cruise-O-Matic. Vinyl convertible tops came in Black (except with trims 52 and 72); White (with all trims); and Blue (with trims 52 and 72 only). All convertible tops included a black headlining.

ENGINES

INTERCEPTOR SPECIAL V-8; BASE THUNDERBIRD V-8: Overhead valve. Cast-iron block. Bore and stroke: 4.00 x 3.50 inches. Displacement: 352 cid. Compression ratio: 9.6:1. Brake hp: 300 at 4600 rpm. Taxable hp: 51.2. Torque: 381 at 2800 rpm. Five main bearings. Hydraulic valve lifters. Crankcase capacity: 5 qt. (add 1 qt. with new oil filter). Cooling system capacity: 19.5 qt. Dual exhaust. Carburetor: Carburetor: Ford-Holley four-barrel Model COAE-9510-J with standard transmission or COAE-9510-K with automatic transmission. Code Y.

NOTE: Not mentioned in early 1960 Ford literature. Aluminum intake. Holley carburetor. Not available in cars with power steering or power brakes.

THUNDERBIRD SPECIAL V-8; OPTIONAL THUNDERBIRD V-8: Overhead valve. Cast-iron block. Bore and stroke: 4.30 x 3.70 inches. Displacement: 430 cid. Compression ratio: 10.0:1. Brake hp: 350 at 4600 rpm. Taxable hp: 59.15. Torque: 490 at 2800 rpm. Five main bearings. Hydraulic valve lifters. Crankcase capacity: 5 qt. (add 1 qt. with new oil filter). Cooling system capacity: 20 qt. with heater (16.5 qt. without heater). Dual exhaust. Carburetor: Carter AFB No. 2992S. Cruise-O-Matic mandatory. Code J.

CHASSIS

Wheelbase: 113 in. Overall length: 205.32 in. Overall width: 77 in. Overall height: (hardtop) 54.5 in., (convertible) 53.1 in. Front headroom: (hardtop) 34.5 in. Rear headroom: (hardtop) 33.3 in. Front shoulder room: 56.2 in. Rear shoulder room: 54.1 in. Front hip room: 59.6 in. Rear hip room: 48.7 in. Front legroom: 43.4 in. Rear legroom: 38.1 in. Road clearance: 5.80 in. Front tread: 60 in. Rear tread: 57 in. Tires: 8.00 x 14 4-ply. Steering ratio: 25.0:1. Chassis type: Welded, integral body and frame. Front suspension: Ball-joints, coil springs and tube shocks. Rear suspension: Outboard-mounted rear leaf springs, shackles and wind-up control rubber bumpers over springs with double-acting shock absorbers. Steering: Re-circulating ball type. Turning circle, curb-to-curb: 40.32 ft. Front brakes: 11-in. diameter double-sealed, ceramic linings. Rear brakes: 11-in. diameter double-sealed, ceramic linings. Brake swept area: 194 sq. in. Standard transmission: Three-speed synchromesh with helical gears. Optional transmission: Planetary overdrive with planetary gears. Optional transmission: Cruise-O-Matic torque converter transmission with planetary gears. Standard rear axle ratio with manual transmission: 3.70. Standard rear axle with overdrive: 3.70. Standard rear axle ratio with 352-cid V-8 and Cruise-O-Matic: 3.10. Standard rear axle ratio with 430-cid V-8 and Cruise-O-Matic: 2.91. Gas tank: 20 gallons (premium fuel required).

OPTIONS

Cruise-O-Matic drive ($242). Overdrive ($144.50). Central console radio and antenna ($112.80). MagicAire heater and defroster ($82.90). Air conditioner ($465.80). Tinted glass ($37.90). 8.00 x 14 rayon whitewall tires ($35.70 extra). 8.00 x 14 nylon white sidewall tires ($63.50 extra). 8.50 x 14 white sidewall tires (Price not available). 350-hp V-8 engine ($177). Master Guide power steering ($75.30). Power windows ($102.10). Swift Sure power brakes ($43.20). Four-way power driver's seat ($92.10). Left- or right-hand OSRV mirror ($5.10). Back-up lights ($9.50). Windshield washers ($13.70). Rear fender shields — skirts ($26.60). Front seat belts ($22.80). Leather interior ($106.20). Heavy-duty 70-amp battery in Hardtop ($7.60).

Cappy collection

This 1960 T-Bird carries a dealer-installed continental kit. It rests between flashy taillight clusters that were new for 1960.

1960 T-Bird hardtops could have optional sunroofs. Such models were dubbed Golde Top models after the company that licensed the sunroofs to Ford. The option cost $212.40.

A T-Bird hardtop being fabricated at the Budd-Detroit Plant.

Tu-Tone paint ($25.80). Underseal ($14.10). Sliding sunroof ($212.40). Two seat belts ($22.80). Two-speed electric windshield wipers (Price not available). Pair of regular floor mats (price not available). Pair of contoured floor mats (price not available). Equa-Lock differential (price not available). Fender-mounted side view mirror (price not available). Visor-vanity mirror (price not available). Clear plastic seat covers (price not available). Antifreeze (price not available). Tissue dispenser (price not available). Full wheel covers (price not available).

EQUIPMENT INSTALLATION RATES

Cruise-O-Matic drive (97.9 percent). V-8 engine (100

The base Thunderbird 352-cid Y-block V-8.

Jerry Heasley photo

Cappy collection

The front end of the 1960 T-Bird got three new vertical dividers in its grille.

percent). Radio (97.8 percent). Heater (99.1 percent). Power steering (96.9 percent). Power brakes (89.1 percent). Power seat (45.6 percent). Power windows (57.3 percent). White sidewall tires (97 percent). Windshield washers (78.4 percent). Tinited windshield (54.7 percent). Backup lights (88 percent). Air conditioning (25 percent). Dual exhaust (100 percent). Overdrive (0.9 percent). Note: The 1960 Thunderbird had the fourth-highest rate of air conditioning installations behind Cadillac, Lincoln, and Imperial. (Note: Based on model-year production.)

HISTORICAL FOOTNOTES

Henry Ford II was president of Ford Motor Company again in 1959. Earnest R. Breech remained chairman of the board. Robert S. McNamara was a Ford Motor Company Group vice president and president of the Car and Truck Division. J. O. Wright was a FoMoCo vice president and general manager of Ford Division.

A total of 92,843 T-Birds, representing 1.5 percent of total industry, were produced for the model year. Calendar-year output of 87,218 T-Birds was up 15.2 percent over 75,723 in 1959 and represented an all-time high for the nameplate. Calendar-year dealer sales were 81,555 T-Birds, which was 5.8 percent of total Ford sales. Research shows that the sunroof model and the Golde Top model were the same car. Production of 1960 T-Birds ended earlier than usual, in July 1960.

The model changeover was pushed up because a total redesign was coming in 1961. Almost as soon as production ended, two special Thunderbirds were built with stainless-steel bodies. Allegheny-Ludlum Steel Co. and Budd Body Co. teamed up to make the two cars a showcase for their product lines. The "Stainless-Steel T-Birds" had to be built as the last 1959 production units, since fabricating the stainless-steel bodies wrecked the dies.

As in 1959, the 430-powered T-Bird was capable of 9-second 0-60 runs, but *Motor Trend* said of the T-Bird: "What it does have is originality, freshness and newness of concept. This is its secret. It has, more than any other current domestic car, the spirit and quality that made the classic roadsters and tourers of the 1930s such memorable favorites." "Uncle" Tom McCahill, the famous automotive writer, said the Thunderbird made him picture a well-off "club woman" arriving at a fancy piano concert in a Duesenberg. "For many people, owning a new T-Bird is a last backwards look at their fleeting youth," he said. "And if they get a bounce out of it, I'm all for it."

After the 1957 Automobile Manufacturer's Association ban on factory participation in auto racing, President Robert S. McNamara was happy to eliminate Ford's racing budget. Over half of the Thunderbird stock cars that raced in 1960 were 1959 models. At least some of these were cars built and prepped by racers John Holman and Ralph Moody. Ford sold its racing parts to Holman & Moody, who continued building Ford race cars.

Cappy collection

The "Square Bird" era came to an end in 1961 with an all-new T-Bird that featured curving, smooth corners. The rear seat tonneau cover arrived in 1962, but many '61s were retro-fitted with the option.

1961 *Thunderbird*

The 1961 T-Bird was all new. Instead of corners and angles, it had smooth, curving lines. Ford's personal-luxury car had a new chassis and a larger, more powerful engine. "To many Thunderbird owners, the greatly restyled 1961 model will look like a bird from another nest," said *Science and Mechanics* magazine in December 1960. "Because this is an age of aerodynamics, high speeds and rockets, we must keep in tune with the times," said George Walker, Ford's vice president of styling.

The downward-curved hood seemed to be moving forward while the car was standing still. Two headlights appeared on either side and were nicely integrated into the upper edge of the grille. Gone were the "eyebrows" that shielded the 1958-1960 headlights. A swept-under grille blended in smoothly with the rest of the torpedo-shaped car. Walker said that sculpturing was dropped from the T-Bird because it added nothing to aerodynamic design.

Despite its departure from earlier T-Birds, the new model did have some traditional design elements, like a sloped nose and a hood scoop. The roof was fairly flat. The rear roof pillars had a "formal" T-Bird-like appearance. Although updated inside, it remained a four-place automobile with bucket seats and a center console. Short,

outward-canted rear fins and round taillights were continued.

Unit construction remained a T-Bird benefit. The frame and body components were welded into an integral unit, rather than bolted together. Ford actually made the car of two unitized sections with a rigid, box-sectioned joint at the cowl area. For the first time, the T-Bird hood was hinged at the rear. It was wider than the 1960 hood, while the fenders were narrower and were bolted on to make body repairs simpler. A new, thin-pillared "straight line" windshield was seen.

Ford offered 19 different "Diamond Lustre" exterior colors and 30 two-tones (including seven reversible combinations). The "Luxury Lounge" interior came in 16 different upholstery combinations and six colors. The 25-percent-smaller center console added legroom. One new idea was gluing the rearview mirror to the windshield.

The convertible featured a fully automatic top-retracting mechanism operated by the turn of a switch on the inside of the left-hand door. The lifting mechanism and pump assembly were relocated to the quarter panels, instead of behind the seat. To raise the top, the trunk lid

BODY COLOR INFORMATION

Color Name	Code	Color Name	Code
Raven Black	A	Diamond Blue +	N
Royal Red +++	B	Green Mist +	O
Aquamarine	C	Natilus Gray +	P
Starlight Blue	D	Silver Gray	Q
Laurel Green Metallic +	E	Cambridge Blue +	R
Desert Gold	F	Mint Green	S
Tawney Beige +++	G	Honey Beige +	T
Chesapeake Blue	H	Rose Glow +++	U
Green Velvet +++	I	Palm Springs Rose ++	V
Monte Carlo Red	J	Garden Turquoise	W
Crystal Grn Metallic +++	K	Heritage Burgundy +	X
Sahara Rose +	L	Mahogany +++	Y
Corinthian White	M	Fieldstone Tan +	Z

+ Also a Lincoln color
++ Also a Lincoln-Mercury color
+++ Special order color

TWO-TONE BODY COLORS

Lower Color/Upper Color	Code	Lower Color/Upper Color	Code
Raven Black/Corinthian White	AM	Laurel Green*/Corinthian White	EM
Corinthian White/Raven Black	MA	Mint Green/Corinthian White	SM
Montecarlo Red/Corinthian White	JM	Garden Turquoise*/Corinthian White	WM
Corinthian White/Montecarlo Red	MJ	Aquamarine/Corinthian White	CM
Nautilus Gray/Corinthian White	PM	Honey Beige*/Field stone Tan	TZ
Silver Gray/Corinthian White	QM	Fieldstone Tan*/Corinthian White	ZM
Silver Gray/Raven Black	QA	Mahogany/Corinthian White	YM
Chesapeake Blue/Corinthian White	HM	Desert Gold/Corinthian White	FM
Cambridge Blue*/Corinthian White	RM	Palm Springs Rose/Raven Black	VA
Starlight Blue/Corinthian White	DM	Palm Springs Rose/Corinthian White	VM
Chesapeake Blue*/Diamond Blue	HN	Heritage Burgundy/Corinthian White	XM
Cambridge Blue*/Diamond Blue	RN		

Colors marked with asterisk available reversed with same interior trim combinations.

TOP COLOR INFORMATION

No. 1: Black satin-grain vinyl with Black headliner and Black frame (available with all interior colors except Blue)
No. 2: White satin-grain vinyl with Black headliner and Black frame (available with all interior colors)
No. 1: Blue satin-grain vinyl with Black headliner and Black frame (available with Blue interior)

INTERIOR TRIM INFORMATION

Crinkle-grain all-vinyl Interiors

Seat Type	Material	Medium Blue	Medium Green	Lt. Pearl Beige	Red	Black	Medium Turquoise
Bucket Seats	Vinyl	52	53	54	55	56	57

Crinkle-grain Vinyl and Nylon Bedford Cloth Interiors

Seat Type	Material	Medium Blue	Medium Green	Lt. Pearl Beige	Black	Medium Turquoise
Bucket Seats	Cloth & Vinyl	72	73	74	76	77

Leather Interiors

Seat Type	Material	Medium Blue	Lt. Pearl Beige	Red	Black	Medium Turquoise
Bucket Seats	Leather	82	84	85	86	87

THUNDERBIRD PRODUCTION

Model Number	Body/Style Number	Body Type & Seating	Factory Price	Shipping Weight	Production Total
71	63A	2d Hardtop-4P	$4,170	3,958 lbs.	62,535
73	76A	2d Convertible-4P	$4,637	4,130 lbs.	10,516

opened to the rear and powerful motors lifted the top, extending it nearly straight up until it lowered over the passenger compartment. This isolated the top-riser mechanism from the passengers and made top operation quieter. A drawback was a noticeable lack of storage space in the trunk when the top was folded and stored there.

STANDARD EQUIPMENT

Built-in dual exhausts, fuel filter, oil filter, 390-cid four-barrel V-8 engine, Lifeguard padded instrument panel and cushioned sun visors, electric clock with sweep second hand, automatic courtesy lights, turn signals, deep-center steering wheel, dual horn and horn rings, individually adjustable front seats, Safety-Swivel day-night tilt type mirror, double-grip door locks, full wheel covers, built-in armrests, floor carpets, full-width foam rubber seat, all-vinyl upholstery, ashtray, cigar lighter, air cleaner, and five black 8.00 x 14 tubeless tires, Cruise-O-Matic transmission, power brakes, power steering, two-speed electric windshield wipers, undercoating, safety belt anchors, coat hooks, parking brake light, glove box light, ashtray light, back-up lights, fully-lined luggage compartment with light, and positive crankcase ventilation system on California cars only.

I.D. NUMBERS

Die-stamped on top of front fender cross-bar to right of hood lock striker plate. First symbol denotes model-year: 1=1961. Second symbol denotes the assembly plant: Y=Wixom (Novi), Michigan. Pilot models possibly built at Pilot Plant, Dearborn, Michigan (Plant code S). Third symbol denotes the car-line: 7=Thunderbird. Fourth symbol denotes body type: 1=Thunderbird Tudor hardtop, 3=Thunderbird two-door convertible. Fifth symbol denotes engine: R=390-cid/275-hp low-compression export-only V-8, Z=390-cid/300-hp Thunderbird V-8, Z 0r Q=390-cid/375-hp Thunderbird Special V-8, Z=390-cid/401-hp Thunderbird Special 6V V-8. Sixth thru 11th symbols denote sequential production number of specific vehicle starting at 100001. Body number plate located on left front body pillar. Serial number: Same as number on VIN tag. Symbols above "BDY" are body symbol code: 63A=Thunderbird hardtop, 76A=Thunderbird convertible. Symbols above "CLR" are paint color code. First symbol indicates lower body color. Second symbol, if used, indicates upper body color on cars with two-tone paint. Symbols above "TRM" are trim combination code. Symbols above "DT" are the production date code. The number indicates the date of the month the car was made. The letters indicate month of manufacture: A=January, B=February, C=March, D=April, E=May, F=June, G=July, H=August, J=September, K=October, L=November, M=December, N=January, and P=February, etc. (Ford listed two-year codes in case the 1960 model run was extended). Symbols above DSO indicate information including the Ford Motor Co. Sales District Code. Symbols above AX indicate rear axle. Axles used on 1960 Thunderbirds were: 1=2.91:1 (also noted as 3.00:1 and 3.56:1), 3=3.10:1, 6=3.00:1, A=3.56:1 Equa Lock, F=3.56:1 Equa-Lock and H=2.91:1 Equa Lock. Symbols above TR indicate type of transmission: All Thunderbirds from 1961 until the 1980s came only with SelectShift Cruise-O-Matic Drive.

ENGINES

THUNDERBIRD 390 SPECIAL BASE V-8: Overhead valve. Cast-iron block. Bore and stroke: 4.05 x 3.78 in. Displacement: 390 cid. Brake hp: 275. Taxable hp: 52.49. Five main bearings. Hydraulic valve lifters. Crankcase capacity: 5 qt. (add 1 qt. with new oil filter). Cooling system capacity: 19 qt. Carburetor: Ford four-barrel Model CIAE-9510-AG with standard transmission or CIAE-9510-AH with automatic transmission. Code Z.

THUNDERBIRD 390 SPECIAL BASE V-8: Overhead valve. Cast-iron block. Bore and stroke: 4.05 x 3.78 in. Displacement: 390 cid. Compression ratio: 9.60:1. Brake hp: 300 at 4600 rpm. Taxable hp: 52.49. Torque: 427 lbs.-ft. at 3200 rpm. Five main bearings. Hydraulic valve lifters.

Crankcase capacity: 5 qt. (add 1 qt. with new oil filter). Cooling system capacity: 19 qt. Carburetor: Ford four-barrel Model CIAE-9510-AG with standard transmission or CIAE-9510-AH with automatic transmission. Code Z.

THUNDERBIRD 390 SPECIAL OPTIONAL V-8: Overhead valve. Cast-iron block. Bore and stroke: 4.05 x 3.78 in. Displacement: 390 cid. Compression ratio: 10.60:1. Brake hp: 375 at 6000 rpm. Taxable hp: 52.49. Torque: 427 lbs.-ft. at 3400 rpm. Five main bearings. Solid valve lifters. Crankcase capacity: 5 qt. (add 1 qt. with new oil filter). Cooling system capacity: 19 qt. Carburetor: Ford four-barrel Model CIAE-9510-AG with standard transmission or CIAE-9510-AH with automatic transmission. Code Q

THUNDERBIRD 390 SPECIAL 6V OPTIONAL V-8: Overhead valve. Cast-iron block. Bore and stroke: 4.05 x 3.78 in. Displacement: 390 cid. Compression ratio: 10.60:1. Brake hp: 401 at 6000 rpm. Taxable hp: 52.49. Torque: 430 lbs.-ft. at 3500 rpm. Five main bearings. Solid valve lifters. Crankcase capacity: 5 qt. (add 1 qt. with new oil filter). Cooling system capacity: 19 qt. Carburetor: Three two-barrel carburetors. Code Q (Early versions may use code Z).

NOTE: Some cars were delivered with the intake manifold and carburetors in the trunk.

CHASSIS

Wheelbase: 113 in. Overall length: 205 in. Overall width: 75.9 in. Overall height (hardtop): 53.9 in. Front headroom (hardtop): 34.2 in. Rear headroom (hardtop): 33.1 in. Front shoulder room (hardtop): 58 in. Rear shoulder room (hardtop): 55.6 in. Front hip room (hardtop): 59 in. Rear hip room (hardtop): 52.3 in. Front legroom (hardtop): 44.4 in. Rear leg room (hardtop): 57.7 in. Front tread: 61 in. Rear tread: 60 in. Tires: 8.00 x 14 4-ply. Steering ratio: 20.31:1.

Turns lock-to-lock: 4.5. Turning circle, curb-to-curb: 40.2 ft. Chassis type: Welded, integral body and frame. Front suspension: Independent SLA (short-and-long-arm) with ball joints and coil springs. Rear suspension: Hotchkiss. Front brakes: 11.03 x 3.00-in. drums. Rear brakes: 11.03 x 2.50-in. drums. Brake swept area: 233.75 sq. in. Standard transmission: SelectShift Cruise-O-Matic Drive. Gas tank: 20 gallons (premium fuel required). Weight distribution: 66 percent front/44 percent rear. Fuel economy: 13-21 mpg. Driving range: 260-420 miles.

OPTIONS

Push-button radio and antenna ($112.80). MagicAire fresh air heater ($82.90). SelectAire conditioner ($462.80). I-

Cappy collection

The "eyebrows" from the previous years were re-placed by a twin-headlight setup that was integrated into the grille.

Cappy collection

The trunk on the 1961 T-Bird was spacious, but not when it housed the convertible roof. Short tail fins and round taillights remained as part of a redesigned back end.

The 1961 T-Bird was considered cool enough to make it as an Indy 500 Festival car.

Rest tinted glass ($43). 8.00 x 14 rayon whitewall tires ($42.10 extra). 8.00 x 14 nylon white sidewall tires ($70.40 extra). Power windows ($106.20). Four-way power driver's seat ($92.10). Four-way power passenger's seat ($92.10). Left- or right-hand OSRV mirror ($5.10). Electric windshield washers ($13.70). Rear fender shields — skirts ($26.60). Lifeguard front seat safety belts ($22.80). Leather interior ($106.20). Heavy-duty 70-amp battery ($7.60). Tu-Tone paint ($25.80). Equa-Lock differential axle ($38.60). Movable Swing-Away steering column ($25.10).

EQUIPMENT INSTALLATION RATES

Cruise-O-Matic drive (100 percent). V-8 engine (100 percent). Radio (98 percent). Heater (99.3 percent). Power steering (100 percent). Power brakes (100 percent). Power seat (46.6 percent). Power windows (75.6 percent). Bucket seats (100 percent). White sidewall tires (97.4 percent). Windshield washers (81.4 percent). Electric windshield wipers (100 percent). Tinted windshield (62 percent). Backup lights (100 percent). Air conditioning (32.6 percent). Dual exhaust (100 percent). Limited-slip axle (7.1 percent). Note: Based on model-year production.

HISTORICAL FOOTNOTES

Henry Ford II was Board Chairman of Ford Motor Company. John Dykstra was president. Lee Iacocca was a FoMoCo vice president and general manager of Ford Division. M.S. McLaughlin was general sales manager of Ford Division.

A total of 73,051 T-Birds, representing 1.4 percent of total industry, was produced for the model year in the Wixom plant. Calendar-year output of 88,207 T-Birds represented another all-time high for the nameplate. Calendar-year dealer sales were 85,142 T-Birds, which was 6.2 percent of total Ford sales.

Motor Trend made a "Special Report" on the all-new 1961 T-Bird in its December 1960 issue, picturing the car with a 1957 two-seat model. Associate editor John Lawlor had praise for everything from the Swing-Away steering wheel to the new springs and wider tread width. He found that riders were well insulated from road shocks and vibrations. The car cornered with less lean than previous T-Birds and had improved brakes. Lawlor was unable to get any hard performance figures, as he was driving a pre-production car at Ford's Dearborn test track. "On the basis of the prototype, though, I believe the '61 model shows a new level of sophistication in its engineering," he wrote. "Without diminishing the particular appeal of the old two-seater nor the trailblazing of the previous four-seater, the latest Thunderbird looks to me like the best one yet."

In February 1961, *Motor Trend* followed up its initial review with a road test article entitled "Thunderbird: A Real Change ... For the Better." The title said it all, as the report praised just about everything except luggage accommodations in the convertible. *Cars* magazine tested a pre-production convertible. A full-bore test of the '61 T-Bird's performance wasn't possible with the prototype. "Those figures registered indicated to our satisfaction that this 300-bhp T-Bird will hold its own with the hottest

The 1961 Thunderbird was advertised as a fitting ride for a formal occasion.

Detroit machinery, excepting the Corvette," said the editors. "We were assured by Ingram Taylor, quality analysis technician and former Ford test driver, that a '61 'Bird in good tune should attain a maximum speed in excess of 130 mph." Other tests recorded a 0 to 60-mph time of 8.5 seconds for a convertible with the 390-cid/300-hp V-8.

Despite its performance numbers, the '61 T-Bird was not competitive in stock car racing. However, some 1959-1960 models continued to race. Many of the cars were battle-worn and fell into the hands of lesser-known drivers with smaller budgets.

Starlight Blue was one of 19 different exterior colors for the 1961 T-Bird. The model had a long list of interior colors and color combinations.

A reworked grille was one of the subtle differences between the 1962 T-Bird and the 1961 model.

1962 *Thunderbird*

Both T-Bird body styles carried over from 1961 had the same "projectile" front end and twin-jet-tube rear design. A reworked radiator grille featured four rows of shiny metal "drawer pulls" between thin horizontal bars. Replacing the four moldings stacked on the rear fender of the '61 model were horizontal "dashes" of ribbed chrome. Late in the spring, some cars were built with a horizontal chrome accessory strip on their body sides. The trademark large round taillights changed from 1961 and also had more chrome to dress them up. The hardtop model's roof was again slightly on the formal side.

The convertible had a flip-up deck and "accordion" top mechanism that Tom McCahill joked about in *Mechanix Illustrated*. "The first time I lowered the top, I thought the car was about to eat itself," he said. "Deck flips open, panels unfold, the top shoots up, all to the accompaniment of a whining noise similar to launching a guided missile. The sight of this operation is enough to cause a coronary in a slightly inebriated 3rd Avenue playboy. The total operation makes Buck Rogers look like a rail-splitting partner of Abe Lincoln's and the end result, though successful in concealing the top, leaves less trunk room than you'll find in a Volkswagen."

A new Landau or Landau Hardtop model featured a black or white vinyl top that looked like a leather-padded carriage top. To further this impression, it had landau irons on the sides of its rear roof panels. An English magazine, *The Motor Sport*, reported, "It's a very pleasing combination, with genuine leather upholstery optional on order." The number of Landaus built was not recorded separately, but the model pushed overall sales of the Thunderbird hardtop up by 7,000 units.

Another new model called the Sports Roadster had a tonneau cover over the rear seats and Kelsey-Hayes wire wheels. Tom McCahill said, "Ford has fielded a convertible T-Bird, called a Sports Roadster, with some real wild innovations that are bound to have eyes popping in Peoria." The tonneau cover could be added or removed in less than three minutes. The headrest section was horseshoe-shaped and fit over the Thunderbird's bucket seats. A quick-release catch secured it to the transmission tunnel between the front seats. Sliding it under the deck lid secured it at the rear. It was possible to raise or lower the convertible top with the tonneau in place. The seat back recessed into the headrest for a smooth, aerodynamic fit. A gap between the bottom edge of the tonneau and the rear seat was provided.

BODY COLOR INFORMATION

Color Name	Code	Color Name	Code
Raven Black ++	A	Corinthian White + and ++	M
Royal Red +++	B	Diamond Blue + and ++	N
Oxford Gray +++	C	Green Mist ++++	O
Patrician Green +	D	Silver Moss Metallic +++	P
Acapulco Blue +	E	Tucson Yellow	R
Skymist Blue +	F	Cascade Green +	S
Silver Mink ++	G	Sandshell Beige ++	T
Caspian Blue +	H	Deep Sea Blue +	U
Castillian Gold ++	I	Chestnut ++	V
Rangoon Red ++	J	Heritage Burgundy +	X
Chalfonte Blue +	K	Fieldstone Tan	Z
Sahara Rose +	L		

+ Also a Lincoln color.
++ Color available on Sport Roadster.
+++ Special order color.
++++ Late-year addition for T-Birds and Lincolns.

TWO-TONE BODY COLORS

Color Panel/Color Overlay	Code	Color Panel/Color Overlay	Code
Raven Black/Corinthian White	AM	Sahara Rose/Corinthian White	LM
Rangoon Red/Corinthian White	JM	Tucson Yellow/Corinthian White	RM
Caspian Blue/Corinthian White	HM	Deep Sea Blue/Corinthian White	UM
Acapulco Blue/Corinthian White	EM	Patrician Green/Corinthian White	DM
Skymist Blue/Corinthian White	FM	Chalfonte Blue/Corinthian White	KM
Fieldstone Tan/Corinthian White	ZM	Chestnut/Corinthian White	VM
Corinthian White/Fieldstone Tan	MZ	Fieldstone Tan/Sandshell Beige	ZT
Sandshell Beige/Corinthian White	TM	Corinthian White/Rangoon Red	MJ
Heritage Burgundy/Corinthian White	XM	Corinthian White/Chestnut	MV
Cascade Green/Corinthian White	SM	Sandshell Beige/Fieldstone Tan	TZ
Castillian Gold/Corinthian White	IM		

CONVERTIBLE TOP COLOR INFORMATION

No. 1: Black satin-grain vinyl with Black headliner and Black frame (available with all exterior colors except Z)
No. 2: White satin-grain vinyl with Black headliner and Black frame (available with all interior and exterior colors)
No. 3: Blue satin-grain vinyl with Black headliner and Black frame (available only with Blue interior)

VINYL TOP COLOR INFORMATION

A: Black (available with all interior and exterior colors)
B: White (available with all interior and exterior colors)

INTERIOR TRIM INFORMATION

Crinkle-grain all-vinyl Interiors

Seat Type	Medium Silver Blue	Medium Blue	Medium Green	Lt. Pearl Beige	Red	Black	Medium Turquoise	Medium Chestnut
Bucket Seats	50	52	53	54	55	56	57	59

Crinkle-grain Vinyl and Nylon Bedford Cloth Interiors

Seat Type	Light Silver Blue/ Medium Silver	Light Blue/ Dark Blue	Lt. Pearl Beige/ Med. Pearl Beige	Black/ Gray	Medium Turquoise
Bucket Seats	70	72	74	76	77

Leather Interiors

Seat Type	Medium Silver Blue	Medium Blue	Lt. Pearl Beige	Red/ Red	Black/ Black	Medium Turquoise	Medium Chestnut
Bucket Seats	80	82	84	85	86	87	89

THUNDERBIRD PRODUCTION

Model Number	Body/Style Number	Body Type & Seating	Factory Price	Shipping Weight	Production Total
71	63A	2d Hardtop-4P	$4,170	3,958 lbs.	62,535
73	76A	2d Convertible-4P	$4,637	4,130 lbs.	10,516

You could slide small items under the cover and onto the rear seat cushion for storage after folding the front seat forward.

Car Life magazine compared the Sport Roadster's long rear end to the deck of the aircraft carrier *USS Enterprise*. "As a prestige car in the true Midwest culture school, this little item should be hard to beat," chimed McCahill. "It won't get a second glance from the Ferrari and E-Jag buffs, but it will singe a lot of wheat in Nebraska." Fender skirts

were not used on Sports Roadsters due to clearance problems with the knock-off hubs, although restorers have found ways to get around this. The open fenders also looked more sports car-like and facilitated brake cooling. The wire wheels did not work well with tubeless tires and required the use of inner tubes.

T-Birds had about 45 lbs. of sound-deadening materials, including aluminum insulation, fiber or mastic felt, undercoating and fiberglass applied to the hood, wheel well housings, dashboard, passenger and trunk floors, roof panels, package tray and quarter panels. On the underbody, the zinc-coated metal had better rust-proofing including a zinc-rich coating, three coats of primer and two finish coats of "never wax" enamel. The aluminized muffler was improved and stainless-steel parts were used in some critical places in the exhaust system, such as the resonators. T-Bird engines featured revised manifolding.

There were 15 improvements to carburetors alone, plus a disposable fuel filter designed to function for 30,000 miles. Oil filter life was also extended to 4,000-6,000 mile intervals by eliminating a crossover valve. T-Birds came with permanent antifreeze that gave protection to minus 35-degrees and had to be changed only every two years or 30,000 miles. A larger master cylinder was said to increase braking efficiency, while reducing pedal pressure. For better durability and fade resistance, new brake lining materials were used. T-Bird seats were low and soft. As in 1961, heater controls and a glove compartment were incorporated into the center console between the seats. A Swing-Away steering wheel moved 10 inches to make getting in and out of the car easier. It functioned only when the gear selector was in Park. In addition to the 390-cid/300-hp base V-8, a limited-edition option was available in 1962. "I am told that under the pressure of thumb-screw and with the possible aid of your congressman, you might be able to order a 'Bird with a hotter engine," joked Tom McCahill. It was a version of the 390 with three progressively linked Holley two-barrel carburetors known as the M-code power plant.

Although the T-Bird was sports-car fast, it came nowhere near handling or braking like a sports car according to *Car and Driver*. *Motor Trend* rated the car higher, but criticized understeer and body roll. The brakes

The Thunderbird script and emblem could be found near the bumper behind the rear wheels.

functioned fine under all conditions, but the linings heated up quickly and caused severe fade if the car was driven hard.

STANDARD EQUIPMENT

Built-in dual exhausts, fuel filter, oil filter, 390-cid four-barrel V-8, Lifeguard padded instrument panel, cushioned sun visors, safety belt anchors, electric clock with sweep second hand, automatic courtesy lights, turn signals, a deep-center steering wheel, dual horns and horn ring, individually adjustable individual front bucket seats, Safety-Swivel day-night tilt type inside rearview mirror, double-grip door locks, coat hooks, full wheel covers, built-in armrests, floor carpet, full-width foam rubber seats, all-vinyl upholstery, fully lined luggage compartment, ashtray, cigar lighter, air cleaner, Cruise-O-Matic automatic transmission, power brakes, power steering, two-speed electric windshield wipers, undercoating, parking brake, glove box, ashtray,

back-up and luggage compartment lights, heater and defroster, movable steering column, console between the front seats, and five black 8.00 x 14 tires. The Convertible Sports Roadster also included the molded tonneau cover with padded headrests, real Kelsey-Hayes chrome wire wheels with knock-off hub caps, a front passenger grab handle with color-keyed vinyl insert, a special insignia under the Thunderbird front fender script and no fender skirts. A Swing-Away steering wheel was standard, except on very early 1961 models.

I.D. NUMBERS

Die-stamped on top of front fender cross-bar to right of hood lock striker plate. First symbol denotes model-year:

Red-on-red made for a flashy interior-exterior combination on the 1962 T-Bird Sports Roadster.

Vinyl was still the material of choice on all 1962 T-Birds.

Critics found some flaws in the 1962 T-Bird's performance, but there was no denying its curb appeal. The Sports Roadster shown here was one of two new models added to the T-Bird lineup. It came with a removable tonneau cover and fancy wire wheels.

Cappy collection

The T-Bird came standard with a 390-cid V-8, dual exhaust, Cruise-O-Matic, power steering and brakes, and a padded dash.

2=1962. Second symbol denotes the assembly plant: Y=Wixom (Novi), Michigan. Third symbol denotes the carline: 8=Thunderbird. Fourth symbol denotes body type: 3=Thunderbird Tudor hardtop, 5=Thunderbird two-door convertible. Fifth symbol denotes engine: Z=390 cid/300-hp Thunderbird V-8, M=390 cid/340-hp Thunderbird Special Six-Barrel V-8. (M code engine introduced in January 1962.) Sixth thru 11th symbols denote sequential production number of specific vehicle starting at 100001. Body number plate located on left front body pillar. Serial number: Same as number on VIN tag. Symbols above "BDY" are body symbol code: 63A=hardtop, 63B=Landau hardtop, 76A=convertible, 76B=Sport Roadster. Symbols above CLR are paint color code. First symbol indicates lower body color. Second symbol indicates upper body color. Symbols above TRM are trim combination code. Symbols above "DT" are the production date code. The number indicates the date of the month the car was made. The letters indicate month of manufacture: A=January, B=February, C=March, D=April, E=May, F=June, G=July, H=August, J=September, K=October, L=November, M=December, N=January, and P=February. Symbols above DSO indicate information including the Ford Motor Co. Sales District Code. Symbols above AX indicate rear axle: 1=3.00:1. Symbols above TR indicate type of transmission: All 1962 Thunderbirds came only with Code 4 SelectShift Cruise-O-Matic Drive.

ENGINES

THUNDERBIRD 390 SPECIAL V-8 (Available only in Thunderbird): Overhead valve. Cast-iron block. Bore and stroke: 4.05 x 3.78 in. Displacement: 390 cid. Compression ratio: 9.60:1. Brake hp: 300 at 4600 rpm. Taxable hp: 52.49. Torque: 427 lbs.-ft. at 2800 rpm. Five main bearings.

Hydraulic valve lifters. Crankcase capacity: 5 qt. (add 1 qt. with new oil filter). Cooling system capacity: 19 qt. Carburetor: Ford four-barrel Model CIAE-9510-AG with standard transmission or CIAE-9510-AH with automatic transmission. Code Z.

THUNDERBIRD 390 SPECIAL 6V V-8: Overhead valve. Cast-iron block. Displacement: 390 cid. Bore and stroke: 4.05 x 3.78 in. Compression ratio: 10.50:1. Brake hp: 340 at 5000 rpm. Torque: 430 lbs.-ft. at 3200 rpm. Five main bearings. Hydraulic valve lifters. Carburetor: Holley three two-barrels. Cooling system capacity: 20.5 qt. with heater. Crankcase capacity: 5 qt. (add 1 qt. with new oil filter). Dual exhaust. Code M.

CHASSIS

Wheelbase: 113 in. Overall length: 205 in. Overall width: 76 in. Overall height (hardtop): 54.2 in. Front seat headroom (hardtop): 34.3 in. Rear seat headroom (hardtop): 33.1 in. Front seat legroom (hardtop): 44.9 in. Rear seat legroom (hardtop): 37.3 in. Front seat shoulder room (hardtop): 58.1 in. Rear seat shoulder room (hardtop): 55.6 in. Front seat hip room (hardtop): 58.8 in. Rear seat hip room (hardtop): 52.3 in. Front tread: 61 in. Rear tread: 60 in. Road axle road clearance: 5.3 in. Body road clearance: 7.2 in. Tires: 8.00 x 14 4-ply. Steering ratio: 20.7:1. Turning diameter: 40.2 ft. Chassis type: Welded, integral body and frame. Front suspension: Independent wishbone type with ball joints and coil springs. Rear suspension: Live rear axle attached to semi-elliptic rear springs. Standard rear axle: 3.00:1. Optional rear axle: 3.00:1 Eqal-Lock. Front brakes: 11.0-in. drums. Rear brakes: 11.0-in. drums. Brake swept area: 234 sq. in. Standard transmission: SelectShift Cruise-O-Matic

Drive. Gas tank: 20 gallons (premium fuel required). Weight distribution: 56 percent front/44 percent rear. Fuel economy: 11-20 mpg. Driving range: 230-420 miles.

OPTIONS

Push-button radio and antenna ($112.80). Rear seat radio speaker with reverb ($15.50). MagicAire heater ($82.90). Thunderbird 390-cid V-8 with triple two-barrel carburetors ($242.10). SelectAire conditioner ($415.10). I-Rest tinted glass ($43). 8.00 x 14 rayon whitewalls ($42.10). 8.00 x 14 nylon whitewalls ($70.40). Power windows ($106.20). One 4-way power front seat ($92.10). Outside rearview mirror ($5.10). Electric windshield washers ($13.70). Rear fender shields ($26.60). Lifeguard front seat belts ($22.80). Leather seat ($106.20). Heavy-duty 70-amp battery ($7.60). Tu-Tone paint ($25.80). Chrome wire wheels ($372.30). Automatic speed control ($80.50). Deluxe wheel covers with simulated knock-off hubs ($15.60). Automatic vacuum door locks ($34.10). Sports side trim ($34.80). Equa-Lock differential ($38.60). (Note: Leather seats included leather seat inserts and bolsters.)

EQUIPMENT INSTALLATION RATES

Cruise-O-Matic drive (100 percent). V-8 engine (100 percent). Radio (96.8 percent). Heater (99.5 percent). Power steering (100 percent). Power brakes (100 percent). Power seat (53.9 percent). Power windows (71.1 percent). Bucket seats (100 percent). Seat belts (15.9 percent). White

The 390-cid/300-hp V-8 received a few improvements for 1962, including a more efficient carburetor and longer-life fuel and oil filters.

Cappy collection

The T-Bird Sport Roadster came with a base sticker price of $5,439 for 1962.

Cappy collection

sidewall tires (97 percent). Windshield washers (82 percent). Electric windshield wipers (100 percent). Tinted windshield (67 percent). Backup lights (100 percent). Air conditioning (39.6 percent). Dual exhaust (100 percent). Limited-slip axle (0.7 percent). (Note: Based on model-year production.)

HISTORICAL FOOTNOTES

Henry Ford II was board chairman of Ford Motor Company. John Dykstra was president. Lee Iacocca was a vice president and general manager of Ford Division. M.S. McLaughlin was general sales manager.

A total of 78,011 T-Birds, representing 1.4 percent of total industry, were produced for the model year in the Wixom plant. Calendar-year output of 75,536 T-Birds represented the first decline in several seasons. Calendar-year dealer sales were 74,306 T-Birds, which was 4.8 percent of total Ford sales. The rare "M" code V-8 had a $171 dealer cost and added $242.10 to the retail price. It was truly hard to get, with a reported total of just 120 M-code Sports Roadsters being put together.

An "M" Roadster could move from 0 to 60 mph in approximately 8.5 seconds and hit a top speed of 125 mph. Most contemporary car magazines dwelled on T-Bird brake fade and the fact that once the brakes faded, they took a long time to cool off and come back.

If T-Birds had trouble stopping, it must have spilled over to the sales department, since there was no stopping the steady increase in demand for '62s. From their introduction on October 12, 1961, the cars sold well. The combination of good looks, advanced styling, many creature comforts, luxury appointments, and reliable performance was a winner in the early 1960s. "Ford's plush style setter has its share of faults and shortcomings," said *Motor Trend*'s technical editor, Jim Wright. "But, it's still the classic example of a prestige car." In addition, other than the limited-production Chrysler 300 letter car, the Thunderbird had the personal-luxury niche to itself. There was no Buick Riviera to contend with in 1962, and the new Pontiac Grand Prix had not yet developed the distinctive styling that would make it a big hit in 1963. On the other hand, Thunderbird's two added models helped fill out the niche and boosted production by 5,000 units. Listed below are some performance figures reported for both open models with the 300-hp or 340-hp V-8s.

1962 THUNDERBIRD PERFORMANCE		
Model	CID/HP	Performance
0-60 mph		
Sports Roadster	390/300	12.4 seconds
Sports Roadster	390/300	9.7 seconds
Convertible	390/300	11.3 seconds
Sports Roadster	390/340	8.5 seconds
1/4-Mile		
Sports Roadster	390/300	19.2 seconds at 78 mph
Sports Roadster	390/300	18.7 seconds
Convertible	390/300	18.6 seconds at 76 mph
Top Speed		
Sports Roadster	390/300	114-116 mph
Convertible	390/300	110 mph (estimated)
Sports Roadster	390/340	125 mph

Cappy collection

The hardtop model remained the most popular among buyers in 1962, with 57,845 shipped.

The 1963 T-Bird retained most of its styling from the previous year, with only a few noticeable changes. This rare Sports Roadster had the 340-hp M Code engine option.

1963

Thunderbird

The 1963 model retained the previous styling with a new sculptured body-side feature line, a modestly revised "electric shaver" grille, new taillights, new side trim and new wheel covers. Inside, buyers found medal-clad brake and accelerator pedals. New options included an AM/FM radio and a tachometer. This was the first T-Bird to use hydraulic windshield wipers powered by the power steering pump. The brakes were more fade-resistant and nearly 100 lbs. of sound-deadening materials were added. Suspension and exhaust improvements, lifetime chassis lubrication and an alternator in place of a generator were other updates.

The grille incorporated a concealed hood latch, eliminating the old cable-operated release. The front fenders had a horizontal crease line that started just behind the grille, passed over the front wheel opening, and continued past the middle of the door, where it slanted downwards for a few inches and faded into the door. Just below the crease line, near the center of the door, were three groupings of forward-slanting chrome hash marks with five strips in each group. *Motor Trend* (October 1962) said these were supposed to remind one of turbine waste gates. Chrome Thunderbird scripts were moved to the rear fenders. New deep-dish wheel covers followed the turbine motif.

There weren't any big changes to the inside of the basic models, although the inner door panels had new white and red courtesy lights for added safety when passengers were entering or exiting the car. Models were the same as in 1962 until February 7, 1963, when a special Limited-Edition Landau made its debut. A single exhaust system was now used with the base 390-cid V-8. It was supposedly a quieter and longer lasting system featuring 2.0-inch diameter laminated tubing (double pipes, one inside the other) and an asbestos-wrapped, aluminized steel muffler. A 1.78-inch-diameter tailpipe was employed.

The 1963 T-Bird front suspension was lubricated for the "life of the car," which Ford estimated as 100,000 miles or seven years. Road noise and vibrations were reduced through use of a newly developed rubber compression-type shock mount for the steering box, plus a flexible coupling between the gear assembly and the steering shaft.

STANDARD EQUIPMENT

Built-in dual exhausts, fuel filter, oil filter, 390-cid four-barrel V-8, padded instrument panel, padded sun visors, electric clock with sweep second hand, courtesy lights, turn signals, deep-center steering wheel, dual horns and horn rings, individually adjustable front seats, day-night tilt-type mirror, double-grip door locks, full wheel covers, built-in armrests, floor carpet, full-width foam rubber seats, all-vinyl upholstery, ashtray, cigar lighter, air cleaner, automatic transmission, power brakes, power steering, electric windshield wipers, undercoating, parking brake, glove box, ashtray, luggage, back-up, and compartment lights, heater and defroster, movable steering column, console between front seats, AM radio and antenna, remote-control left-hand outside rearview mirror, and five black 8.00 x 14 tubeless tires. The Convertible Sports Roadster, which came only in eight colors, also included special front fender insignias, a molded tonneau cover with padded headrests, bolt-on chrome wire wheels with simulated knock-off hubs, a Swing-Away steering wheel, a passenger-assist handle, and no fender skirts. The 1963 Landau offered Black, White, Brown, and Blue vinyl tops, simulated walnut interior trim, and a simulated walnut steering wheel. The Limited-Edition Landau featured White leather upholstery, a White steering wheel, simulated rosewood interior trim, a Rose Beige (maroon) vinyl top, and special wheel covers with simulated knock-off hubcaps.

I.D. NUMBERS

Die-stamped on top of front fender cross-bar to right of hood lock striker plate. First symbol denotes model-year: 3=1963. Second symbol denotes the assembly plant: Y=Wixom (Novi), Michigan. Third symbol denotes the carline: 8=Thunderbird. Fourth symbol denotes body type: 3=Thunderbird Tudor hardtop, 5=Thunderbird two-door convertible, 7=Two-door Landau hardtop, 9=Sports Roadster. Fifth symbol denotes engine: 9=390-cid low-

Daniel B. Lyons photo

Only 37 Sports Roadsters had the M Code engine. Such cars can be worth more than 10 times their original sticker price today.

BODY COLOR INFORMATION

Color Name	Code	Color Name	Code
Raven Black +++	A	Diamond Blue + and +++	N
Oxford Gray ++++	C	Green Mist +	O
Patrician Green +	D	Spanish Red ++++	Q
Acapulco Blue +	E	Tucson Yellow ++	R
Silver Mink + and +++	G	Cascade Green +	S
Caspian Blue +	H	Sandshell Beige +++	T
Champagne + and +++	I	Deep Sea Blue	U
Rangoon Red +++	J	Chestnut +++	V
Chalfonte Blue	K	Rose Beige	W
Sahara Rose +	L	Heritage Burgundy	X
Corinthian White + and +++	M	Fieldstone Tan	Z

+ Color also offered on Lincolns.
++ Color also offered on Lincolns and Mercurys.
+++ Color offered on Sports Roadster model
++++ Special order color

TWO-TONE BODY COLORS

Color Panel/Color Overlay	Code	Color Panel/Color Overlay	Code
Raven Black/Corinthian White	AM	Sahara Rose/Corinthian White	LM
Rangoon Red/Corinthian White	JM	Tucson Yellow/Corinthian White	RM
Caspian Blue/Corinthian White	HM	Deep Sea Blue/Corinthian White	UM
Acapulco Blue/Corinthian White	EM	Patrician Green/Corinthian White	DM
Skymist Blue/Corinthian White	FM	Chalfonte Blue/Corinthian White	KM
Fieldstone Tan/Corinthian White	ZM	Chestnut/Corinthian White	VM
Corinthian White/Fieldstone Tan	MZ	Fieldstone Tan/Sandshell Beige	ZT
Sandshell Beige/Corinthian White	TM	Corinthian White/Rangoon Red	MJ
Heritage Burgundy/Corinthian White	XM	Corinthian White/Chestnut	MV
Cascade Green/Corinthian White	SM	Sandshell Beige/Fieldstone Tan	TZ
Castillian Gold/Corinthian White	IM		

CONVERTIBLE TOP COLOR INFORMATION

No. 1: Black satin-grain vinyl with Black headliner and Black frame (available with all interior and exterior colors except Z on convertible or T on Sport Roadster)
No. 2: White satin-grain vinyl with Black headliner and Black frame (available with all interior colors)
No. 3: Blue satin-grain vinyl with Black headliner and Black frame (available with Blue interior)

VINYL TOP COLOR INFORMATION

A: Black (available with all interior and exterior colors)
B: White (available with all interior and exterior colors)
C: Brown (available with exterior colors I, M, R or Z
D: Blue (available with exterior colors E, G, H, M or N)
E: Maroon (available on Limited Edition Landau model only)

INTERIOR TRIM INFORMATION

Crinkle-grain all-vinyl interiors

Seat Type	Medium Silver/Blue/Light Silver	Light Rose Beige/Blue/Light Rose Beige	Medium Blue/Light Blue	Light Pearl Beige/Light Pearl Beige
Bucket Seats	50	51	52	54

Seat Type	Red/Red	Black/Black	Medium Turquoise/Light Turquoise	Lt. Gold/Lt. Gold	Medium Chestnut/Medium Chestnut
Bucket Seats	55	56	57	58	59

Crinkle-grain vinyl/Silver stripe broadcloth interiors

Seat Type	Light Blue/Dark Blue	Light Pearl Beige/Medium Beige	Black/Black	Light Turquoise/Medium Turquoise
Bucket Seats	72	74	76	77

Crinkle/Vachette Leather Interiors

Seat Type	Light Blue/Light Blue	White/White	Light Pearl Beige/Light Pearl Beige	Red/Red	Black/Black
Bucket Seats	82	83	84	85	86

* Code 83 white leather upholstery exclusive to 1963 1/2 Limited Edition Thunderbird Landau introduced in Monaco. This package also included Corinthian White exterior finish and Rose Beige roof of deeply grained vinyl. Interior had White and Rose Beige accents and White leather seat upholstery.

THUNDERBIRD PRODUCTION

Model Number	Body/Style Number	Body Type & Seating	Factory Price	Shipping Weight	Production Total
83	63A	2d Hardtop-4P	$4,445	4,195 lbs.	42,806
87	63B	2d Landau-4P	$4,548	4,320 lbs.	14,139
85	76A	2d Convertible-4P	$4,912	4,205 lbs.	5,913
89	76B	2d Spt Roadster-4P	$5,563	4,395 lbs.	455

NOTE 1: A total of 2,000 Limited-Edition "Princess Grace" Landau hardtops are included above.

The tonneau cover again gave 1963 T-Birds a unique profile.

compression Thunderbird V-8 (for export), Z=390 cid/300-hp Thunderbird V-8, M=390 cid/340-hp Thunderbird Special Six-Barrel V-8. Sixth thru 11th symbols denote sequential production number of specific vehicle starting at 100001. Body number plate located on left front body pillar. Serial number: Same as number on VIN tag. Symbols above "BDY" are body symbol code: 63A=hardtop, 63B=Landau hardtop, 76A=convertible, 76B=Sport Roadster. Symbols above CLR are paint color code. First symbol indicates lower body color. Second symbol indicates upper body color. Symbols above TRM are trim combination code.

Symbols above "DT" are the production date code. The number indicates the date of the month the car was made. The letters indicate month of manufacture: A=January, B=February, C=March, D=April, E=May, F=June, G=July, H=August, J=September, K=October, L=November, M=December. Symbols above DSO indicate information including the Ford Motor Co. Sales District Code. Symbols above AX indicate rear axle. 1=3.00:1. Symbols above TR indicate type of transmission: All 1963 Thunderbirds came only with SelectShift Cruise-O-Matic Drive Code 4.

The biggest changes for the 1963 Thunderbird were probably the improvements in its exhaust and suspension. The upgrades weren't enough to keep it from being a disappointing seller, however.

Daniel B. Lyons photo

The 1963 T-Birds were considered by many to be the most handsome of three-year era, but sales dipped and a redesign was on the way for the following year.

ENGINES

INTERCEPTOR 390 BASE V-8: Overhead valve. Cast-iron block. Displacement: 390 cid. Bore and stroke: 4.05 x 3.78 in. Compression ratio: 9.60:1. Brake hp: 300 at 4600 rpm. Torque: 427 lbs.-ft. at 2800 rpm. Five main bearings. Hydraulic valve lifters. Carburetor: Ford four-barrel C2AF-9510. Cooling system capacity: 20.5 qt. with heater. Crankcase capacity: 5 qt. (add 1 qt. with new oil filter). Dual exhaust. Code Z.

THUNDERBIRD SPECIAL 390 6V OPTIONAL V-8: Overhead valve. Cast-iron block. Displacement: 390 cid. Bore and stroke: 4.05 x 3.78 in.. Compression ratio: 10.50:1. Brake hp: 340 at 5000 rpm. Torque: 430 lbs.-ft. at 3200 rpm. Five main bearings. Hydraulic valve lifters. Carburetor: Holley three Model 2300 two-barrel. Cooling system capacity: 20.5 qt. with heater. Crankcase capacity: 5 qt. (add 1 qt. with new oil filter). Dual exhaust. Code M.

CHASSIS

Wheelbase (all): 113.2 in. Overall length (all): 205 in. Overall width (all): 76.5 in. Overall height (hardtop): 52.5 in. Front tread: 61 in. Rear tread: 60 in. Front seat headroom (hardtop): 34.3 in. Rear seat headroom (hardtop): 33.1 in. Front seat legroom (hardtop): 44.9 in. Rear seat legroom (hardtop): 37.3 in. Front hip room: 2 x 21.5 in. Rear hip room: 52.3 in. Front overhang: 38.3 in. Box volume: 476 cu. ft. Front overhang: 38.3 in. Front Approach Angle: 20.6 degrees. Rear overhang: 53.6 in. Rear departure angle: 12.7 degrees. Road axle road clearance: 5.6 in. Body road clearance: 7.2 in. Tires: 8.00 x 14 4-ply. Steering: Power-assisted link type 3.6 turns lock-to-lock. Steering ratio: 20.3:1. Turning diameter: 40.2 ft. Chassis type: Welded, integral body and frame. Front suspension: Independent wishbone type with ball joints and coil springs (with a ride rate of 105 lb.-in.) and 0.660-in. anti-roll bar. Rear suspension: Live rear axle attached to 2.5 x 60-in.

semi-elliptic rear springs with ride rate of 105 lb.-in. Telescoping 1/19-in. piston diameter shocks were mounted on the T-Bird suspension front and rear. Standard rear axle: 3.00:1. Front brakes: 11 x 3-in. drums. Rear brakes: 11 x 2.5-in. drums. Brake swept area: 234 sq. in. Weight distribution: 56 percent front/44 percent rear. Electrical: Autolite alternator with 2.25:1 drive ratio and maximum 40-amp. charge rate. Standard transmission: SelectShift three-element Cruise-O-Matic automatic transmission with Park/Reverse/Neutral/Drive-1/Drive-2/Low quadrant layout, 2.10:1 stall ratio and 5.04:1 ratio at breakaway. Transmission gears: (first) 2.40:1, (second) 1.47:1, (third) 1.0:1 and (reverse) 2.00:1. The transmission had a maximum upshift speed of 70 mph and a maximum kick-down speed of 65 mph. Gas tank: 20 gallons (premium fuel required). Fuel economy: 11-20 mpg. Driving range: 230-420 miles.

OPTIONS

Rear speakers in hardtop and Landau ($15.60). AM/FM push-button radio and antenna ($83.70). Rear radio speaker, hardtop only ($15.50). Reverb-type rear radio speaker, hardtops only ($54.10). Thunderbird 390-cid/340-hp 6V V-8, includes dual exhaust ($242.10). Dual exhaust system with standard V-8 ($31.90). SelectAire air conditioner, except with 6V engine ($415.10). Banded tinted glass ($43). Concentric whitewall tires ($51.90). Five 8.00 x 14 rayon whitewalls ($42.10). Five 8.00 x 14 nylon whitewalls ($70.40). Power windows ($106.20). One 4-Way power front seat ($92.10). Power door locks ($34.10). Windshield washers ($13.70). Rear fender shields, except with wire wheels ($26.60). Front seat belts ($16.80). Leather seat ($106.20). Heavy-duty 70-amp battery ($.7.60). Tu-Tone paint ($25.80). Chrome wire wheels ($372.30). Automatic speed control system ($80.50). Sports tachometer ($56.80). Deluxe wheel covers with simulated knock-off hubs ($15.60). (Note: Leather seats included leather seat inserts and bolsters.) Heavy-duty alternator.

EQUIPMENT INSTALLATION RATES

Cruise-O-Matic drive (100 percent). V-8 engine (100 percent). Radio (100 percent). Heater (100 percent). Power steering (100 percent). Power brakes (100 percent). Power seat (52.4 percent). Power windows (70.9 percent). Bucket seats (100 percent). Seat belts (24.4 percent). White sidewall tires (97.3 percent). Windshield washers (83.6 percent). Electric windshield wipers (100 percent). Tinted windshield (69.7 percent). Backup lights (100 percent). Air conditioning (43.5 percent). Dual exhaust (100 percent). Limited-slip axle (1.2 percent). Wheel covers (100 percent) (Note: Based on model-year production.)

HISTORICAL FOOTNOTES

Henry Ford II was board chairman of Ford Motor Company. Arjay R. Miller was president. Lee Iacocca was a vice president and general manager of Ford Division. O.F.

Black on black was a sharp color combination for 1963 convertible T-Birds.

Cappy collection

57

Cappy collection

Five different vinyl top covers were available on the 1963 Landau models, including white.

Yand was general sales manager of Ford Division.

A total of 63,313 T-Birds, representing .09 percent of total industry, were produced for the model year in the Wixom plant. Calendar-year output of 66,681 T-Birds represented .09 percent of industry. Calendar-year dealer sales were 66,681 T-Birds, which was 4.1 percent of total Ford sales.

The four carryover T-Bird models were introduced to the public on September 28, 2002. On February 7, 1963, the special 1963 1/2 Limited-Edition Thunderbird Landau made its debut in Monaco. Princess Grace of Monaco was given car number one. This model was then dubbed the "Princess Grace" model by Ford salesmen. Only 2,000 were built and all were painted white. One Thunderbird factory "dream car" was built this year for display at auto shows. It was called the Italien and had to be one of the sleekest T-

Bird styling exercises ever built. When viewed from the side it looked like a fastback, but it actually had a notchback roofline like the original 1965 Mustang 2+2. The car had wire wheels, unique taillight trim and special trim on the front fenders and doors.

The 1963 Thunderbird is considered by many to be the best-looking of the three-year group, primarily because of its new grille. Unfortunately, the party was over. With new competitors in the marketplace, the '63s sold the worst of the bunch. Hardtop deliveries tumbled to just 42,806 units. The total output of regular Landaus was recorded separately this year and came to 12,139. That did not include the 2,000 "Princess Grace" Limited-Edition Landaus. The regular convertible saw production of 5,913 units. Only 455 Sports Roadsters were built, including a mere 37 with the optional M-code engine. Overall, nearly 10,000 fewer Thunderbirds were built.

One magazine said the all-new 1964 T-Bird featured "every creature comfort imaginable." What had started out as a sporty two-seater nine years earlier had officially become a big, plush, four-seater.

1964 *Thunderbird*

The 1964 T-Bird had new styling with a longer hood and shorter roofline. The hood was raised and blended in with the front fenders. There were "mirror-image" upper and lower feature lines at the belt line and lower body sides. *Car Life* (October 1963) noted "While the basic understructure — unit-body inner and floor pan sections — probably do remain much the same as the '63s (and the '61s-62s, too), virtually all of the outer sheet metal stampings are new and different."

The convertible had an all-vinyl, wrinkle-resistant top that retracted under the power-operated deck lid. It was automatically stacked in the trunk, eliminating the need for an outside top boot. Options could be purchased to turn the convertible into a Sports Roadster-type car. Ford dealers sold wire wheels for $415 and a new headrest Sports Tonneau cover was $269. The factory produced a few dozen cars with both options.

A "Chinese pagoda" shape characterized the Thunderbird's grille and textured horizontal bars made up the grille insert. "Thunderbird" was spelled out along the lip of the hood in widely spaced chrome letters. Amber-colored rectangular parking lamps were recessed into the bumper directly under the headlights. The dual headlights sat side by side under the sculptured eyebrows. A dual directional light indicator system was standard. There were little indicator lamps on the front fenders for the driver to visualize when turning. Side sculpturing created a kind of flat "Parker pen" shaped indentation on the upper body sides. Thunderbird styling trademarks included a scooped hood (with a larger scoop), chrome Thunderbird script nameplates behind the front wheel openings and a formal-style roof. The hardtop's wide sail panels were decorated with T-Bird emblems. Full wheel covers of a new design were standard.

The rear of the car was shaped like an electric razor without blades. The large, rectangular taillights sported bright frames and a T-Bird symbol in the middle. Some said they were the industry's largest taillights because Ford planned to make them flash sequentially. The company had

BODY COLOR INFORMATION

Color Name	Code	Color Name	Code
Raven Black +++	A	Diamond Blue +	N
Pagoda Green	B	Silver Green +	O
Princeton Gray ++++	C	Prairie Bronze	P
Dynasty Green ++++	D	Brittany Blue + and +++	Q
Silver Mink + and +++	E	Phonecian Yellow	R
Arcadian Blue +	F	Cascade Green +	S
Prairie Tan +++	G	Navajo Beige	T
Caspian Blue +	H	Patrician Green +	U
Florentine Green	I	Sunlight Yellow ++	V
Rangoon Red +++	J	Rose Beige +	W
Samoan Coral +++	L	Vintage Burgundy	X
Wimbledon White +++	M	Chantilly Beige	Z

+ Color also used on Lincolns.
++ Color also used on Lincolns and Mercurys
+++ Color available on Sports roadster.
++++ Special-order color
Prairie Tan and Phoenician Yellow were deleted at midyear.
Prairie Bronze and Sunlight Yellow were added at midyear.

CONVERTIBLE TOP COLOR INFORMATION

No. 1: Black satin-grain vinyl with Black headliner and Black frame (available with all interior and exterior colors)
No. 2: White satin-grain vinyl with Black headliner and Black frame (available with all interior and exterior colors)
No. 4: Blue satin-grain vinyl with Black headliner and Black frame (available with Light Blue interior only)

LANDAU VINYL TOP COLOR INFORMATION

A: Black (available with all interior and exterior colors)
B: Black (available with all interior and exterior colors)
C: Brown (available with specific interiors only)
D: Blue (available with specific interiors only)

TONNEAU COLOR INFORMATION

Sports Tonneau covers came in Raven Black 1 (Code A), Wimbledon White 17 (Code M), Rangoon Red 12 (Code J), Silver Mink 5 (Code E), Brittany Blue 19 (Code Q), Patrician Green 23 (Code U), Prairie Bronze 9 (Code G) and Samoan Coral 15 (Code L). All tops have Black headlining.

INTERIOR TRIM INFORMATION

All-vinyl Interiors

Seat Type	Light Rose Beige/ Dark Rose Beige	Light Silver Blue/ Black	Light Blue/ Dark Blue	White Pearl/ Black
Bucket Seats	50/50A	51/51A	52/52A	53/53A

Seat Type	Light Beige/ Medium Beige	Black/ Black	Light Turquoise/ Dark Turquoise	Light Gold/ Dark Gold	Medium Palomino
Bucket Seats	54/54A	55/55A	57/57A	58/58A	59/59A

Vinyl/Pompell Cloth Interiors

Seat Type	Light Silver Blue/ Medium Blue	Light Medium Blue	Light Beige	Black
Bucket Seats	71/71A	72/72A	74/74A	76/76A

Leather Interiors

Seat Type	Light Blue/ Dark Blue	White Pearl/ Black	Red/ Black	Black/ Black	Medium Palomino
Bucket Seats	82/82A	83/83A	85/85A	86/86A	89/89A

A suffix indicates reclining passenger seat with adjustable headrest

THUNDERBIRD PRODUCTION

Model Number	Body/Style Number	Body Type & Seating	Factory Price	Shipping Weight	Production Total
83	63A	2d Hardtop-4P	$4,486	4,431 lbs.	60,552
87	63B	2d Landau-4P	$4,589	4,586 lbs.	22,715
85	76A	2d Convertible-4P	$4,953	4,441 lbs.	9,198

NOTE 1: A total of 45 convertibles left the factory with wire wheels and a sports tonneau

this technology ready to go, but some state laws prohibited sequential lamps in 1964. Between the taillights was a white center piece bearing the Thunderbird name. An optional Safety-Convenience panel had toggle switches for safety flashers and automatic door locks, plus lights to indicate low fuel, door ajar and safety flasher operation.

A restyled "Flight-Deck" instrument panel was one of

the 1964 T-Bird's big selling features. The complete interior sported an aircraft look. The instruments were mounted in separate pods and illuminated by soft green lighting. New thin-shell front bucket seats with headrests were featured. A front passenger seat with a fully reclining backrest was optional. The bucket seats were mounted on pedestals, which increased rear passenger legroom. Wider doors and a difference in the roofline made getting in and out of the T-Bird noticeably easier. New crank-type vent windows aided ventilation. The "Silent-Flo" fresh air circulation system let air into the car through vents at the base of the windshield. It exited through a grille vent just below the rear window. A new asymmetric full-length console was offset to the driver's side, where it blended into the instrument panel. Between the front seats, the console rose up to double as a center foam-padded armrest. It also separated the all-new wraparound lounge-style rear seats, which had a fold-down center armrest. Safety and convenience were stressed in the new interior. A two-spoke steering wheel made the controls and gauges easier to see. It incorporated a padded hub. The dashboard and sun visors were also padded. The speedometer was of drum design with progressive illumination. A red indicator light grew in size as speed increased. All control levers, buttons and wheels for operating the heater, air conditioner, cruise control, radio, air vents and power windows were clustered around the console. The gearshift lever was on the steering column for greater safety. There were stronger new "bear hug" door latches to hold the larger doors shut. Flood-type reading lamps, mounted in the rear roof pillars behind the seats, enhanced both safety and convenience. New inertia reels were provided to retract the outboard front seat belts and make them easier to store and use. The Landau model's vinyl top now had corner creases that gave it a crisper appearance.

The only engine changes included microscopically smaller intake and exhaust valve diameters, a reduction in exhaust pipe diameter from 2.5 in. to 2.0 in., a corresponding reduction in tailpipe diameter from 2.0 in. to 1.75 in. and some ignition timing revisions. Another improvement was that the main bearing thrust surface was increased 1/4 in. in diameter for increased durability and ruggedness. A transistorized ignition system was a new option. Ford said it could increase ignition points and spark plug life to 48,000 miles. Part of the fuel system was a new 22-gallon gas tank. One of its biggest advantages was that its new location provided a deep, wide well and more space in the luggage compartment.

Continuing its quest of the "lifetime" car, Ford promoted 24,000-mile wheel bearing lubrication intervals, 100,000-mile chassis lubes, and 6,000-mile oil changes for T-Birds this year. The smooth-shifting Cruise-O-Matic transmission had no specifications changes. There was a new integral power steering system.

T-Birds switched to 15-in. wheels and 8.15 x 15 low-profile tires. These had a special tread and composition developed specifically for T-Birds. Convertibles with optional wire wheels had to use 8.00 x 14 tires. Another change in 1964 was the availability of a long list of rear axle options.

STANDARD EQUIPMENT

300-hp/390-cid four-barrel V-8, Cruise-O-Matic transmission, power steering, power brakes, movable

The trim pieces present on the doors of the 1963 T-Birds were gone for 1964, adding to the car's sleeker look.

steering column, padded instrument panel, padded sun visors, hydraulic windshield wipers, electric clock, push-button radio and antenna, heater, automatic parking brake release, turn signals, seat belts with retractors, wheel covers, undercoating, back-up lights, glove box light, ashtray light, courtesy light, map light, luggage compartment light, remote-control mirror, windshield wipers-washers, alternator, full instrumentation, automatic parking brake release and Silent-Flow fresh-air circulation system. The Landau model had a padded vinyl top and had landau bars attached to its roof sail panels. Although they had the traditional S-shape with chrome finish, the landau irons carried a new horizontal oval badge at their center. The Landau hardtop's vinyl top came in Black, White, Brown, and Blue. Simulated walnut graining on the instrument panel and interior doorsills returned, but Rosewood trim was no longer offered.

The Thunderbird's power top in action.

I.D. NUMBERS

Die-stamped on top of front fender cross-bar to right of hood lock striker plate. First symbol denotes model-year: 4=1964. Second symbol denotes the assembly plant: Y=Wixom (Novi), Michigan. Third symbol denotes the car-line: 8=Thunderbird. Fourth symbol denotes body type: 3=Thunderbird Tudor hardtop, 5=Thunderbird two-door convertible, 7=Two-door Landau hardtop. Fifth symbol denotes engine: 9=390-cid low-compression Thunderbird V-8 (for export), Z=390 cid/300-hp Thunderbird V-8. Sixth thru 11th symbols denote sequential production number of specific vehicle starting at 100001. Body number plate located on left front body pillar. Serial number: Same as number on VIN tag. Symbols above "BDY" are body symbol code: 63A=hardtop, 63B=Landau hardtop, 76A=convertible. Symbols above CLR are paint color code. First symbol indicates lower body color. Second symbol indicates upper body color. Symbols above TRM are trim combination code. Symbols above "DT" are the production date code. The number indicates the date of the month the car was made. The letters indicate month of manufacture: A=January, B=February, C=March, D=April, E=May, F=June, G=July, H=August, J=September, K=October, L=November, M=December. Symbols above DSO indicate information including the Ford Motor Co. Sales District Code. Symbols above AX indicate rear axle. 1=3.00:1, 4=3.25:1, A=3.00:1 Equa Lock and D=3.25:1 Equa Lock. Symbols above TR indicate type of transmission: All 1964 Thunderbirds came only with SelectShift Cruise-O-Matic Drive code 4.

ENGINES

THUNDERBIRD 390 V-8 (LOW-COMPRESSION EXPORT-ONLY): Overhead valve. Cast-iron block. Displacement: 390 cid. Bore and stroke: 4.05 x 3.78 in. Compression ratio: 9.6:1. Brake hp: 275. Five main bearings. Hydraulic valve lifters. Carburetor: Four-barrel. Cooling system capacity: 20 qt. with heater. Crankcase capacity: 5 qt. (add 1 qt. with new oil filter). Dual exhaust. Code Z.

THUNDERBIRD 390 BASE V-8: Overhead valve. Cast-iron block. Displacement: 390 cid. Bore and stroke: 4.05 x 3.78 in.. Compression ratio: 10.8:1. Brake hp: 300 at 4600 rpm. Torque: 427 lbs.-ft. at 2800 rpm. Five main bearings. Hydraulic valve lifters. Carburetor: Four-barrel. Cooling system capacity: 20 qt. with heater. Crankcase capacity: 5 qt. (add 1 qt. with new oil filter). Dual exhaust. Code Z.

CHASSIS

Wheelbase (all): 113.2 in. Overall length (all): 205.4 in. Overall width (all): 77.1 in. Overall height (hardtop and Landau hardtop): 52.5 in., (convertible) 53.3 in. Front tread: 61 in. Rear tread: 60 in. Front hip room: 2 x 21.5 in. Rear hip room: 49.9 in. Box volume: 482 cu. ft. Front area: 22.4 sq. ft. Front overhang: 37.7 in. Front approach angle: 19.5 degrees. Rear overhang: 54.5 in. Rear departure angle: 12.9 degrees. Road axle road clearance: 5.56 in. Body road clearance: 9.0 in. Tires: 8.15 x 15 4-ply (8.00 x 14 with wire wheels). Steering: Power-assisted link type 3.6 turns lock-to-lock. Steering ratio: 20.3:1. Turning diameter: 40.2 ft. Chassis type: Welded, integral body and frame. Front suspension: Independent wishbone type with ball joints and coil springs. Rear suspension: Live rear axle attached to semi-elliptic rear springs. Telescoping shocks were mounted on the T-Bird suspension front and rear. Standard rear axle: 3.00:1. Front brakes: 11.09 x 3-in. drums. Rear brakes: 11 x 2.5-in. drums. Brake swept area: 381 sq. in. Weight distribution: 56 percent front/44 percent rear. Standard transmission: SelectShift three-element Cruise-O-Matic automatic transmission. Gas tank: 22 gallons (premium fuel required). Fuel economy: 11.1 (averaged 8.3 mpg to 14.5 mpg.) Driving range: 242-308 miles.

Ford photo

The tonneau cover again gave the T-Bird a sports-car look.

Ford photo

The 1964 convertible came with a new wrinkle-resistant top that folded up under a power deck lid.

OPTIONS

4-way power driver's seat ($92.10). 4-way power driver and passenger seats ($184.10). Power windows ($106.20). SelectAire air conditioner ($415.10). AM/FM push-button radio with antenna ($83.70). Rear seat speaker ($15.50). StudioSonic reverb sound system ($54.10). 8.15 x 15 white sidewall tires ($42.10 additional). Tu-Tone paint ($25.80). Sports side trim ($34.80). Tonneau cover, for convertible only ($269). Contoured vinyl floor mats ($15.25). Sports tachometer ($43.10). Kelsey-Hayes sports-style chrome wire wheels and 8.00 x 14 white sidewall tires ($415.20). Deluxe wheel covers ($15.60). Leather seat trim ($106.20). Reclining passenger seat with adjustable headrest ($38.60). Heavy-duty battery ($7.60). Rear fender shields ($26.60). Tinted glass with banded windshield glass ($43). Transistorized ignition system ($51.50). Safety Convenience Control Panel, includes vacuum door locks, door ajar warning light, low fuel warning light, and simultaneous flashing parking and taillights ($45.10). Speed control system ($63.40). Equa Lock limited-slip rear axle. Optional rear axle ratios: 3.00:1, 3.25:1, 3.00:1 Equa Lock, and 3.25:1 Equa Lock. Right-hand outside rearview mirror ($6.95). Door edge guards ($4.40). License plate frame ($6.10). Accent striping ($13.90).

EQUIPMENT INSTALLATION RATES

Cruise-O-Matic drive (100 percent). V-8 engine (100 percent). Radio (100 percent). Heater (100 percent). Power steering (100 percent). Power brakes (100 percent). Power seat (52.4 percent). Power windows (75 percent). Bucket seats (100 percent). Moveable type steering wheel (100 percent). White sidewall tires (96.6 percent). Windshield washers (100 percent). Tinted windshield (72.6 percent). Backup lights (100 percent). Air conditioning (50.6 percent). Dual exhaust (100 percent). Wheel covers (100 percent) (Note: Based on model-year production.)

HISTORICAL FOOTNOTES

Henry Ford II was board chairman of Ford Motor Company. Arjay R. Miller was president. Lee Iacocca was a FoMoCo vice president and general manager of Ford Division. M.S. McLaughlin was back as general sales manager of Ford Division.

The Thunderbird posted a 26 percent retail sales increase and celebrated its 10th anniversary on October 21, 1964. Calendar-year output leaped 35 percent. A total of 92,465 T-Birds, representing 1.2 percent of total industry output, were produced for the model year in the Wixom factory. That just missed the all-time record, set in 1960, of 92,843. Calendar-year output of 90,239 T-Birds represented 1.1 percent of industry. Calendar-year dealer sales were 90,239 T-Birds, which was a huge 2 percent gain.

"What it is is a heavy, luxurious, prestige four-seater that gives its owner a soft, smooth ride and every imaginable creature comfort," *Motor Trend* said in February 1964. "Granted, it's not everyone's cup of tea, but for 'Bird lovers, it's the 'only way to fly.'" Magazines aimed at 1960s sports car buffs always seemed to be a bit more critical of the T-Bird. *Car and Driver* (August 1964), complained, "The Thunderbird is 205.5 in. of steel and chrome with one purpose: gratification of the ego." Along with the rest of Ford Motor Company's Total Performance Products, the Thunderbird shared *Motor Trend* magazine's "Car of the Year" award for "the best possible use of high-performance testing in bringing to the motoring public a product that lives up to the claims of the maker: Total Performance."

A Thunderbird show car called the "Golden Palomino" made its way around the circuit this year. It was a Landau with roof sections that flipped up. The car had both genuine wire wheels and fender skirts. While touring the country it was put on display at many Ford dealerships nationwide.

Ford photo

The hardtop remained the most popular T-Bird, outselling the Landau models more than 2 to 1. The hardtops came with a base price of $4,486.

1965 *Thunderbird*

The 1965 T-Bird had no drastic appearance changes. Thunderbird lettering on the edge of the hood was replaced with a stylized T-Bird emblem. Wide-spaced vertical moldings were added to the former horizontal-bars grille. The script plate with the model name moved from the front fender to the rear fender. There were dummy air vents (Ford called them "simulated waste gates") on both sides of the body, just behind the front wheel openings. New emblems with a stylized Thunderbird partly encircled by a chrome ring adorned the roof sail panels. The center section of the rear bumper had a Thunderbird crest replacing the name spelled out across it. The broad taillights were divided into six square segments by short vertical chrome moldings.

The doors could now be locked without using a key and the keys went into the door locks with either edge up. A "fasten seat belt" light now went off when the driver's belt was pulled out and latched. (In 1964, the light had stayed lit.)

The engine was virtually the same as 1964 and earlier 390s, but the oil filler tube in front of the manifold was replaced with a breather cap and filler tube on the driver's side valve cover. Two engine mount bosses were added on each side of the block casting, due to the use of a new engine-mounting system. A vacuum-operated trunk release was a new accessory.

The headrest-style Sports Tonneau cover was dropped. However, the '64 Sports Tonneau fit the '65 convertible and, for buyers who demanded one, a cover could often be obtained from some Ford dealer's parts inventory. Red band tires, another new option, were $44 extra. Only 15-in. tires

were offered in 1965. New disc brakes did not work with wire wheels, so that option was dropped.

The hardtop, Landau hardtop and convertible models returned. A limited-edition Special Landau was released in March 1965.

Inside the T-Bird was an instrument panel inspired by aircraft design motifs. *Car Life* quipped that driving a T-Bird for the first time at night could "remind its driver of the main drag of Las Vegas, if all the lights are blinking in front of him." At the rear, new sequential taillights were a real attention getter. They operated through an arrangement of multiple taillight bulbs that flashed, in order, from the inner side of the broad red lens to its outer edge. The T-Bird's 390-cid/300-hp V-8 had a new carburetor.

STANDARD EQUIPMENT

Built-in dual exhausts and aluminized stainless-steel muffler, fuel filter, oil filter, 390-cid/300-hp four-barrel V-8, Cruise-O-Matic Drive, double-sided keys, keyless door locking, variable-speed hydraulic windshield wipers, electric windshield washers, crank-type vent windows, front seat belts, padded instrument panel, padded sun visors, electric clock with sweep second hand, courtesy lights, safety-courtesy door lights, sequential turn signals, Swing-Away deep-center steering wheel, dual horns and horn rings, individually adjustable shell-contour front bucket seats, front armrest on top of center console, rear center folding armrest, floating day-night tilt type mirror, double-grip door locks, full wheel covers, power front disc brakes, built-in armrests, floor carpet, full-width foam rubber seats, MagicAire heater and defroster, Silent-Flo ventilation

BODY COLOR INFORMATION

Color Name	Code	Color Name	Code
Raven Black	A	Brittany Blue +	Q
Midnight Turquoise	B	Ivy Green	R
Honey Gold	C	Charcoal Gray +	S
Silver Mink +	E	Navajo Beige	T
Arcadian Blue +	F	Patrician Green +	U
Pastel Yellow +	G	Ember-Glo ++++	V
Caspian Blue	H	Rose Beige	W
Rangoon Red	J	Vintage Burgundy	X
Lilac Mist +++	L	Chantilly Beige	Z
Wimbledon White	M	Frost Turquoise +	4
Diamond Blue +	N	Phoenician Yellow	7
Prairie Bronze	P	Springtime Yellow ++	8

+ Also a Lincoln color
++ Indicates midyear color addition. The Landau Special model came only in this color with Parchment (Code 70) interior trim
+++ Special order color
++++ Available only on Special Landau

CONVERTIBLE TOP COLOR INFORMATION

No. 1: Black with Black headliner and Black frame (available with all interior and exterior colors)
No. 2: White with Black headliner and Black frame (available with all interior and exterior colors)
No. 3: Tan with Black headliner and Black frame (available with specific interior colors only)
No. 4: Blue with Black headliner and Black frame (available with specific interior colors only)

LANDAU VINYL TOP COLOR INFORMATION

A: Black (available with all interior and exterior colors)
B: Black (available with all interior and exterior colors)
C: Brown (available with specific interiors only)
D: Blue (available with specific interiors only)
H: Parchment (available with specific interiors only)

INTERIOR TRIM INFORMATION

All-vinyl Interiors

Seat Type	White Pearl/ Black	Light Silver Blue/ Black	Light Blue/ Dark Blue	Burgundy/ Med. Beige	Light Beige/ Black
Buckets or/ Optiona seat	20/50	21/51	22/52	23/53	24/54

Seat Type	Red/ Burgundy	Black/ Black	Light Turq./ Dark Turq.	Light Gold/ Dark Gold	Med. Palomino
Buckets or/ Optiona seat	25/55	26/56	27/57	28/58	29/59

Seat Type	White Pearl/ Light Blue	White Pearl/ Burgundy	White Pearl/ Light Beige	White Pearl/ Red	White Pearl/ Blk. & Wht.
Buckets or/ Optiona seat	G2/P2	G3/P3	G4/P4	G5/P5	G6/P6

Seat Type	White Pearl/ Aqua	White Pearl/ Light Ivy Gold	White Pearl/ Medium Palomino	Parchment/ Ember-Glo
Buckets or/ Optiona seat	G7/P7	G8/P8	G9/P9	7D/XD

Vinyl/Pompell Cloth Interiors

Seat Type	Light Blue/ Medium Blue	Black	Med Palomino	White Pearl Leather/Blk
Buckets or/ Optiona seat	12/42	16/46	19/49	30/60

Seat Type	Light Blue/ Dark Blue	Burgundy	Red/ Burgundy	Black	Med. Palomino (leather print)
Buckets or/ Optiona seat	32/62	33/63	35/65	36/66	39/69

Seat Type	White Pearl/ Light Blue	White Pearl/ Burgundy	White Pearl/ Light Beige	White Pearl/ Red	White Pearl/ Black & White
Buckets or/ Optiona seat	H2/Q2	H3/Q3	H4/H4	H5/H5	H6/H6

Seat Type	White Pearl/ Aqua	White Pearl/ Light Ivy Gold	White Pearl/ Medium Palomino
Buckets or/ Optiona seat	H7/H7	H8/H8	H9/H9

Color ahead of slash is upholstery color/color behind slash is color of appointments.
Code ahead of slash is for bucket seat/color behind slash is for optional reclining passenger seat with headrest.

THUNDERBIRD PRODUCTION

Model Number	Body/Style Number	Body Type & Seating	Factory Price	Shipping Weight	Production Total
8	63A	2d Hardtop-4P	$4,486	4,470 lbs.	42,652
8	63B	2d Landau-4P	$4,589	4,478 lbs.	20,974
8	63D	2d Spl Landau-4P	$4,639	4,478 lbs.	4,500
8	76A	2d Convertible-4P	$4,953	4,588 lbs.	6,846

system (except convertible), all-vinyl upholstery, ashtray, cigar lighter, air cleaner, automatic transmission, power brakes, integral power steering, undercoating, automatic parking brake release, map light, glove box light, ignition light, ashtray light, fully-lined luggage compartment, luggage compartment light, back-up lights, compartment lights, convertible roof bow light, transistor-type AM radio and antenna, remote-control left-hand outside rearview mirror, five black 8.15 x 15 tubeless tires, full wheel covers, rear fender shields (fender skirts) and shielded alternator. [Special Landau] The limited-edition Thunderbird Special Landau also featured Ember-Glo exterior finish, Ember-Glo dashboard trim, Ember-Glo carpeting, special wheel discs with Ember-Glo trim, a Parchment vinyl roof, a Parchment steering wheel, Parchment dashboard and console trim, a Parchment headliner, Parchment vinyl upholstery, burled walnut vinyl accents on the doors and instrument panel and a plate affixed to the console with the owner's name and "Limited Edition" engraved on it. (Note: At least one Thunderbird Special Landau had White finish.)

I.D. NUMBERS

Die-stamped on top of front fender cross-bar to right of hood lock striker plate. First symbol denotes model-year: 5=1965. Second symbol denotes the assembly plant: Y=Wixom (Novi), Michigan. Third symbol denotes the carline: 8=Thunderbird. Fourth symbol denotes body type: 1=Two-door Landau Special hardtop, 3=Thunderbird Tudor hardtop, 5=Thunderbird two-door convertible, 7=Two-door Landau hardtop. Fifth symbol denotes engine: 9=390-cid low-compression Thunderbird V-8 (for export), Z=390 cid/300-hp Thunderbird V-8. Sixth thru 11th symbols denote sequential production number of specific vehicle starting at 100001. Body number plate located on left front body pillar. Serial number: Same as number on VIN tag. Symbols above "BDY" are body symbol code: 63A=hardtop, 63B=Landau hardtop, 63D=Landau Special hardtop and 76A=convertible. Symbols above "CLR" are paint color code. First symbol indicates lower body color. Second symbol indicates upper body color. Symbols above TRM are trim combination code. Symbols above "DT" are the production date code. The number indicates the date of the month the car was made. The letters indicate month of manufacture: A=January, B=February, C=March, D=April, E=May, F=June, G=July, H=August, J=September, K=October, L=November, M=December. Symbols above DSO indicate information including the Ford Motor Co. Sales District Code. Symbols above AX indicate rear axle. 1=3.00:1, 4=3.25:1, 5=3.50:1, 6=2.80:1, A=3.00:1 Equa Lock, D=3.25:1 Equa Lock, E=3.50:1 and F=2.80:1. Symbols above TR indicate type of transmission: All 1965 Thunderbirds came only with SelectShift Cruise-O-Matic Drive code 4 or code 6.

ENGINES

THUNDERBIRD SPECIAL BASE V-8: Overhead valve. Cast-iron block. Displacement: 390 cid. Bore and stroke: 4.05 x 3.78 in. Compression ratio: 10.0:1. Brake hp: 300 at 4600 rpm. Torque: 427 lbs.-ft. at 2800 rpm. Five main bearings. Hydraulic valve lifters. Carburetor: Four-barrel. Cooling system capacity: 20 qt. with heater. Crankcase capacity: 5 qt. (add 1 qt. with new oil filter). Engine weight: 660 lbs. Dual exhaust. Code Z. (Code 9 low-compression engine used in export units).

This 1965 Special Landau hardtop was just one of 4,500 built.

CHASSIS

Wheelbase: 113.2 in. Overall length: 205.4 in. Overall width: 77.1 in. Overall height (hardtop): 52.5 in., (Landau) 52.7 in., (convertible) 53.3 in. Front tread: 61 in. Rear tread: 60 in. Front hip room: 2 x 21.5 in. Rear hip room: 49.9 in. Box volume: 482 cu. ft. Front area: 22.5 sq. ft. Front overhang: 37.7 in. Front approach angle: 19.5 degrees. Rear overhang: 54.5 in. Rear departure angle: 12.9 degrees. Road axle road clearance: 5.5 in. Body road clearance: 9.0 in. Tires: 8.15 x 15 4-ply. Steering: Power-assisted link type 3.6 turns lock-to-lock. Steering ratio: 20.4:1. Turning diameter: 40.2 ft. Chassis type: Welded, integral body and frame. Front suspension: Independent wishbone type with coil springs. Rear suspension: Live rear axle attached to semi-elliptic rear springs. Telescoping shocks were mounted on the T-Bird suspension front and rear. Standard rear axle: 3.00:1. Front brakes: 11.87-in. Kelsey-Hayes ventilated four-piston caliper discs. Rear brakes: 11 x 2.5-in. drums with 412 sq. in. of swept area. Brake lining gross area: 133 sq. in. Weight Distribution: 56 percent front/44 percent rear. Standard transmission: SelectShift three-element

Ford photo

The 1965 T-Bird had large, rectangular taillights with the T-Bird symbol in between.

The convertible remained in the 1965 Thunderbird lineup, but the tonneau cover was no longer available. Non-functional air vents were added behind the front wheels – one of the few styling differences from 1964.

Cruise-O-Matic automatic transmission. Gas tank: 22 gallons (premium fuel required). Average fuel economy: 11.1 mpg (averaged 8.3 mpg to 14.5 mpg.) Driving Range: 242-308 miles.

OPTIONS

SelectAire air conditioner ($424.90). Heavy-duty 70-amp battery ($7.60). California type closed emission system ($5.30). Automatic deck lid release, except Convertible ($12.90). Limited-slip differential ($47.70). Extra-cooling package ($7.90). Rear fender shields—skirts ($32.70). Tinted glass with banded windshield ($43). Leather seat bolsters and inserts ($106.20). Tu-Tone paint ($25.80). Sports side trim ($34.80). Retracting power antenna ($29.60). 4-way power driver's seat ($92.10). 4-way power driver and passenger seats ($184.10). Power windows and power vent windows ($159.40). Power windows ($106.20). AM/FM push-button radio and antenna ($83.70). Safety Convenience Control Panel includes: vacuum door locks, door ajar light, low fuel light, and safety flashers ($58). Reclining passenger seat with headrest ($45.10). Rear seat speaker ($16.90). Studiosonic rear seat speaker ($54.10). Speed control system ($63.40). Heavy-duty suspension with front and rear heavy-duty springs and shock absorbers ($28.60). Five rayon 8.15 x 15 whitewall tires ($43.90 additional). Five rayon 8.15 x 15 Red Band tires ($51.98 additional). Transistorized ignition system ($76). Deluxe wheel covers with simulated knock-off hubs ($15.60). Automatic headlight dimmer ($45.60). Extra-cooling package ($7.90). Color-keyed floor mats ($15.25). Door edge guards ($4.40). Right-hand outside rearview mirror ($6.95). License plate frame ($6.10). Fuel filler door edge guard ($3.35).

EQUIPMENT INSTALLATION RATES

Cruise-O-Matic drive (100 percent). V-8 engine (100 percent). Radio (100 percent). Heater (100 percent). Power steering (100 percent). Power brakes (100 percent). Power seat (100 percent). Power windows (100 percent). Bucket seats (3.7 percent). Moveable type steering wheel (100 percent). Seat belts (98.2 percent). White sidewall tires (100 percent). Windshield washers (100 percent). Tinted windshield (97.5 percent). Backup lights (100 percent). Air conditioning (90.6 percent). Dual exhaust (100 percent). Limited-slip axle (17.7 percent). Wheel covers (100 percent). Power antenna (21.1 percent). Speed control (7.6 percent). Disc brakes (100 percent). (Note: Based on model-year production.)

HISTORICAL FOOTNOTES

Henry Ford II was board chairman of Ford Motor Company. Arjay R. Miller was president of FoMoCo. Donald N. Frey was a vice president and the new general manager of Ford Division. Lee A. Iacocca moved to the Ford Truck Group. M.S. McLaughlin was now assistant general manager of Ford Division Sales and Marketing.

Calendar-year output fell to 75,710 units representing 0.81 percent of industry. A total of 74,972 T-Birds, representing 0.9 percent of total industry output, were produced for the model year in the Wixom factory. Calendar-year dealer sales were 72,132 T-Birds, representing 0.8 percent of industry sales. Despite the calendar-year sales and production declines, Ford built more Thunderbirds in October 1965 than in any other single month in T-Bird history. The 10,339 cars sold that month (mostly 1966 models) beat the previous monthly sales record of 9,753 units set in October 1962.

Car Life found the 1965 T-Bird's optional thin-shell bucket seats "an aid to the continual ease of riding" and strongly recommended the optional reclining passenger seat with pull-up headrest. "The seats provide a fine compromise between wrap-around support and lounge chair squirm room," reported *Car Life.* "Once tried, the 'Bird's accommodations actually invite long (and normally dreary) drives, rather than discouraging them."

The new Kelsey-Hayes vented disc brakes featured four-piston calipers and brought a vast improvement in T-Bird braking performance. "Deceleration rates and stopping distances are nothing short of phenomenal for a 5,000-lb. car," said *Car Life.* The disc brake system was the same one used in the Lincoln Continental, except that the T-Bird did not have a front wheel pressure-limiting valve. A proportioning valve was used in the system to balance pressure to the lightly loaded rear wheels. The disc brake pads were advertised to last 30,000 miles.

With countless gadgets and accessories running, *Car Life* reported, "So quiet and effortless was the running that the red ribbon type speedometer all too often crept past the 80-mph mark." As usual, the T-Bird was assessed as being "hard-pressed to exhibit much control with less than ideal road surfaces." But the magazine said that the car had to be admired for inspiring "dozens of lesser imitations which, by their very imitation, prove the 'Bird a better beast."

1965 THUNDERBIRD PERFORMANCE		
Model	**CID/HP**	**Performance**
0-60 mph		
Landau	390/300	10.3 seconds
1/4-Mile		
Landau	390/300	17.5 seconds at 79 mph
Top Speed		
Landau	390/300	115
Hardtop	390/300	117 mph (calculated)

Ford photo

The T-Bird was sometimes criticized for its lack of handling and dexterity on the road, but it drew high praise for its amenities and smooth, effortless ride.

Ford photo

The 1966 T-Bird received a mild facelift, but the big redesign was still a year away.

1966 *Thunderbird*

The headlights on the 1966 T-Bird had a bright metal faceplate around them and the rest of the front end had a more aggressive wedge shape. The hood grew longer and the hood scoop was flatter and more sharply pointed. The front lip of the hood had no decorative trim and the heavy chrome grille surround was eliminated. An "ice cube tray" grille carried a big stylized T-Bird ornament right in its center. There was a much slimmer bumper with the splash pan showing below it and parking lamps in the splash pan. Ford removed the fake "waste gates" from the front fenders, but the "Thunderbird" name stayed on the rear body sides. Thin chrome moldings highlighted the front and rear wheel openings. Fender skirts were optional. When skirts were ordered, the rear wheel arch moldings were eliminated and the skirts had chrome bottom moldings.

A full-width rear end treatment had the back-up lights in the middle of the sequential taillight lenses. The taillights had a series of side-by-side square segments, but the individual squares no longer had chrome moldings. New pentastar wheel covers with a "mag" wheel look and color-coordinated sections that matched the body color were used on some new models.

The Town hardtop and Town Landau were new models with a roof featuring wider sail panels and no rear quarter windows. Both carried Thunderbird insignias on the roof sail panels, while the Town Landau carried S-shaped landau irons in the same location. The Landau hardtop was dropped.

The 390-cid engine was tuned to give 315 hp and a new 428-cid/345-hp V-8 was optional. Another new option was a stereo tape player that was built into the AM radio. It provided up to 80 minutes of music per cartridge. Four speakers were included with this sound system. A Safety-Convenience Control Panel was standard in "Town" models and optional in hardtops and convertibles. In the Town hardtop and Town Landau it was incorporated into an overhead roof console.

STANDARD EQUIPMENT

Built-in dual exhausts with aluminized stainless-steel mufflers, fuel filter, oil filter, 390-cid/315-hp four-barrel V-8, Cruise-O-Matic Drive, double-sided keys, keyless door locks, retractable front seat belts with reminder light, color-keyed rear seat belts, front and rear folding center armrests, padded instrument panel, padded sun visors, crank-type vent windows, automatic parking brake release, electric clock with sweep second hand, courtesy lights, sequential turn signals, shielded alternator, Safety-Courtesy door lights, deep-center steering wheel, dual horns and horn rings, individually adjustable shell-contour front bucket seats, floating type day-night tilt type mirror, double-grip door locks, full wheel covers, built-in armrests, floor carpet, full-width foam rubber seats, all-vinyl upholstery, ashtray, cigar lighter, air cleaner, automatic transmission, power front disc brakes, integral power steering, variable-speed hydraulic windshield wipers, electric windshield washers, undercoating, parking brake light, map light, glove box light, ashtray light, fully lined luggage compartment with light, roof bow light (convertible only), back-up lights, compartment lights, MagicAire heater and defroster, Swing-Away movable steering column, transistorized AM push-button radio with antenna, remote-control left-hand outside rearview mirror, five black 8.15 x 15 tubeless tires, Silent Flo ventilation system (except convertible), complete underbody sound coating, and full wheel covers. (Town models) Overhead Safety Panel.

I.D. NUMBERS

Die-stamped on top of front fender cross-brace to right of hood lock striker plate. First symbol denotes model year: 6=1966. Second symbol denotes the assembly plant: Y=Wixom (Novi), Michigan. Third symbol denotes the carline: 8=Thunderbird. Fourth symbol denotes body type: 1=Two-door Town hardtop (blind rear roof quarters with painted top), 3=Two-door hardtop, 5=Thunderbird two-door convertible, 7=Two-door Town Landau (blind rear roof quarters with vinyl top). Fifth symbol denotes engine: Z=390 cid/300-hp Thunderbird V-8, 8=428-cid/265-hp V-8 for export only, Q=428-cid/345-hp Thunderbird Special V-8. Sixth thru 11th symbols denote sequential production number of specific vehicle starting at 100001. Body number plate located on left front body pillar. Serial number: Same as number on VIN tag. Symbols above "BDY" are body symbol code: 63A=hardtop, 63C=Town hardtop, 63D=Town Landau hardtop and 76A=convertible. Symbols above CLR are paint color code. First symbol indicates lower body color. Second symbol indicates upper body color. See the table below. Symbols above TRM are trim combination code. See table below. Symbols above "DT" are the production date code. The number indicates the date of the month the car was made. The letters indicate month of manufacture: A=January, B=February, C=March, D=April, E=May, F=June, G=July, H=August, J=September, K=October, L=November, M=December. Symbols above DSO indicate information including the Ford Motor Co. Sales District Code. Symbols above AX indicate rear axle. The rear axles used were: 1=3.00:1, 3=3.20:1, 6=2.80:1, 01=3.00:1, 11=3.00:1, A=3.00:1 Equa Lock, F=2.80:1 Equa Lock, 0A=3.00:1 Equa Lock, 1A=3.00:1 Equa Lock and 6A=2.80:1 Equa Lock. Symbols above TR indicate type of transmission: All 1966 Thunderbirds came only with SelectShift Cruise-O-Matic Drive code 4 or code 8.

BODY COLOR INFORMATION

Color Name	Code	Color Name	Code
Raven Black	A	Brittany Blue	Q
Sundust Beige	B	Ivy Green	R
Silver Mink	E	Clearcoat Frost	S
Arcadian Blue	F	Candyapple Red	T
Sapphire Blue	G	Tahoe Turquoise	U
Sahara Beige	H	Ember-glo	V
Nightmist Blue	K	Vintage Burgundy	X
Honeydew Yellow	L	Sauterne Gold	Z
Wimbledon White	M	Silver Rose	1
Diamond Blue	N	Mariner Turquoise	2
Silver Rose	O	Springtime Yellow	8
Antique Bronze	P		

TU-TONE BODY COLOR INFORMATION

Color Name	Code	Color Name	Code
Raven Black/Wimbledon White	AM	Silver Rose/Raven Black	OA
Sundust Beige/Raven Black	BA	Silver Rose/Wimbledon White	OM
Sundust Beige/Wimbledon White	BM	Antique Bronze/Wimbledon White	PM
Silver Mink/Raven Black	EA	Brittany Blue/Arcadian Blue	QF
Silver Mink/Wimbledon White	EM	Brittany Blue/Nightmist Blue	QK
Silver Mink/Diamond Blue	EN	Brittany Blue/Wimbledon White	QM
Arcadian Blue/Nightmist Blue	FK	Ivy Green/Wimbledon White	RM
Arcadian Blue/Wimbleton White	FM	Candyapple Red/Raven Black	TA
Sapphire Blue/Wimbeldon White	GM	Candyapple Red/Wimbledon White	RM
Shara Beige/Raven Black	HA	Tahoe Turquoise/Wimbledon White	UM
Sahara Beige/Wimbledon White	HM	Ember-glo/Wimbledon White	VM
Nightmist Blue/Arcadian Blue	KF	Vintage Burgundy/Raven Black	XA
Nightmist Blue/Wimbledon White	FM	Vintage Burgundy/Wimbledon White	XM
Honeydew Yellow/Raven Black	LA	Sauterne Gold/Raven Black	ZA
Honeydew Yellow/Wimbledon White	LM	Sauterne Gold/Wimbledon White	ZM
Honeydew Yellow/Ivy Green	LR	Sauterne Gold/Ivy Green	ZR
Diamond Blue/Wimbledon White	NM	Mariner Turquoise/Wimbledon White	M

CONVERTIBLE TOP COLOR INFORMATION

Code S:	Black with Black headliner and Black frame (available with all interior and exterior colors)
Code T:	White with Black headliner and Black frame (available with all interior and exterior colors)
Code V:	Blue with Black headliner and Black frame (available with specific interior colors only)

LANDAU VINYL TOP COLOR INFORMATION

Code 2:	Black (available with all interior and exterior colors)
Code 3:	White (available with all interior and exterior colors)
Code 7:	Sage Gold (available with specific interiors only)
Code 8:	Parchment (available with specific interiors only)

INTERIOR TRIM INFORMATION

All-vinyl Interiors

Seat type	Silver Mink	Dark Blue	Burgundy	Ember-glo	Red
Bucket seats or/ Optional seat	21/51	22/52	23/53	24/54	25/55

Seat type	Black	Aqua	Ivy Gold	White Pearl/ Silver Mink	
Bucket seats or/ Optional seat	26/56	27/57	28/58	G1/P1	

Seat type	White Pearl/ Dark Blue	White Pearl/ Burgundy	White Pearl/ Ember-glo	White Pearl/ Black & White	White Pearl/ Turquoise
Bucket seats or/ Optional seat	G2/P2	G3/P3	G4/P4	G6/P6	G7/P7

Seat type	White Pearl/ Aqua	White Pearl/ Ivy Gold	White Pearl/ Med. Palomino	Parchment/ Dark Blue	Parchment/ Burgundy
Bucket seats or/ Optional seat	G7/P7	G8/P8	G9/P9	B2/K2	B3/K3

Seat type	Parchment/ Ember-glo	Parchment/ Black	Parchment/ Turquoise	Parchment/ Ivy Gold	Parchment/ Palomino
Bucket seats or/ Optional seat	B4/K4	B5/K5	B7/K7	B8/K8	B9/K9

Vinyl & cloth interiors

Seat type	Dark Blue	Black	Parchment
Bucket seats or/ Optional seat	12/42	16/46	1D/4D

Leather Interiors

Seat Type	Dark Blue	Red	Black Dark Blue	Parchment/ Burgundy	Parchment
Bucket seats or/ Optional seat	62	65	66	L2	L3

Seat type	Parchment/ Ember-glo	Parchment/ Black	Parchment/ Turquoise	Parchment/ Ivy Gold	Parchment/ Palomino
Bucket seats or/ Optional seat	L4	L6	L7	L8	L9

Color ahead of slash is upholstery color/color behind slash (if used) is color of appointments.
Code ahead of slash is for bucket seat/color behind slash is for optional reclining passenger seat with headrest.

THUNDERBIRD PRODUCTION

Model Number	Body/Style Number	Body Type & Seating	Factory Price	Shipping Weight	Production Total
8	63A	2d Hardtop-4P	$4,395	4,582 lbs.	13,389
8	63C	2d Twn Hardtop-4P	$4,452	4,560 lbs.	15,633
8	63D	2d Twn Landau-4P	$4,552	4,568 lbs.	35,105
8	76A	2d Convertible-4P	$4,845	4,692 lbs.	5,049

ENGINES

THUNDERBIRD SPECIAL 390 BASE V-8: Overhead valve. Cast-iron block. Displacement: 390 cid. Bore and stroke: 4.05 x 3.78 in. Compression ratio: 10.5:1. Brake hp: 315 at 4600 rpm. Torque: 427 lbs.-ft. at 2800 rpm. Five main bearings. Hydraulic valve lifters. Carburetor: Four-barrel. Cooling system capacity: 20.5 qt. with heater. Crankcase capacity: 4 qt. (add 1 qt. with new oil filter). Dual exhaust. Code Z.

THUNDERBIRD SPECIAL 428 EXPORT V-8: Overhead valve. Cast-iron block. Displacement: 428 cid. Bore and stroke: 4.13 x 3.98 in. Compression ratio: 8.9:1. Brake hp: 265 at 4400 rpm. Torque: 462 lbs.-ft. at 2800 rpm. Five main bearings. Hydraulic valve lifters. Carburetor: Four-barrel. Cooling system capacity: 20.5 qt. with heater. Crankcase capacity: 4 qt. (add 1 qt. with new oil filter). Dual exhaust. Engine weight: 680 lbs. Code 8.

THUNDERBIRD SPECIAL 428 BASE V-8: Overhead valve.

Cast-iron block. Displacement: 428 cid. Bore and stroke: 4.13 x 3.98 in. Compression ratio: 10.50:1. Brake hp: 345 at 4600 rpm. Torque: 462 lbs.-ft. at 2800 rpm. Five main bearings. Hydraulic valve lifters. Carburetor: Four-barrel. Cooling system capacity: 20.5 qt. with heater. Crankcase capacity: 4 qt. (add 1 qt. with new oil filter). Dual exhaust. Engine weight: 680 lbs. Code Q.

CHASSIS

Wheelbase (all): 113.0 in. Overall length (all): 205.4 in. Overall width (all): 77.3 in. Overall height: (hardtop) 52.5 in., (Town hardtop) 52.6 in., (Town Landau) 52.7 in., (convertible) 52.5 in. Front tread: 61 in. Rear tread: 60 in. Front hip room: 2 x 21.5 in. Front shoulder room: 57 in. Front headroom: 37.4 in. Rear hip room: 49.9 in. Rear shoulder room: 54 in. Rear leg room: 33.2 in. Rear headroom: 37.6 in. Road axle road clearance: 6.4 in. Body road clearance: 9.0 in. Box volume: 482 cu. ft. Front area: 22.5 sq. ft. Front overhang: 37.7 in. Front approach angle: 19.5 degrees. Rear overhang: 54.5 in. Rear departure angle:

Mike Mueller photo

The 1966 T-Bird continued the model's tradition of style and convenience. Among the notable options for the year were a new 428-cid/345-hp V-8 and an 8-track tape player.

12.9 degrees. Tires: 8.15 x 15 4-ply. Steering: Power-assisted link type 3.6 turns lock-to-lock. Turning diameter: 42.6 ft. Steering ratio: 20.4:1. Front suspension: Independent wishbone type with coil springs and ball joints. Rear suspension: Live rear axle attached to semi-elliptic rear springs. Telescoping shocks were mounted on the T-Bird suspension front and rear. Front brakes: 11.87-in. Kelsey-Hayes ventilated four-piston caliper discs. Rear brakes: 11.09 x 2.50 -in. drums with 412 sq. in. of swept area. Weight distribution: (with 390-cid V-8) 56 percent front/44 percent rear. Weight distribution: (with 428-cid V-8) 53.9 percent front/56.1 percent rear. Standard transmission: SelectShift three-element Cruise-O-Matic automatic transmission. Gas tank: 22 gallons (premium fuel required). Average fuel economy: 11.1 mpg (averaged 8.3 mpg to 14.5 mpg.) Driving range: 242-308 miles. Axle (390 V-8): 3.00 (standard), 3.25 (optional); Axle (428 V-8): 2.80 (standard); 3.00/3.50 (optional). Average fuel economy: (390 V-8) 13-16 mpg, (428 V-8) 12-14 mpg. Driving range: (390 V-8) 286-352 miles, (428 V-8) 264-308 miles.

OPTIONS

428-cid/345-hp V-8 ($64.77). 6-way power driver's seat ($96.62). 6-way power driver and passenger seats ($193.73). Power windows ($103.95). Power windows including vent windows ($156.40). Retracting power antenna ($29.60). Heavy-duty 80-amp battery, standard with 428-cid V-8 ($7.44). Limited-slip differential ($46.35). Transistorized ignition system with 428-cid V-8 only ($75.50). Highway-Pilot speed control ($128.72). Safety Convenience Control Panel includes vacuum door locks, door ajar light, low fuel light, and safety flashers, standard in Town hardtop and Town Landau ($56.36). Tinted glass ($42.09). SelectAire conditioner ($412.90). AM/FM radio with antenna ($81.55). Remote deck lid release, except convertible ($12.90). AM radio and Stereosonic 8-track tape player ($127.56). Rear fender shields—skirts ($32.70). License plate frames ($6.10). Leather seat trim, includes reclining seat ($147.03). Tu-Tone paint ($25.07). White sidewall tires ($42.93). White sidewall tires with red band ($51.98). Deluxe wheel covers with simulated knock-off hubs ($15.60). Reclining passenger seat with headrest ($43.83). Rear seat speaker ($16.90). StudioSonic rear seat speaker ($53.50). California closed crankcase emissions control system ($5.30). Exhaust emissions control system ($49.45). Extra-cooling package ($7.90). Heavy-duty suspension ($28.60). Right-hand outside rearview mirror ($6.95). Chrome deck lid luggage rack ($32.44). Retractable rear seat belts ($7.10). Door edge guards ($4.40). Fuel filler door edge guard ($3.35). Contour floor mats ($15.25). Body-side moldings ($34.80). Special order paint ($34.70).

EQUIPMENT INSTALLATION RATES

Cruise-O-Matic drive (100 percent). V-8 engine (100 percent). Radio (100 percent). Heater (100 percent). Power steering (100 percent). Power brakes (100 percent). Power seat (48.4 percent). Power windows (79.1 percent). Bucket seats (100 percent). Moveable type steering wheel (100 percent). White sidewall tires (96.6 percent). Windshield washers (100 percent). Tinted windshield (77.0 percent). Backup lights (100 percent). Air conditioning (63.7 percent). Dual exhaust (100 percent). Limited-slip axle (4.7 percent). Wheel covers (100 percent). Power antenna (21.7 percent). Speed control (10.7 percent). Front disc brakes (100 percent). (Note: Based on model-year production.)

If buyers ponied up just $64.77 more, they could get the big 428-cid/345-hp engine option.

HISTORICAL FOOTNOTES

Calendar-year output was 72,734 units representing 0.8 percent of industry. A total of 69,176 T-Birds, representing 0.8 percent of total industry output, were produced for the model year in the Wixom factory. Calendar-year dealer sales were 68,816 T-Birds, representing 0.8 percent of industry sales.

"The flying-carpet-on-autopilot" is how *Car Life* (June 1966) referred to the Thunderbird that it tested. "Aladdin himself would be astounded at the things this Ford-built 'jinni' can do — and without all that tiresome rubbing of lamps." The writers, of course, were referring to the car's "bells and whistles," which they had the opportunity to try out during a cruise from Los Angeles to Las Vegas. Their "magic carpet" was described as a Town Landau carrying "Aquamarine Blue lower body paint, a pebbled White vinyl-covered top with aluminized plastic Landau bars at the windowless rear quarter panel, special tires with both red and white striping, Beige leather-like vinyl upholstery, interior trim of chromium and walnut, loop pile nylon carpeting in a matching blue-green shade, and a Beige molded fiberglass headliner." It was loaded with the 428-cid V-8, air conditioning, California emission controls, vacuum door locks, a door warning light, a low-fuel warning lamp, emergency flashers, power seats, speed control, and a special steering wheel for the speed control. Naturally, this was all in addition to such standard features as Cruise-O-Matic transmission, power steering, power front disc brakes, AM radio, bonded mirror, heater, hydraulic wipers, and Swing-Away steering wheel. *Car Life*, in its test, had nothing but praise for the Thunderbird. This included advice that the car with power front discs drew quickly to a halt, in a straight line, hardly screeching the tires. The steering was assessed as "a definite surprise when compared to mushy, imprecise, and slow-turning assisted systems." The magazine liked the car's "steering only" (with speed control on) operation, plus its Swing-Away steering wheel, electric seat, power windows and air conditioning system. It did, however, note the shortage of rear seat legroom and some wind rumble at speeds above 60 mph.

With the big engine the car could do 0 to 30 mph in 3.1 seconds, 0 to 50 in 6.8 seconds, and 0 to 100 in 29 seconds. Moving from 30 to 70 mph in passing gear took 9.3 seconds.

Standard T-Bird interiors were already loaded, and most buyers added air conditioning and power windows to boot.

1966 THUNDERBIRD PERFORMANCE		
Model	CID/HP	Performance
0-60 mph		
Town Landau	390/315	11.4 seconds
Town Landau	428/345	9.4 seconds
1/4-Mile		
Town Landau	390/315	18.3 seconds at 77 mph
Town Landau	428/345	16.9 seconds at 82 mph
Top Speed		
Town Landau	428/345	117 mph

Cappy collection

One magazine test compared the 1966 T-Bird to a "flying-carpet-on-autopilot."

Cappy collection

73

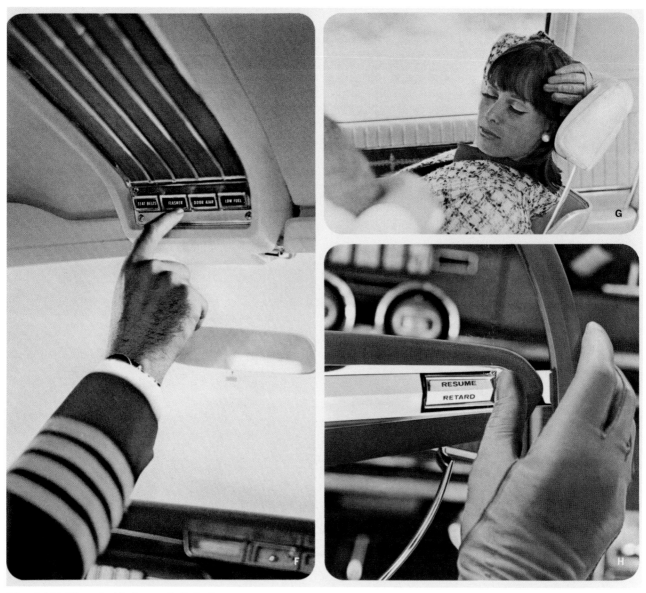

The 1966 Thunderbird was definitely stocked with conveniences. Among the options Ford touted were the "Overhead Safety Panel" with four warning lights, reclining seats, and steering wheel "Highway Pilot Controls."

Cappy collection

The full-width rear taillight assembly had backup lights between sequential signal lights.

Cappy collection

The front end of the 1966 T-Bird featured an ice cube tray grille with a more wedge-shaped design and large emblem in the center.

Mike Mueller photo

The Thunderbird's radical 1967 redesign brought four doors to the model for the first time, and the doors were center opening.

1967
Thunderbird

The '67 T-Bird was completely redesigned with a perimeter frame, a semi-unit body and an all-coil-spring suspension. The convertible was replaced by a four-door Landau. The sporty four-door, with center-opening doors, was viewed as a competitor for the Jaguar Mark II (known as the 340 beginning in 1967), and the Maserati Quatroporte. Also available was a two-door hardtop and two-door Landau.

The new T-birds had long-hood/short-deck styling with a long front overhang. Full-radius wheel openings and the lack of fender skirts gave an "open-wheel" look. A full-width oval bumper housed a lattice-work grille, "Hide-Away" headlights and a T-Bird-shaped center trim piece. One-piece curved door glass eliminated vent windows. Two-door

hardtops had rear quarter windows that retracted by sliding horizontally. Both Landau models had roofs with wide "C" pillars that gave them a close-coupled appearance. All models had a "Coke-bottle" profile and wall-to-wall sequential taillights at the rear. Landaus had vinyl tops and S-shaped landau irons with center medallions.

The T-Bird interior had a smoother and cleaner dashboard with four dials across the dash. A new Tilt-Away steering wheel swung aside or tilted to make it easy for the driver to enter or leave the car. The 1967 T-Bird took driver and passenger safety to new levels. In addition to a padded, shock-absorbing steering wheel, padded dashboard and back-up braking system, Ford provided front seat shoulder harnesses that stowed above the doors with Velcro

BODY COLOR INFORMATION

Color Name	Code	Color Name	Code
Raven Black	A	Brittany Blue (Metallic)	Q
Frost Turquoise	B	Ivy Green(Metallic)	R
Charcoal Gray (Metallic)	C	Candyapple Red	T
Beige Mist (Metallic)	E	Tahoe Turquoise (Metallic)	U
Arcadian Blue	F	Burnt Amber (Metallic)	V
Diamond Green	H	Vintage Burgundy (Metallic)	X
Nightmist Blue (Metallic)	K	Sauterne Gold (Metallic)	Z
Wimbledon White	M	Phoenician Yellow	2
Diamond Blue	N	Silver Frost (Metallic)	4
Pewter Mist (Metallic)	P	Pebble Beige	6

ALL-VINYL INTERIOR TRIM INFORMATION

Seat type	Black	Blue	Red	Saddle	Ivy Gold	Aqua	Ivy Parchment
Bucket seats	2A/4A	2B/4B	2D/4D	2F/4F	2G/4G	2K/4K	2U/4U

First code for regular seat, second code for reclining passenger seat with adjustable headrest.

CLOTH-AND-VINYL INTERIOR TRIM INFORMATION

Seat type	Black	Blue	Red	Ivy Gold	Aqua	Silver	Parchment
Bucket seats	5A/8A	5B/8B	5D/8D	5G/8G	5K/8K	5L/8L	5U/8U

First code for regular seat, second code for reclining passenger seat with adjustable headrest.

LEATHER INTERIOR TRIM INFORMATION

Seat type	Black
Bucket seat	HA/LA

First code for regular seat, second code for reclining passenger seat with adjustable headrest.

VINYL ROOF COLOR INFORMATION

Black	Parchment (White)	Dark Blue	Brown
A	U	B	F

THUNDERBIRD PRODUCTION

Model Number	Body/Style Number	Body Type & Seating	Factory Price	Shipping Weight	Production Total
1	65A	2d Hardtop-4P	$4,603	4,348 lbs.	15,567
2	65C	2d Landau-4P	$4,704	4,256 lbs.	37,422
4	57D	4d Landau-4P	$4,552	4,348 lbs.	24,967

NOTE: Hardtop production includes five "Apollos" built for Abercrombie & Fitch.

Mike Mueller photo

The four-door Landau replaced the convertible in the 1967 Thunderbird lineup. There was little on the car that was recognizable from the previous year.

Ford photo

The two-door Landau was the most popular T-Bird for 1967, with 37,422 produced.

fasteners, plus recessed sun visors, pliable rubber door grab handles, and front fender trim pieces.

Underneath, the '67s were the first T-Birds in 10 years not to have unit-body construction. Computer-tuned mounting pads carried the T-Bird's semi-unit body on the frame, allowing it to "float" on the mountings. The '67 T-Bird had a steering column gear selector with a shift pattern similar to the Fairlane GTA's, which was arranged like a manual gearshift. The '67s were described as "quiet-riding cars on the highway." The new bodies were extremely rigid, due to their stamped-in floor pan stiffeners, heavy sheet metal cross members and full-length drive shaft tunnel. A 14-point body mounting system reduced noise and vibration. All mounts were of bridge-type design and all were located ahead of or behind the passenger compartment. The T-Bird's disc brakes continued to get high marks.

The new four-door Landau was initially a big success, with production higher than the combined total of 1964-1966 T-Bird convertibles.

STANDARD EQUIPMENT

Comfort Stream ventilation system, MagicAire heater and defroster, Unipane side glass, sliding quarter windows in coupes, reversible keys, keyless door locking, ignition lock light, suspended accelerator pedal, retractable headlamp doors, built-in dual exhausts, windshield washers, front and rear seat belts with front retractors and warning light, 4-way emergency flashers, signal lights with lane-change feature, automatic brake release, impact-absorbing steering wheel, padded instrument panel, padded sun visors, padded windshield pillars, electric clock, instrument panel courtesy light, sequential turn signals, adjustable front bucket seats, front seat center console with lighted ashtray and stowage compartment, rear seat folding center armrest, door courtesy lights, non-glare day-night tilt-type mirror, full wheel covers, SelectShift Cruise-O-Matic drive, dual

hydraulic brake system, self-adjusting power front disc/rear drum brakes, power steering, variable-speed hydraulic windshield wipers, undercoating, parking brake light, map light, glove box light, ashtray light, luggage compartment light, back-up lights, heater and defroster, Tilt-Away movable steering column, AM push-button radio and antenna, fully-trimmed luggage compartment, remote-control left-hand OSRV mirror, Safety-Yoke door latches, positive locking door buttons, five 8.15 x 15 tubeless tires, 390-cid/315-hp V-8 engine, alternator, and all standard FoMoCo safety features. Landau models came with a vinyl top as standard equipment.

I.D. NUMBERS

Die-stamped on right-hand side of cowl top panel tab. First symbol denotes model-year: 7=1967. Second symbol denotes the assembly plant: Y=Wixom (Novi), Michigan. Third symbol denotes the car-line: 8=Thunderbird. Fourth symbol denotes body type: 1=Two-door hardtop painted roof, 2=Two-door Landau, 4=four-door Landau. Fifth symbol denotes engine: Z=390 cid/315-hp Thunderbird V-8, Q=428-cid/345-hp Thunderbird Special V-8, 8=428-cid Thunderbird Special low-compression V-8 for export. Sixth thru 11th symbols denote sequential production number of specific vehicle starting at 100001. Body number plate located on front body pillar. Serial number: Same as number on VIN tag. Symbols above "BODY" are body symbol code: 65A=hardtop, 65B=Landau hardtop and 57B=Landau sedan. Symbols above CLR are paint color code. First symbol indicates lower body color. Second symbol indicates upper body color. Symbols above TRM are trim combination code. Symbols above "DT" are the production date code. The number indicates the date of the month the car was made. The letter indicates month of manufacture: A=January, B=February, C=March, D=April, E=May, F=June, G=July, H=August, J=September, K=October, L=November, M=December. Symbols above DSO indicate information including the Ford Motor Co. Sales District Code. Symbols above AX indicate rear axle:

1=3.00:1 conventional, 6=2.80:1 conventional and A=3.00:1 limited-slip. Symbols above TR indicate type of transmission: All 1967 Thunderbirds came only with C6 SelectShift Cruise-O-Matic Drive code U.

ENGINES

THUNDERBIRD SPECIAL 390 BASE V-8: Overhead valve. Cast-iron block. Displacement: 390 cid. Bore and stroke: 4.05 x 3.78 inches. Compression ratio: 10.5:1. Brake hp: 315 at 4600 rpm. Torque: 427 lbs.-ft. at 2800 rpm. Five main bearings. Hydraulic valve lifters. Carburetor: Single four-barrel C7AF-AD. Cooling system capacity: 20.5 qt. with heater. Crankcase capacity: 4 qt. (add 1 qt. with new oil filter). Dual exhaust. Code Z.

THUNDERBIRD SPECIAL 428 BASE V-8: Overhead valve. Cast-iron block. Displacement: 428 cid. Bore and stroke: 4.13 x 3.98 inches. Compression ratio: 10.50:1. Brake hp: 345 at 4600 rpm. Torque: 462 lbs.-ft. at 2800 rpm. Five main bearings. Hydraulic valve lifters. Carburetor: Single four-barrel C7AF-AD. Cooling system capacity: 20.5 qt. with heater. Crankcase capacity: 4 qt. (add 1 qt. with new oil filter). Dual exhaust. Code Q.

NOTE: 428-cid export V-8 also available in export units.

CHASSIS

Wheelbase (two-door): 114.7 in., (four-door) 117.2 in. Overall length (two-door): 206.9 in., (four-door) 209.4. Overall width (all): 77.2 in. Overall height (two-door): 52.8 in., (four-door) 53.7 in. Front tread: 62 in. Rear tread: 62 in. Front hip room: 2 x 22.5 in. Effective headroom: 38.4 in. Rear hip room: 54.3 in. Box volume: 505.1 cu. ft. Front area: 22.8 sq. ft. Tires: 8.15 x 15 4-ply. Steering: Power-assisted link type. Steering ratio: 20.4:1. Turn diameter: 40.2 ft. Front suspension: Independent SLA type with drag strut, ball joints and rubber-bushed stabilizer. Rear suspension: Three-link type with coil springs and rubber-bushed lateral track bar. Telescoping shocks were mounted on the T-Bird suspension front and rear. Standard rear axle: 3.00:1. Front brakes: 11.87 x 1.125 in. power front disc. Rear brakes: 11.03-in. X 2.25 in. drums. Effective area 398 sq. in. Standard transmission: SelectShift three-element Cruise-O-Matic automatic transmission. Gas tank: 24.1 gallons (premium fuel required).

This 1967 ad claimed that "A Thunderbird with four doors is still a Thunderbird."

OPTIONS

Body side accent stripe ($13.90). SelectAire air conditioner ($421.49). Tinted glass ($47.49). 80-amp heavy-duty battery ($7.44). Limited-slip differential ($46.69). California-type emissions control system with EECS only ($5.19). Exhaust emission control system, California type ($49.45). 428-cid 345-hp V-8 with Cruise-O-Matic transmission, extra charge over base V-8 ($90.68). Extra heavy-duty cooling package, standard with air conditioning ($7.73). Tinted glass with banded windshield ($47.49). Tu-Tone paint, on Tudor hardtop only ($25.25). Retracting power antenna ($28.97). Power deck lid release ($12.63). 6-way power driver's seat ($97.32). Power windows ($103.95). Two-door Protection Group ($25.28). Four-door Protection Group ($29.17). (Note: Protection Groups include front and rear color-keyed floor mats, license plate frames, and door edge guards.) AM/FM Multiplex stereo radio with speakers ($163.17). AM manual Stereosonic tape system ($128.49). AM/FM radio with dual rear speakers ($89.94). Overhead Convenience Control Panel, includes speed-actuated power door locks, door ajar light, low-fuel light, and emergency flashers ($77.73 for two-door models, $101.10 for four-door models). Reclining passenger seat with headrests ($57.08). Shoulder harness ($27.27). Dual rear speaker for AM radio only ($33.07). Highway Pilot fingertip speed control, including specific steering wheel ($129.55). Heavy-duty suspension includes front and rear heavy-duty springs and shocks ($27.99). 8.15 x 15 four-ply tires, whitewall with red band ($51.98). 8.15 x 15 four-ply tires, whitewall ($43.12). Split leather trim interior with unique seat trim style and wood-grain accents ($201.06). Deluxe wheel covers with spinners ($19.48). Styled steel wheel covers with chrome lug nuts ($35.70).

EQUIPMENT INSTALLATION RATES

Cruise-O-Matic drive (100 percent). V-8 engine (100 percent). Radio (78.9 percent). Power steering (100 percent). Disc brakes (100 percent). Power seat (52 percent). Power windows (83.8 percent). Bucket seats (100 percent). Moveable type steering wheel (100 percent). White sidewall tires (95.4 percent). Tinted windshield (83.8 percent). Vinyl top: (80 percent). Air conditioning (74.9 percent). Dual exhaust (100 percent). Limited-slip axle (9.5 percent). Wheel covers (100 percent). Power antenna (34.1 percent). Speed control (11.4 percent). AM/FM radio (21.1 percent). Clock (100 percent). (Note: Based on model-year production.)

HISTORICAL FOOTNOTES

The 1967 Thunderbird was introduced on September 22, 1966. Henry Ford II was board chairman of Ford Motor Company. Arjay R. Miller was president. Donald N. Frey was a vice president and the new general manager of Ford Division. M.S. McLaughlin was now vice president and general manager of Ford Division. J.B. Naughton was assistant general sales manager.

Calendar-year output was 59,640 units or 0.8 percent of industry. This was a 16.7 percent drop from the previous year, although much of this was due to a 61-day strike against Ford. A total of 77,956 T-Birds, representing 1 percent of industry output, were produced for the model year in the Wixom factory. Model-year output was up 12.7 percent from 1966. Calendar-year dealer sales amounted to 57,913 T-Birds, representing 0.7 percent of industry sales.

The 1967 Thunderbird was a fairly good performer. With the optional 428-cid engine, it was even more fun to drive. "While no dragster, the (428) test car's accelerative ability was at least adequate for all present-day driving needs," noted *Car Life*. "Zero to 60 mph acceleration in 10 seconds will take care of the exigencies of on-ramp maneuvering, while sprinting to 82 mph within a quarter-mile's space certainly implies more briskness than most drivers will ever require or employ."

Five Thunderbird two-door hardtops were specially ordered by Abercrombie & Fitch for display in the company's department stores in New York, San Francisco, Chicago, Miami, and Palm Beach. These cars were converted into two-door Landau models with sliding sunroofs, with the work being done by Andy Hotten's Detroit Steel Tubing Company at a cost of approximately $15,000 per car. They were loaded up with options and painted Apollo Blue. The cars had serial numbers 7Y81Q122570-7Y81Q122574, and at least three of them survive.

1967 THUNDERBIRD PERFORMANCE		
Model	**CID/HP**	**Performance**
0-60 mph		
Four-door Landau	390/315	12 seconds
Four-door Landau	428/345	9.8 seconds
1/4-Mile		
Four-door Landau	390/315	17.8 seconds @ 78 mph
Four-door Landau	428/345	16.4 seconds @ 82 mph
Top Speed		
Four-door Landau	390/315	111 mph estimated
Four-door Landau	428/345	120 mph
Two-door Hardtop	390/315	118 mph

The T-Bird line continued to include a four-door model in 1968. Ford produced more than 21,000 of the four-door Landau models.

1968 *Thunderbird*

The 1968 T-Bird was mildly revised. The full-width grille had more widely spaced openings. Instead of a large T-Bird emblem in the center, there were smaller ones on the grille sides of the rotating headlight doors. The lower part of the narrower new two-piece bumper was painted body color and had large slots below it, one on either side, that provided increased air flow. The parking lamps were set into these slots.

A two-door hardtop and two- and four-door Landaus returned along with a new four-door Town Sedan. The Town Sedan's roof was painted, instead of vinyl, and wider S-shaped Landau bars decorated its sail panels. Federally mandated front fender side marker lamps were seen. The rear fenders had red reflectors that served a similar purpose. Much thinner rocker panel moldings were used.

Other new government-required safety features included a non-tilting energy-absorbing steering column (the Tilt-Away wheel became optional equipment), hazard flasher lights, recessed instruments and windshield washers. Shoulder belts, which were previously a $23.38 option, were added to the standard equipment list, effective January 1, 1968. A three-passenger Flight Bench front seat was now standard. Bucket seats, a center console, and a console-mounted gear selector lever were optional. The T-Bird also featured new squeeze-type inside door handles. Rear seat legroom was increased due to a lower floor tunnel, which was made possible by a new type of universal joint.

At the start of the model-year the 390-cid V-8 was the base engine. A new IMCO exhaust emission control system was used. It incorporated a different carburetor with a preheated air feature and ignition modifications designed to provide more complete fuel combustion. A new option was a 429-cid "Thunderjet" thin-wall V-8 rated at 360 hp. Based on Ford's lightweight 289-cid V-8, this "big-block" version provided more horsepower with lower emissions. Effective January 1, 1968, the 429 became standard equipment in T-Birds and the 390 was discontinued. Other technical changes for 1968 included new "floating" caliper front disc/rear drum brakes. There were no major changes in the 1968 T-Bird chassis. *Motor Trend* (November 1967) described it as "the ideal car for pleasant journeying."

STANDARD EQUIPMENT

Comfort Stream ventilation system, MagicAire heater and defroster, Unipane side glass, sliding quarter windows in coupes, reversible keys, keyless door locking, ignition switch light, suspended accelerator pedal, retractable headlight doors, built-in dual exhausts, dual-stream windshield wipers, front and rear seat belts with front retractors and warning light, shoulder belts for front outboard passengers (effective January 1, 1968), 4-way emergency flashers, front side marker lights and rear side reflectors, sequential turn signal instrument panel indicator (early production only), signal lights with lane-change feature, automatic brake release, impact-absorbing steering wheel, energy-absorbing instrument panel, padded safety sun visors, padded windshield pillars, electric clock, instrument panel courtesy light, interior rear courtesy light, sequential turn signals, full-width three-passenger front seat, self-locking folding seats, front seat center console with lighted ashtray and stowage compartment, rear seat folding center armrest, door courtesy lights, non-glare day-night tilt-type mirror, full wheel covers, SelectShift Cruise-O-Matic drive, dual hydraulic brake system, self-adjusting power front disc/rear drum brakes, power steering, variable-speed hydraulic windshield wipers, underbody sound coating, parking brake light, map light, glove box light, ashtray light, luggage compartment light, back-up lights, heater and defroster, AM push-button radio and antenna, fully-trimmed luggage compartment, remote-control left-hand OSRV mirror, corrosion-resistant brake lines, Safety-Yoke door latches, positive locking door buttons, five 8.15 x 15 tubeless tires on two-door models or five 8.45 x 15 four-ply-rated black sidewall tires on four-door models, (early) Thunderbird 390 Special 315-hp V-8 engine, (after January 1) Thunderjet 429-cid/360-hp V-8, alternator, and all standard FoMoCo safety features. Landau models came with a vinyl top as standard equipment.

I.D. NUMBERS

VIN stamped on aluminum tab riveted to dashboard on passenger side and observable through the windshield from outside the car. First symbol denotes model-year: 8=1968. Second symbol denotes the assembly plant: Y=Wixom (Novi), Michigan and J=Los Angeles, California. Third symbol denotes the car-line: 8=Thunderbird. Fourth symbol denotes body type: 3=Two-door hardtop, 4=Two-door Landau, 7=four-door Landau. Fifth symbol denotes engine: Z=390 cid/315-hp Thunderbird V-8, N=429-cid/360-hp Thunder-Jet V-8. Sixth thru 11th symbols denote sequential production number of specific vehicle starting at 100001. Body number plate located on front door hinge pillar. Serial number: Same as number on VIN tag. Symbols above "BODY" are body symbol code: 65C=hardtop, 65D=Landau hardtop and 57C=Landau sedan. Symbols above CLR are paint color code. First symbol indicates lower body color. Second symbol indicates upper body color. Symbols above TRM are trim combination code. Symbols above "DT" are the production date code. The number indicates the date of the month the car was made. The letters indicate month of manufacture: A=January, B=February, C=March, D=April, E=May, F=June, G=July, H=August, J=September, K=October, L=November, M=December. Symbols above DSO indicate information including the Ford Motor Co. Sales District Code. Symbols above AX indicate rear axle: 0=standard 2.50:1, 3=optional 2.80:1, 5=optional 3.00:1, C=optional 2.80:1 limited-slip and E=optional 3.00:1

limited-slip. TR indicated type of transmission: All 1968 T-Birds came only with SelectShift Cruise-O-Matic Drive code U.

ENGINES

THUNDERBIRD 390 FOUR-BARREL BASE V-8: Overhead valve. Cast-iron block. Displacement: 390 cid. Bore and stroke: 4.05 x 3.78 in. Compression ratio: 10.5:1. Brake hp: 315 at 4600 rpm. Torque: 427 lbs.-ft. at 2800 rpm. Five main bearings. Hydraulic valve lifters. Carburetor: Four-barrel. Cooling system capacity: 20.5 qt. with heater. Crankcase capacity: 5 qt. (add 1 qt. with new oil filter). Dual exhaust. Code Z.

THUNDER JET 429 V-8: Overhead valve. Cast-iron block. Displacement: 429 cid. Bore and stroke: 4.36 x 3.59 in. Compression ratio: 10.50:1. Brake hp: 360 at 4600 rpm. Torque: 480 lbs.-ft. at 2800 rpm. Five main bearings. Hydraulic valve lifters. Carburetor: Motorcraft four-barrel. Cooling system capacity: 19.4 qt. Crankcase capacity: 5 qt. (add 1 qt. with new oil filter). Dual exhaust. Code N.

CHASSIS

Wheelbase (two-door): 114.7 in., (four-door) 117.2 in. Overall length (two-door): 206.9 in., (four-door) 209.4. Overall width (all): 77.3 in. Overall height: (two-door) 52.6 in., (four-door) 53.4 in. Front tread: 62 in. Rear tread: 62 in. Front hip room: 2 x 22.5 in. Effective headroom: 38.1 in. Rear hip room: 54.3 in. Box volume: 505.1 cu. ft. Front area: 22.8 sq. ft. Tires: 8.15 x 15 4-ply. Steering: Power-assisted link type. Ratio: 21.9:1. Turning diameter: 42.0 ft. Front suspension: Independent SLA type with coil springs and ball joints. Rear suspension: Four-link type with coil springs. Telescoping shocks were mounted on the T-Bird suspension front and rear. Standard rear axle: 3.00:1. Front brakes: 11.80 x 1.125 in. power front disc. Rear brakes: 11.03-in. X 2.25 in. drums. Effective area 373 sq. in. Standard transmission: SelectShift three-element Cruise-O-Matic automatic transmission. Gas tank: 24 gallons (premium fuel required).

BODY COLOR INFORMATION

Color Name	Code	Color Name	Code
Raven Black	A	Brittany Blue (Metallic)	Q
Royal Maroon	B	Highland Green (Metallic)	R
Beige Mist (Metallic)	E	Candyapple Red	T
Diamond Green	H	Tahoe Turquoise (Metallic)	U
Lime Gold (Metallic)	I	Alaska Blue	V
Midnight Aqua	J	Meadowlark Yellow	W
Silver Pearl (Metallic)	L	Presidential Blue (Metallic)	X
Wimbledon White	M	Sunlit Gold (Metallic)	Y
Diamond Blue	N	Oxford Gray (Metallic)	Z
Pewter Mist (Metallic)	P	Pebble Beige	6

ALL-VINYL INTERIOR TRIM INFORMATION

Seat Type	Black	Dark Blue	Red	Saddle	Ivy Gold	Aqua	Parchment	Nugget Gold
Bench Seat	4A	4B	—	4F	—	—	4U	4Y
Bucket Seat	2A	2B	2D (*)	2F	2G (*)	2K	2U	2Y

(*) Two-door only

BROUGHAM CLOTH-AND-VINYL INTERIOR TRIM INFORMATION

Seat Type	Black	Blue	Red	Ivy Gold	Aqua	Nugget Gold
Bench Seat	3A (+)	3B (+)	3D (+)	3G (+)	3K (+)	3Y (+)
Bucket Seats	1A (*)	1B (*)	1D (*)	1G (*)	1K (*)	1Y (*)

(+) Four-door only
(*) Two-door only

LEATHER INTERIOR TRIM INFORMATION

Seat Type	Black	Saddle
Bucket Seats	8A	8F

VINYL ROOF COLOR INFORMATION

Black	Parchment (White)	Dark Blue	Ivy Gold
A	U	B	G

THUNDERBIRD PRODUCTION

Model Number	Body/Style Number	Body Type & Seating	Factory Price	Shipping Weight	Production Total
3	65A	2d Hardtop-4P	$4,716	4,327 lbs.	9,977
4	65B	2d Landau-4P	$4,845	4,337 lbs.	33,029
7	57B	4d Landau-4P	$4,924	4,427 lbs.	21,925

NOTE 1: Factory prices shown are from January 1, 1968; earlier prices were $4,339 for Model 65A, $4,768 for Model 65B, and $4,847 for Model 57B.
NOTE 2: Production total above includes 5,420 Model 65A with bucket seats, $19,105 Model 65B with bucket seats, and 4,674 Model 57B with bucket seats.

This two-door Landau came in Diamond Green, one of 20 different colors available.

OPTIONS

429-cid ThunderJet V-8 engine, prior to January 1, 1968 ($53.18). Limited-slip rear axle ($46.69). High-ratio axle, standard with 429-cid engine ($46.69). Heavy-duty battery, standard with 429-cid engine ($7.44). Two-door Brougham interior trim with bucket seats ($129.54). Four-door Brougham interior trim with bench seats ($161.98). Brougham leather interior for models with Black or Saddle colored bucket seats ($194.31). (Note: Brougham interior trim includes unique seat trim style, wood-grain appointments, door courtesy lights, cut-pile carpets, unique door trim panels, door pull handles, and rear seat center arm rest.) Deluxe front or rear shoulder belts ($15.59). Deluxe front shoulder belts ($18.22). Deluxe rear shoulder belts ($18.22). Passenger side reclining seat ($41.49). Adjustable front headrests ($42.75). Tilt-Away steering wheel ($66.14). Heavy-duty suspension with front and rear heavy springs and shocks ($27.99). Deluxe wheel covers ($57.08). Extra charge for non-standard tires on two-door models without air conditioning: 8.15 x 15 4-ply whitewalls ($43.12). 8.15 x 15 4-ply red band whitewalls ($51.98). 8.45 x 15 4-ply black sidewalls ($18.07). 8.45 x 15 4-ply whitewalls ($61.26). 8.45 x 15 4-ply red band whitewalls ($70). 8.45 x 15 (215 R15) radial-ply whitewalls ($117.64). Extra charge for non-standard tires on two-door models with air conditioning and all four-door models: 8.45 x 15 4-ply whitewalls ($43.19). 8.45 x 15 4-ply red band whitewalls ($52.04). 8.45 x 15 (215 R15) radial-ply whitewalls ($101.30). Appearance Protection Group, including door edge guards, license plate frame and vinyl floor mats front and rear, on two-door ($25.28); on four-door ($29.17). Body-side protection molding ($45.40). Spare Tire Cover ($5.25). Styled steel wheel covers with chrome lug nuts ($35.70). Body accent stripe in Red, White or Black ($13.90). Supplemental brake lamp ($33.70) Front Cornering Lamps ($33.70). Convenience Check Group two-door ($77.73); four-door ($101.10). Rear lamp monitor ($25.91). Four note horn ($15.59). Rear window defogger ($22.33). Complete tinted glass ($47.49). SelectAire Conditioner ($427.07). SelectAire Conditioner with Automatic Climate Control ($499.22). Dual rear seat speakers with AM radio only ($33.07). AM-FM push-button stereo radio ($150.29). AM push-button radio/StereoSonic tape system ($128.49). Power radio antenna ($28.97). Highway Pilot speed control, requires Tilt-Away steering wheel ($97.21). Power deck lid release ($14.85). 6-way power seat, bench or driver's side bucket ($97.32). Power windows ($103.95). Visor-vanity mirror ($3.79). Automatic headlight dimmer ($51.20 special order). Automatic ride control ($89.94).

EQUIPMENT INSTALLATION RATES

Cruise-O-Matic drive (100 percent). V-8 engine (100 percent). AM radio (55.8 percent). Power steering (100 percent). Disc brakes (100 percent). Power seat (53.6 percent). Power windows (84 percent). Bucket seats (45 percent). Moveable type steering wheel (61.7 percent). White sidewall tires (95.4 percent). Tinted windshield (85.6 percent). Vinyl top: (84.6 percent). Air conditioning (82.7 percent). Dual exhaust (100 percent). Limited-slip axle (8.4 percent). Wheel covers (100 percent). Power antenna (34.1 percent). Speed control (12.1 percent). AM/FM radio (24.9 percent). Clock (100 percent). Stero tape player (19.3 percent) Note: Based on model-year production.

HISTORICAL FOOTNOTES

The 1968 T-Bird was introduced on September 22, 1967. Henry Ford II was board chairman of Ford Motor Company. Arjay R. Miller was vice chairman. J.B. Naughton was a vice president and the general manager of Ford Division. G.B. MacKenzie was assistant general sales manager. Lee A. Iaccoca was named executive vice president in charge of North American Operations for Ford Motor Company.

Calendar-year output was 76,789 units or 0.9 percent of industry. This was a 28.8 percent rise from the previous year. A total of 64,391 T-Birds, representing 0.8 percent of industry output, were produced. Only 51,429 of these cars were made in the Wixom assembly plant. The additional 13,502 cars were made in Ford's Los Angeles, California factory. Model-year output was down 16.7 percent from 1967. Calendar-year dealer sales amounted to 67,373 T-Birds, representing 0.8 percent of industry sales and a 17.6 percent gain over '67.

In December 1967, *Motor Trend* magazine published an article titled "How the 429 really performs." In it, editor Steve Kelly drove a 429-powered 1968 T-Bird two-door Landau at the Ford test track in Dearborn, Michigan. The car had only 500 miles on its odometer. A 2.80:1 final drive ratio allowed it to cruise at 27.6 mph per 1000 rpm, keeping engine speed down and gas mileage up. With two people on board, 150 lbs. of test equipment, and a full tank of gas, the car moved from 0-60 mph in 9.5 seconds and covered the quarter-mile in 17.4 seconds at 84 mph. "The times were very good, but below those of a 428-cid V-8-powered 'Bird tested in the August '67 *MT*," said Kelly. "The 428 car, though, had nearly 5,000 miles of careful break-in, and from what we learned of the new engine from behind the wheel and from the engineering department, we can safely predict that the 429 will reveal itself a better performer than the earlier 428. In our judgment, not only is the 429 V-8 a breakthrough in low emission design power plants, it is an amazingly good performer with reserve power and reliability."

A historical milestone was marked this year when T-Birds were produced in two different factories. Another significant event in the history of Ford Motor Co. occurred this year in the hiring of "Bunkie" Knudsen, a veteran General Motors executive, as FoMoCo's new president. He came to Dearborn on February 6, 1968. This was too late to influence product changes scheduled for 1969, but, even though his tenure at Ford turned out to be very brief, Knudsen would have a role in planning the fifth-generation T-Birds that bowed in 1970.

1968 THUNDERBIRD PERFORMANCE		
Model	**CID/HP**	**Performance**
0-60 mph		
Two-door Landau	429/360	9.5 seconds
1/4-Mile		
Two-door Landau	429/360	17.4 seconds at 84 mph
Top Speed		
Two-door Landau	390/315	118 mph

Ford photo

Among the subtle changes on the 1968 'Birds were the side-marker lamps, rear reflectors, and thinner rocker panel moldings.

Ford photo

All T-Birds were lowered one-half inch for 1969, and the two-door models received an improved suspension package.

1969 *Thunderbird*

Ford's new boss, "Bunkie" Knudsen, arrived too late to change the 1969 T-Bird in any significant way. The front and rear were modestly updated for the new model year. A new formal roof treatment with wider "C" pillars graced the Landau coupe, giving it a more stately look. A new die-cast radiator grille featured a full-width horizontal center bar and three widely spaced vertical bars that crossed it to form eight slim rectangular segments. Each segment had a horizontally textured background and the outer grille segments (actually the headlamp doors) had additional segmentation. There was a large Thunderbird emblem in the center of the grille. The front bumper had indentations cut into the air slots for housing the rectangular parking lamps.

At the rear of the car, full-width taillights were gone. Instead a single, large, red rectangular lens on each side carried the T-Bird emblem in its center. Sequential taillight bulbs were used, but the center rear panel section that had the Thunderbird name lettered across it was no longer illuminated. New front side marker lamps had a simpler design and the red reflectors on the rear fenders were smaller. Three body styles were offered again.

Like all 1969 Ford products, T-Birds came with FoMoCo's package of "Lifeguard Design Safety Features." This was the name for some two dozen safety items, some required by federal law. They ranged from outside rearview mirrors to "safety" coat hooks. Another new safety feature found on all Ford front seats were headrests.

There were standard vinyl bench and bucket seat options, Brougham bucket and bench options and a Brougham leather option for bucket seat interiors only. A center console was included when bucket seats were ordered. The consoles swept upwards, in front, to integrate with the dashboard and included two extra storage boxes to supplement the glove compartment in the dash. Bucket seats with standard vinyl trim were not provided in four-door Landaus, but you could get bucket seats with fancier trims in that model. Reclining seat mechanisms were optional and available on all seats at extra cost. Specific seat trims were available in up to six color choices and vinyl tops came in Black, White, Dark Blue and Ivy Gold. Interiors included a recessed, five-pod gauge cluster with full instrumentation as standard equipment.

Also standard in Thunderbirds was a 429-cid/360-hp V-8 and SelectShift Cruise-O-Matic automatic transmission. The big engine featured dual exhausts as regular equipment. Ford's biggest automatic transmission had a P-R-N-D-2-1 shift pattern that provided a choice of manual-style or fully automatic gear selection. Several new options were introduced this year. One was a wire-in-glass type rear window defroster and the other was a push-button sliding electric sunroof. Constructed entirely of metal, the sunroof

BODY COLOR INFORMATION

Color Name	Code	Color Name	Code
Raven Black	A	Brittany Blue (Metallic)	Q
Dark Royal Maroon	B	Morning Gold	R
Black Jade (Metallic)	C	Champagne Gold (metallic)	S
Lilac Frost (Metallic)	G	Candyapple Red	T
Diamond Green	H	Tahoe Turquoise (Metallic)	U
Lime Gold (Metallic)	I	Copper Flame (Metallic)	V
Midnight Aqua (Metallic)	J	Meadowlark Yellow	W
Midnight Orchid (Metallic)	K	Presidential Blue (Metallic)	X
Wimbledon White	M	Indian Fire (Metallic)	Y
Diamond Blue	N	Oxford Gray (Metallic)	Z

BODY COLOR INFORMATION

Color Name	Code	Color Name	Code
Raven Black	A	Brittany Blue (Metallic)	Q
Dark Royal Maroon	B	Morning Gold	R
Black Jade (Metallic)	C	Champagne Gold (metallic)	S
Lilac Frost (Metallic)	G	Candyapple Red	T
Diamond Green	H	Tahoe Turquoise (Metallic)	U
Lime Gold (Metallic)	I	Copper Flame (Metallic)	V
Midnight Aqua (Metallic)	J	Meadowlark Yellow	W
Midnight Orchid (Metallic)	K	Presidential Blue (Metallic)	X
Wimbledon White	M	Indian Fire (Metallic)	Y
Diamond Blue	N	Oxford Gray (Metallic)	Z

ALL-VINYL INTERIOR TRIM INFORMATION

Seat Type	Black	Dark Blue	Red	Ivy Gold	White	Nugget Gold
Bench Seat (all models)	4A	4B	4D	—	4W	4Y
Bucket Seat (two-door models)	2A	2B	2D	2G	2W	2Y

BROUGHAM CLOTH-AND-VINYL INTERIOR TRIM INFORMATION

Seat Type	Black	Blue	Red	Ivy Gold	Nugget Gold
Bench Seat (all models)3A	3B	3D (+)	3G	3Y	
Bucket Seats (two-door models)	1A	1B	1D (*)	1G	1Y

(+) Four-door only
(*) Two-door only

LEATHER INTERIOR TRIM INFORMATION

Seat Type	Black	White
Bucket Seats	8A	8W

VINYL ROOF COLOR INFORMATION

Black	White	Dark Blue	Ivy Gold	Dark Brown
A	U	B	G	F

THUNDERBIRD PRODUCTION

Model Number	Body/Style Number	Body Type & Seating	Factory Price	Shipping Weight	Production Total
3	65A/65C	2d Hardtop-4P	$4,807	4,348 lbs.	5,913
4	65B/65D	2d Landau-4P	$4,947	4,360 lbs.	27,664
8	57B/57C	4d Landau-4P	$5,026	4,460 lbs.	15,650

NOTE 1: 65A=two-door hardtop with bucket front seats; 65C=two-door hardtop with front bench seat; 65B=two-door Landau with blind quarter roof and front bucket seats; 65D=two-door Landau with blind rear quarter roof and front bench seat; 57B=four-door Landau with front bucket seats; 57C=four-door Landau with front bench seat.
NOTE 2: Prices increased by $17 on February 1, 1969, after front headrests became standard federally mandated equipment.
NOTE 3: Production totals above include 2,361 Model 65A with bucket seats, 12,125 Model 65B with bucket seats, and 1,983 Model 57B with bucket seats.

(last offered in 1960) was power-operated. A small button on the bottom portion of the dash activated it. *Motor Trend* (February 1969) said, "The roof itself is a solid, well-built unit that seals tightly into place when closed." Also noted was a lack of turbulence with the roof open and the fact that the car stayed warm when the roof was rolled back on chilly, but sunny days. A crank was provided to operate the roof in case of electrical failure.

Technical improvements for 1969 were mainly refinements. All T-Birds came equipped with an Autolite "Sta-Ful" battery, Autolite "Power-Tip" spark plugs, Autolite shock absorbers and an Autolite 6,000-mile oil filter. Ford promoted "Twice-A-Year Maintenance" based on the fact that recommended oil change intervals were 6,000 miles or six months. Coolant replacement was called for at 24 months and major chassis lubrication was supposed to be good for 36,000 miles. "The '69 Thunderbird needs so little service it's just good sense to see that it gets the best — at your Ford dealer's," said the sales catalog.

There were some important suspension modifications on 1969 two-door models and all T-Birds were lowered one-half inch. Coupes got what amounted to a heavy-duty suspension package. It included stiffer springs with a ride rate of 135 lb.-in. up front and 123 lb.-in. in the rear, larger shock absorbers and a fatter 0.812-in. diameter anti-roll bar. While this gave a ride that was still on the traditional "T-Bird-soft" side, it was firmer than in the past. "Ride and handling characteristics are vastly improved in the two-door models due to suspension modifications," *Motor Trend* reported. "The change in suspension has reduced roll and gives a flatter, smoother ride when cornering."

STANDARD EQUIPMENT

ThunderJet 429-cid/360-hp V-8, SelectShift Cruise-O-Matic drive, Unipane side glass, reversible keys, keyless locking, lighted ignition switch, full-width three-passenger front seat, power steering, AM radio, electric clock, MagicAire heater and defroster, suspended accelerator pedal, lockable lighted glove box, map light, instrument panel courtesy light, rear interior courtesy lights, power front disc/rear drum brakes, sequential turn signals, lined and lighted luggage compartment, underbody soundcoating, full wheel covers, dual hydraulic brake system with warning light, front and rear seat belts with front outboard retractors, floating day/night breakaway inside rearview mirror, energy-absorbing instrument panel, padded safety sun visors, variable-speed hydraulic windshield wipers, windshield washers, 4-way emergency flasher, back-up lights, side marker lights, self-locking folding front seat backs, shoulder belts for outboard front seat passengers, remote-control left-hand outside rearview mirror, retractable headlight doors that open automatically if vacuum system fails, power ventilation, directional signals with lane-change feature, adjustable headrests (after January 1, 1969) and cornering side lights (optional on very early-production cars).

I.D. NUMBERS

VIN stamped on aluminum tab riveted to dashboard on passenger side and observable through the windshield from outside the car. First symbol denotes model-year: 9=1969. Second symbol denotes the assembly plant: Y=Wixom (Novi), Michigan and J=Los Angeles, California. Third symbol denotes the car-line: 8=Thunderbird. Fourth symbol denotes body type: 3=Two-door hardtop, 4=Two-door Landau, 7=four-door Landau. Fifth symbol denotes engine: N=429-cid/360-hp Thunder-Jet V-8. Sixth thru 11th symbols denote sequential production number of specific vehicle starting at 100001. Body number plate located on front body pillar. Serial number: Same as number on VIN tag. Symbols above "BODY" are body symbol code: 65A=two-door hardtop with bucket front seats, 65C=two-door hardtop with front bench seat; 65B=two-door Landau with blind quarter roof and front bucket seats; 65D=two-door Landau with blind rear quarter roof and front bench

THUNDERBIRD
ALWAYS GAVE YOU
THE MOON AND THE STARS...

FOR 1969
THUNDERBIRD GIVES YOU
THE SUN.

Take a new way to the sun: push the button
opening Thunderbird's optional sliding
sunroof. Go the Bird's way of long, low
exterior design, interior décor to match every
shade of opinion about luxury, power to
answer all demands. Among personal-luxury
cars only, the Bird offers a choice of rooflines,
body styles and seating arrangements.
Go Thunderbird for all this. And heaven, too.

1969 Thunderbird 2-door Landau.

THUNDERBIRD *Ford*

**Perhaps the biggest news for the 1969 Thunderbird was the optional push-button sliding electric
sunroof.**

Ford photo

It might have been a stretch to market the four-door Landau T-Bird as a hunting vehicle, but the big Ford was definitely roomy and nice to travel in.

seat; 57B=four-door Landau with front bucket seats; 57C=four-door Landau with front bench seat. Symbols above CLR are paint color code. First symbol indicates lower body color. Second symbol indicates upper body color. See the table below. Symbols above TRM are trim combination code. See table below. Symbols above "DT" are the production date code. The number indicates the date of the month the car was made. The letters indicate month of manufacture: A=January, B=February, C=March, D=April, E=May, F=June, G=July, H=August, J=September, K=October, L=November, M=December. Symbols above DSO indicate information including the Ford Motor Co. Sales District Code. Symbols above AX indicate rear axle: 4=2.80:1, 6=3.00:1, M=2.80:1 limited-slip and O=3.00:1 limited-slip. Symbols above TR indicate type of transmission: All 1968 T-Birds came only with SelectShift Cruise-O-Matic Drive C6 (Code U) or SelectShift automatic C6 Special (Code Z).

ENGINES

THUNDERJET 429 FOUR-BARREL V-8: Overhead valve. Cast-iron block. Displacement: 429 cid. Bore and stroke: 4.36 x 3.59 inches. Compression ratio: 10.50:1. Brake hp: 360 at 4600 rpm. Torque: 480 lbs.-ft. at 2800 rpm. Five main bearings. Hydraulic valve lifters. Carburetor: Motorcraft four-barrel. Cooling system capacity: 19.4 qt.. Crankcase capacity: 5 qt. (add 1 qt. with new oil filter). Dual exhaust. Code N.

CHASSIS

Wheelbase (two-door): 114.7 in., (four-door): 117.2 in.

Overall length (two-door): 206.9 in., (four-door): 209.4. Overall width (all): 77.3 in. Overall height (two-door): 52.3 in., (four-door): 53.4 in. Front tread: 62 in. Rear tread: 62 in. Front hip room: 2 x 23 in. Front headroom: 37.1 in. Rear hip room: 53.5 in. Rear headroom: 36.7 in. Door opening width: 40.5 in. Tires: 8.45 x 15 4-ply. Steering: Integral with power-assist, 4.0 turns lock-to-lock. Steering ratio: 21.8 to 1. Turning diameter: 42 ft. Front suspension: Independent wishbone type with coil springs and ball joints. Rear suspension: Four-link type with coil springs. Telescoping shocks were mounted on the T-Bird suspension front and rear. Standard rear axle: 3.00:1. Front brakes: 11.72 x 1.77 in. power front disc. Rear brakes: 11.03-in. X 2.25 in. drums. Rear brake swept area 373.2 sq. in. Standard transmission: SelectShift three-element Cruise-O-Matic automatic transmission. Gas tank: 24.1 gallons (premium fuel required).

OPTIONS

SelectAire air conditioner ($427.07). SelectAire conditioner with automatic climate control ($499.22). Electric sunroof in Landau model ($453.30). Sure Track anti-lock braking system ($194.31). Flight Bucket seats and console ($64.77). Reclining front passenger seat ($41.49). 6-way power seat ($98.89). Power window lifts ($109.22). Power trunk lid release ($14.85). Power retracting antenna ($28.97). Rear window defogger ($22.23). Electric defroster and tinted rear window ($84.25). Tinted glass ($47.49). Highway-Pilot speed control, requires Tilt-Away steering wheel ($97.21). Tilt-Away steering wheel ($66.14). Four-door convenience group ($101.10). Two-door convenience group ($77.73). AM/FM stereo with speakers ($150.29). Stereo sonic AM radio with tape player ($128.49). Dual rear speakers, standard with stereo sonic or stereo ($33.07). Limited-slip differential axle ($46.69) Four-note horn ($15.59). Brougham cloth and vinyl interior trim with bucket seats ($129.54). Brougham cloth and vinyl interior trim with bench seats ($161.98). Brougham vinyl and leather interior for models with Black or Saddle colored bucket seats ($194.31). (Note: Brougham interior trim includes unique seat trim style, wood-grain appointments, door courtesy lights, cut-pile carpets, unique door trim panels, door pull handles, and rear seat center arm rest.) Deluxe seat belts with warning light ($15.59). Deluxe front and rear shoulder belts ($15.60). Rear lamp monitor ($25.91). High-level rear window brake lamp, supplemental, four-door Landaus only ($33.70). Two-door Protection Group ($25.28). Four-door Protection Group ($29.17). Heavy-duty suspension ($27.99). Deluxe wheel covers ($57.08). Simulated styled wheel covers with chrome lug nuts, finished in Argent Silver, Brittany Blue, Candyapple Red, Champagne Gold, Midnight Aqua or Oxford Gray ($35.70). Extra charge for non-standard tires: 8.55 x 15 whitewalls ($42.88). 8.55 x 15 red band whitewalls ($52.04). Size 215-B15 A (6.55 x 15) steel-belted radial whitewall tires ($101.30). Fiberglass-belted white sidewall tires ($75.43). 215-R15 Michelin radial-ply white sidewall tires ($101.30). Goodyear Power-Cushion Life Guard dual-chamber tires with unique whitewall design ($196.80). Adjustable head restraints prior to January 1, 1969 ($17). Cornering sidelights ($33.70, but became standard early in the production run). Rear lamp monitor ($25.91). Rear shoulder belts ($27.06). Body-side protection moldings ($45.40). Spare tire cover ($5.25). Body accent stripe in Red, White, or Black ($13.90). Right-hand outside rearview mirror ($6.95). Visor-vanity mirror ($3.79). Deck lid luggage rack ($32.45). Automatic headlight dimmer, special order ($51.20) and Automatic Red Control ($89.94).

EQUIPMENT INSTALLATION RATES

Cruise-O-Matic drive (100 percent). V-8 engine (100 percent). AM radio (43.9 percent). Power steering (100 percent). Power front disc brakes (100 percent). Power door locks: (40.4 percent). Power seat (59.7 percent). Power windows (86.6 percent). Bucket seats (34 percent). Moveable type steering wheel (67.2 percent). White sidewall tires (96.1 percent). Tinted windshield (88.8 percent). Vinyl top (88 percent). Air conditioning (89 percent). Dual exhaust (100 percent). Limited-slip axle (9 percent). Standard wheel covers (69.4 percent). Optional wheel covers (30.6 percent). Power antenna (34.4 percent). Speed control (15.2 percent). AM/FM radio (39.8 percent). Clock (100 percent). Stereo tape player (16.3 percent). (Note: Based on model-year production.)

Ford photo

Among the T-Bird's standard features for 1969 were a 429-cid/360-hp V-8, SelectShift Cruise-O-Matic drive, bench front seat, retractable headlight doors, and keyless locking with reversible keys.

HISTORICAL FOOTNOTES

The 1969 T-Bird was introduced on September 27, 1968. Henry Ford II was board chairman of Ford Motor Company. Arjay R. Miller was vice chairman. Lee A. Iacocca was executive vice president. J.B. Naughton was a FoMoCo vice president and the general manager of Ford Division. G.B. MacKenzie was assistant general sales manager.

Calendar-year output was 50,143 units. This was a 34.7 percent drop from the previous year. A total of 49,272 T-Birds, representing 0.6 percent of industry output, were produced in the model year. This was a decline of 24.1 percent. Of these units, 40,571 were made in the Wixom assembly plant and 8,701 were made in Ford's Los Angeles, California factory. Calendar-year dealer sales amounted to 49,381 T-Birds, representing 0.58 percent of industry sales and a 26.7 percent drop from 1968.

The 1969 T-Bird was designed to do battle with personal-luxury cars like the Buick Riviera, Cadillac Eldorado, Oldsmobile Toronado, Dodge Charger and Pontiac Grand Prix, all of which had arrived in the market since 1962. Considering that the T-Bird was the "old buzzard" of the bunch, the competition actually strengthened its image. "Ford hasn't just 'added on' to the '69 'Bird, but has made definite and worthwhile improvements right down the line—in ride, handling, comfort and convenience," *Motor Trend* reported. "It has that elusive, diffident air known as class."

While the 1969 T-Bird was the "class of its class," it was still basically a 1967 model and its aging did have a negative effect on sales in a new-product-driven marketplace. In fact, Thunderbird model-year production dropped to its lowest point since 1958. It included 1,983 four-door Landaus with bucket seats, 13,712 four-door Landaus with bench seats, 2,361 two-door hardtops with bucket seats, 3,552 two-door hardtops with bench seats, 12,425 two-door Landaus with bucket seats and 15,239 two-door Landaus with bench seats. Even this low production total—49,272 units—outpaced the production of front-wheel-drive Eldorados (27,100) and Toronados (28,500) and came within striking distance of the 52,700 Rivieras built. However, the less expensive Charger (69,000) and the all-new Pontiac Grand Prix (112,500) found many more buyers.

Change was needed and was on its way. Unfortunately, coming T-Bird revisions did not last very long for two reasons. First, they had virtually no effect on the car's popularity. Sales climbed microscopically in 1970, then plummeted again in 1971. Second, they were changes that Ford's new general manager "Bunkie" Knudsen brought in with his GM thinking and Knudsen was fired even before they hit the market. In August 1969, the former GM executive was let go after a personality conflict with FoMoCo Chairman Henry Ford II erupted in Dearborn. Some observers blamed his firing on the fact that Knudsen wanted to involve Ford in motorsports and HFII did not want to go that route. Others said that Knudsen's management concepts went against the Ford family's concept of centralized control of the company. Whatever the reason, Knudsen's departure was probably good for the Thunderbird, since he seemed incapable of understanding what made the car sell.

1969 THUNDERBIRD PERFORMANCE		
Model	**CID/HP**	**Performance**
0-60 mph		
Two-door Landau	429/360	9.8 seconds
Two-door Landau	429/360	9.0 seconds
1/4-Mile		
Two-door Landau	429/360	16.75 seconds @ 85.66 mph
Top Speed		
Two-door Landau	429/360	126 mph
Two-door Landau	429/360	140 mph (estimated)

The changes in the 1970 T-Bird were easy to spot. The car had a lower profile and roof line, new front end, and gained six inches in length.

Ford photo

1970

Thunderbird

The 1970 T-Birds are often called "Bunkie" Birds because their bold, dramatically different formal appearance reflected the influence of Semon E. "Bunkie" Knudsen. Knudsen had left General Motors to take over the reins at Ford, but he clashed with Henry Ford II and his tenure at the firm bearing HFII's name was very short. He did, however, stick around long enough to help develop the 1970 T-Bird.

With all-new front-end sheet metal, the T-Bird was six inches longer and one inch lower to the ground. Its new radiator grille stuck way out and came to a point. Some said it had a Pontiac-like look. Unfortunately, its protruding center section proved prone to damage, inspiring insurance companies to charge T-Bird owners higher premiums. Hide-Away headlights were discontinued, but the radio antenna and windshield wipers were now tucked out of sight. Full-width taillights returned. They had a new inverted-U appearance and sequential turn signals. The length and lowness of the T-Bird was accented by a single horizontal feature line along the mid body sides. A full-width vinyl "Flight Bench" front seat was standard. A Special Brougham option featured hopsack-and-vinyl upholstery. Ford's "better idea" Swing-Away steering wheel was gone. A Tilt-Away type was optional. Color-keyed wheel covers added to the rich look of T-Birds with the Brougham package. The T-Bird engine was again the 429-cid/360-hp V-8. Dual exhausts and SelectShift Cruise-O-Matic transmission were standard.

The T-Bird's strong body-on-frame design consisted of a front end assembly, a rear end assembly and four torque box assemblies connected by formed center rails (which were longer on the four-door model). The frame featured rugged ladder-type construction with five reinforced cross-members. Node-point body mounting at 14 computer-designed positions resulted in superior noise and vibration suppression characteristics. Up front, the suspension used drag-struts and ball joints, plus a rubber-bushed stabilizer bar. The rear suspension was by a three-link coil spring system with a long-and-short mounting link arrangement. A lateral track bar centered the axle. All of the links, as well as the track bar, had rubber bushings. Integral-design power steering was featured. The self-adjusting brakes used floating caliper discs in front and drum-shoe brakes at the rear. The drums were cross-ribbed and flared. True-Center wheels on precision-machined hubs carried the radial-ply tires.

STANDARD EQUIPMENT

ThunderJet 429-cid/360-hp V-8, SelectShift Cruise-O-Matic transmission, integral Fluidic-Control power steering, self adjusting front disc/rear drum brakes, dual exhausts, full instrumentation, remote-control lefthand outside rearview mirror, radial tires, Flight Bench seats with fold-down center armrest, power ventilation system, concealed electric windshield wipers, Uni-Lock safety harness, sequential turn signals, cornering lights, ventless side glass, reversible keys, keyless door locking, electric clock, MagicAire heater and defroster, lockable lighted glove box, map light with automatic time delay (early production units), lined and lighted luggage compartment, full wheel

BODY COLOR INFORMATION

Color Name	Code	Color Name	Code
Black	A	Red	T
Maroon (Metallic)	B	Dark Blue (Metallic)	X
Dark Ivy Green (Metallic)	C	Chestnut Bronze (Metallic)	Y
Light Blue	E	Dark Gray (Metallic)	Z
Dark Aqua (Metallic)	F	Light Ivy Yellow	2
Deep Blue (Metallic)	J	Medium Brown (Metallic)	5
Light Gray (Metallic)	L	Light Gold	8
White	M	Pastel Yellow	9
Medium Ivy Green (Metallic)	P	Green Fire (optional at extra cost)	19
Medium Brown (Metallic)	Q	Olive Fire (optional at extra cost)	09
Dark Brown (Metallic)	R	Burgundy Fire (optional at extra cost)	59
Medium Gold (Metallic)	S	Bronze Fire (optional at extra cost)	89

STANDARD GLOVE SOFT ALL-VINYL INTERIOR TRIM INFORMATION

Seat Type	Black	Dark Blue	Ivy (Dk Green)	White (Black Trim)
Bench Seat (all models)	4A	4B	4G	4W
Bucket Seat (two-door models)	2A	2B	2G	2W

BROUGHAM QUILTED CLOTH AND VINYL INTERIOR TRIM INFORMATION

Seat Type	Black	Dark Blue	Red	Ginger	Ivy (Dark Green)	Nugget (Gold)
Bench Seat (two-door models)	3A	3B	3D	3F	3G	3Y

BROUGHAM QUILTED CLOTH AND VINYL INTERIOR TRIM INFORMATION

Seat Type	Black	Dark Blue	Red	Ivy (Dk Green)	Nugget Gold	Tobbacco
Split Bench Seats (four-door models)	5A	5B	5D	5G	5Y	5Z

BROUGHAM LEATHER INTERIOR TRIM INFORMATION

Seat Type	Dark Blue	Red	Ginger
Bucket Seats (two-door models)	8B	8D	8F

BROUGHAM LEATHER INTERIOR TRIM INFORMATION

Seat Type	Black	Red	Tobacco
Split Bench Seats (four-door models)	6A	6D	6Z

SPECIAL BROUGHAM HOPSACK CLOTH AND VINYL INTERIOR TRIM INFORMATION

Seat Type	Black	Blue	Red	Ivy (Dark Green)	Ginger
(*) Bucket Seats (two-door models)	1A	1B	1D	1G	1F

(*) Available only with specific exterior colors

VINYL ROOF COLOR INFORMATION

Black	White	Blue	Green	Brown
A	U	B	G	F

THUNDERBIRD PRODUCTION

Model Number	Body/Style Number	Body Type & Seating	Factory Price	Shipping Weight	Production Total
3	65A/65C	2d Hardtop-4P	$4,916	4,354 lbs.	5,116
4	65B/65D	2d Landau-4P	$5,104	4,630 lbs.	36,847
8	57B/57C	4d Landau-4P	$5,182	4,464 lbs.	8,401

NOTE 1: 65A=two-door hardtop with front bucket seats; 65C=two-door hardtop with front bench seat; 65B=two-door Landau with blind quarter roof and front bucket seats; 65D=two-door Landau with blind quarter roof and front bench seat; 57B=four-door Landau with front bucket seats; 57C=four-door Landau with front bench seat.
NOTE 2: Production totals above include 1,925 Model 65A with bucket seats, 16,953 Model 65B with bucket seats and 5,005 Model 57B with bucket seats.

covers, articulated accelerator pedal, front and rear ashtrays, back-up lights, cigarette lighter, coat hooks, courtesy lights, floor carpeting, all-vinyl color-keyed headlining, day/night rearview mirror, teak-toned appliqué on instrument panel and all Ford Motor Company Lifeguard Design safety features.

I.D. NUMBERS

VIN stamped on aluminum tab riveted to dashboard on passenger side and observable through the windshield from outside the car. Prefix indicates manufacturer: F=Ford. First symbol denotes model-year: 0=1970. Second symbol denotes the assembly plant: Y=Wixom (Novi), Michigan and J=Los Angeles, California. Third symbol denotes the car-line: 8=Thunderbird. Fourth symbol denotes body type: 3=two-door hardtop, 4=two-door Landau, 7=four-door Landau. Fifth symbol denotes engine: N=429-cid/360-hp ThunderJet V-8. Sixth thru 11th symbols denote sequential production number of specific vehicle starting at 100001. Body certification label located on rear face of driver's door. The top part of the label indicates that the Thunderbird was manufactured by Ford Motor Company. Directly below this is the month and year of manufacture, plus a statement that the car conforms to federal motor vehicle safety standard in effect on the indicated date of manufacture. The VIN appears first on the first line of encoded information. It matches the 1st to 11th symbols on VIN tag. The body style code appears to the right of the VIN on the same line. The Thunderbird codes for this model-year are: 57B=four-door Landau with front split-bench seat; 57C=four-door Landau with front bench seat; 65A=two-door hardtop with front bucket seats; 65B=two-door Landau with front bucket seats; 65C=two-door hardtop with front bench seat; 65D=two-door Landau with front bench seat. The color code(s) appears to the right of the body style code. Conventional colors are identified by a single letter or number. Optional Glamour Paints are identified by two numbers. The trim code appears on the far left-hand side of the second line of encoded information. The axle code appears to the right of the trim code in the second position on the second line of encoded information. Axle codes were: 2=2.75:1, 4=2.80:1, 6=3.00:1, K=2.75:1 limited-slip, M=2.80:1 limited-slip and O=3.00:1 limited-slip. Transmission codes were: U=SelectShift Cruise-O-Matic C6 three-speed automatic, Z= SelectShift Cruise-O-Matic C6 special three-speed automatic. The transmission code appears to the right of the axle code in the third position on the second line of encoded information. The District Special Equipment (DSO) code appears to the right of the transmission code in the far right-hand position on the second line of encoded information. (Note: The abbreviations VIN/BDY/CLR/TRM/AX/TR/DSO do not appear on the certification label itself. The specific application of the codes is determined by where they are located on the vehicle certification label.)

ENGINES

THUNDERJET 429 FOUR-BARREL V-8: Overhead valve. Cast-iron block. Displacement: 429 cid. Bore and stroke: 4.36 x 3.59 in. Compression ratio: 10.50:1. Brake hp: 360 at 4600 rpm. Torque: 480 lbs.-ft. at 2800 rpm. Five main bearings. Hydraulic valve lifters. Carburetor: Motorcraft four-barrel. Cooling system capacity: 19.4. Crankcase capacity: 5 qt. (add 1 qt. with new oil filter). Dual exhaust. Code N.

CHASSIS

Wheelbase (two-door): 114.7 in., (four-door): 117.2 in. Overall length (two-door): 212.5 in., (four-door): 215 in. Overall width; (two-door): 78 in., (four-door): 77.4 in. Overall height (two-door): 51.4 in., (four-door): 53.6 in. Front tread: 62 in. Rear tread: 62 in. Tires: 215R15 radial.

Steering: Integral with power-assist, 3.6 turns lock-to-lock. Overall steering ratio: 21.9 to 1. Turning diameter: (two-door) 42.7 ft., (four-door) 43.4 ft. Front suspension: Coil spring and drag-strut ball-joint type with rubber-bushed stabilizer. Rear suspension: Three-link coil-spring with long-and-short mounting link and lateral track bar (all rubber-bushed). Telescopic shock absorbers front and rear. Standard rear axle: 2.8:1. Front brakes: Power front disc. Rear brakes: Power drums.

OPTIONS

SelectAire air conditioner ($427.07). SelectAire air conditioner with automatic climate control ($499.22). Electric sunroof in Landau model ($453.30). Sure Track anti-lock braking system ($194.31). Flight Bucket seats and console ($64.77). Reclining front passenger seat ($41.49). 6-way power seat ($98.89) Power window lifts ($109.22). Power trunk lid release ($14.85). Power retracting antenna ($28.97). Rear window defogger ($22.23). Electric defroster ($84.25). Tinted windows ($47.49). Highway-Pilot speed control, requires Tilt-Away steering wheel ($97.21). Tilt-Away steering wheel ($66.14). Four-door convenience group ($101.10). Two-door convenience group ($77.73). AM/FM stereo with speakers ($150.29). Stereo sonic AM radio with tape player ($128.49). Dual rear speakers, standard with stereo sonic or stereo ($33.07). Limited-slip differential axle ($46.69) Four-note horn ($15.59). Brougham cloth and vinyl interior trim with bucket seats ($129.54). Brougham cloth and vinyl interior trim with bench seats ($161.98). Brougham vinyl and leather interior for models with Black or Saddle colored bucket seats ($194.31). (Note: Brougham interior trim includes unique seat trim style, wood-grain appointments, door courtesy lights, cut-pile carpets, unique door trim panels, door pull handles, and rear seat center arm rest.) Deluxe seat belts with warning light ($15.59). Rear lamp monitor ($25.91).

High-level rear window brake lamp, supplemental, four-door Landaus only ($33.70). Two-door Protection group ($25.28). Four-door protection group ($29.17). Heavy-duty suspension ($27.99). Simulated styled steel wheel covers ($57.08). Extra charge for non-standard tires: 8.55 x 15 whitewalls ($42.88). 8.55 x 15 red band whitewalls ($52.04). Size 215-B15A (6.55 x 15) steel-belted radial whitewall tires ($101.30).

EQUIPMENT INSTALLATION RATES

Cruise-O-Matic drive (100 percent). V-8 engine (100 percent). AM radio (33 percent). Power steering (100 percent). Power front disc brakes (100 percent). Power door locks (46.6 percent.) Power seat (64.6 percent). Power windows (88.7 percent). Bucket seats (37.4 percent). Moveable type steering wheel (71.5 percent). White sidewall tires (96.7 percent). Tinted windshield (93.8 percent). Vinyl top (89.6 percent). Air conditioning (93.7 percent). Dual exhaust (100 percent). Limited-slip axle (9.4 percent). Standard wheel covers (75.4 percent). Optional wheel covers (24.6 percent). Power antenna (10.1 percent). Speed control (20.7 percent). AM/FM radio (50.3 percent). Clock (100 percent). Stereo tape player (16.7 percent). Reclining front seats: (14.1 percent). (Note: Based on model-year production.)

HISTORICAL FOOTNOTES

The 1970 T-Bird was introduced on September 19, 1969. Henry Ford II was board chairman of Ford Motor Company. Lee A. Iaccoca was the new executive vice president and president of North American Auto Operations. J.B. Naughton was a vice president and general manager of Ford Division. G.B. MacKenzie was general marketing manager for Ford Division.

Ford photo

The Thunderbird was no muscle car, but the top speed for the two-door Landau model was reported to be a respectable 125 mph. The ThunderJet 429-cid V-8 was the lone engine option.

Ford photo

Some observers thought the new protruding nose design on the 1970 T-Bird made it resemble the Pontiacs of its era.

Calendar-year output was 40,512 units. This was a 23.8-percent drop from the previous year. A total of 50,364 T-Birds were produced in the model year. Of these units, 30,830 were made in the Wixom assembly plant and 19,534 were made in Ford's Los Angeles, California factory. Calendar-year dealer sales amounted to 40,868 T-Birds, representing 0.6 percent of industry sales.

In November 1969, *Motor Trend* did a comparison road test pitting the T-Bird against the Chevrolet Monte Carlo and Pontiac Grand Prix. "The '70 'Bird is practically an entirely new car, even without what should be called a major change" suggested writer Bill Sanders with a bit of wordsmithing. He was talking about its lower height and new body-hugging roofline. "The first thing that comes to mind when looking at the two-door in profile is the beautiful custom work of the late '40s and early '50s," chimed Sanders. "The '70 'Bird is reminiscent of some of those early creations and looks like it has been chopped and channeled." Mentioned in the article was the T-Bird's adoption of the Lincoln Mark III's sound insulation package to reduce noise inside the car, the fact that the seats had additional comfort padding, and the use of an in-the-windshield wire-type radio antenna.

Despite its larger size and heavier weight, the 1970 model performed almost exactly the same as the 1969 edition. "Unlike the Monte Carlo or Grand Prix, the 'Bird is not specifically a performance-oriented car, but is more at home with the luxury aspects," said Sanders. "For instance, acceleration may not be as rapid, but it is fluid smooth with no quick shifting movements." With its new suspension and radial tires, the car was a better handler than previous Thunderbirds. It had very little understeer and driver control was described as "uncanny." All in all, the car was summarized as combining a custom luxury feeling with outstanding ride and handling abilities.

1970 THUNDERBIRD PERFORMANCE		
Model	CID/HP	Performance
0-60 mph		
Two-door Landau	429/360	9.0 seconds
1/4-Mile		
Two-door Landau	429/360	16.9 seconds @ 84.6 mph
Top Speed		
Two-door Landau	429/360	125 mph

There were some minor trim and color changes on the 1971 T-Bird, but it was very similar to the 1970 models. Two-door hardtop, two-door Landau (above), and four-door Landau models were offered.

1971 *Thunderbird*

The 1971 Thunderbird was the 1970 model with minor trim revisions. The grille had slightly wider bright metal blades at every third rung, which gave it a horizontally segmented look. There were nine vertical bars in the new grille. Front side marker lamps with a one-piece lense were introduced. In addition, the front bumper had more massive wraparound edges. A few bits of chrome were revised. Some new exterior appearance options were color-keyed wheel covers, body-side moldings with color-keyed protective vinyl inserts and wheel opening moldings. These all came as part of the Brougham interior option.

The same three Thunderbird body styles were offered. H78 x 15 belted bias-ply tires were standard. Michelin 215R15 steel-belted radials were standard with the Special Brougham option. In 1971, the T-Bird was the only U.S. car offered with radial tires as an option. This was the only year that the four-door Landau model was not available with optional front bucket seats. A front bench seat was also standard in two-door models, but bucket seats were optional. Front seating options included standard vinyl bench seats (all models), vinyl bucket seats (optional in two-door models), Brougham bench seat (optional in two-door models), Brougham split bench seat (optional in four-door models), Brougham leather bucket seats (optional in two-door models), Brougham leather bench seat (optional in four-door models), and Special Brougham bucket seats (optional in two-doors models).

STANDARD EQUIPMENT

All standard FoMoCo safety, anti-theft, convenience items and emissions control equipment, sequential rear turn signals, Uni-Lock harness, remote-control left-hand OSRV mirror, locking steering column with ignition key reminder buzzer, electric clock, front cornering lights, AM radio, power ventilation, 100 percent nylon carpeting, automatic parking brake release, carpeting, padded five-pod instrument panel cluster with full gauges, non-reversing odometer, Safety Design front end, head rests or high-back seats and shoulder belts for front outboard passengers, padded sun visors, energy-absorbing steering column, yield-away day/night inside rearview mirror, fuel evaporative emission control system, hydraulic wipers with electric washers, courtesy lights, energy-absorbing steering column, 4-way emergency flasher, back-up lights, flashing side marker lights, safety coat hooks, MagicAire heater and defroster, glove box light, map light, luggage compartment light, Flight Bench seats with bright seat shields, front seat center arm rest, pleated all-vinyl interior fabric, SelectShift Cruise-O-Matic transmission, power steering, power front disc brakes, dual hydraulic master cylinder, brake warning light, 429-cid/360-hp four-barrel V-8 engine, and H78-15 black sidewall bias-ply tires. Landau models included a Cayman Grain vinyl roof.

95

BODY COLOR INFORMATION (U.S. & CANADA)

Color Name	Code	Color Name	Code
Black	A	Red ++	T
Maroon (Metallic)**	B	Light Pewter (Metallic)	V
Bright Aqua (Metallic)	F	Yellow ++	W
Dark Green ++	G	Dark Blue (Metallic)	X
Light Green	H	Deep Blue (Metallic)	Y
Dark Gray (Metallic)	K	Grabber Green (Metallic)	Y
White ++	M	Tan ++	2
Pastel Blue ++	N	Medium Brown (Metallic) ++	5
Light Yellow Gold ++	O	Burgandy Fire (extra-cost option) ++	C9
Medium Green (Metallic) ++	P	Blue Fire (extra-cost option) ++	D9
Medium Blue (Metallic) ++	Q	Green Fire (extra-cost option) ++	E9
Dark Brown (Metallic)	R	Walnut Fire (extra-cost option) ++	39
Gray Gold (Metallic) ++	S	Maroon**	7

++ Indicates colors used with Special Brougham option.
** Maroon Metallic was deleted and Maroon was added during the model-run.

PLEATED VINYL INTERIOR TRIM INFORMATION

Seat Type	Black	Dark Blue	Dark Green	White
Low-Back Bench Center Armrest (all)	4A	4B	4R	4W
High-Back Bucket with Console (two-door)	2A	2B	2R	2W

BROUGHAM QUILTED CLOTH AND VINYL INTERIOR TRIM INFORMATION

Seat Type	Black	Dark Blue	Dark Red	Medium Ginger	Dark Green	Light Gray Gold
Low-Back Bench Center Armrest (two-door)	CA	CB	CD	CF	CR	CY

BROUGHAM QUILTED CLOTH AND VINYL INTERIOR TRIM INFORMATION

Seat Type	Black	Dark Blue	Dark Red	Dark Green	Light Gray Gold	Dark Tobacco
High-Back Split Bench Dual Armrest (four-door)	EA	EB	ED	ER	EYE	Z

BROUGHAM LEATHER-AND-VINYL INTERIOR TRIM INFORMATION

Seat Type	Black	Dark Red	Medium Ginger
High-Back Bucket (two-door)	8A	8D	8F

BROUGHAM LEATHER-AND-VINYL INTERIOR TRIM INFORMATION

Seat Type	Black	Medium Red	Tobacco
High-Back Split Bench Dual Armrest (four-door)	FA	FD	FZ

SPECIAL BROUGHAM HOPSACK CLOTH AND VINYL INTERIOR TRIM INFORMATION (*)

Seat Type	Black	Dark Blue	Dark Red	Medium Ginger	Dark Green
High-Back Bucket Seats With Console (two-door)	AA	AB	AD	AF	AR

(*) Available only with specific exterior colors.

THUNDERBIRD PRODUCTION

Model Number	Body/Style Number	Body Type & Seating	Factory Price	Shipping Weight	Production Total
3	65A/65C	2d Hardtop-4P	$5,295	4,399 lbs.	9,146
4	65B/65D	2d Landau-4P	$5,438	4,370 lbs.	20,356
7	57B/57C	4d Landau-4P	$5,516	4,509 lbs.	6,553

NOTE 1: 65A=two-door hardtop with bucket front seats; 65C=two-door hardtop with front bench seat; 65B=two-door Landau with blind quarter roof and front bucket seats; 65D=two-door Landau with blind rear quarter roof and front bench seat; 57B=four-door Landau with front bucket seats; 57C=four-door Landau with front bench seat.
NOTE 2: Production totals above include 2,992 Model 65A with bucket seats, 8,133 Model 65B with bucket seats and 4,238 Model 57B with split bench seats.

I.D. NUMBERS

VIN stamped on aluminum tab riveted to dashboard on passenger side and observable through the windshield from outside the car. Prefix indicates manufacturer: F=Ford. First symbol denotes model-year: 1=1971. Second symbol denotes the assembly plant: Y=Wixom (Novi), Michigan and J=Los Angeles, California. Third symbol denotes the car-line: 8=Thunderbird. Fourth symbol denotes body type:

3=two-door hardtop, 4=two-door Landau, 7=four-door Landau. Fifth symbol denotes engine: N=429-cid/360-hp Thunder-Jet V-8. Sixth thru 11th symbols denote sequential production number of specific vehicle starting at 100001. Body certification label located on rear face of driver's door. The top part of the label indicates that the Thunderbird was manufactured by Ford Motor Company. Directly below this is the month and year of manufacture, plus a statement that the car conforms to federal motor vehicle safety standard in effect on the indicated date of manufacture. The VIN appears first on the first line of encoded information. It matches the 1st to 11th symbols on VIN tag. The body style code appears to the right of the VIN on the same line. The Thunderbird codes for this model-year are: 57B=four-door Landau with front bucket seats; 57C=four-door Landau with front bench seat; 65A=two-door hardtop with front bucket seats; 65B=two-door Landau with front bucket seats; 65C=two-door hardtop with front bench seat; 65D=two-door Landau with front bench seat. The color code(s) appears to the right of the body style code. Conventional colors are identified by a single letter or number. Optional Glamour Paints are identified by two numbers. The trim code appears on the far left-hand side of the second line of encoded information. The axle code appears to the right of the trim code in the second position on the second line of encoded information: 2=2.75:1, 4=2.80:1, 6=3.00:1, K=2.75:1 limited-slip, M=2.80:1 limited-slip and O=3.00:1 limited-slip. The transmission code appears to the right of the axle code in the third position on the second line of encoded information: U=SelectShift Cruise-O-Matic C6 three-speed automatic, Z=SelectShift Cruise-O-Matic C6 special three-speed automatic. The District Special Equipment (DSO) code appears to the right of the transmission code in the far right-hand position on the second line of encoded information. (Note: The abbreviations VIN/BDY/CLR/TRM/AX/TR/DSO do not appear on the certification label itself. The specific application of the codes is determined by where they are located on the vehicle certification label.)

ENGINE

THUNDERJET 429 FOUR-BARREL V-8: Overhead valve. Cast-iron block. Displacement: 429 cid. Bore and stroke: 4.36 x 3.59 in. Compression ratio: 10.50:1. Brake hp: 360 at 4600 rpm. Torque: 480 lbs.-ft. at 2800 rpm. Five main bearings. Hydraulic valve lifters. Carburetor: Motorcraft four-barrel. Cooling system capacity: 19.4. Crankcase capacity: 5 qt. (add 1 qt. with new oil filter). Dual exhaust. Code N.

CHASSIS

Wheelbase (two-door): 114.7 in., (four-door) 117.2 in. Overall length (two-door): 212.5 in., (four-door) 215 in. Overall width; (two-door): 78 in., (four-door) 77.4 in. Overall height (two-door): 51.9 in., (four-door) 53.7 in. Front tread: 62 in. Rear tread: 62 in. Tires: H78 x 15. Steering: Integral with power-assist, 3.6 turns lock-to-lock. Overall ratio: 21.9:1. Turning diameter: (two-door) 42.7 ft., (four-door) 43.4 ft. Front suspension: Coil spring and drag-strut ball-joint type with rubber-bushed stabilizer. Rear suspension: Three-link coil-spring with long-and-short mounting link and lateral track bar (all rubber-bushed). Telescopic shock absorbers front and rear. Standard rear axle: 3.0:1. Front brakes: Power front disc. Rear brakes: Power drums.

OPTIONS

SelectAire conditioner ($448). Automatic temperature control with 55-amp alternator and electric rear window defroster ($519). Traction-Lok differential ($49). Sure Track brake control system ($194). Rear window defogger ($26). Electric rear window defroster, includes interior light located in the heater control ($84). Complete tinted glass ($52). Glamour paint ($130). Front and rear bumper guards with rubber inserts ($20). Vinyl-insert body side protection moldings, includes wheel lip moldings, but standard with Brougham package and exterior appearance group ($34). Power antenna ($31). 6-way power full-width seat or 6-way power driver's high-back bucket seat ($104). 6-way power driver and passenger high-back bucket seats ($207). Power side windows ($133). AM/FM stereo radio including dual front and rear seat speakers ($150). Vinyl roof, except standard on Landau models ($141). High-back bucket seats and center console for two-door Thunderbirds, except standard with Brougham option ($78). Manual reclining passenger seat, except standard with Turnpike group ($41). Dual rear seat speakers, standard with AM/FM stereo radio or tape system ($33). Fingertip speed control including Rim-Blow deluxe three-spoke steering wheel (standard with Turnpike group, otherwise ($97). Tilt steering wheel ($52). Trailer towing package ($50). Stereophonic tape system with AM radio only ($150). Power-operated sunroof, requires vinyl roof on Hardtop ($518). Heavy-duty suspension with heavy front and rear springs and shocks, front stabilizer bar ($28). Deluxe wheel covers, not available with Special Brougham package or Exterior Appearance group ($52). Power trunk lid release ($14). Exterior appearance group, included with Special Brougham option ($78). Deluxe color-keyed seat belts ($16). Convenience check group including seat belt light, low fuel flasher and door ajar light, vacuum power door locks, front lights-on warning light and buzzer, and automatic seat back release, for two-doors only ($101). Michelin single-band white sidewall steel-belted radial tires, standard with Turnpike Convenience group ($101). Dual-band white sidewall bias-belted tires, standard with Special Brougham option ($30). Turnpike convenience group includes fingertip speed control, manual reclining passenger seat, and Michelin steel-belted radial-ply whitewall tires with 40,000-mile tread life guarantee on Thunderbirds with Brougham option ($196). Turnpike convenience group includes fingertip speed control, manual reclining passenger seat, and Michelin steel-belted radial-ply whitewall tires with 40,000-mile tread life guarantee on Thunderbirds without Brougham option ($227). Exterior appearance group includes color-keyed stone shields and grille finish panels, body side moldings with color-keyed vinyl inserts, color-keyed wheel covers, and wheel lip moldings ($61 only with specific selected exterior colors and not available teamed with special wheel covers, Brougham option, or special paint colors). Protection group includes color-keyed floor mats, license plate frames, and door edge guards for two-doors ($26), for four-doors ($30). Special Brougham option for two-door, includes hopsack-and-vinyl high-back bucket seats, matching door panels, center rear armrest, 3-spoke Rim-Blow deluxe steering wheel, plush cut-pile carpeting, door-pull handles, courtesy lights, color-keyed stone shield and grille finish panels, full-length color-keyed body-side moldings, wheel-lip moldings, bias-belted double-band white sidewall tires and color-coordinated wheel covers. Brougham low-back bench seat cloth-and-vinyl interior for two-door models ($162). Brougham high-back split-bench seat cloth-and-vinyl interior for four-door models ($162). Brougham bucket seat leather-and-vinyl interior for two-door models ($227). Brougham split-bench seat leather-and-vinyl interior for two-door models ($227).

The base price of the two-door Landau T-Bird grew to $5,438 for 1971.

Ford photo

Ford photo

The 1971 T-Bird stacked up favorably to its competition in magazine testing, but sales lagged and a new direction was being planned for the model.

EQUIPMENT INSTALLATION RATES

Cruise-O-Matic drive (100 percent). V-8 engine (100 percent). AM radio (26.9 percent). AM/FM radio (59.6 percent). Stereo tape player (13.5 percent). Power steering (100 percent). Power front disc brakes (100 percent). Power door locks: (46.3 percent.) Power seat (71 percent). Power windows (89.5 percent). Bucket seats (23.6 percent). Moveable type steering wheel (69.7 percent). White sidewall tires (98.5 percent). Tinted windshield (97 percent). Vinyl top: (94 percent). Automatic temperature control (24.2 percent. Manual air conditioning (73.9 percent). Dual exhaust (100 percent). Limited-slip axle (8.7 percent). Standard wheel covers (87.8 percent). Optional wheel covers (12.2 percent). Power antenna (36 percent). Speed control (27.1 percent). Clock (100 percent). Reclining front seats (16.2 percent). (Note: Based on model-year production.)

HISTORICAL FOOTNOTES

The 1971 T-Bird was introduced on September 18, 1970. Henry Ford II was Ford's chairman of the board. Lee A. Iacocca was promoted to president of Ford Motor Company. J.B. Naughton was a vice president and general manager of Ford Division. G.B. MacKenzie was general marketing manager for Ford Division.

Calendar-year output was 46,277 units. A total of 36,055 T-Birds were produced in the model year. Of these units, 29,733 were made in Michigan and 6,322 were made in California. Calendar-year dealer sales amounted to 41,801 T-Birds, representing 0.5 percent of industry sales. The T-Bird was the only 1971 Ford to increase calendar-year dealer sales over 1970.

In December 1970, *Motor Trend* published an article by Jim Brokaw entitled "Almost a Limousine." It was a comparison road test featuring 1971 versions of the "boat tail" Riviera, the front-drive Oldsmobile Toronado, and the Brougham-optioned Thunderbird two-door Landau. It was the first of a series of annual articles that compared various cars, but almost always included the T-Bird. The 1971 model tested had a list price of $6,649.71, which compared to $6,667.72 for the Buick and $6,457.15 for the Oldsmobile. "These cars are expensive," said the writer. "If you have to check your budget to see whether you can handle the payments, you can't afford one." The five-page story pointed out that the Thunderbird's four-coil suspension differed from that of the other two cars in how the lateral and longitudinal restraints were handled with drag-strut bars up front and three control arms and one track bar at the rear. The T-Bird's system was rated the firmest, but it also exhibited much less roll control than the "Riv" and the "Toro." Brokaw concluded, "The 'Bird requires a bit of attention going into a corner at high speed, but produces no surprises after the initial turn is passed." Of the three cars, the T-Bird was fastest in the quarter-mile acceleration test and the quickest to stop from 30 mph (27 ft.) and 60 mph (129 ft.).

Part of the reason for the model year's poor showing may have been that sales of the "Bunkie" Knudsen-designed 1971 models were the responsibility of Iacocca, who had a totally different concept of what a Thunderbird should be. Iacocca would soon give the car a new personality and turn the sales trend around.

1971 THUNDERBIRD PERFORMANCE		
Model	**CID/HP**	**Performance**
0-60 mph		
Two-door Landau	429/360	9.2 seconds
1/4-Mile		
Two-door Landau	429/360	16.4 seconds @ 85.6 mph
Top Speed		
Two-door Landau	429/360	118 mph (calculated)

This two-door Landau was the 1 millionth Thunderbird built. It is owned by R.D. Peterson of Cedar Rapids, Iowa.

1972
Thunderbird

The 1972 T-Birds were restyled. They were the biggest T-Birds ever. Lee Iacocca created these cars on the "the bigger-is-better" principal. He based them on a new Lincoln Continental Mark IV.

The two cars shared chassis and sheet metal. Only a two-door hardtop with a long hood and short rear deck was offered. The grille had a neo-classic look with horizontal bars above and below a massive bumper. The horizontal-bars texture was also used in the headlamp housings. There was a Thunderbird emblem on the car's nose. Notches in the leading edges of the front fenders held the parking lamps, which doubled as sidemarker lamps. Separate sidemarker lights and signal lights for the front fender sides were optional.

The T-Bird's large, thick doors had guard beams built into them to protect occupants during side-impact collisions. A low semi-fastback roof bridged the extremely wide "C" pillars. A single wall-to-wall taillight lens contributed to a very massive rear end appearance. There were 10 taillight bulbs that lit up the car like a light bar. T-Birds came in 24 colors and the optional Glamour colors—Burgundy Fire, Blue Fire, Green Fire, Lime Fire, Walnut Fire, Cinnamon Fire, Copper Fire and Gold Fire—were particularly brilliant. They came in packages that included color-coordinated wheel covers and moldings, hood and body-side pin striping, and tooled-silver S-shaped Landau bars on cars with vinyl tops. There was a new dashboard and full instrumentation was abandoned in favor of warning lights.

The T-Bird's 429-cid four-barrel V-8 was de-tuned to operate on unleaded gas and rated at 212 net horsepower. The T-Bird body was mounted at computer-designated points for noise and vibration suppression characteristics. A new rear stabilizer bar improved roll stiffness. T-Bird brakes had now been accepted as perhaps the best system in the sports-personal car market segment. ABS brakes were optional. A heavier-duty 9.38-in. rear axle ring gear was used with this system, as ABS tended to create some rear axle chattering that could wreck the standard 9-inch ring gear.

STANDARD EQUIPMENT

429-cid V-8, SelecShift Cruise-O-Matic transmission, power steering, power front disc brakes, automatic parking brake release, Michelin 40,000-mile black sidewall steel-belted radial tires, electric clock, split bench front seat, front seat center armrest, seat belt reminder buzzer, cut-pile floor carpeting, power ventilation system, MagicAire heater and defroster, remote-control left-hand outside rearview mirror, vinyl-insert body-side moldings, dome light, door courtesy lights, under dash light, glove compartment light, front ash tray light, fully insulated body, fully-trimmed trunk, luggage compartment light, full wheel covers, side-guard door rails, energy-absorbing steering column, energy-absorbing steering wheel, energy-absorbing instrument panel, padded sun visors, two-speed electric windshield wipers, windshield washers, 4-way hazard flasher, back-up lights, self-locking front seat backs, non-reversing odometer, locking steering column, and ignition key buzzer.

BODY COLOR INFORMATION (U.S. & CANADA)

Color Name	Code	Color Name	Code
Light Gray Metallic	1A	Yellow	6D
Black	1C	Gray Gold Metallic	6J
Maroon	2J	White	9A
Light Blue	3B	Burgundy Fire*	2G
Medium Blue Metallic	3D	Blue Fire*	3C
Dark Blue Metallic	3H	Green Fire*	4D
Pastel Lime	4A	Lime Fire*	4G
Burnt Green Gold Metallic	4B	Walnut Fire*	5C
Medium Green Metallic	4P	Cinnamon Fire*	5D
Dark Green Metallic	4Q	Copper Fire*	5G
Dark Brown Metallic	5F	Gold Fire*	6G
Light Yellow Gold	6B		

* Optional at extra cost.

STANDARD LAMONT CLOTH AND VINYL INTERIOR TRIM INFORMATION

Seat Type	Black	Dark Blue	Dark Red	Dark Green	Tobacco (Dark Brown)
Low-Back Split Bench	HA	HB	HD	HR	HZ

OPTIONAL HOPSACK CLOTH AND VINYL INTERIOR TRIM INFORMATION

Seat Type	Black	Dark Blue	Dark Red	Ginger	Dark Green
High-Back Bucket with Console	GA	GB	GD	GF	GR

OPTIONAL LEATHER AND VINYL INTERIOR TRIM INFORMATION

Seat Type	Black	Dark Blue	Dark Red	Ginger	Dark Green	Tobacco (Dark Brown)
Low-Back Split Bench	KA	KB	KD	KF	KR	KZ

OPTIONAL LEATHER AND VINYL INTERIOR TRIM INFORMATION

Seat Type	White w/Black	White w/Blue	White w/Green	White w/Tobacco
Low-Back Split Bench	KW	KL	K5	K9

ALLIGATOR GRAIN VINYL ROOF COLOR INFORMATION

Black	White	Dark Blue	Dark Green	Dark Brown
A	W	B	R	Z

THUNDERBIRD - (V-8) - SERIES H

Model Number	Body/Style Number	Body Type & Seating	Factory Price	Shipping Weight	Production Total
86	5K	2d Hardtop-4P	$5,293	4,420 lbs.	57,814

I.D. NUMBERS

VIN stamped on aluminum tab riveted to dashboard on passenger side and observable through the windshield from outside the car. Prefix indicates manufacturer: F=Ford. First symbol denotes model-year: 2=1972. Second symbol denotes the assembly plant: Y=Wixom (Novi), Michigan and J=Los Angeles, California. Third symbol denotes the carline: 8=T-Bird. Fourth symbol denotes body type: 7=Two-door hardtop. Fifth symbol denotes engine: N=429-cid/212-hp Thunderbird V-8, A=460-cid/224-hp Thunderbird V-8. Sixth thru 11th symbols denote sequential production number of specific vehicle starting at 100001. Body certification label located on rear face of driver's door. The top part of the label indicates that the T-Bird was manufactured by Ford Motor Company. Directly below this is the month and year of manufacture, plus a statement that the car conforms to federal motor vehicle safety standard in effect on the indicated date of manufacture. The VIN appears first on the first line of encoded information. It matches the first to 11th symbols on VIN tag. The body style code appears to the right of the VIN on the same line. The T-Bird code for this model year is: 65K=two-door hardtop. The color code(s) appears to the right of the body style code. The trim code appears on the far left-hand side of the second line of encoded information. The axle code appears to the right of the trim code in the second position on the second line of encoded information: K=2.75:1 Traction-Lok, M=2.80:1 Traction-Lok, O=3.00:1 Traction-Lok, R=3.25:1 Traction-Lok, 2=2.75:1, 4=2.80:1, 6=3.00:1 and 9=3.25:1. The transmission code appears to the right of the axle code in the third position on the second line of encoded information: U=C-6 three-speed automatic, Z=C-6 special three-speed automatic. The District Special Equipment (DSO) code appears to the right of the transmission code in the far right-hand position on the second line of encoded information. (Note: The abbreviations VIN/BDY/CLR/TRM/AX/TR/DSO do not appear on the certification label itself. The specific application of the codes is determined by where they are located on the vehicle certification label.)

ENGINE

THUNDERBIRD 429 FOUR-BARREL V-8: Overhead valve. Cast-iron block. Displacement: 429 cid. Bore and stroke: 4.36 x 3.59 in. Compression ratio: 8.50:1. Brake nhp: 212 at 4400 rpm. Torque: 327 lbs.-ft. at 2600 rpm. Five main bearings. Hydraulic valve lifters. Carburetor: Four-barrel. Cooling system capacity: 18.8 qt. with heater. Crankcase capacity: 5 qt. (add 1 qt. with new oil filter). Dual exhaust. Code N.

THUNDERBIRD 460 FOUR-BARREL V-8: Overhead valve. Cast-iron block. Displacement: 460 cid. Bore and stroke: 4.36 x 3.85 in. Compression ratio: 8.50:1. Brake nhp: 224 at 4400 rpm. Torque: 342 lbs-ft. at 2600 rpm. Five main bearings. Hydraulic valve lifters. Carburetor: Four-barrel. Cooling system capacity: 18.8 qt. with heater. Crankcase capacity: 5 qt. (add 1 qt. with new oil filter). Dual exhaust. Code A.

CHASSIS

Wheelbase: 120.4 in. Overall length: 216 in. Overall width: 79.3 in. Overall height: 51.3 in. Trunk volume: 13.9 cu. ft. Front tread: 63 in. Rear tread: 62.8 in. Tires: 215R-15 steel-belted radial. Steering: Integral with power-assist. Turning diameter: 43 ft. Front suspension: Independent drag-strut, ball-joint type with coil springs. Rear suspension: Four-link rubber-cushioned with integral stabilizer bar. Standard rear axle: 2.75:1. Front brakes: Power front disc brakes, swept area 232 sq. in. Rear brakes: Power drums, swept area: 155.9 sq. in. Total swept area: 387.9 sq. in. Fuel tank capacity: 22.5 gal.

OPTIONS

460-cid V-8 engine (SelectAire conditioner required) $75.97. SelectAire conditioner ($436.52). Automatic temperature control with 61-amp alternator and electric rear window defroster ($505.68). Traction-Lok differential ($47.71 without optional axle ratio, $60.33 with optional axle ratio). Deluxe seat belts with warning light ($35.94). Bumper guards front and rear, except standard with protection group ($36.97). Electric rear window defroster, includes 65-amp alternator and panel light ($81.91). 460-cid four-barrel V-8, air conditioning required ($75.97). California emissions system ($15.14). Complete tinted glass ($50.74). Rocker panel moldings ($25.37). Color Glow paint ($37.99). Dual accent body side stripes ($12.62). Power antenna ($30.17). Door lock group, includes remote deck lid release ($59.45). 6-way power driver's seat ($101.34). 6-way power driver and passenger seats ($201.67). Power side windows ($129.60). Power trunk lid release ($13.63). AM/FM stereo radio including dual front and rear seat speakers ($146.14). Vinyl roof ($137.43). (Note: Vinyl roof includes "S" landau bars with wood-grain inserts (or tooled silver Landau bar inserts when Glamour paint is ordered) on T-Birds.) Manual reclining passenger seat, except standard with Turnpike group ($40). High-back bucket seats and console ($75.97). Spare tire cover ($86.32). Dual rear seat speakers, standard with AM/FM stereo radio or tape system ($32.18). Fingertip speed control including rim-blow deluxe three-spoke steering wheel (standard with Turnpike group, otherwise $103.14). Deluxe three-spoke rim-blow steering wheel ($37.99). Tilt steering wheel ($50.74). Stereosonic tape system with AM radio only ($146.14). Power-operated sunroof, requires vinyl roof on hardtop ($504.80). Heavy-duty suspension with heavy front and rear springs and shocks, front stabilizer bar ($27.26). Leather trim for split-bench seats ($63.65). Deluxe wheel covers, except not available with Glamour Paint option ($87.07). Intermittent windshield wipers, requires recessed windshield wipers ($25.37). Convenience group includes low fuel and door ajar light and buzzer, dual overhead map lights, engine compartment light ($43.79). Glamour Paint option, includes color-keyed wheel covers, dual body side and hood paint stripes, tooled silver Landau bar inserts without vinyl roof ($161.79). Protection group includes color-keyed floor mats, license plate frames, and door edge guards ($25.37). Heavy-duty trailer towing package, includes heavy-duty suspension, extra-cooling package, wiring harness, high-ratio axle, and trailer towing decal ($45.82). Turnpike convenience group includes fingertip speed control, manual reclining passenger seat, and trip odometer ($132.51). Michelin 215-15R steel-belted radial-ply single band whitewall tires with 40,000-mile tread life guarantee (Michelin black sidewalls were standard and the whitewalls were $31.17 extra).

EQUIPMENT INSTALLATION RATES

Cruise-O-Matic drive (100 percent). Standard V-8 engine (79.6 percent). Optional V-8 engine (20.4 percent). AM radio (17.5 percent). AM/FM radio (69.2 percent). Stereo tape player (13.3 percent). Power steering (100 percent). Power front disc brakes (100 percent). Power door locks: (48.8 percent.) Power seat (77.4 percent). Power windows (90.4 percent). Bucket seats (13.9 percent). Moveable type steering wheel (74.5 percent). White sidewall tires (99.9 percent). Tinted glass (97.7 percent). Vinyl top (98.3 percent). Sunroof: (3.4 percent). Automatic temperature control (29.6 percent). Manual air conditioning (69.3 percent). Dual exhaust (100 percent). Limited-slip axle (7.1 percent). Standard wheel covers (79.3 percent). Optional wheel covers (20.7 percent). Speed control (36.6 percent). Clock (100 percent). Reclining front seats (27.1 percent). Slid control device (0.9 prcent) (Note: Based on model-year production.)

HISTORICAL FOOTNOTES

The 1972 T-Bird was introduced on September 24,

The 1972 T-Birds were a far cry from their 1950s "Small Bird" roots. The cars were the same size as the Lincoln Continental and averaged between 9 and 11 mpg with their 429- and 460-cid V-8s.

With Lee Iacocca taking charge of the redesign, the Thunderbird grew larger than ever before for 1972. Only a two-door hardtop was offered.

1971. Henry Ford II was Ford's chairman of the board. Lee A. Iaccoca was promoted to president. J.B. Naughton was a vice president and general manager of Ford Division. G.B. MacKenzie became general sales manager for Ford Division.

Calendar-year output was 58,582 units. A total of 57,814 T-Birds were produced in the model year. This represented 0.7 percent of the industry total. Of these units, 35,585 were made in Michigan and 22,229 were made in California. Calendar year dealer sales amounted to 58,731 T-Birds, representing 0.6 percent of industry sales. Ford had originally planned to use a 400-cid two-barrel V-8 as the standard 1972 T-Bird power plant. Sales catalog no. 5303 dated 8/71 lists this smaller engine as standard equipment and the 429-cid four-barrel V-8 as an option. However, a new version of the 429-4V was used and Lincoln's big 460-cid four-barrel V-8 was optional. "Evidently, the 400-2V engine's performance was not what they hoped it would be," said *Road Test* magazine. "The 460-4V can be expected to give slightly better acceleration, but decreased gas mileage."

Body and frame construction was reintroduced in the new model. The 429-4V normally averaged about 9.0 to 9.1 mpg. *Road Test* magazine averaged 10.6 mpg for its entire trial, but had a low figure of 8.2 mpg during acceleration testing. *Motor Trend* (December 1971) averaged 11.67 mpg, also with the 429-4V. The 460-4V engine was good for 10-10.6 mpg on average. When the '72 models were about 10 years old, the editors of *Consumer Guide* said that the T-Bird was "A possible collector's item one day, but awful mileage means you'll spend more time looking at it than driving it." *Motor Trend's* December article was an unusual three-way comparison between the Buick Riviera, the T-Bird, and the Jaguar XJ6. The buff book made the point that

America's personal luxury cars had grown as large as its four-door sedans, thereby justifying—in its "editorial mind" at least—stacking the pair of destroyer-sized domestics against one of Britain's hottest "sports saloon" models (saloon meaning four-door sedan in the King's English). The conclusion arrived at through this methodology was nearly as unique as the underlying concept. "You can bet your bottom dollar that the next generation of both Thunderbird and Riviera will be smaller and will handle better," predicted writer Jim Brokaw. "...take a peek at tomorrow and promote a ride in an XJ6."

A significant historical milestone was marked during the year when the 1 millionth T-Bird ever built was assembled. It was specially finished with Anniversary Gold paint and wore a White vinyl-clad landau roof. The wheel covers had color-coordinated gold accents. Up front was a gold-finished radiator grille. Commemorative "Millionth Thunderbird" emblems were found on the right-hand side of the instrument panel, and in the center of the S-shaped landau bars on either side of the roof. The car was presented to a member of the Classic Thunderbird Club International to use for one year. The following year it was purchased by George Watts, the collector who owns the earliest production T-Bird known to have been built.

The Thunderbird continued to grow in popularity in 1973 with more than 90,000 cars built for the calendar year—almost double the number made just two years earlier.

1973

The 1973 T-Bird continued sharing the Lincoln Mark IV body. There was a new egg-crate grille, plus a stand-up hood ornament. The grille no longer showed through below a new energy-absorbing bumper that was designed to withstand 5-mph impacts. This massive "Twin I-Beam" bumper had a shelf-like appearance and added nearly three inches of length. Vertical guards near the center of the bumper were standard. The Thunderbird name was spelled out on the car's nose.

The dual headlamps were mounted in separate square bezels on each side of the grille. New three-deck parking lights were notched into the front fenders and viewable from the side. Wider body side moldings with color-keyed protective vinyl inserts were seen. Initially, opera windows were optional and they eliminated a blind spot caused by massive "C" pillars. The opera windows were basically of a low, rectangular shape, but the trailing edge was slanted to match the rear roofline. A midyear sales catalog (5402 Rev. 6/73) added opera windows as standard equipment, along with SelectAire air conditioning, tinted glass, power side windows, an automatic seatback release (that unlatched the seat when you opened the door to simplify entering the car with bulky packages), power steering and a vinyl roof. Landau bars were no longer offered. The 1973 wheel covers

had some detail changes.

Wall-to-wall taillights again graced the T-Bird's rear end, with a winged Thunderbird emblem in the center of each lens. The huge lens had more of a wedge shape than an inverted U-shape. The "vacation-size" trunk offered 13.9 cu. ft. of luggage capacity. The rear bumper was massive and wrapped around the body corners. Two large vertical guards flanked a huge license plate "frame" in the center. The energy-absorbing rear bumper system met new federal safety standards.

Exteriors could be finished in any of 15 standard colors or eight optional Glamour paints. The Glamour paints contained a higher amount of metallic particles for greater reflectivity and iridescence. Odense Grain vinyl tops (available on cars having the Exterior Décor Group option) came in Copper, White, Blue, Green and Brown. Individually adjustable, deep-cushioned spilt bench front seats with fold-down armrests were standard in all T-Birds. Also featured was cut-pile carpeting on the floor, lower seatbacks and lower door panels. Cloth-and-vinyl interior trims were standard for the split bench seat. Optional all-vinyl trim was available in all seven colors. Leather-and-vinyl trim was available for the split bench seat. Optional

BODY COLOR INFORMATION (U.S. & CANADA)

Color Name	Code	Color Name	Code
Light Gray (Metallic)	1A	Light Green	4S
Black	1C	Emerald Fire*	4U
Burgundy Fire*	2G	Cinnamon Fire*	5D
Maroon	2J	Dark Brown (Metallic)	5F
Pastel Blue	3A	Almond Fire*	5K
Medium Blue (Metallic)	3D	Tan	5L
Dark Blue (Metallic)	3G	Mahogany Fire*	5P
Silver Blue Fire*	3L	Light Yellow Gold	6B
Green Fire*	4D	Yellow	6D
Lime Fire*	4G	Gold Fire*	6G
Medium Green (Metallic)	4P	Medium Gold (Metallic)	6L
Dark Green (Metallic)	4Q	White	9A

* Optional at extra cost.

STANDARD CLOTH AND VINYL INTERIOR TRIM INFORMATION

Seat Type	Black	Dark Blue	Ginger	Dark Green	Gold	Tobacco
Split Bench	GA	GB	GF	GR	HY	HZ

OPTIONAL ALL- VINYL INTERIOR TRIM INFORMATION

Seat Type	Black	Dark Blue	Ginger	Dark Green	Gold	Tobacco
Split Bench	JA	JB	JF	JR	JY	JZ

OPTIONAL LEATHER TRIM INFORMATION

Seat Type	Black	White w/Blue	Dark Green	Tobacco	White w/Black	White w/Green	White w/Tobacco
Split Bench	KA	KQ	KR	KZ	KW	K5	K9

OPTIONAL CLOTH AND VINYL INTERIOR TRIM INFORMATION

Seat Type	Black	Dark Blue	Ginger	Dark Green
High-Back Bucket Seats	GA	GB	GF	GR

VINYL TOP COLOR INFORMATION

Alligator-grain Cayman vinyl tops were available for cars without the Exterior Décor Group and came in Black, White, Dark Blue, Dark Green, Brown, Beige, Gold, and Light Blue.
Odense grain tops were used only on cars that also had the Exterior Décor Group and came in Copper, White, Blue, Green, and Brown.

THUNDERBIRD PRODUCTION

Model Number	Body/Style Number	Body Type & Seating	Factory Price	Shipping Weight	Production Total
7	65K	2d Hardtop-4P	$5,577	4,572 lbs.	87,269

NOTE 1: Price increased to $6,414 when six additional items listed above became standard equipment on June 11, 1973.

bucket seats came only in cloth-and-vinyl.

The 1973 T-Birds had an improved impact-absorbing laminated safety glass windshield. Other product improvements included suspension system refinements, increased front and rear headroom and whitewall steel-belted radial tires as standard equipment. An inside hood release and spare tire lock were also new.

The standard 429-cid four-barrel V-8 was designed to operate on regular gasoline with an octane rating of at least 91 with the engine adjusted to factory specifications. The 460-cid four-barrel V-8 was optional.

STANDARD EQUIPMENT

All regulation safety, anti-theft, convenience items and emissions control equipment, dual hydraulic brake system with warning light, Uni-Lock shoulder and lap belts with reminder, side-door steel guard rails, energy-absorbing front and rear bumpers, 429-cid four-barrel regular fuel V-8, SelectShift Cruise-O-Matic transmission with uniform transmission shift quadrant, power front disc/rear drum brakes, rubber-insert-type front bumper guards, body-side moldings with protective vinyl inserts, bright window reveal moldings, remote-control left-hand OSRV mirror, full wheel covers, individually adjustable split-bench front seat with two folding armrests, self-locking front seat backs with padding, non-reversing odometer, Aurora cloth seat trim with vinyl facings, headrests or high-back seats for front outboard passengers, cut-pile carpeting, energy-absorbing steering column and wheel, locking steering column with warning buzzer, two-speed windshield wipers, windshield washers, 4-way hazard warning flashers, turn signals with lane-change feature, fully lined and lighted luggage compartment, wood-tone interior dress up accents, deluxe arm rests, interior courtesy lights (dome, door, under-panel, glove box and front ashtray), steel-belted radial white sidewall tires, power front disc/rear drum brakes, power ventilation system, 80-amp battery, inside the car hood release, constant-ratio power steering, AM radio, MagicAire heater and defroster, electric clock, spare tire lock, back-up lights, side marker lights, unique T-Bird identification and ornamentation, hood ornament, bright moldings at rear of hood, door belts, drip rails and wheel lips, 61-amp alternator maintains battery charge even at low engine speeds, automatic parking brake release, aluminized muffler with stainless-steel components and choice of 23 exterior colors. Added to standard equipment list on June 11, 1973 were SelectAire conditioner, opera windows, power windows, tinted glass, vinyl roof, and automatic seat back release.

I.D. NUMBERS

VIN stamped on aluminum tab riveted to dashboard on passenger side and observable through the windshield from outside the car. Prefix indicates manufacturer: F=Ford. First symbol denotes model year: 3=1973. Second symbol denotes the assembly plant: Y=Wixom (Novi), Michigan and J=Los Angeles, California. Third symbol denotes the car-line: 8=T-Bird. Fourth symbol denotes body type: 7=two-door hardtop. Fifth symbol denotes engine: N=429-cid/208-hp Thunderbird V-8, A=460-cid/219-hp Thunderbird V-8. Sixth thru 11th symbols denote sequential production number of specific vehicle starting at 100001. Suffix: Denotes manufacturer, F=Ford. Body certification label located on rear face of driver's door. The top part of the label indicates that the T-Bird was manufactured by Ford Motor Company. Directly below this is the month and year of manufacture, plus a statement that the car conforms to federal motor vehicle safety standard in effect on the indicated date of manufacture. The VIN appears first on the first line of encoded information. It matches the 1st to 11th symbols on VIN tag. The body style code appears to the right of the VIN on the same line. The T-Bird code for this model-year is: 65K=two-door hardtop. The color code(s) appears to the right of the body style code. The trim code appears on the far left-hand side of the second line of encoded information. The axle code appears to the right of the trim code in the second position on the second line of encoded information: 2=2.75:1, 6=3.00:1, 9=3.25:1, K=2.75:1 Traction-Lok, O=3.00:1 Traction-Lok and R=3.25:1 Traction-Lok. The transmission code appears to the right of the axle code in the third position on the second line of encoded information: U=SelectShift Cruise-O-Matic three-speed automatic and Z=SelectShift Cruise-O-Matic Special three-speed automatic. The District Special Equipment (DSO) code appears to the right of the transmission code in the far right-hand position on the second line of encoded information. (Note: The abbreviations VIN/BDY/CLR/TRM/AX/TR/DSO do not appear on the certification label itself. The specific application of the codes is determined by where they are located on the vehicle certification label.)

ENGINE

THUNDERBIRD 429 FOUR-BARREL V-8: Overhead valve. Cast-iron block. Displacement: 429 cid. Bore and stroke: 4.36 x 3.59 in. Compression ratio: 8.50:1. Brake hp: 201 at 4400 rpm. Torque: 327 lbs.-ft. at 2800 rpm. Five main bearings. Hydraulic valve lifters. Carburetor: Four-barrel. Cooling system capacity: 18.8 qt. with heater. Crankcase capacity: 5 qt. (add 1 qt. with new oil filter). Dual exhaust. Code N.

THUNDERBIRD 460 FOUR-BARREL V-8: Overhead valve. Cast-iron block. Displacement: 460 cid. Bore and stroke: 4.36 x 3.85 in. Compression ratio: 8.50:1. Brake hp: 219 at 4400 rpm. Torque: 338 lbs.-ft. at 2600 rpm. Five main bearings. Hydraulic valve lifters. Carburetor: Four-barrel. Cooling system capacity: 18.8 qt. with heater. Crankcase capacity: 5 qt. (add 1 qt. with new oil filter). Dual exhaust. Code A.

CHASSIS

Wheelbase: 120.4 in. Overall length: 218.9 in. Overall width: 79.7 in. Overall height: 53.1 in. Trunk volume: 13.9 cu. ft. Front tread: 63 in. Rear tread: 63.1 in. Tires: 230R-15 steel-belted radial. Steering: Integral with power-assist, 21.73:1 overall ratio. Turning diameter: 43 ft. Ground clearance: 5.4 in. Front suspension: Coil springs, stabilizer, shocks, axial strut. Rear suspension: Coil spring, shocks and stabilizer. Standard rear axle: 2.75:1. Front brakes: Power front disc brakes, swept area 232 sq. in. Rear brakes: Power drums, swept area: 155.9 sq. in. Total swept area: 387.9 sq. in. Fuel tank capacity: 22.5 gal.

OPTIONS

Power side windows, prior to June 11, 1973 ($129.60). 460-cid/219-hp V-8 engine ($75.79). Vinyl roof, prior to June 11, 1973 ($137). SelectAire Conditioner, prior to June 11, 1973 ($436.52). SelectAire Conditioner with automatic temperature control ($505.68). Traction-Lok differential with standard axle ratio ($47.71). Traction-Lok differential with high-ratio axle ($60.33). Sure-Track brake control system ($197). Deluxe bumper group including front and rear bumper guards with rubber inserts and full-width rub strips ($51). Opera windows, prior to June 11, 1973 ($81.84). Glamour Paint Group, includes higher amount of metallic particles in paint, dual body-side stripes, twin hood stripes and color-keyed wheel covers ($161.79). Electric rear window defroster, including panel indicator light and 70-amp alternator ($81.91). California emissions testing ($21). Dual exhaust system, including sound package ($53). Dual body side and hood stripes ($18). Fire Metallic paint ($131). Starfire Metallic paint ($172). Dual body-side accent stripes ($18). Power antenna ($30.17). Power door locks group including remote trunk release ($59.45). 6-way power full-width driver and passenger seats ($201.67). 6-way power driver seat ($1201.34). Power sunroof, vinyl top required ($504.80). AM/FM stereo radio ($146). AM/FM stereo radio with tape player ($311). Dual rear seat speakers (standard with stereo radio or tape system, otherwise $32.18). Manual reclining passenger seat, standard with Turnpike convenience group ($40). High-back bucket seats with central console ($75.97). Fingertip speed control, including rim-blow steering wheel and standard with Turnpike convenience group ($103.14). Rim-blow steering wheel alone ($37.99). Tilt steering wheel ($51). Heavy-duty suspension includes heavy front and rear springs and shocks ($27.26). Heavy-duty trailer-towing package, includes heavy-duty suspension ($45.82). Front cornering lamps ($43). Deluxe bumper group ($51). Super-soft vinyl seat trim ($35). Luggage compartment trim ($57). Leather and vinyl trim ($35). Deluxe wheel covers ($64). Convenience Light Group including: high-intensity map lights, warning lights for headlamps on, low fuel warning light, door ajar light, headlamps on buzzer, and engine compartment light ($43.79). Tinted glass ($50.74). Turnpike convenience group, including: visor-vanity mirror, interval windshield wipers, right- and left-hand remote-control mirrors, speed control, manual reclining passenger seat, and trip odometer ($132.51). Theft-Foil alarm system with alarm and decals ($79). Interval windshield wipers ($25.37). Deluxe color-keyed seat belts ($50.49). Remote-control right-hand rearview mirror ($26.67). Vinyl seat trim ($35). Rim-blow steering wheel ($37.99). Appearance Protection group with: door edge guards, license plate frames, spare tire lock and cover, and front and rear floor mats with carpet inserts (with exterior décor group $68, without exterior décor group $75). Class III trailer towing package with heavy-duty handling suspension, heavy-duty alternator, wiring harness, extra-cooling package, coolant recovery system, heavy-duty frame, and trailer towing decal ($48, but not offered for cars registered in California). LR78 steel-belted radial-ply whitewall tires ($33 extra). Burgundy luxury group, including Burgundy Victorian velour or Red leather seats and door trim, deluxe luggage compartment trim, gold insert Thunderbird opera window ornaments, Burgundy Fire Metallic paint, simulated wire wheel covers, gold paint stripes, and Dark Red Odense grain vinyl roof ($411).

EQUIPMENT INSTALLATION RATES

Cruise-O-Matic drive (100 percent). Standard V-8 engine (28.7 percent). Optional V-8 engine (71.3 percent). AM radio (8.2 percent). AM/FM radio (69.2 percent). Stereo tape player (28.9 percent). Power steering (100 percent). Power front disc brakes (100 percent). Power door locks (61.5 percent.) Power seat (85.9 percent). Power windows (99.2 percent). Bucket seats (4.6 percent). Adjustable steering column (75.8 percent). Tinted glass (97.9 percent). Vinyl top (99.4 percent). Sunroof: (4.8 percent). Automatic temperature control (37 percent). Manual air conditioning (62.4 percent). Limited-slip axle (6.9 percent). Standard steel-belted radial whitewall tires (100 percent). Standard wheel covers (15.2 percent). Optional wheel covers (84.8 percent). Speed control (50.1 percent). Clock (100 percent). Skid control device (5.9 percent). Rear window defogger (46.9 percent). Remote-control rearview mirror (100 percent). Reclining front seats: (53.2 percent). (Note: Based on model-year production of 82,711 units for the U.S. market, which is less than model-year output.)

HISTORICAL FOOTNOTES

The 1973 T-Bird was introduced on September 22, 1972. Henry Ford II (chairman) and. Lee A. Iaccoca (president) again held the top two corporate positions at Ford Motor Company. B.E. Bidwell was Ford Division's new vice president and general manager. W.J. Oben became general sales manager for the division.

Calendar-year output was 90,404 units. A total of 87,269 T-Birds were produced in the model year. This represented 0.9 percent of the industry total. Of these units, 46,676 were made in Michigan and 40,593 were made in California. Calendar-year dealer sales amounted to 74,759 T-Birds, representing 0.8 percent of industry sales. With the government and insurance companies cracking down on automotive performance, 1973 Ford sales catalogs said nothing about horsepower or torque ratings.

Motor Trend did a four-car comparison (June 1973) of a T-Bird, Pontiac Grand Prix, Buick Riviera, and Oldsmobile Toronado. The T-Bird was the most expensive of the quartet. Although it used the optional 460-4V engine, it had the lowest horsepower rating. Nevertheless, it was second fastest from 0 to 60 mph. It also had the second-fastest terminal speed in the quarter-mile, but the third-lowest elapsed time. Writer Jim Brokaw found the T-Bird's handling good, but sensitive to tire inflation. He joked about its cigarette lighter having more stages than a Saturn V rocket and said, "If you threw it out the window in Belfast, you'd clear the streets in three seconds." Brokaw especially noted the 460-cid V-8 was a good low-end torquer that could easily burn rubber. He actually rated it second-highest in performance, next to the 455-cid/250-hp Grand Prix. Criticisms were directed at a too-small ashtray and glove box and excessive wind noise for a Ford product. He also gave the T-Bird his top rating in the "prestige" department.

Model-year production was nearly 30,000 units higher than the previous year, an impressive endorsement of the Lincoln-like "T-Bird." Ford published separate T-Bird literature for dealers in Canada, although all of the 1973 models were built in the United States. Under a free trade agreement that went into effect around 1970, cars could be shipped across the border, in either direction, duty-free. This allowed automakers to avoid sourcing cars from both countries to avoid tariffs and helped them make more efficient use of their production facilities. There are no dramatic differences in the wording of the U.S. and Canadian sales catalogs, although at least three small differences appear in Canadian literature. First, the phrase "1973 Federal Motor Vehicle Standards" is changed to "1973 Canadian Motor Vehicle Standards." Second, instead of mentioning specific mileage intervals for service operations, Canadian catalogs say: "details are contained in the Owner's Manual." Third, instead of listing a "22.5-gal." fuel tank, the Canadian literature says "18.7 gal."

1973 THUNDERBIRD PERFORMANCE		
Model	**CID/HP**	**Performance**
0-60 mph		
Two-door hardtop	429/201	9.0 seconds
1/4-Mile		
Two-door hardtop	429/201	17.4 seconds @ 85 mph
Top Speed		
Two-door hardtop	429/212	120 mph

A transparent moon roof was one of the new options on the 1974 Thunderbird.

1974
Thunderbird

In most details, the 1974 T-Bird was changed very little from 1973, but there were a number of refinements. The bumpers and bumper guards were slightly altered and there was a new rear appearance with the addition of an impact-absorbing bumper and redesigned full-width taillights. The 460-cid four-barrel V-8 became standard equipment. It had a new solid-state ignition system and a 220-hp rating. The solid-state ignition replaced ignition parts like the points, cam, and condenser with highly reliable, low-maintenance electronic components. The results were a stronger spark, reduced maintenance, more dependable cold-weather starting, lower emissions, and the virtual elimination of misfiring. New luxury options included an electrically heated quick-defrost windshield and rear window, plus a transparent moonroof. T-Bird interiors featured simulated wood-tone accents and deluxe seat belts.

On the outside all T-Birds had full wheel covers, a unique T-Bird hood ornament, moldings on the hood edge, doors, belt line, drip rails and wheel openings and vinyl-insert body side moldings. Initially, 21 exterior colors were offered on '74 T-Birds and eight were optional Glamour Colors. In January 1974, the Autumn Fire Glamour Paint color was deleted.

Also in January, a pair of Special Edition T-Birds was added. The Burgundy Luxury Group model included all basic T-Bird equipment, plus dual body-side and hood stripes, special body-side moldings, and simulated wire wheel covers. An exclusive Dark Red Odense grain vinyl top was also featured. The White and Gold Special Edition Thunderbird came with color-coordinated wide body-side moldings, color-keyed wheel covers, body side accent stripes, hood and deck lid accent stripes, and an exclusive Gold Levant grain vinyl top. Both special T-Birds also offered Glamour colors and luggage compartment trim as standard equipment.

All Comfort and Convenience features found on mid-1973 T-Birds were standard, including the adjustable split-bench front seat with fold-down center armrest. Front outboard retractable lap/shoulder belts with the infamous starter interlock system, as required by the National Highway Traffic Safety Administration (NHTSA) were so unpopular that the new safety rule was canceled by Congress at the end of the year. The ignition interlock system prevented an engine from starting if belts for occupied front seats were not buckled in the proper sequence. A warning buzzer (after January a warning light and buzzer) reminded outboard passengers to buckle up. Additionally, a logic circuit prevented the engine from starting if passengers attempted to beat the system by extending the harness before sitting or by buckling the belts together.

STANDARD EQUIPMENT

All regulation safety, anti-theft, convenience items and

BODY COLOR INFORMATION (U.S.)

Color Name	Code	Color Name	Code
Black	1C	Autumn Fire*	5R
Silver Cloud (Metallic)	1E	Medium Beige	5S
Burgundy Fire*	2G	Buff	5V
Pastel Blue	3A	Gold Fire*	6G
Medium Blue (Metallic)	3D	Medium Gold (Metallic)	6L
Dark Blue (Metallic)	3G	Dark Olive Gold (Metallic)	6M
Silver Blue Fire*	3L	Medium Ivy Yellow	6N
Blue Sarfire*	3P	Polar White	9C
Pastel Lime	4A	Cinnamon Starfire*	51
Green Starfire*	4Y	Mahogany Starfire*	52
Dark Brown (Metallic)	5Q		

* Optional at extra cost.

STANDARD AURORA CLOTH AND VINYL INTERIOR TRIM INFORMATION

Seat Type	Black	Medium Blue	Dark Red	Medium Green	Tan	Saddle
Split Bench	HA	HB	HD	HR	HU	HZ

OPTIONAL SUPER-SOFT VINYL INTERIOR TRIM INFORMATION

Seat Type	Black	Medium Blue	Dark Red	White w/ Dk Red	White Med Blue	w/Medium Green	Tan
Split Bench	JA	JB	JD	JN	JQ	JR	JU

Seat Type	White w/ Black	Gold	White w/ Med. Green	White w/ Gold	White w/ Saddle
Split Bench	JW	JY	J5	J8	J9

OPTIONAL PICARDY CLOTH NTERIOR TRIM INFORMATION

Seat Type	Medium Blue	Tan	Gold
Split Bench	FB	FU	FY

OPTIONAL LEATHER AND VINYL TRIM INFORMATION

Seat Type	Medium Black	Dark Blue	White w/ Red	White w/ Dk Red	Medium Med Blue	White w/ Green	Tan	Black
Split Bench	KA	KB	KD	KN	KQ	KR	KU	KW

Seat Type	Gold	White w/ Saddle	White w/ Med Green	Medium Gold	Saddle
Split Bench	KY	KZ	K5	K8	K9

SPECIAL EDITION LUXURY GROUP INTERIOR TRIM INFORMATION

	Burgundy Content	White-and-Gold Content
Paint:	Burgundy Fire Metallic Glamour	Polar White with Gold
Trim:	Dark Red Victoria Velour with Dark Red Leather seating surfaces	Wh. Leather w/ Gold vinyl trim
Striping:	Gold (body side and hood)	Gold (side, hood and trunk)
Roof:	Dark Red Odense Grain Vinyl	Gold Levant Grain
Other:	Gold T-Bird insignia in window	Gold insignia in window
Wheels:	Simulated wires	Color-Keyed Deluxe wheel covers
Trunk:	Deluxe trim	Deluxe trim

VINYL TOP COLOR INFORMATION

Alligator-grain Cayman vinyl tops were available for cars without the Exterior Décor Group and came in Brown, Copper, Medium Green, Tan, Black, Medium Silver Blue, Gold, White, Dark Blue, and Dark Red with Burgundy Luxury Group only.
Gold Levant Grain vinyl top supplied with White and Gold Luxury Group only.

THUNDERBIRD PRODUCTION

Model Number	Body/Style Number	Body Type & Seating	Factory Price	Shipping Weight	Production Total
7	65K	2d Hardtop-4P	$7,221	5,033 lbs.	58,443

emissions control equipment, Thunderbird hood ornament, power steering, solid-state ignition, power windows, power ventilation system, automatic seatback release, inside hood release, dome light, door courtesy light, under-panel light, glove box light, front ashtray light, ignition light, map lights, SelectShift transmission, 460-cid V-8 engine, power front disc/rear drum brakes, AM radio, electric clock, cut-pile carpeting, Odense vinyl roof, opera windows, individually-adjustable split bench front seat with fold-down center armrests, Aurora cloth and vinyl interior trim, wood-tone accents, extensive soundproofing, seat belt-ignition interlock system, remote-control left-hand OSRV mirror, deluxe seat belts, protective body-side moldings with vinyl inserts, lined and lighted trunk, LR78/15 steel-belted radial white sidewall tires, spare tire lock, full wheel covers, manual SelectAire conditioner, tinted glass, rear hood edge molding, door belt moldings, drip rail moldings, wheel lip moldings, 61-amp alternator, automatic parking brake release, front bumper guards and full coil spring suspension.

I.D. NUMBERS

VIN stamped on aluminum tab riveted to dashboard on passenger side and observable through the windshield from outside the car. Prefix indicates manufacturer: F=Ford. First symbol denotes model-year: 4=1974. Second symbol denotes the assembly plant: Y=Wixom (Novi), Michigan and J=Los Angeles, California. Third symbol denotes the carline: 8=T-Bird. Fourth symbol denotes body type: 7=Two-door hardtop. Fifth symbol denotes engine: A=460-cid/220-hp Thunderbird V-8. Sixth thru 11th symbols denote sequential production number of specific vehicle starting at 100001. Suffix: denotes manufacturer, F=Ford. Body certification label located on rear face of driver's door. The top part of the label indicates that the T-Bird was manufactured by Ford Motor Company. Directly below this is the month and year of manufacture, plus a statement that the car conforms to federal motor vehicle safety standard in effect on the indicated date of manufacture. The VIN appears first on the first line of encoded information. It matches the 1st to 11th symbols on VIN tag. The body style code appears to the right of the VIN on the same line. The T-Bird code for this model-year is: 65K=two-door hardtop. The color code(s) appears to the right of the body style code. Conventional colors are identified by a single letter or number. Optional Glamour Paints are identified by two numbers. The trim code appears on the far left-hand side of the second line of encoded information. The axle code appears to the right of the trim code in the second position on the second line of encoded information: K=2.75:1 limited-slip, O=3.00:1 limited-slip, R=3.25:1 limited-slip, 2=2.75:1, 6=3.00:1 and 9=3.25:1. The transmission code appears to the right of the axle code in the third position on the second line of encoded information: U=C6 SelectShift three-speed automatic, Z=C6 special SelectShift three-speed automatic. The District Special Equipment (DSO) code appears to the right of the transmission code in the far right-hand position on the second line of encoded information. (Note: The abbreviations VIN/BDY/-CLR/TRM/AX/TR/DSO do not appear on the certification label itself. The specific application of the codes is determined by where they are located on the vehicle certification label.)

ENGINE

THUNDERBIRD 460 FOUR-BARREL V-8: Overhead valve. Cast-iron block. Displacement: 429 cid. Bore and stroke: 4.36 x 3.85 in. Compression ratio: 8.00:1. Brake hp: 220 at 4000 rpm. Torque: 355 lbs.-ft. at 2600 rpm. Five main bearings. Hydraulic valve lifters. Carburetor: Four-barrel. Cooling system capacity: 18.8 qt. with heater. Crankcase capacity: 5 qt. (add 1 qt. with new oil filter). Dual exhaust. Code A.

Ford photo

The oil embargo made a huge impact on the sales of the big 1974 Thunderbird and its rivals. Sales were down by more than 30,000 cars as the buying public began looking for more economical vehicles.

CHASSIS

Wheelbase: 120.4 in. Overall length: 224.8. Overall width: 79.7 in. Overall height: 53 in. Trunk volume: 13.4 cu. ft. Front tread: 63 in. Rear tread: 63.1 in. Tires: 230R-15 steel-belted radial. Steering: Integral with power-assist. Turning diameter: 43 ft. Front suspension: Coil springs, stabilizer, shocks and axial strut. Rear suspension: Coil spring, shocks and stabilizer. Standard rear axle: 3.00:1. Front brakes: Power disc. Rear brakes: Power drum. Fuel tank capacity: 26 gal.

OPTIONS

Automatic temperature control air conditioner ($74). Traction-Lok differential ($50). Deluxe bumper group including front and rear bumper guards with rubber inserts and full-width rub strips ($51). Quick-defrost windshield and rear window ($315). Electric rear window de-icer including panel indicator light and 70-amp alternator ($85). California emissions testing ($21). Dual exhaust system, including sound package ($53). Dual body-side and hood stripes ($18). Fire Metallic paint ($131). Starfire Metallic paint ($172). Power antenna ($31). Power door locks group including remote trunk release ($62). 6-way power full-width seat ($210). 6-way power split-bench seat, driver's side only ($105). Front cornering lamps, included in Exterior Décor Group ($43). Power moonroof ($798). Power mini-vent windows ($70). AM/FM stereo radio ($152). AM/FM stereo radio with tape player ($311). Dual rear seat speakers (standard with stereo radio or tape system, otherwise $33). Manual reclining passenger seat, standard with Turnpike convenience group ($42). High-back bucket seats with central console ($120). Fingertip speed control, including rim-blow steering wheel and standard with Turnpike convenience group ($103). Rim-blow steering wheel alone ($40). Tilt steering wheel ($53). Power-operated sunroof ($525). Sure-Track brake control system ($197). Heavy-duty suspension includes heavy front and rear springs and shocks ($28). Trailer equalizing hitch, requires trailer towing package ($90). Super-soft vinyl seat trim ($35). Deluxe luggage compartment trim ($57). Picardy velour cloth trim ($64). Leather seat trim ($105). Deluxe wheel covers ($64). Color-keyed standard wheel covers ($20). Simulated wire wheel covers ($85). Rear window quick defrost ($315). Anti-Theft Group, includes lockable hood latch ($79). Auto lamp on/off delay system, included in Light Group ($34). Convenience group, including interval windshield wipers and right-hand remote-control OSRV mirror ($53). Turnpike convenience group, including visor-vanity mirror, interval windshield wipers, right- and left-hand remote-control mirrors, speed control, manual reclining passenger seat, and trip odometer ($138). Convenience light group, including illuminated visor mirror, headlights-on light and buzzer, low fuel warning light, door opening warning light, overhead map light, and engine compartment light ($138). Light Group includes: dual overhead map lights, illuminated visor vanity mirror, warning lights for headlamps on, buzzer for headlamps on, low-fuel light, door ajar light, engine compartment light, and Autolamp system ($160). Exterior Décor group, including: partial wheel lip moldings, front cornering lights, and wide lower body-side moldings with padded grain-tone vinyl inserts ($141). Protection group with: door edge guards, license plate frames, spare tire lock and cover, and front and rear floor mats with carpet inserts (with exterior décor group $68, without exterior décor group $75). Class III trailer towing package with heavy-duty handling suspension, heavy-duty alternator, wiring harness, extra-cooling package, coolant recovery system, heavy-duty frame, and trailer towing decal ($48, but not offered for cars registered in California). Theft-Foil alarm system with alarm and decals ($79). LR78 steel-belted radial-ply whitewall tires ($33 extra). Burgundy luxury group, including: Burgundy Victorian velour or Red leather seats and door trim, deluxe luggage compartment trim, gold insert Thunderbird opera window ornaments, Burgundy Fire Metallic paint, simulated wire wheel covers, gold paint stripes, and Dark Red Odense grain vinyl roof ($411). White and Gold Luxury Group ($546). Space Saver spare tire ($86).

EQUIPMENT INSTALLATION RATES

Cruise-O-Matic drive (100 percent). Standard V-8 engine (100 percent). AM radio (4.6 percent). AM/FM radio (63.5 percent). Stereo tape player (31.9 percent). Power steering (100 percent). Power front disc brakes (100 percent). Power door locks: (72.6 percent.) Power seat (90.9 percent). Power windows (100 percent). Reclining seats (62.4 percent). Adjustable steering column (81 percent). Tinted glass (100 percent). Vinyl top (100 percent). Sunroof (10.4 percent). Automatic temperature control: (53.1 percent). Manual air conditioning (46.9 percent). Limited-slip axle (7.4 percent). Standard steel-belted radial whitewall tires (100 percent). Standard wheel covers (34.4 percent). Optional wheel covers (65.6 percent). Speed control (64.4 percent). Clock (100 percent). Skid control device (6.8 percent). Rear window defogger (55.4 percent). Remote-control rearview mirror (100 percent). Reclining front seats (53.2 percent). Dual exhausts (30.6 percent). (Note: Based on production of 53,843, which is less than model-year output.)

HISTORICAL FOOTNOTES

The 1974 T-Bird was introduced on September 20, 1973. Henry Ford II (chairman) and Lee A. Iaccoca (president) again held the top two corporate positions at Ford Motor Company. B.E. Bidwell was Ford Division's new vice president and general manager. W.J Oben was General Sales manager for the division.

Calendar-year output was 49,074 units. A total of 58,443 T-Birds were produced in the model year. This represented 0.72 percent of the industry total. Of these units, 37,943 were made in Michigan and 20,500 were made in California. Calendar-year dealer sales amounted to 54,112 T-Birds, representing 0.6 percent of industry sales. The 460-4V engine retained its 8.0:1 compression ratio to permit operation on 91 octane gas.

Although the 1974 T-Bird averaged just 11.6 mpg on a 73-mile loop of city, suburban, freeway and hilly roads driving conducted by *Motor Trend* magazine (March 1974), Ford sales literature included a list of "Economy and Durability" features. Self-adjusting brakes, two-year coolant, a long-life Motorcraft Sta-Ful battery, a corrosion-resistant aluminized muffler, zinc-coatings on underbody parts and the fact that the 460 operated on regular fuel were highlighted as "economy" features. In the durability department, Ford promoted its 36,000-mile major chassis lubrication, 6,000-mile oil changes and 12,000-mile (after the first time) oil filter changes.

This year's Jim Brokaw road test in *Motor Trend* continued the practice of comparing the T-Bird to other American personal-luxury cars. It featured eight vehicles—the most ever—of which three were new models. The T-Bird had faced off against the Riviera, Toronado, Grand Prix, and Monte Carlo in previous competitions. Now it was being stacked up against the AMC Matador "Oleg Cassini" model, the Mercury Cougar, and the Ford Torino Elite. The T-Bird was the most expensive and heaviest car in the group. It had the most cubic inches, but only the sixth-highest net horsepower rating. Though tied for second in torque, the T-Bird's fuel economy was on the very bottom. Brokaw concluded that all eight models shared the same basic features and a high level of execution. "It's really a matter of product loyalty and styling tastes," he felt about picking one over the other.

After the Arab oil embargo caused a severe energy shortage in the U.S. from January-March 1974, the big T-Bird's long-term popularity dropped. The 1974 T-Bird lost about 30,000 customers and two-tenths of a point of market share. No T-Birds were built in Canada, although a separate Canadian sales catalog was issued in August 1973. It was the same as the July 1973 U.S. catalog, except for one difference that some collectors might be interested in: Cars sold in Canada (although made in the U.S.) were *not* required to have the seat belt/starter interlock system.

Ford described the '74 T-Bird as "A magnificent expression of personal car luxury, which has long been a hallmark of Thunderbird." An informative piece of factory literature entitled *Thunderbird: An engineering achievement*, talked about the engineers, designers, and assembly line workers who built the car and their desire to achieve a higher standard of quality. It suggested that this was reflected in the fit of T-Bird parts, the look of the paint, an exceptionally smooth and quiet ride, and painstaking attention to detail.

All the 1975 Thunderbirds were considered "20th Anniversary" models. The big 'Birds were largely unchanged from 1974.

1975

Thunderbird

The physical appearance of the 1975 T-Bird was virtually unchanged from 1974, except that the front bumper guards were spaced further apart to improve the car's crash worthiness. There was also a new steering wheel with a center hub with outer ends that angled downward. Separate body and frame construction was featured. The T-Bird's strong, durable frame featured closed box-section members and five cross-members. Self-adjusting rear brakes, a long-life battery, an aluminized muffler and zinc-coated chassis parts were standard equipment.

All 1975 T-Birds were considered "20th Anniversary" models. Twenty exterior colors were originally offered, but others were added during the year. The standard interior featured Aurora cloth-and-vinyl trim in four colors. Picton velour cloth-and-vinyl, Super Soft vinyl and leather seats with vinyl trim were available. The standard Odense grain vinyl roof came in 11 colors: Black, White, Blue, Silver Blue, Green, Brown, Tan, Gold, Red, Copper, and Silver. Silver and Copper Luxury trim options joined last year's Gold and White Luxury options.

BODY COLOR INFORMATION (U.S.)

Color Name	Code	Color Name	Code
Black	1C	Dark Brown (Metallic)	5Q
Silver Starfire**	1J	Gold Starfire*	6G
Medium Red (Metallic)	2G	Medium Ivy Yellow	6N
Dark Red	2M	Dark Gold (Metallic)	6Q
Dark Blue (Metallic)	3G	Light Jade Starfire*	7B
Blue Starfire*	3P	Jade Starfire	7F
Pastel Blue	3Q	Polar White	9D
Silver Blue Starfire*	3R	Emerald Starfie*	41
Dark Yellow Green (Metallic)	4V	Cinnamon Starfire*	51
Light Green Gold (Metallic)	4Z	Copper Starfire*	52
Light Green	47	Bronze Starfire*	54

* Optional at extra cost.
** Available only with optional Silver Luxury Group.

STANDARD AURORA CLOTH AND VINYL INTERIOR TRIM INFORMATION

Seat Type	Black	Medium Blue	Medium Green	Saddle
Split Bench	HA	HB	HG	HZ

PICTON VELOUR CLOTH AND VINYL INTERIOR TRIM INFORMATION

Seat Type	Medium Blue	Dark Red	Medium Green	Saddle
Split Bench	FB	FD	FG	FZ

MEDIA VELOUR CLOTH AND VINYL INTERIOR LUXURY GROUP TRIM INFORMATION

Seat Type	Copper	Jade
Split Bench	MC	NR

OPTIONAL SUPER-SOFT VINYL INTERIOR TRIM INFORMATION

Seat Type	Black	Medium Blue	Dark Red	Medium Green	White w/ Dk Red	White w/ Med Blue	Saddle Tan
Split Bench	JA	JB	JD	JG	JN	JQ	JU*

Seat Type	White w/ Black	Saddle	White w/ Med. Green	White w/ Copper	White w/ Saddle
Split Bench	JW	JZ**	J5	J6	J9

*JU=vinyl

**JZ =leather and vinly

OPTIONAL LEATHER AND VINYL TRIM INFORMATION

Seat Type	Black	Medium Blue	Copper Luxury	Dark Red	Medium Green	White w/ Dk Red	Silver Luxury	White w/ Md Blue	Saddle/ Tan
Split Bench	KA	KB	KC	KD	KG	KN	KP	KQ	KU

Seat Type	White w/ Black	Saddle	White w/ Green	White w/ Copper	White w/ Saddle	White w/ Jade (Luxury)
Split Bench	KW	KZ	K5	K6	K9	P5

VINYL TOP INFORMATION

	Black	Blue	Copper	Red	Green	Silver	Jade	Silver Blue	Tan	Brown	White	Gold
	A	B	C	D	G	P	R	S	U	W		Y

Four types of vinyl tops were offered: F=Normande Grain full vinyl roof, L=Normande Grain half vinyl roof, G=Odense Grain full vinyl top and H=Odense Grain half vinyl top on Copper and Silver Luxury Groups. A full vinyl top was mandatory with sunroof or moonroof.

THUNDERBIRD PRODUCTION

Model Number	Body/Style Number	Body Type & Seating	Factory Price	Shipping Weight	Production Total
7	65K	2d Hardtop-4P	$7,701	5,101 lbs.	42,685

To make the 20th Anniversary T-Bird more distinctive, Ford added a Jade Luxury Group option at midyear. This package featured new colors, new textures and new fabrics in three exterior and two interior décor combinations. The All-Jade version had a Normande grain padded vinyl half-top, color-keyed vinyl-clad rear window moldings, color-keyed roof moldings, a silver Thunderbird opera window insignia, color-keyed wide body-side moldings, Jade Starfire glamour finish, dual hood and body-side stripes and wire wheel covers. In addition to the all-green version, the Jade Thunderbird came in two alternate combinations. One featured Polar White exterior finish smartly topped with a Jade half-vinyl roof. Another offered Jade Starfire glamour finish with a white half-vinyl top. Jade Thunderbirds also featured a choice of White leather seating surfaces or Jade Media Velour upholstery, both with Jade vinyl trim and color-keyed components. A half-vinyl roof was standard with Copper, Silver and Jade Luxury groups.

The T-Bird engine was again the 460-cid four-barrel V-8. Horsepower wasn't given in sales catalogs and various sources show different ratings.

STANDARD EQUIPMENT

All regulation safety, anti-theft, convenience items, and emissions control equipment, body and frame construction with closed box-section members and five cross-members, power steering, ignition and map lights, Cruise-O-Matic transmission, 460-cid V-8 engine, self-adjusting power front disc/rear drum brakes, three-year coolant and antifreeze, long-life Motorcraft Sta-Ful battery, corrosion-resistant aluminized muffler, zinc-coated underbody parts, AM radio, electric clock, split-bench front seat, vinyl roof, opera windows, full front seat with arm rests, standard cloth and vinyl seat trim, cut-pile carpeting, remote-control left-hand OSRV mirror, protective body-side moldings with vinyl inserts, all courtesy lights, all door light switches, ash tray and trunk lights, LR78/15 steel-belted radial white sidewall tires, full wheel covers, SelectAire conditioner, tinted glass, front bumper guards and full coil spring suspension. Copper Starfire or White exterior, Copper padded vinyl half roof with color-coordinated wrap-over moldings, color-keyed vinyl insert body-side moldings, Gold-toned T-Bird insignia. The Copper Luxury Group substituted or added: Copper Starfire or Polar White exterior finish, Copper Odense grain padded vinyl half roof with color-coordinated wrap-over moldings, color-keyed vinyl insert body-side moldings, Gold-toned T-Bird insignia on opera windows, color-accented cast-aluminum wheels, color-keyed pin stripes on hood and body belt, Copper velour cloth or Copper leather interior trim, Copper dash, door panel and headliner accents, Copper floor carpeting, and Copper-colored trunk compartment trim. The Silver Luxury Group substituted or added: Silver Starfire exterior finish, Silver Odense grain padded vinyl half roof with color-coordinated wrap-over moldings, color-keyed vinyl insert body side moldings, silver silk-screened T-Bird insignia on opera windows, choice of Red velour, Red leather or Silver leather deluxe interior trim and color-coordinated trunk compartment trim. The Jade Luxury Group substituted or added: choice of Polar White exterior body finish with Jade Green half vinyl roof, or Jade Starfire Glamour paint exterior body finish with Jade Green half vinyl roof, or Jade Starfire Glamour paint exterior body finish with White half vinyl roof, plus wide body-side molding color-keyed to roof, opera window Thunderbird insignia, rear window and roof moldings also color-keyed, dual hood and body side paint stripes, wire wheel covers and rich White leather seating (code P5) with Jade vinyl trim and components, or deep-cushioned seats tailored in plush Jade Green Media velour cloth trim (Code NR) with Jade vinyl trim and color-keyed components.

I.D. NUMBERS

VIN stamped on aluminum tab riveted to dashboard on passenger side and observable through the windshield from outside the car. Prefix indicates manufacturer: F=Ford. First

Ford photo

Despite some subtle upgrades from the previous model year, Thunderbird sales were off sharply in 1975. The biggest change was an optional four-wheel disc brake system.

symbol denotes model-year: 5=1975. Second symbol denotes the assembly plant: Y=Wixom (Novi), Michigan and J=Los Angeles, California. Third symbol denotes the car-line: 8=T-Bird. Fourth symbol denotes body type: 7=two-door hardtop. Fifth symbol denotes engine: A=460-cid/220-hp Thunderbird V-8. Sixth thru 11th symbols denote sequential production number of specific vehicle starting at 100001. Suffix: denotes manufacturer, F=Ford. Body certification label located on rear face of driver's door. The top part of the label indicates that the T-Bird was manufactured by Ford Motor Company. Directly below this is the month and year of manufacture, plus a statement that the car conforms to federal motor vehicle safety standard in effect on the indicated date of manufacture. The VIN appears first on the first line of encoded information. It matches the first to 11th symbols on VIN tag. The body style code appears to the right of the VIN on the same line. The T-Bird code for this model-year is: 65K=two-door hardtop. The color code(s) appears to the right of the body style code. The trim code appears to the right of the color and vinyl roof codes in the third position on the second line of encoded information The transmission code appears to the right of the trim code in the fourth position on the second line of encoded information: U=C6 XPL automatic transmission, Z=C6 Special XPL automatic transmission. The axle code appears to the right of the transmission code in the fifth position on the second line of encoded information: K=2.75:1 limited-slip, 2=2.75:1 and 6=3.00:1. The District Special Equipment (DSO) code appears to the right of the transmission code in the far right-hand position on the second line of encoded information. (Note: The abbreviations VIN/BDY/CLR/-TRM/AX/TR/DSO do not

appear on the certification label itself. The specific application of the codes is determined by where they are located on the vehicle certification label.)

ENGINE

THUNDERBIRD 460 FOUR-BARREL V-8: Overhead valve. Cast-iron block. Displacement: 460 cid. Bore and stroke: 4.36 x 3.85 in. Compression ratio: 8.50:1. Brake hp: 194 at 3800 rpm. Torque: 355 lbs.-ft. at 2600 rpm. Five main bearings. Hydraulic valve lifters. Carburetor: Four-barrel. Cooling system capacity: 18.8 qt. with heater. Crankcase capacity: 5 qt. (add 1 qt. with new oil filter). Dual exhaust. Code A.

CHASSIS

Wheelbase: 120.4 in. Overall length: 225.8. Overall width: 79.7. Overall height: 53 in. Trunk volume: 13.4 cu. ft. Front tread: 62.9 in. Rear tread: 62.8 in. Tires: 230R-15 steel-belted radial. Steering: Integral with power-assist. Turning diameter: 43 ft. Front suspension: Coil springs, stabilizer, shocks and axial strut. Rear suspension: Coil spring, shocks and stabilizer. Standard rear axle: 3.00:1. Front brakes: Power disc. Rear brakes: Power drum. Fuel tank capacity: 26.5 gal.

OPTIONS

Copper Luxury Group ($624). Silver Luxury Group ($337). Power-operated glass moonroof ($798). Power-operated sunroof ($617). AM/FM stereo radio with tape player

($249). Power antenna ($32). Dual body-side and hood paint stripes ($33). Trunk dress-up kit ($59). Protection Group with: color-coordinated carpet-insert floor mats front and rear, license plate frames, door edge guards, rocker panel moldings and spare tire cover ($79 on cars with trunk dress-up kit; on other cars includes parts of the trunk dress-up kit and costs $87). Wide vinyl-insert body-side moldings ($121). Deluxe wheel covers ($67, but included with Silver Luxury Group). Simulated wire wheel covers ($88). Deep-dish aluminum wheels ($251, but standard with Copper Luxury Group). Wide-band white sidewall tires ($59). Leather seating with vinyl trim ($239, but available at no extra cost for cars with Silver Luxury Group or Copper Luxury Group). Picton velour cloth trim ($96, but standard with Silver Luxury Group). Super-Soft vinyl trim ($55). Anti-theft alarm system, includes inside locking hood release ($84). Security Lock Group, includes inside locking hood release and locking gas cap ($18). Manual reclining passenger seat ($70). Tilt steering wheel ($68). Convenience Group, includes remote-control right-hand outside rearview mirror and interval windshield wipers ($84). Fingertip speed control ($120). Light Group, includes Autolamp on/off delay system, lighted visor-vanity mirror, twin overhead map lights, low fuel reminder, door-ajar warning light, headlights-on warning light and buzzer and under-hood light ($164). Power Lock Group, includes electric door locks and electric trunk lid release ($86). 6-way power driver's seat ($132). 6-way power front seats for driver and passenger ($250). Power mini-vent windows ($79). Space-Saver spare tire ($86). Optional ratio axles ($14). Traction-Lok differential ($54). Four-wheel disc brakes ($184). Sure-Track brake control system, includes four-wheel disc brakes ($378). Dual exhaust ($53). Heavy-duty suspension ($28). Fuel monitor warning light ($20). Class II trailer tow package ($48). Automatic Temperature Control system ($74). Quick-Defrost windshield and rear window ($355). Electric rear window defroster ($99). Starfire glamour paint ($204). Turnpike Group, including: manually reclining passenger seat, Fingertip speed control and trip odometer ($180).

EQUIPMENT INSTALLATION RATES

Cruise-O-Matic drive (100 percent). Standard V-8 engine (100 percent). AM/FM radio (57.8 percent). Stereo tape player (42.2 percent). Power steering (100 percent). Power front disc brakes (100 percent). Power door locks (76.3 percent.) Power seat (90.4 percent). Power windows (100 percent). Reclining seats (67.2 percent). Adjustable steering column (80.3 percent). Tinted glass (100 percent). Vinyl top (100 percent). Sunroof (11.1 percent). Automatic temperature control (50.6 percent). Manual air conditioning (49.4 percent). Limited-slip axle (8.7 percent). Standard steel-belted radial whitewall tires (100 percent). Standard wheel covers (20.9 percent). Optional wheel covers (61.9 percent). Styled wheels (17.2 percent). Speed control (79 percent). Clock (100 percent). Skid control device (4.4 percent). Rear window defogger (58.4 percent). Remote-control rearview mirror (100 percent). Reclining front seats (67.2 percent). Dual exhausts (40.5 percent). (Note: Based on partial model-year output of 38,506 cars.)

HISTORICAL FOOTNOTES

The 1974 T-Bird was introduced on September 27, 1974. Henry Ford II (chairman) and Lee A. Iaccoca (president) again held the top two corporate positions at Ford Motor Company. W.P. Benton was Ford Division's vice president and general manager. W.J. Oben was general sales manager for the division.

Calendar-year output was 37,557 units. A total of 42,685 T-Birds were produced in the model year. This represented 0.65 percent of the industry total. Of these units, 24,455 were made in Michigan and 18,230 were made in California. Calendar-year dealer sales amounted to 36,803 T-Birds, representing 0.5 percent of industry sales.

According to *Ward's Automotive Yearbook 1975*, the specification was 194 nhp at 3800 rpm. Other sources say 216 hp, 218 hp, and 220 hp. In reality, the early net horsepower ratings used in the industry were relative to vehicle weight, so the fully loaded T-Bird could, theoretically, have less horsepower than the base model. Therefore, all of these ratings could be "correct."

The biggest technical innovation of 1975 was an optional four-wheel disc brake system powered by Ford's new Hydro-Boost hydraulic brake booster. It included the Sure Trac rear brake anti-skid package. In addition, the anti-freeze was now advertised to last three years, instead of two. All 1975 T-Birds were manufactured in U.S. plants, but not all were produced for the U.S. market. Export units may have had minor differences. For instance, the sales literature issued by Ford of Canada did not include a paragraph that appeared in U.S. catalogs saying that T-Birds were designed to operate on unleaded gas. Also, the American literature specified mileage intervals for oil changes and major chassis lubrication, while Canadian catalogs eliminated such references. Sales and production saw another decline and the Thunderbird's share of market dropped, too. Model-year production was about 15,800 less than the previous year.

The 1976 Thunderbird didn't have much in the way of restyling. A roomy two-door model was the only one offered, but buyers had several different luxury option packages to pick from that included a variety of trim and interior combinations.

1976

Thunderbird

Ford described the 1976 T-Bird as "Possibly the best luxury car buy in the world today."

No drastic product changes were made. The T-Bird came only as a roomy two-door hardtop on the same chassis as before. It had a cavernous trunk. Seventeen exterior colors were offered and seven were optional Starfire finishes. Odense grain or Creme Normande grain vinyl roofs were standard. Four styles of wheel covers were available: Base, Deluxe (not available with Luxury groups), simulated wire (included with Bordeaux and Lipstick Red Luxury groups) and deep-dish aluminum wheels (included with the Crème and Gold Luxury package). Buyers of the latter could swap the aluminum wheels for the simulated wire wheels and receive a credit.

Silky Aurora nylon cloth-and-vinyl trim was standard on the deep-cushioned split-bench seats. The interior included assist straps, burled walnut wood-tone appliqués and plush cut-pile carpeting. Kasman cloth trim, which had the look and feel of cashmere, was optional in four colors. T-Bird buyers could also pick from super-soft vinyl trims in 11 single and two-tone combinations or over a dozen optional trims featuring genuine leather seating surfaces. A new Lipstick Red and White Luxury group, as listed in the *1976 Color & Trim* book, had a Lipstick Red Normande grain half-vinyl roof with Lipstick Red exterior finish. Also featured in this package were color-keyed body-side, border, and back window moldings and color-keyed paint and tape

stripes. White with Lipstick Red accents were available in both vinyl or vinyl-and-leather interiors. If the buyer wanted the optional Silver moonroof, a color-keyed full vinyl roof was required.

A "feature car" for 1976 was the T-Bird with a Lipstick Red Luxury group that included the same Lipstick Red exterior color, but came with a Bright Red Odense grain vinyl half-top, color-keyed border and wide body moldings, dual body and hood paint stripes, wire wheel covers, White leather seating surfaces or White super-soft vinyl upholstery, Red and White door trim panels, color-keyed interior components, 24-oz. cut-pile carpeting, and color-keyed luggage compartment trim. The Bordeaux luxury package included Bordeaux Starfire exterior finish, a Dark Red or Silver Odense grain vinyl half-top, color-keyed border and wide body side moldings, dual body and hood paint stripes, wire wheel covers, rich Red leather or plush Red velour Media cloth seats, color-keyed interior components, 24-oz. cut-pile carpeting and a color-keyed luggage compartment.

The Creme and Gold luxury group was an ultra-luxurious option. It included Gold Starfire glamour paint on the body sides, Creme paint on the hood, deck and front half of the roof, unique double tape stripes along the upper fender edges, a fully padded Gold Odense grain half-vinyl roof, color-keyed border moldings, wide Creme body-side moldings, Gold Thunderbird emblems in the opera

BODY COLOR INFORMATION (EARLY)

Color Name	Code	Color Name	Code
Black	1C	Dark Brown (Metallic)	5Q
Silver Starfire*	1J	Creme	6P
Dark Red	2M	Tan	6U
Bordeaux Starfire*	2S	Gold Starfire*	6Y
Lipstick Red	2U	Light Jade (Metallic)**	7A
Dark Blue (Metallic)	3G	Medium Jade (Metallic)*	7F
Blue Starfire*	3P	Polar White	9D
Silver Blue Starfire*	3R	Dark Jade (Metallic)	46
Light Blue	3S	Cinnamon Starfire*	51

* Optional at extra cost.
** During the model-run Light Jade Starfire (7B) was added and Light Jade 7A was deleted.

BODY COLOR INFORMATION (LATE)

Color Name	Code	Color Name	Code
Black	1C	Dark Brown (Metallic)	5Q
Silver Starfire*	1J	Creme	6P
Dark Red	2M	Tan	6U
Bordeaux Starfire*	2S	Gold Starfire*	6Y
Lipstick Red	2U	Light Jade **	7A
Dark Blue Metallic	3G	Jade Starfire*	7F
Blue Starfire*	3P	Polar White	9D
Light Blue	3S	Dark Jade (Metallic)	46
Silver Blue Starfire*	3R	Cinnamon Starfire*	51

* Optional at extra cost.
** Light Jade is crossed out in some factory literature and may have been discontinued late in the year.

STANDARD AURORA CLOTH AND VINYL INTERIOR TRIM INFORMATION

Seat Type	Black	Medium Blue	Medium Jade	Saddle
Split Bench	HA	HB	HR	HZ

KASMAN CLOTH AND VINYL INTERIOR TRIM INFORMATION

Seat Type	Medium Blue	Red	Jade	Gold	Saddle w/ Tan
Split Bench	FB	FD	FR	FY	FZ

OPTIONAL SUPER-SOFT VINYL INTERIOR TRIM INFORMATION

Seat Type	Black	Blue	Red	White w/ Red	White w/ Med Blue	Jade
Split Bench	JA	JB	JD	JN	JQ	JR

Seat Type	White w/ Black	White w/ Gold	Saddle w/ Tan	White w/ Jade	White w/ Saddle
Split Bench	JW	JY	JZ	J5	J9

OPTIONAL LEATHER AND VINYL TRIM INFORMATION

Seat Type	Black	Medium Blue	Dark Red	White w/ Dk Red	White w/ Md Blue	Jade	White w/ Black
Split Bench	KA	KB	KD	KN	KQ	KR	KW

Seat Type	Gold	Saddle w/ Tan	White w/ Jade	White W/ Saddle	Red Bordeaux Luxury	Crème-Gold Luxury
Split Bench	KY	KZ	K5	K9	RD	RY

SPECIAL EDITION LUXURY GROUP INTERIOR TRIM INFORMATION

	Crème-Gold Luxury Group	Bordeaux Luxury Group	Lipstick Luxury Group
Paint:	Gold Starfire and Crème	Bordeaux Starfire	Lipstick Red
Striping:	Unique beltline striping	Dual body and hood	Dual body and hood
Trim:	Crème/Gold Leather/ Gold Media Cloth	Red Leather/ Red Media Cloth	White Leather or SS Vinyl
Dash:	Gold appliqué	NA	NA
Roof:	Gold Odense Grain Vinyl	Dk Red or Silver Odense Grain	Bright Red Odense Grain
Other:	Crème body-side moldings	Color-key wide body moldings	Color-key wide body moldings
	Gold T-Bird insignia in opera window	Color-key components	Color-key components
Wheels:	Deep-Dish Aluminum	Simulated wire wheel covers	Simulated wire wheel covers
Trunk:	Dress-up Trim	Deluxe trim	Deluxe trim
Carpet:	24-oz. color-keyed cut-pile	24-oz. color-keyed cut-pile	24-oz. color-keyed cut-pile

VINYL TOP INFORMATION

Black	Blue	Dark Red	Bright Red	Silver	Dark Jade	Brown	Creme
A	B	D	N	P	R	T	V

Three types of vinyl tops were offered: G=Odense Grain full vinyl top, H=Odense Grain half vinyl top on Luxury Groups only and L=Mormande full vinyl in Crème color only. A full vinyl top was mandatory with sunroof or moonroof.

THUNDERBIRD PRODUCTION

Model Number	Body/Style Number	Body Type & Seating	Factory Price	Shipping Weight	Production Total
76	5K	2d Hardtop-4P	$7,790	4,808 lbs.	52,935

windows, and deep-dish aluminum wheels. Interior touches included Creme and Gold leather seating or plush Gold velour Media cloth trim, a gold instrument panel appliqué, color-keyed 24-oz. cut-pile carpeting and a luggage compartment dress-up package.

Under the T-Bird's hood was a huge 7.5-liter V-8 with a four-barrel carburetor. Road testers were able to chirp the tires with this engine and Cruise-O-Matic transmission.

STANDARD EQUIPMENT

460-cid V-8, solid-state ignition, SelectShift Cruise-O-Matic transmission, power steering, power front disc brakes, manual SelectAire Conditioning, automatic parking brake release, AM radio with driver and front passenger door speakers, power window lifts, heavy-duty 61-amp alternator, burled walnut wood-tone interior appliqués, inside hood release, power ventilation system, door courtesy lights, under panel light, glove box light, front ashtray light, individually-adjustable split-bench seat with dual folding center armrest, Aurora cloth-and-vinyl upholstery, electric clock, 24-oz. cut-pile carpeting, color-keyed deluxe safety belts, sound insulation, Odense Grain full vinyl roof, opera windows with T-Bird emblems, remote-control left-hand outside rearview mirror, stand-up hood ornament, hood rear edge molding, door belt molding, bright drip rail moldings, bright body-side moldings with color-keyed vinyl inserts, partial wheel opening moldings, Deluxe bumper group (including front and rear bumper guards with white insert strips), steel-belted radial white sidewall tires, and full wheel covers.

I.D. NUMBERS

VIN stamped on aluminum tab riveted to dashboard on passenger side and observable through the windshield from outside the car. Prefix indicates manufacturer: F=Ford. First symbol denotes model-year: 6=1976. Second symbol denotes the assembly plant: Y=Wixom (Novi), Michigan and J=Los Angeles, California. Third symbol denotes the car-line: 8=T-Bird. Fourth symbol denotes body type: 7=Two-door hardtop. Fifth symbol denotes engine: A=460-cid/202-hp Thunderbird V-8. Sixth thru 11th symbols denote sequential production number of specific vehicle starting at 100001. Suffix: Denotes manufacturer, F=Ford. Body certification label located on rear face of driver's door. The top part of the label indicates that the T-Bird was manufactured by Ford Motor Company. Directly below this is the month and year of manufacture, plus a statement that the car conforms to federal motor vehicle safety standard in effect on the indicated date of manufacture. The VIN appears first on the first line of encoded information. It matches the 1st to 11th symbols on VIN tag. "PASSENGER" now appears to the right of the VIN to denote passenger vehicle. The body style code now appears on the far left-hand side of the second line of encoded information. The only Thunderbird code for this model-year is: 65K=2-door hardtop. The color and vinyl roof type/color code appears to the right of the body style code in the second position on the second line of encoded information. See table below. The trim code appears to the right of the color and vinyl roof codes in the third position on the second line of encoded information. See table below. The transmission code appears to the right of the trim code in the fourth position on the second line of encoded information: U=XPL C6 three-speed automatic, Z=XPL C6 Special three-speed automatic. The axle code appears to the right of the transmission code in the fifth position on the second line of encoded information: K=2.75:1 limited-slip, L=2.79:1 limited-slip, M=3.18:1 limited-slip, N=3.07:1 limited-slip, O=3.00:1 limited-slip, P=3.40:1 limited-slip, R=3.25:1 limited slip. The District Special Equipment code appears to the right of the transmission code in the far right-hand position on the second line of encoded information. (Note: The abbreviations VIN/BDY/CLR/TRM/TR/AX/DSO do not appear on the certification label itself. The specific application of the codes is determined by where they are located on the vehicle certification label.)

ENGINE

THUNDERBIRD 460 FOUR-BARREL V-8: Overhead valve. Cast-iron block. Displacement: 429 cid. Bore and stroke: 4.36 x 3.85 in. Compression ratio: 8.50:1. Brake hp: 202 at 3800 rpm. Torque: 352 lbs.-ft. at 1600 rpm. Five main bearings. Hydraulic valve lifters. Carburetor: Four-barrel Motorcraft 9510 or Ford 4350A 9510. Cooling system capacity: 18.8 qt. with heater. Crankcase capacity: 5 qt. (add 1 qt. with new oil filter). Dual exhaust. Code A.

CHASSIS

Wheelbase: 120.4 in. Overall length: 225.7. Overall width: 79.7. Overall height: 52.8 in. Trunk volume: 13.9 cu. ft. Front tread: 63 in. Rear tread: 63.1 in. Tires: JR78-15 steel-belted radial. Steering: Integral with power-assist. Turning diameter: 43 ft. Front suspension: Coil springs, stabilizer, shocks and axial strut. Rear suspension: Coil spring, shocks and stabilizer. Steering: Integral power-assist. Standard rear axle: 3.00:1. Front brakes: Power disc. Rear brakes: Power drum. Fuel tank capacity: 26.5 gal.

OPTIONS

Bordeaux luxury group ($624-$700). Créme and Gold luxury group ($717-$793). Lipstick luxury group ($337-$546). Turnpike group ($180). Convenience group including remote-control right-hand outside rearview mirror, interval windshield wipers and automatic seatback release ($84). Protection group including: front and rear color-keyed floor mats with carpet inserts, license plate frames, door edge guards, spare tire cover, and rocker panel moldings ($79 without rocker panel molding or $87 with). Light group including: Autolamp On/Off delay system, passenger lighted visor-vanity mirror, dual overhead map/dome lights, engine compartment light, low fuel and door ajar warning lights, headlamps-on alert buzzer, and automatic headlamp dimmer ($164). Power lock group including electric door locks and trunk opener ($86). Security lock group including locking gas cap, spare tire lock and lockable inside hood release ($18). Automatic temperature control air conditioning ($488). Anti-theft alarm system ($84). Electric rear defroster ($99). Electric windshield/rear window defroster ($355). Fingertip speed control ($120). Tinted glass ($29-$66). Power mini-vent windows ($79). Power 6-way power driver's seat ($132). Power 6-way driver and passenger seat ($250). Power lumbar support seats ($86). Manual reclining passenger seat ($70). Automatic seat back release ($30). Tilt steering wheel ($68). Fuel monitor warning light ($20). Front cornering lamps ($43). Lighted driver's visor vanity mirror ($43). AM/FM stereo radio ($145). AM/FM stereo radio with tape player ($249). AM/FM stereo radio with search function ($298). AM/FM quadrosonic radio with tape player ($382). Power antenna ($32). Power-operated glass moonroof in Gold, Silver, Brown or Rose ($879). Power-operated sunroof ($716). Starfire Glamour paint ($204). Wide color-keyed vinyl insert body-side moldings ($121). Dual body-side and hood paint stripes ($33). Leather seat trim ($239). Kasman cloth seat trim ($96). Super-soft vinyl seat trim ($55). Trunk dress-up package ($59). Deluxe wheel covers ($67). Simulated wire wheel covers, except with Gold and Créme package ($88). Simulated wire wheel covers (with Gold and Créme package $163 credit). Deep-dish aluminum wheels, except with Bordeaux/Lipstick groups ($251). Deep-dish aluminum wheels with Bordeaux/Lipstick groups ($163). JR78 x 15 steel-belted radial whitewall tires ($41). LR78 x 15 steel-belted radial wide white sidewall tires ($59). Space-Saver spare tires ($86). Optional axle ratio ($14). Traction-Lok axle ($55). Four-wheel disc brakes ($184). Sure-Track brake control system, includes four-wheel disc brakes ($378). Dual exhaust system ($72). Engine block heater ($18). Heavy-duty suspension ($29).

EQUIPMENT INSTALLATION RATES

Automatic transmission (100 percent). Standard V-8 engine (100 percent). AM radio (7.4 percent). AM/FM radio (44.6 percent). Stereo tape player (48 percent). Power steering (100 percent). Power front disc brakes (100 percent). Power door locks (79.1 percent.) Power seat (90.7 percent). Power windows (100 percent). Reclining seats (76.1 percent). Adjustable steering column (82.3 percent). Tinted glass (97 percent). Vinyl top (100 percent). Sunroof (11.3 percent). Automatic temperature control: (49.9 percent). Manual air conditioning (50.1 percent). Limited-slip axle (7.2 percent). Standard steel-belted radial whitewall tires (100 percent). Standard wheel covers (20.3 percent). Optional wheel covers (61.4 percent). Styled wheels (18.3 percent). Speed control (85.4 percent). Clock (100 percent). Rear window defogger (57.8 percent). Remote-control left-hand rearview mirror (100 percent). Remote-control right-hand rearview mirror (82.9 percent). Reclining front seats (76.1 percent). Dual exhausts: (43.7 percent). (Note: Based on 47,949 units produced in the model year for the U.S. market only.)

HISTORICAL FOOTNOTES

The 1976 T-Bird was introduced on October 3, 1975. Henry Ford II (chairman) and. Lee A. Iaccoca (president) again held the top two corporate positions at Ford Motor Company. W.P. Benton was Ford Division's vice president and general manager. W.J. Oben was general sales manager for the division.

The 1976 T-Bird was the last of the early- and mid-1970s "Big Birds." The following year, the car was restyled and downsized.

Calendar-year output was 106,962 units and included production of the all-new, down-sized 1977 T-Bird. A total of 52,935 T-Birds were produced in the model year. This represented 0.65 percent of the industry total. Of these units, 37,777 were made in Michigan and 15,158 were made in California. Calendar-year dealer sales amounted to 100,658 T-Birds, representing 1.2 percent of industry sales.

During late June and early July of 1976, the country was in a fever pitch with the Bicentennial Celebration theme. It was from this celebration that a "Commemorative" model T-Bird evolved. Only 32 of these cars were made. These cars had many special features and a sticker price of nearly $10,000.

Motor Trend's Tony Swan said that his deepest affection for the T-Bird surfaced while stuck in rush hour traffic jams or dashing across Interstate highways through Nebraska. He described the T-Bird as "a car for people who like to ride, not drive." It was the best-insulated and quietest car built by Ford at the time. The silence experienced in the interior helped to isolate the driver from his or her surroundings. The conclusion reached in *Motor*

Trend was: "Big Birds rank high in the lists of all-time opulent glamour boats and they're habit-forming in the extreme. They'll be missed." Other experts found the car's performance pretty good. Its recall history and repair record were also not all that bad. Overall reliability of the 1976 model was rated "better than average" by *Consumer Guide*. In his *Illustrated Thunderbird Buyer's Guide*, Ford expert Paul G. McLaughlin wrote, "The 1976 T-Birds were fine cars in their own right, but the time had come for them to take on a new image, an image more in tune with the needs of late-1970s society. The T-Birds that would follow were smaller, more agile, lighter and more performance-oriented. They'll never be more luxurious, though, because as far as luxury goes in a T-Bird package, the epitome was reached in 1976."

1976 THUNDERBIRD PERFORMANCE		
Model	CID/HP	Performance
0-60 mph		
Two-door hardtop	460/202	11.0 seconds
1/4-Mile		
Two-door Landau	460/202	17.4 seconds @ 79.5 mph

An exterior option package that accented the T-Bird's roof could be ordered on 1977 models. The front fender louvers were functional.

1977

Thunderbird

The all-new 1977 T-Bird was a mid-size—rather than full-size—luxury car with the same six-passenger accommodations as before. All new sheet metal and sharp styling hid the fact that the shrunken T-Bird was based on the Ford LTD II.

The car's profile was pleasantly different. A chrome wrap-over roof molding and small opera windows with beveled-glass decorated the "B" pillars, which separated the front door windows from large coach windows at the far rear end of the "greenhouse." Distinctive T-Bird features included concealed headlights (hidden behind large flip-up doors) and functional front fender louvers. The chrome crosshatch grille had the same design theme, but horizontal bars were more dominant. It had a bright surround and a lower edge designed to swing back, under impact, to avoid slow-speed collision damage. The parking and signal light lenses were notched into the front fender tips.

At the rear of the car were tall, full-width taillights and a sculptured deck lid. A Thunderbird nameplate dressed up the deck section that extended down between the taillights. A 302-cid (5.0-liter) V-8 with DuraSpark ignition was standard. California cars came with a cleaner-burning 351-cid V-8. Both 351- and 400-cid V-8s were optional in federal

(non-California) cars. To improve handling, the 1977 T-Bird had higher-rate springs, a larger front stabilizer bar and a standard rear stabilizer bar. There was less standard equipment overall, but a coolant recovery system was added.

The T-Bird interior featured bench seats with Wilshire cloth and vinyl upholstery. There was a new five-pod instrument cluster with European-type graphics. Instruments included an 85-mph speedometer, a trip odometer, a 0-6000-rpms tachometer, an amp gauge, a fuel gauge, a temperature gauge, an oil pressure gauge, and a clock. Warning lights were provided, as were directional signal and high-beam indicators. Other lights indicated when the hand brake was on, if the door was ajar, when the seat belts were in use and whether the rear defogger was being used. Simulated engine-turned trim or simulated burled wood-grain accents were used on the dashboard. The stitching pattern on the standard bench seat was brand new. A split-bench seat or bucket seats were optional. Also available was a front center console with twin storage bins.

An optional exterior décor package could be ordered to accent the T-Bird's roof. Also optional was an interior décor group option. It contained Ardmore and Kasman knit cloth

119

BODY COLOR INFORMATION (EARLY)

Color Name	Code	Color Name	Code
Black	1C	Creme	6P
Silver Metallic	1G	Bright Saddle Metallic	8K
Dove Gray	1N	Champagne Metallic	8Y
Dark Red	2M	Polar White	9D
Lipstick Red	2U	Rose Glow*	2Y
Dark Blue Metallic	3G	Burnt Blue Glow*	3V
Dark Jade Metallic	46	Light Jade Glow*	7L
Dark Brown Metallic	5Q	Chamois Glow*	8W

* Optional colors.

BODY COLOR INFORMATION (LATE)

Color Name	Code	Color Name	Code
Black	1C	Creme	6P
Silver Metallic	1G	Pastel Beige**	86
Dove Gray	1N	Champagne Metallic	8Y
Dark Red	2M	Bright Saddle Metallic	8K
Lipstick Red	2U	Polar White	9D
Dark Blue Metallic	3G	Rose Glow*	2Y
Dark Jade Metallic	46	Chamois Glow*	8W
Dark Brown Metallic	5Q		

* Optional colors.
** Unique to Town Landau.

upholstery choices, fold-down center armrests, a reclining passenger seat, a visor vanity mirror and color-keyed seat belts.

Two personalized versions of the T-Bird arrived in the spring. One was the Silver/Lipstick Feature Package and the other was an all-new T-Bird Town Landau. The Silver/Lipstick feature package was basically a paint and vinyl trim option. A flyer showed the base vehicle price of $5,063, and prices for three separate options (vinyl roof at $132, interior décor group at $299, and all-vinyl trim at $22). They added up to $5,516. However, the same flyer also noted that a vinyl roof was not required, so you could get a Silver or Lipstick car with an all-steel roof for as little as $5,384. It's doubtful that many (if any) were ordered without a vinyl roof, which was a popular feature. The décor package's actual content included a Silver Metallic exterior color or Lipstick Red exterior color. Both were usually combined with a vinyl roof in a choice of the matching or contrasting color. This added up to six combinations, since buyers could get either color of paint without a vinyl top or with a choice of a Silver or Lipstick Red vinyl top. You also got a Dove Gray all-vinyl interior with a choice of a split bench seat or bucket seats up front. This interior featured Lipstick Red accent straps and belts, Dove Gray door and quarter trim with Lipstick Red carpets, moldings, and components, plus Dove Gray trim above the belt line. This package could be teamed with all other T-Bird regular production options, except leather seat trims and Tu-tone paint treatments.

The Town Landau was a separate model.

STANDARD EQUIPMENT

1977 Thunderbird: All standard FoMoCo safety, anti-theft, convenience items, and emissions control equipment, 302-cid two-barrel V-8 (or 352-cid/149-hp V-8 in California), DuraSpark ignition system, SelectShift automatic transmission, power steering, power front disc/rear drum brakes, HR78 x 15 black sidewall belted radial tires, chrome-plated swing-away grille, fender louvers, concealed two-speed windshield wipers, wiper-mounted washer jets, coolant recovery system, inside hood release, concealed headlights, full-width taillights, opera windows, dual note

INTERIOR TRIM INFORMATION

Seat Type	Material	Blue	Red	Jade	Dove Gray	Cham.	Saddle	White/Blue
Standard								
Bench Seat	Cloth & Vinyl	AB	AD	AR	AS	AT	AZ	—
Bench Seat	All-vinyl	BB	BD	BR	BS	BT	BZ	—
Bucket Seats	Cloth & Vinyl	HB	HD	HR	HS	HT	HZ	—
Bucket Seats	All-vinyl	CB	CD	CR	CS	CT	CZ	CQ
Décor Group								
Bucket Seats	Cloth & Vinyl	JB	JD	JR	JS	JT	JZ	—
Bucket Seats	All-vinyl	GB	GD	GR	GS	GT	GZ	GQ
Split-Bench	Cloth & Vinyl	DB	DD	DR	DS	DT	DZ	—
Split-Bench	All-vinyl	EB	ED	ER	ES	ET	EZ	—
Split-Bench	Leather/vinyl	FB	FD	FR	FS	FT	FZ	FQ
Interior Luxury Group								
Split-Bench	Velour Cloth	RB	RD	RR	RS	RT	RZ	
Split-Bench	US Leather -vinyl	SB	SD	SR	SS	ST	SZ	
Town Landau & Luxury Interior								
Split-Bench	Velour Cloth	RB	RD	RR	RS	RT	RZ	
Split-Bench	US Leather-vinyl	SB	SR	SS	ST	SZ	SQ	

Seat Type	Material	W. & Red	W. & Jade	W. & Cham.	W. & Saddle	Saddle & W.	W. & Lipstick
Standard							
Bucket Seats	All-vinyl	CN	C5	C2	C9	C3	—
Décor Group							
Bucket Seats	All-vinyl	G5	G2	G9	G3	—	—
Split-Bench	All-Vinyl	EN	E5	E2	E9	E3	EL
Split-Bench	Leather/vinyl	FN	F5	F2	F9	F3	FL
Town Landau & Luxury Interior							
Split-Bench	US Leather-vinyl	SN	S5	S2	S9	SL	—

Legend: W. means White. Cham. means Chamois. US Leather-vinyl means Ultra-Soft leather and vinyl.

THUNDERBIRD PRODUCTION

Model Number	Body/Style Number	Body Type & Seating	Factory Price	Shipping Weight	Production Total
THUNDERBIRD - (V-8)					
87	60H	2d Hardtop-4P	$5,063	3,907 lbs.	Note 1
THUNDERBIRD TOWN LANDAU - (V-8)					
87	60H	2d Hardtop-4P	$7,990	4,104 lbs.	Note 1

NOTE 1: Production of both models combined was 318,140.

horn, bright rocker panel moldings, bright wheel lip moldings, full wheel covers, bright window, door belt, and roof drip moldings, heater and defroster, full-flow ventilation, deluxe steering wheel, day/night mirror, bench seats, carpeting, instrument panel with wood-tone appliqués, inside hood release, and cigar lighter. **1977 1/2 Thunderbird Town Landau:** Most of the features above, with these differences or additions: Brushed aluminum roof wrap-over appliqué, color-keyed roof cross-over moldings (when optional vinyl top is ordered), color-coordinated translucent hood ornament insert, four cast aluminum wheels with accent paint, opera windows with a Town Landau insignia, accent stripes on body-sides, hood, and grille opening panel, deck lid, headlight doors, and fender

One of the most noticeable differences in the 1977 T-Bird was its hidden headlights. The car also sported new sheet metal, a slightly different grille, and different overall dimensions.

louvers, whitewall steel-belted radial tires, wide color-keyed vinyl insert body-side moldings with partial wheel lip moldings, front cornering lamps, deluxe bumper group (including front and rear bumper guards and horizontal rub strips), a luxury sound insulation package, Town Landau insignia on instrument panel appliqué, 22-karat gold finish plaque engraved with owner's name, 6-way power driver's seat, power side windows, power lock group (including door locks and remote trunk release), manual-control SelectAire Conditioner, Interior luxury group including convenience group (with left- and right-hand remote control mirrors, interval windshield wipers, automatic parking brake release, and trip odometer) and light group (with dual-beam map lights, under-dash lights, glove box light, ashtray light, trunk light, engine compartment light, door ajar light, and headlights on light), tinted glass, AM/FM stereo search radio (with twin front door mounted speakers and dual rear speakers), and a tilt steering wheel.

I.D. NUMBERS

VIN stamped on aluminum tab riveted to dashboard on passenger side and observable through the windshield from outside the car. Prefix indicates manufacturer: F=Ford. First symbol denotes model-year: 7=1977. Second symbol denotes the assembly plant: G=Chicago, Illinois and J=Los Angeles, California. Third symbol denotes the car-line: 8=T-Bird. Fourth symbol denotes body type: 7=two-door hardtop. Fifth symbol denotes engine: F=302-cid (5.0L)/130- to 137-hp V-8, H=351-cid (5.8L)/149-hp V-8, Q=Modified 351-cid (5.8L)/152-hp V-8, S=400-cid (6.6L)/173-hp V-8. Sixth thru 11th symbols denote sequential production number of specific vehicle starting at 100001. Suffix: Denotes manufacturer, F=Ford. Body certification label located on rear face of driver's door. The top part of the label indicates that the Thunderbird was manufactured by Ford Motor Company. Directly below this is the month and year of manufacture, plus a statement that the car conforms to federal motor vehicle safety standard in effect on the indicated date of manufacture. The VIN appears first on the first line of encoded information. It matches the 1st to 11th symbols on VIN tag. PASSENGER appears to the right of the VIN to denote passenger vehicle. The body style code now appears on the far left-hand side of the second line of encoded information. The only Thunderbird code for this model year is: 60H=2-door pillared hardtop. The color and vinyl roof type/color code appears to the right of the body style code in the second position on the second line of encoded information. The trim code appears to the right of the color and vinyl roof codes in the third position on the second line of encoded information. The transmission code appears to the right of the trim code in the fourth position on the second line of encoded information. The axle code appears to the right of the transmission code in the fifth position on the second line of encoded information. The District Special Equipment code appears to the right of the transmission code in the far right-hand position on the second line of encoded information. (Note: The abbreviations VIN/BDY/-CLR/TRM/TR/AX/DSO do not appear on the certification label itself. The specific application of the codes is determined by where they are located on the vehicle certification label.)

ENGINE

THUNDERBIRD BASE V-8 (FEDERAL): 90-degree. Overhead valve. Cast-iron block and head. Displacement: 302 cid (5.0 liters). Bore and stroke: 4.00 x 3.00 in. Compression ratio: 8.4:1. Brake hp: 130-137 at 3400-3600 rpm. Torque: 243-245 lbs.-ft. at 1600-1800 rpm. Five main bearings. Hydraulic valve lifters. Carburetor: Motorcraft 2150 two-barrel. Serial number code: F.

THUNDERBIRD BASE V-8 (CALIFORNIA): 90-degree. Overhead valve. Cast iron block and head. Displacement: 351 cid (5.8 liters). Bore and stroke: 4.00 x 3.50 in. Compression ratio: 8.3:1. Brake hp: 149 at 3200 rpm. Torque: 291 lbs.-ft. at 1600 rpm. Five main bearings. Hydraulic valve lifters. Carburetor: Motorcraft 2150 two-barrel. Windsor engine. Serial number code: H.

THUNDERBIRD OPTIONAL V-8 (FEDERAL): 90-degree. Overhead valve. Cast-iron block and head. Displacement: 351 cid (5.8 liters). Bore and stroke: 4.00 x 3.50 in. Compression ratio: 8.0:1. Brake hp: 161 at 3600 rpm. Torque: 285 lbs.-ft. at 1800 rpm. Five main bearings. Hydraulic valve lifters. Carburetor: Motorcraft 2150 two-barrel. Windsor engine. Serial number code: Q.

THUNDERBIRD OPTIONAL V-8 (FEDERAL): 90-dgree. Overhead valve. Cast-iron block and head. Displacement: 400 cu. in (6.6 liters). Bore and stroke: 4.00 x 4.00 in. Compression ratio: 8:0.1. Brake hp: 173 at 3800 rpm. Torque: 326 lbs. at 1600 rpm. Five main bearings. Hydraulic valve lifters. Carburetor: Motorcraft 2150 two-barrel. Serial number code: S.

CHASSIS

Wheelbase: 114 in. Overall length: 215.5. Overall width: 78.5. Overall height: 53 in. Front headroom: 37.3 in. Front legroom: 42.1 in. Rear headroom: 36.2 in. Rear legroom: 32.6 in. Trunk capacity: 15.6 cu. ft. Front tread: 63.2 in. Rear tread: 63.1 in. Wheels: 15 x 6.5 in. Tires: H78-15 steel-belted radial. Steering: Integral with power-assist. Steering ratio: 21.9:1. Turning diameter: 43.1 ft. Front suspension: Independent, upper and lower control arms, coil springs, tubular shocks and anti-roll bar. Rear suspension: Live axle, four-link control arms, coil springs, tubular shocks, anti-roll bar. Steering: Recirculating ball, power-assist. Standard rear axle: 2.50:1. Weight distribution: 57/43. Front brakes:

Power vented disc. Rear brakes: Power drum. Brakes swept area: 372.3 sq. in. Fuel tank capacity: 21 gal.

OPTIONS

351-cid/161-hp V-8 engine ($66). 400-cid V-8 engine ($155). Manual air conditioner ($505). Automatic air conditioner in base Hardtop ($546). Automatic air conditioner in Town Landau or Diamond Jubilee (N/A) Heavy-duty 90-amp alternator ($45). Optional ratio axle ($14). Traction-Lok differential axle ($54). Heavy-duty 77-amp. battery ($17). Color-keyed deluxe seat belts ($18). Front license plate bracket (no charge). Deluxe bumper group ($72). Day and date clock ($20). Convenience group for models with bucket seat and floor shift ($88), for other models ($96). Front cornering lights ($43). Exterior décor group for models with convenience group or interior luxury group ($317), for other models ($368). Interior décor group ($299). Electric rear window defroster ($87). California emissions equipment ($70). Illuminated entry system ($51). Complete tinted glass ($61). High-altitude equipment ($22). Instrumentation group for Sports models with convenience group ($103), for other models ($111). Light group ($46). Power lock group ($92). Interior luxury group ($724). Dual sport mirrors from models with convenience or interior luxury groups (no charge), for other models ($51). Remote-control left OSRV chrome mirror ($14). Illuminated right-hand visor-vanity mirror for models with interior décor group ($42), for other models ($46). Black vinyl insert body-side moldings ($39). Bright wide body-side moldings ($39). Color-keyed wide body-side moldings ($51). Power moonroof ($888). Metallic glow paint ($62). Protection group for models with front license plate bracket ($47), for other models ($43). AM/FM manual radio ($59). AM/FM stereo radio ($120). AM/FM stereo search radio ($276). AM/FM radio with quadrosonic tape player in base hardtop ($326), in Town Landau ($50). AM/FM stereo with tape player ($193). Two-piece vinyl roof ($132). Six-way power full-width front seat ($143). Six-way power driver's seat only ($143). Bucket seats and console with interior décor group (no charge), all others ($158). Automatic seatback release ($52). Space Saver spare tire (no charge to $13 credit, depending on type of tires). Dual rear seat speakers ($43). Fingertip speed control in models with sports instrumentation group or interior luxury group ($93), all other models ($114). Leather steering wheel in models with sports instrumentation group ($39), all other models ($61). Tilt steering wheel ($63). Handling suspension ($79). Dual accent paint stripes ($39). Heavy-duty trailer towing package ($138). Leather seat trim ($241). Vinyl seat trim ($22). Tu-Tone paint treatment ($49). Wire wheel covers with exterior décor group ($47 credit), other models ($99). Four turbine-spoke cast aluminum wheels, with exterior décor group ($88), all other models ($234). Power side windows ($114). AM radio delete ($72 credit). Tire options (followed by extra charge for models having five HR78 x 15 steel-belted black sidewall tires as standard equipment): HR78 x 15 radial whitewalls ($45 extra), HR78 x 15 radial white band whitewalls ($61 extra), and HR70 x 17 white oval whitewalls ($67 extra).

EQUIPMENT INSTALLATION RATES

Automatic transmission (100 percent). Standard V-8 engine (17.5 percent). Optional V-8 engine (82.5 percent). AM radio: (35.7 percent). AM/FM radio (5.8 percent). Stereo tape player (36.6 percent). Radio with tape player (25.3

percent). Power steering (100 percent). Power front disc brakes (100 percent). Power door locks (29.1 percent.) Power seat (33.9 percent). Power windows (43.5 percent). Adjustable steering column (44.5 percent). Tinted windshield only (2.7 percent). All tinted glass (93 percent). Vinyl top: (89.6 percent). Sunroof (4.2 percent). Automatic air conditioning (14 percent). Manual air conditioning (81.4 percent). Limited-slip axle (3.5 percent). Standard steel-belted radial tires (100 percent). Electric rear window defogger (36.1 percent). Standard wheel covers (66 percent). Optional wheel covers (28.2 percent). Styled wheels: (5.8 percent). Rear window defogger (67.7 percent). Remote-control left-hand rearview mirror (90.8 percent). Remote-control right-hand rearview mirror (82.9 percent). Reclining front seats (25 percent). Analog clock (73.1 percent). Digital clock (26.9 percent). Speed control (51.2 percent). (Note: Based on 295,779 units produced in the model year for the U.S. market only.)

HISTORICAL FOOTNOTES

The 1977 T-Bird was introduced on September 30, 1976. Henry Ford II (chairman) and Lee A. Iacocca (president) again held the top two corporate positions at Ford Motor Company.

Demand for T-Birds soared and Ford scrambled to keep up with a six-fold increase in production. Calendar-year output was 365,986 units. A total of 318,144 T-Birds were produced in the model year. This represented 3.49 percent of the industry total. Of these units, 235,884 were made in Chicago and 82,256 were made in Los Angeles. Calendar-year dealer sales amounted to 325,153 T-Birds, representing 3.6 percent of industry sales.

"New Ford Thunderbird: The Best in 15 Years," announced the cover of the April 1977 issue of *Road Test* magazine. The magazine explained that Ford had made the right decision by taking the T-Bird "off the hill of the custom built homes" and rolling it down the road "where it can punch it out with all the Monte Carlos, Grand Prixs, Cordobas and Cougars." The magazine was loaned a Sport version of the T-Bird with a 400-cid V-8 that averaged 17 mpg. While summing up the T-Bird's appearance as "practically every styling cliché known to civilized Western man," the magazine stressed how much T-Bird buyers were getting for the car's now-more-affordable price tag. It said that the car was "qualitatively no different" than a Mercury Cougar. "But in a market where you sell quantity, this new T-Bird is a lot of car," the testers concluded. "You can roll that thing into your driveway and the whole neighborhood can tell it says Thunderbird."

On a scale of 0 to 100, *Road Test* rated acceleration at 79 points. The brakes were scored 89 points. Handling warranted 73 points. Interior noise levels (92 points) and tire reserve (100 points) where the highest-rated categories. Fuel economy got 30 points. Overall, the 1977 T-Bird earned 76 points. This was only two to three points under the three best cars that had been tested, which were the VW Super Scirocco, the Saab EMS, and the Porsche Turbo Carrera.

From a contemporary buyer's standpoint, these cars were a vast improvement over the "Big 'Birds" of the past few years, in terms of maneuverability and economy. The cars had no major mechanical problems, but the bodies of the 1977 models proved very prone to rust. The 1978 and 1979 editions had improved rust protection. Cars of 1977 vintage with tilt steering were also the subject of a recall, since some had been built with Ford truck tilt steering parts. This caused some of the cars to start with the gear selector in neutral.

While these T-Birds lack the degree of distinction from other Ford products that earlier T-Birds reflected, they were tremendously well received by the car-buying public and T-Bird production saw a huge increase. The Los Angeles assembly plant put together more 'Birds than it had in the last three years combined. This was over twice as many T-Birds as had ever been made there in a single year. The grand total of 318,144 T-Birds in the model year, over 60,000 higher than Ford had built in the first six years of the T-Bird's history. Of these, 295,779 were made for the U.S. market and the rest were shipped to Canada and other countries.

1977 THUNDERBIRD PERFORMANCE		
Model	CID/HP	Performance
0-60 mph		
Hardtop	402/173	10.3 seconds
1/4-Mile		
Hardtop	402/173	17.7 seconds @ 78.6 mph
Top Speed		
Hardtop	402/173	110 mph

Ford photo

The T-roof convertible option was a midyear addition for the 1978 Thunderbird.

1978 *Thunderbird*

Ford added T-Bird emblems to the headlight doors in 1978. Six new body colors, four added vinyl roof colors, bold striped cloth bucket seat trim, and a new Russet interior option were promoted. Technical improvements included a more efficient torque converter, a new lighter-weight battery, revisions to the engine air induction system, and a new lighter-weight power steering pump with quick-disconnect hydraulic fittings.

A T-roof convertible option was a midyear innovation. However, the biggest news of the year was the limited-availability Diamond Jubilee Edition commemorating Ford's 75th year of making cars. New options included a power radio antenna and a 40-channel CB radio.

The 302-cid V-8 was again base engine. A slightly hotter "modified" version of the 351-cid V-8 with a four-barrel carburetor, plus the 400-cid (actually 402 cid) two-barrel V-8 remained optional. The base engine provided about 15.1 mpg on average. The 351 used as standard equipment in California cars averaged around 14.1 mpg. The more powerful version of the 351-cid V-8 was good for about 13.6 mpg overall. The larger 400-cid engine averaged around 12.8 mpg.

T-Birds came with deep-cushioned bench seats wearing knit-cloth-and-vinyl trim. Heavy carpeting, full-length door armrests and burled walnut wood tone accents gave even

the base model a rich look inside. Optional bucket seats came in all-vinyl or cloth and vinyl. An interior décor package with special door panels was a separate option. A front split-bench seat was included with the Town Landau model and the interior luxury group option. It came with either standard velour cloth trim or optional Ultra-Soft leather-and-vinyl trim and both included interior décor type door trim panels. The Diamond Jubilee Edition T-Bird featured an interior done in one of two exclusive colors of luxury cloth with a split bench style front seat.

New this year was a sports décor option that added a bold grille with blacked-out vertical bars, unique imitation deck lid straps, paint stripes, twin remote sport mirrors, spoke-style road wheels, HR70 x 15 raised white letter tires, polycoated Chamois color paint and a tan vinyl roof with color-keyed rear window moldings. The Thunderbird Town Landau returned in 1978 and came in 14 body colors. Crushed velour upholstery and a split-bench seat with fold-down center armrest were part of the Town Landau interior package.

Billed as "the most exclusive Thunderbird you can buy," the $10,106 Diamond Jubilee anniversary model included several items never before offered on a Thunderbird. It had an exclusive monochromatic exterior done in Diamond Blue Metallic or Ember Metallic paint. Diamond Blue models had blue luxury cloth upholstery.

BODY COLOR INFORMATION

Color Name	Code	Color Name	Code
Black	1C	Russet Metallic	81
Silver Metallic	1G	Light Chamois*	83
Dove Gray	1N	Pastel Beige	86
Dark Midnight Blue	3A	Champagne Metallic**	8Y
Light Blue**	3U	White	9D
Dark Jade Metallic	46	Burnt Blue Glow (Opt.)**	3V
Ember Metallic**	5Y	Light Jade Glow (Opt.)**	7L
Dark Brown Metallic	5Q	Chamois Glow (Opt.)**	8W

* Available on Town Landau only.
** Not available on Town Landau.

DIAMOND JUBILEE EDITION COLOR INFORMATION

Color Name	Code	Color Name	Code
Diamond Blue	3E	Ember Metallic	5Y

INTERIOR TRIM INFORMATION

Seat Type	Material	Blue	Russet	Jade	Dove Gray	Cham.	Saddle	White w/ Blue
Standard								
Bench Seat	Cloth & Vinyl	AB	AE	AR	AS	AT	AZ	—
Bench Seat	All-vinyl	RR	RF	BR	BS	BT	BZ	—
Bucket Seats	Cloth & Vinyl	HB	HE	HR	HS	HT	HZ	—
Bucket Seats	All-vinyl	CB	CE	CR	CS	CT	CZ	CQ
Décor Group								
Bucket Seats	Cloth & Vinyl	JB	JE	JR	JS	JT	JZ	—
Bucket Seats	All-vinyl	GB	GE	GR	GS	GT	GZ	GQ
Town Landau & Luxury Interior								
Split-Bench	Velour Cloth	RB	RE	RR	RS	RT	RZ	—
Split-Bench	US Leather-vinyl	SB	SE	SR	SS	ST	SZ	—
Diamond Jubilee Edition								
Split-Bench	Luxury Cloth	TB	TT	—	—	—	—	—

Seat Type	Material	W. & Russet	W. & Jade	W. & Cham.	W. & Saddle
Standard					
Bench Seat	Cloth & Vinyl	—	—	A2	—
Bucket Seats	All-vinyl	C7	C5	C2	C9
Décor Group					
Bucket Seats	All-vinyl	G7	G5	G2	G9
Town Landau & Luxury Interior					
Split-Bench	US Leather-vinyl	S7	S5	S2	S9

Legend: W. & means White and the color below. Cham. means Chamois. US Leather-vinyl means Ultra-Soft leather and vinyl.

THUNDERBIRD PRODUCTION

Model Number	Body/Style Number	Body Type & Seating	Factory Price	Shipping Weight	Production Total
THUNDERBIRD - (V-8)					
87	60H	2d Hardtop-4P	$5,411	3,907 lbs.	Note 1
THUNDERBIRD TOWN LANDAU - (V-8)					
87	60H	2d Hardtop-4P	$8,420	4,104 lbs.	Note 1
THUNDERBIRD DIAMOND JUBILEE - (V-8)					
87	60H	2d Hardtop-4P	$10,106	4,200 lbs.	18,994

NOTE 1: Production of both the Thunderbird and Thunderbird Town Landau combined was 333,757.

Diamond Ember models had chamois-colored cloth seats. Some collectors say the production totals included just under 19,000 Diamond Jubilee Editions.

STANDARD EQUIPMENT

All standard FoMoCo safety, anti-theft, convenience items, and emissions control equipment, 302-cid two-barrel V-8 (or 352-cid/149-hp V-8 in California), DuraSpark ignition system, SelectShift automatic transmission, power steering, power front disc/rear drum brakes, front and rear stabilizer bars, H78 x 15 black sidewall belted radial tires, chrome-plated swing-away grille, fender louvers, concealed two-speed windshield wipers, wiper-mounted washer jets, coolant recovery system, inside hood release, concealed headlights, full-width taillights, opera windows, dual note horn, bright rocker panel moldings, bright wheel lip moldings, full wheel covers, bright window, door belt, and roof drip moldings, heater and defroster, full-flow ventilation, deluxe steering wheel, day/night mirror, deep-cushioned bench seats with knit cloth/vinyl trim, color-keyed 10-oz. cut-pile carpeting, full-length door armrests, all-vinyl door trim with burled walnut wood-tone appliqués, instrument panel with burled walnut wood-tone appliqués, inside hood release, cigar lighter, AM radio, and electric clock. **1978 Thunderbird Town Landau Standard Equipment:** Most of the features above, with these differences or additions: Brushed aluminum roof wrap-over appliqué, color-keyed roof cross-over moldings (when optional vinyl top is ordered), color-coordinated translucent hood ornament insert, four cast-aluminum wheels with accent paint, opera windows with a Town Landau insignia, accent stripes on body sides, hood, and grille opening panel, deck lid, headlight doors, and fender louvers, whitewall steel-belted radial tires, wide color-keyed vinyl insert body-side moldings with partial wheel lip moldings, front cornering lamps, deluxe bumper group (including front and rear bumper guards and horizontal rub strips), a luxury sound insulation package, Town Landau insignia on instrument panel appliqué, 22-karat gold finish plaque engraved with owner's name, 6-way power driver's seat, power side windows, power lock group (including door locks and remote trunk release), manual-control SelectAire Conditioner, Interior luxury group including convenience group (with left- and right-hand remote control mirrors, interval windshield wipers, automatic parking brake release, and trip odometer) and light group (with dual-beam map lights, under-dash lights, glove box light, ashtray light, trunk light, engine compartment light, door ajar light, and headlights on light), tinted glass, AM/FM stereo search radio (with twin front door mounted speakers and dual rear speakers), and a tilt steering wheel. **1978 1/2 Thunderbird Diamond Jubilee Edition Standard Equipment:** Most of the features above except/or in addition to: An exclusive monochromatic exterior done in Diamond Blue Metallic or Ember Metallic paint, a matching thickly padded vinyl roof, a color-keyed grille texture, a Diamond Jubilee opera window insignia, the owner's initials on the door, color-keyed cast aluminum wheels, color-keyed bumper rub strips, a power radio antenna, an illuminated left-hand visor-vanity mirror, an instrumentation cluster with Ebony wood-tone appliqué, unique front split-bench seat with biscuit design all cloth trim and Thunderbird ornamentation on the upper seat bolsters, door and front seat-back assist straps, hand-stitched leather-covered pad on instrument panel, ebony wood-tone appliqués on instrument panel, knobs, door and quarter trim panels, and steering wheel, molded door and quarter trim armrests with extra padding, 36-oz. cut-pile floor carpeting, bright metal pedal trim accents, unique car keys with wood-tone inserts, color-keyed 18-oz. trunk carpets, molded rear deck liner, and seat belt warning chime.

I.D. NUMBERS

VIN stamped on aluminum tab riveted to dashboard on passenger side and observable through the windshield from outside the car. Prefix indicates manufacturer: F=Ford. First symbol denotes model-year: 8=1978. Second symbol denotes the assembly plant: G=Chicago, Illinois and J=Los Angeles, California. Third symbol denotes the car-line: 8=T-Bird. Fourth symbol denotes body type: 7=Two-door hardtop. Fifth symbol denotes engine: F=302-cid (5.0L)/134-hp V-8, H=351-cid (5.8L)/144-hp V-8, Q=Modified 351-cid (5.8L)/152-hp V-8, S=400-cid (6.6L)/173-hp V-8. Sixth thru 11th symbols denote sequential production number of specific vehicle starting at 100001. Suffix: Denotes manufacturer, F=Ford. Body certification label located on rear face of driver's door. The top part of the label indicates that the T-Bird was manufactured by Ford Motor Company. Directly below this is the month and year of manufacture, plus a statement that the car conforms to federal motor vehicle safety standard in effect on the indicated date of manufacture. The VIN appears first on the first line of encoded information. It matches the 1st to 11th symbols on VIN tag. PASSENGER appears to the right of the VIN to denote passenger vehicle. The body style code now appears on the far left-hand side of the second line of encoded information. The only Thunderbird code for this model-year is: 60H=2-door pillared hardtop. The color and vinyl roof type/color code appears to the right of the body style code in the second position on the second line of encoded information. The trim code appears to the right of the color and vinyl roof codes in the third position on the second line of encoded information. The transmission code appears to the right of the trim code in the fourth position on the second line of encoded information. The axle code appears to the right of the transmission code in the fifth position on the second line of encoded information. The District Special Equipment code appears to the right of the transmission code in the far right-hand position on the second line of encoded information. Note: The abbreviations VIN/BDY/CLR/TRM/TR/AX/DSO do not appear on the certification label itself. The specific application of the codes is determined by where they are located on the vehicle certification label.

ENGINE

THUNDERBIRD BASE V-8 (FEDERAL): 90-degree. Overhead valve. Cast-iron block and head. Displacement: 302 cid (5.0 liters). Bore and stroke: 4.00 x 3.00 in.

The special Diamond Jubilee Edition Thunderbird had a monochromatic metallic paint treatment and other badging and detailing that set it apart from the other T-Birds.

Mike Mueller photo

Compression ratio: 8.4:1. Brake hp: 134 at 3400 rpm. Torque: 248 lbs.-ft. at 1600 rpm. Five main bearings. Hydraulic valve lifters. Carburetor: Motorcraft 2150 two-barrel. Serial number code: F.

THUNDERBIRD BASE V-8 (CALIFORNIA): 90-degree. Overhead valve. Cast-iron block and head. Displacement: 351 cid (5.8 liters). Bore and stroke: 4.00 x 3.50 in. Compression ratio: 8.3:1. Brake hp: 145 at 3400 rpm. Torque: 277 lbs.-ft. at 1600 rpm. Five main bearings. Hydraulic valve lifters. Carburetor: Motorcraft 2150 two-barrel. Windsor engine. Serial number code: H.

THUNDERBIRD OPTIONAL V-8 (FEDERAL): 90-degree. Overhead valve. Cast-iron block and head. Displacement: 351 cid (5.8 liters). Bore and stroke: 4.00 x 3.50 in. Compression ratio: 8.0:1. Brake hp: 152 at 3600 rpm. Torque: 278 lbs.-ft. at 1800 rpm. Five main bearings. Hydraulic valve lifters. Carburetor: Motorcraft 2150 two-barrel. Windsor engine. Serial number code: Q.

THUNDERBIRD OPTIONAL V-8 (FEDERAL): 90-degree. Overhead-valve. Cast-iron block and head. Displacement: 400 cu. in (6.6 liters). Bore and stroke: 4.00 x 4.00 in. Compression ratio: 8:0.1. Brake hp: 166 at 3800 rpm. Torque: 319 lbs.-ft. at 1800 rpm. Five main bearings. Hydraulic valve lifters. Carburetor: Motorcraft 2150 two-barrel. Serial number code: S.

CHASSIS

Wheelbase: 114 in. Overall length: 215.5 in. Overall width: 78.5 in. Overall height: 53 in. Front headroom: 37.3 in. Front legroom: 42.1 in. Rear headroom: 36.2 in. Rear legroom: 32.6 in. Trunk capacity: 15.6 cu. ft. Front tread: 63.2 in. Rear tread: 63.1 in. Wheels: 15 x 6.5 in. Tires: HR78-15 steel-belted radial. Steering: Integral with power-assist. Steering ratio: 21.9:1. Turning diameter: 43.1 ft. Front suspension: Independent, upper and lower control arms, coil springs, tubular shocks and anti-roll bar. Rear suspension: Live axle, four-link control arms, coil springs, tubular shocks, anti-roll bar. Steering: Recirculating ball, power-assist. Standard rear axle: 2.50:1. Weight distribution: 57/43. Front brakes: Power vented disc. Rear brakes: Power drum. Brakes swept area: 372.3 sq. in. Fuel tank capacity: 21 gal.

OPTIONS

351-cid/161-hp V-8 engine ($157). 400-cid V-8 engine ($283). Traction-Lok differential axle ($50). Manual air conditioner ($543). Automatic air conditioner in base Hardtop ($588). Automatic air conditioner in Town Landau or Diamond Jubilee ($45) Power antenna ($45). Heavy-duty battery ($18). Color-keyed deluxe seat belts ($21). Front license plate bracket (no charge). Deluxe bumper group ($78). Day and date clock ($22). Convenience group for models with bucket seat and floor shift ($93), for other models ($103). Front cornering lights ($46). Exterior décor group for models with convenience group or interior luxury group ($332), for other models ($382). Interior décor group ($316). Sports décor group for models with convenience group ($396), for other models (446). Electric rear window defroster ($93). California emissions equipment ($75). T-roof convertible option ($699). Illuminated entry system $54). Complete tinted glass ($66). Sports instrumentation group for models with convenience group ($111), for other models ($118). Luxury sound insulation package ($29). Light group ($49). Power lock group ($100). Interior luxury group ($783). Dual Sport mirrors for models with convenience or interior luxury groups ($8), for other models ($58). Remote-control left OSRV mirror ($16). Illuminated visor-vanity mirror for models with interior décor group ($33), for other models ($37). Rocker panel moldings ($29). Bright wide body-side moldings ($42). Color-keyed wide body-side moldings ($54). Power moonroof ($691). Metallic Glow paint ($62). Protection group for models with front license plate bracket ($50), for other models ($46). AM/FM monaural radio ($53). AM/FM stereo radio ($113). AM/FM stereo search radio ($270). 40-channel citizens band radio ($295), AM/FM radio with quadrosonic tape player in base hardtop ($320), in Town Landau and Diamond Jubilee models ($50). AM/FM stereo with tape player ($187). Radio flexibility group ($105). Two-piece vinyl roof ($138). Bucket seats and console with interior décor group ($37), all others ($211). Automatic seatback release ($33). Dual rear seat speakers ($46). Fingertip speed control, Town Landau or Diamond Jubilee with Sports instrumentation group or interior luxury group ($104), all other models ($117). Leather steering wheel in models with Sports instrumentation group ($51), all other models ($64). Tilt steering wheel ($70). Heavy-duty suspension ($20) Dual accent paint stripes ($46). Inflatable spare tire with HR78 black sidewall tires (no charge). Heavy-duty trailer towing package ($184). Leather and vinyl seat trim ($296). Luggage compartment trim ($39). Vinyl seat trim ($24). Tu-Tone paint treatment ($79). Wire wheel covers ($112). Four styled road wheels ($159). Four cast aluminum wheels on models with exterior décor group ($132), all other models ($291). Power side windows ($126). Heavy-duty alternator ($50). Front and rear bumper guards ($42). Sports instrumentation group on Town Landau or models with interior luxury group ($75), models with convenience group ($111), all other models ($118). Vinyl body-side moldings ($42). Tinted windshield glass ($28) Front floor mats ($20). Tire options for base hardtop with five GR78 x 15 tires as standard equipment included GR78 x 15 radial whitewalls ($46 extra), HR78 x 15 black sidewalls ($22 extra), HR78 x 15 radial whitewalls ($68 extra), HR78 x 15 radial white-band whitewalls ($88 extra), and HR70 x 17 white oval whitewalls ($90 extra). Tire

The Town Landau T-Bird had pin striping and color accents on the roof, body-side moldings, and wheel covers.

options for the Diamond Jubilee with five standard HR78 x 15 steel-belted whitewall radials as standard equipment included HR78 x 15 radial wide band whitewalls ($20 extra), and HR70 x 15 whitewall wide oval radials ($22 extra).

EQUIPMENT INSTALLATION RATES

Automatic transmission (100 percent). Standard V-8 engine (32.1 percent). Optional V-8 engine (67.9 percent). AM radio (19.9 percent). AM/FM radio (5.9 percent). Stereo tape player (38.7 percent). AM/FM with 8-Track tape player: (23.5 percent). AM/FM stereo cassette (2.3 percent). Power steering (100 percent). Power front disc brakes (100 percent). Power door locks (32.5 percent). Power seat (34.4 percent). Power windows (44.7 percent). Adjustable steering column (48.3 percent). Tinted windshield only (1.5 percent). All tinted glass (94.6 percent). Vinyl top (83.9 percent). Sunroof (3.9 percent). Automatic air conditioning (9.9 percent). Manual air conditioning (86.4 percent). Limited-slip axle (2.5 percent). Standard steel-belted radial tires (100 percent). Electric rear window defogger (37 percent). Standard wheel covers (47.8 percent). Optional wheel covers (20.1 percent). Steel styled wheels (26.8 percent). Aluminum styled wheels 5.3 percent). Speed control (55 percent). Remote-control left-hand rearview mirror (91.9 percent). Remote-control right-hand rearview mirror (72.9 percent). Reclining front seats: (68.2 percent). Bucket seats (6.3 percent). Analog clock (80 percent). Digital clock (20 percent). (Note: Based on 324,192 units produced in the model year for the U.S. market only.)

HISTORICAL FOOTNOTES

The 1978 T-Bird was introduced on October 6, 1977. Henry Ford II (chairman), Phillip Caldwell (vice chairman) and Lee A. Iaccoca (president) held the top three corporate positions at Ford Motor Company. W.S. Walla was Ford Division's vice president and general manager. B.L. Crumpton was general sales manager for the division.

Demand for T-Birds was the highest ever and brought a new all-time production record for an annual model. Calendar-year output was 326,873 units. A total of 352,751 T-Birds were produced in the model year. This represented 3.94 percent of the industry total. Of these units, 260,792 were made in Chicago and 91,959 were made in Los Angeles. Calendar-year dealer sales amounted to 304,430 T-Birds, representing 3.3 percent of industry sales.

An estimated 20,000 of the T-Birds made in the U.S. were destined for the export market and were shipped to Canada and other countries. These offered almost the same equipment, color schemes, and trim as the cars made for the U.S. market. However, they were not necessarily 100 percent identical. For example the "California" version of the 351-cid two-barrel V-8 was not offered in cars marketed in Canada. Also the Canadian version of the Diamond Jubilee Edition did not include a power antenna. In Canadian literature the gas tank capacity was expressed in Imperial gallons (17.3), the trunk space was expressed in liters (402), and other measurements were given in millimeters. Interestingly, service mileage intervals used in the U.S. did not apply to Canadian cars, but the cars sold in Canada were backed by a no-extra-charge Duraguard system that offered 36-month protection against sheet metal rust-through. There was no such program offered in the U.S.

During calendar-year 1978, a total of 144 additional Thunderbirds were actually put together in a factory in Canada. As far as we can tell, these were the first cars bearing the Thunderbird name to be manufactured in Canada. They were early 1979 models, however, and not 1978 models.

It was, however, the 1978 Thunderbird that brought the marque back into NASCAR racing. Drivers Bobby Allison, Dick Brooks, and Jody Ridley found the new down-sized T-Bird well-suited to Grand National competition with the proper modifications. It had been 18 years—1960—since the T-Bird's last appearance in a major stock car race. 1978 would be only the beginning of the T-Bird's latter-day motorsports history. Allison's number 15 T-Bird, built by Bud Moore, took the checkered flag in events like the NAPA 400 at Riverside, California. That particular event was conducted in 103-degree weather, and Allison's car held up until his clutch linkage broke. However, he managed to keep the T-Bird going and came home 32.9 seconds in front of Darrell Waltrip.

1978 THUNDERBIRD PERFORMANCE		
Model	**CID/HP**	**Performance**
0-60 mph		
Hardtop	402/173	10.3 seconds
1/4-Mile		
Hardtop	402/173	17.7 seconds @ 78.6 mph
Top Speed		
Hardtop	402/173	110 mph

T-Birds again sported a heavy-looking front end, hidden headlights, and a forward-sloping wrap-over roof for 1979.

1979
Thunderbird

A bolder, heavier-looking grille greeted T-Bird customers in 1979. It had a neo-classic look with a heavy chrome shell around it. Three thin horizontal moldings criss-crossed three vertical bars to form large rectangular openings arranged in a four across-by-four high pattern. The hidden headlight doors were double-framed with chrome moldings and had large chrome Thunderbird insignias at their centers. There was a script nameplate on the left one.

A massive, angular front bumper carried heavy, low bumper guards. A new spoiler went below the front bumper. Clear fender-notched parking lamp lenses with adjoining amber-colored marker lenses each held three horizontal divider strips. Each front fender sported a set of six simulated vertical louvers just behind the front wheel opening. Horizontal cornering lamps that mounted low on the fenders, just ahead of the wheel opening, were optional

or included as part of décor packages.

A forward-slanting wrap-over roof was becoming a T-Bird trademark. The wrap-over section showed narrow, slanting opera windows. Standard inside the base T-Bird was a comfort-contoured Flight Bench front seat with Rossano cloth seating surfaces and vinyl trim. A large, fold-down armrest hid in the center of the seatback.

There were six solid interior colors and five Tu-Tone combinations with White as the base color. Specific color choices were offered in various materials: Vinyl, vinyl and cloth, standard cloth, luxury cloth or ultra-soft leather. Eight body colors, five vinyl roof colors, and four interior colors were all-new for 1979.

Bucket seats in vinyl or cloth and vinyl were an extra-cost item. Optional split-bench seats came with these same

129

BODY COLOR INFORMATION

Color Name	Code	Color Name	Code
Black	1C	Light Medium Blue	3F
Polar White	9D	Dove Grey	1N
Dark Red	2M	Light Chamois	83
Midnight Blue Metallic	3L	Maroon**	2J
Silver Metallic	1G	Medium Blue Glow*	3H
Dark Jade Metallic	46	Burnt Orange Glow*	5N
Dark Cordovan Metallic	8N	Chamois Glow*	8W
Pastel Chamois	5P	Light Jade Glow*	7L
Light Gray	12	Red Glow*	2H

* Optional Glow Colors.
** Available on Heritage Edition only.
Dove Grey (1N) is deleted and Light Gray (12) is added during the model run.

VINYL TOP COLOR INFORMATION

Black Valino Grain	A	Dove Grey Valino Grain	S
White Valino Grain	W	Dark Red Valino Grain	D
Dark Jade Valino Grain	R	Maroon Valino Grain **	9
Midnight Blue Valino Grain	Q	Light Medium Blue Lugano Grain **	2
Silver Valino Grain	P	Chamois Valino Grain	T
Cordovan Valino Grain ***	F		

** Available on Heritage only.
***F indicates Dark Cordovan Lugano Grain on Town Landau.

PAINT STRIPE COLORS (EXCEPT TOWN LANDAU)

Black	1	Dark Jade	6
White	2	Chamois	7
Red	3	Light Cordovan	8
Silver	4	Gold**	9
Dark Blue	5		

** Available on Heritage only.

PAINT STRIPE COLORS (TOWN LANDAU)

Gold	1	Red	3
Brown	2		

INTERIOR TRIM INFORMATION)

Seat Type	Material	Dove Grey	Dark Red	Blue	Jade	Chamois	Cordovan
Flight Bench	Cloth & Vinyl	KS	KD	KB	KR	KT	KF
Flight Bench	All-Vinyl	LS	LD	LB	LR	LT	LF
Bucket	Cloth & Vinyl	HS	HD	HB	HR	HT	HF
Bucket	All-Vinyl	CS	CD	CB	CR	CT	CF
T-Bird Interior Décor							
Split-Bench	Cloth & Vinyl	DS	DD	DB	DR	DT	DF
Split-Split Bench	All-Vinyl	ES	ED	EB	ER	ET	EF
Bucket	Cloth & Vinyl	JS	JD	JB	JR	JT	JF
Bucket	All-Vinyl	GS	GD	GB	GR	GT	GF
Interior Luxury & Town Landau							
Split-Bench	Cloth	RS	RD	RB	RR	RT	RF
Split-Bench	U-Soft Leather	SS	SD	SB	SR	ST	SF
Heritage Edition							
Split-Bench	Luxury Cloth	TD	TB				
Split Bench	U-Soft Leather	UD	UB				

TU-TONE INTERIOR INFORMATION

Seat Type	Material	White/ Red	White/ Blue	White/ Jade	White/ Cham.	White/ Cordovan
Bucket	All-Vinyl	CN	CQ	C5	C2	C6
T-Bird Interior Décor						
Split-Split Bench	All-Vinyl	EN	EQ	E5	E2	E6
Bucket	All-Vinyl	GN	GQ	G5	G2	G6
Interior Luxury & Town Landau						
Split-Bench	U-Soft Leather	SN	SQ	S5	S2	S6

Legend: U-Soft Leather means Ultra-Soft Leather

THUNDERBIRD PRODUCTION

Model Number	Body/Style Number	Body Type & Seating	Factory Price	Shipping Weight	Production Total
THUNDERBIRD - (V-8)					
87	60H	2d Hardtop-4P	$5,877	3,893 lbs.	Note 1
THUNDERBIRD TOWN LANDAU - (V-8)					
87	60H	2d Hardtop-4P	$8,866	4,284 lbs.	Note 1
THUNDERBIRD HERITAGE EDITION - (V-8)					
87	60H	2d Hardtop-4P	$10,687	4,178 lbs.	Note 1

NOTE 1: Production of the three models combined was 284,141.

materials, plus regular cloth, luxury cloth or ultra-soft leather. On the floor was 10-oz. cut-pile carpeting color-keyed to match the upholstery. The door panels had full-length armrests.

At the rear of most models were large, swept-back side windows. Separate large, rectangular-shaped two-piece taillights characterized the rear of 1979 T-Birds. These replaced the former full-width units and looked like rectangles within rectangles. A winged T-Bird emblem was in the center. A single back-up light stood between the taillights. It was centered over the new rear bumper guards, which were standard equipment.

Ford's 75th anniversary year had ended and the Diamond Jubilee model disappeared. A new Heritage Edition T-Bird was designed to take its place. Two monochromatic color schemes were available for this luxury car. One was Maroon and the other Light Medium Blue. A matching Lugano grain formal-style padded vinyl roof was featured. The split-bench seats had unique biscuit design all-cloth upholstery and a T-Bird insignia on the upper seatback bolsters. The Heritage Edition's roof had a unique solid quarter panel appearance instead of rear quarter windows. Chrome Heritage scripts decorated the solid panels.

Returning as a Thunderbird option package was the Sports décor group. It included a Chamois vinyl roof with color-keyed backlight moldings, Chamois dual accent paint stripes, Chamois hood/GOP and fender louver paint stripes, Chamois deck lid straps, styled road wheels with Chamois paint accents, dual sport mirrors, and blacked-out vertical

grille bars. It was available on cars with Black, Polar White, Midnight Blue Metallic, Dark Cordovan Metallic, Burnt Orange Glow, Dark Jade Metallic, or Pastel Chamois exterior finish. Chamois-colored interior trims were available with all exterior body colors. Chamois and White trims were offered with Polar White or Dark Cordovan Metallic exteriors. Chamois or Cordovan trims came in cars with Dark Cordovan Metallic exteriors. Also available were Chamois or Jade upholstery trims in cars with Dark Jade Metallic bodies. The deck lid straps gave these cars a hint of the classic image embodied in the sporty Stutz and Bentley touring coupes of the 1930s.

On the technical front, T-Birds had a new electronic voltage regulator. The carburetor on the base 302-cid V-8 was also a refined two-barrel design. Door and ignition locks were modified for better theft protection. Corrosion

Ford photo

Sales of the beautiful Thunderbird slipped a bit in 1979, but more than 284,000 vehicles in the three-model line were still produced—a far cry from the lean years of the early 1970s.

protection was also becoming a factor in the U.S. market. Ford used pre-coated steels—such as galvanized steel and chromium/zinc-rich primer coated steel—vinyl sealers, aluminized wax, and enamel top coats to combat rust.

STANDARD EQUIPMENT

All standard FoMoCo safety, anti-theft, convenience items, and emissions control equipment, 302-cid two-barrel V-8 (or 352-cid/149-hp V-8 in California), DuraSpark ignition system, SelectShift automatic transmission, power steering, power front disc/rear drum brakes, front and rear stabilizer bars, GR78 x 15 black sidewall belted radial tires, chrome-plated swing-away grille, chrome plated front and rear bumpers, chrome plated rear bumper guards, fender louvers, concealed two-speed windshield wipers, wiper-mounted washer jets, coolant recovery system, inside hood release, concealed headlights, full-width taillights, opera windows, dual note horn, bright rocker panel moldings, bright wheel lip moldings, full wheel covers, bright window, door belt, and roof drip moldings, heater and defroster, full-

flow ventilation, deluxe steering wheel, day/night mirror, Flight Bench seat, three-point seat and shoulder belts with retractors, color-keyed 10-oz. cut-pile carpeting, full-length door armrests, all-vinyl door trim with burled walnut wood-tone appliqués, instrument panel with burled walnut wood-tone appliqués, inside hood release, cigar lighter, AM radio, and electric clock. **1979 Thunderbird Town Landau Standard Equipment:** Most of the features above, with these differences or additions: HR78 x 15 steel-belted radial whitewall tires, air conditioning, luxury sound insulation package, power lock group, 6-way driver's power seat, power side windows, tilt steering wheel, tinted glass, trip odometer, windshield wipers with interval control, deluxe bumper group, dual sport remote-control mirrors, wide color-keyed vinyl insert body-side moldings, integral partial wheel lip moldings, brushed aluminum roof wrap-over appliqué, cast aluminum wheels, upgraded carpeting, quartz crystal day and date clock, illuminated visor-vanity mirror on passenger side, AM/FM stereo radio, split bench seat with manual recliner, and automatic seatback releases. **1979 Thunderbird Heritage Edition Standard Equipment:**

In addition to base equipment: HR78 x 15 whitewall steel-belted radial tires, air conditioning, illuminated entry system, luxury sound insulation package, power antenna, power lock group, 6-way power driver's seat, power side windows, speed control, tilt steering wheel, tinted glass, trip odometer, interval windshield wipers, deluxe bumper group, dual remote-control mirrors, wide color-keyed vinyl body-side moldings, integral wheel lip moldings, vinyl roof, cast aluminum wheels, upgraded carpeting, illuminated visor-vanity mirrors on both sides, AM/FM stereo search radio, split bench seat with manual recliner, automatic seatback release, and sport instrumentation.

I.D. NUMBERS

VIN stamped on aluminum tab riveted to dashboard on passenger side and observable through the windshield from outside the car. Prefix indicates manufacturer: F=Ford. First symbol denotes model-year: 9=1979. Second symbol denotes the assembly plant: G=Chicago, Illinois and J=Los Angeles, California. Third symbol denotes the car-line: 8=T-Bird. Fourth symbol denotes body type: 7=two-door pillared hardtop. Fifth symbol denotes engine: F=302-cid (5.0L)/133-hp V-8, H=351-cid (5.8L)/135-142-hp V-8, Q=modified 351-cid (5.8L)/151-hp V-8. Sixth thru 11th symbols denote sequential production number of specific vehicle starting at 100001. Body certification label located on rear face of driver's door. The top part of the label indicates that the T-Bird was manufactured by Ford Motor Company. Directly below this is the month and year of manufacture, plus a statement that the car conforms to federal motor vehicle safety standard in effect on the indicated date of manufacture. The VIN appears first on the first line of encoded information. It matches the 1st to 11th symbols on VIN tag. PASSENGER appears to the right of the VIN to denote passenger vehicle. The color and vinyl roof type/color code now appears in the far left-hand position on the second line of encoded information. The District Special Order code appears to the right of the body style code in the second position on the second line of encoded information. The body style code now appears on the far left-hand side of the second line of encoded information. The only Thunderbird code for this model-year is: 60H=two-door pillared hardtop. The trim code appears to the right of the body style code in the fourth position on the second line of encoded information. The Scheduled Build Date is a new code. It appears to the right of the trim code in the fifth position on the second line of encoded information. The axle code appears to the right of the Scheduled Build Date in the sixth position on the second line of encoded

Ford photo

This Maroon-colored 'Bird was a special Heritage Edition T-Bird that came out in 1979 and replaced the Diamond Jubilee 'Bird.

The Sport Décor group gave the T-Bird a flashy exterior, complete with deck lid straps.

information. The transmission code appears to the right of the axle code in the seventh position on the second line of encoded information. The air conditioning code appears to the right of the transmission code in the eighth position on the second line of encoded information. The abbreviations VIN/BDY/CLR/-TRM/TR/AX/DSO do not appear on the certification label itself. The specific application of the codes is determined by where they are located on the vehicle certification label.

ENGINE

THUNDERBIRD BASE V-8 (FEDERAL): 90-degree. Overhead valve. Cast-iron block and head. Displacement: 302 cid (5.0 liters). Bore and stroke: 4.00 x 3.00 in. Compression ratio: 8.4:1. Brake hp: 133 at 3400 rpm. Torque: 245 lbs.-ft. at 1600 rpm. Five main bearings. Hydraulic valve lifters. Carburetor: Motorcraft 2150 two-barrel. Serial number code: F.

THUNDERBIRD BASE V-8 (CALIFORNIA): 90-degree. Overhead valve. Cast-iron block and head. Displacement: 351 cid (5.8 liters). Bore and stroke: 4.00 x 3.50 in. Compression ratio: 8.3:1. Brake hp: 135-142 at 3200 rpm. Torque: 286 lbs.-ft. at 1400 rpm. Five main bearings. Hydraulic valve lifters. Carburetor: Motorcraft 2150 two-barrel. Windsor engine. Serial number code: H.

THUNDERBIRD OPTIONAL V-8 (FEDERAL): 90-degree. Overhead valve. Cast-iron block and head. Displacement: 351 cid (5.8 liters). Bore and stroke: 4.00 x 3.50 in. Compression ratio: 8.0:1. Brake hp: 151 at 3600 rpm. Torque: 270 lbs.-ft. at 2200 rpm. Five main bearings. Hydraulic valve lifters. Carburetor: Motorcraft 2150 two-barrel. Windsor engine. Serial number code: Q.

CHASSIS

Wheelbase: 114 in. Overall length: 217.2. Overall width: 78.5. Overall height: 52.8 in. Front headroom: 37.3 in. Front legroom: 42.1 in. Rear headroom: 36.2 in. Rear legroom: 32.6 in. Trunk capacity: 15.6 cu. ft. Front tread: 63.2 in. Rear tread: 63.1 in. Wheels: 15 x 6.5 in. Tires: 215-R15 steel-belted radial. Steering: Integral with power-assist. Steering ratio: 21.9:1. Turning diameter: 43.1 ft. Front suspension: Independent, upper and lower control arms, coil springs, tubular shocks, and anti-roll bar. Rear suspension: Live axle, four-link control arms, coil springs, tubular shocks, anti-roll bar. Steering: Recirculating ball, power-assist. Standard rear axle: 2.50:1. Weight distribution: 57/43. Front brakes: Power vented disc. Rear brakes: Power drum. Brakes swept area: 372.3 sq. in. Fuel tank capacity: 21 gal.

OPTIONS

351-cid/161-hp V-8 engine ($263). Traction-Lok differential axle ($64). Auto Temperature Control air conditioner, in base Hardtop ($607), in Town Landau or Heritage Edition ($45). Manual air conditioner ($562). Heavy-duty battery ($20). Color-keyed deluxe seat belts ($22). Lower body-side protection, models with rocker panel moldings ($33), Other models ($46). Front license plate bracket (no charge). Bumper rub strips ($37). Day and date clock ($24). Convenience group for models with bucket seat and floor shift ($108), for other models ($117). Front cornering lights ($49). Exterior décor group for models with convenience group or interior luxury group ($346), for other models ($406). Interior décor group ($322). Sports décor group for models with convenience group ($459), for other models ($518). Mud and stone deflectors ($25). Electric rear window defroster ($99). California emissions equipment ($83). High-altitude emissions system ($83). Extended range fuel tank ($36). Illuminated entry system ($57). Complete tinted glass ($70). Sports instrumentation group for Town Landau or cars with interior luxury group ($88), for models with convenience group ($121), for other models ($129). Light group ($51). Power lock group ($111). Luggage compartment trim ($43). Luxury sound insulation package ($30). Interior luxury group ($816). Illuminated passenger side visor-vanity mirror for cars with interior décor group ($34), for other cars ($39). Left-hand remote-control OSRV mirror ($18). Color-keyed wide body-side moldings ($54). Dual sport mirrors, on models with convenience group or interior luxury group ($9), on other models ($68). Rocker panel moldings ($29). Wide bright body-side moldings ($42). Power moonroof ($691). Metallic Glow paint ($64). Protection group for models with front license plate bracket ($53), for other models ($49). Power radio antenna ($47). AM radio delete ($79 credit). AM/FM monaural radio ($59). AM/FM stereo radio ($120). AM/FM stereo search radio ($276). AM/FM radio with 8-track tape player ($193). 40-channel citizens band radio ($329). AM/FM radio with quadrosonic tape player in base Hardtop ($326), in Town Landau and Heritage Edition models ($50). AM/FM stereo with cassette tape player, in two-door Hardtop ($187), in Town Landau or Heritage Edition ($83 credit). Radio flexibility group ($105). Two-piece vinyl roof ($132). Seat belt warning chime ($22). Bucket seats and console with interior décor group ($37), all others ($211). Automatic seatback release ($37). Dual rear seat speakers ($46). Fingertip speed control, Town Landau or Heritage Edition with sports instrumentation group or interior luxury group ($1,134), all other models ($126). Tilt steering wheel ($75). Heavy-duty suspension ($22) Dual accent paint stripes ($46). Inflatable spare tire with HR78 black sidewall tires (no charge). All-vinyl seat trim ($26). Ultra-soft leather seat trim, in Heritage Edition ($243), in other models ($309). T-roof convertible option ($747). Tu-Tone paint treatment ($62). Wire wheel covers ($118). Four styled road wheels ($132). Four cast-aluminum wheels on models with exterior décor group ($150), all other models ($316). Power side windows ($132). Tire options for base hardtop with five GR78 x 15 steel-belted radial black sidewall tires as standard equipment included GR78 x 15 radial whitewalls ($47 extra), HR78 x 15 black sidewalls ($25 extra), HR78 x 15 radial whitewalls ($72 extra), and HR70 x 17 white oval whitewalls ($100 extra). Tire options cards with five standard HR78 x 15 steel-belted whitewall radials as standard equipment included HR70 x 15 whitewall wide oval radials ($29 extra). Color-keyed front floor mats ($20). Tinted windshield only ($28). Engine block heater ($14). Vinyl body-side moldings ($42).

EQUIPMENT INSTALLATION RATES

Automatic transmission (100 percent). V-8 engine (100 percent). AM radio (16.4 percent). AM/FM radio (4.2 percent). Stereo tape player (39.3 percent). AM/FM with 8-Track tape player (12.8 percent). AM/FM stereo cassette (4.4 percent). AM/FM stereo with CB radio (0.7 percent). AM/FM stereo with 8-track tape player and CB (0.1 percent). AM/FM Quadratrack 8-track with CB (0.3 percent). Power steering (100 percent). Power front disc brakes (100 percent). Power door locks (29.5 percent). Power seat (29.7 percent). Power windows (43.5 percent). Adjustable steering column (49.2 percent). Tinted windshield only (1.8 percent). All tinted glass (94.3 percent). Vinyl top (76 percent). Sunroof (8 percent). Automatic air conditioning (7.4 percent). Manual air conditioning (89.2 percent). Limited-slip axle (2.7 percent).

Standard steel-belted radial tires (100 percent). Electric rear window defogger (39.4 percent). Standard wheel covers (48.4 percent). Optional wheel covers (18.9 percent). Steel styled wheels (27.5 percent). Aluminum styled wheels 5.2 percent). Speed control (55.9 percent). Remote-control left-hand rearview mirror (97 percent). Remote-control right-hand rearview mirror (73 percent). Reclining front seats (62.9 percent). Bucket seats (5.1 percent). Analog clock (83.3 percent). Digital clock (16.7 percent). (Note: Based on 256,584 units produced in the model year for the U.S. market only.)

HISTORICAL FOOTNOTES

The 1979 T-Bird was introduced on October 6, 1978. Henry Ford II (chairman), Phillip Caldwell (vice chairman), and William O'Borke (executive VP of North American Automotive Operations) were the top three executives at Ford Motor Company after Lee Iacocca was fired from the presidency by HFII. William Clay Ford was named chairman of the Executive Committee and vice president of Product Design. Walter S. Walla was Ford Division's vice president and general manager and Bernard L. Crumpton was general sales manager for the division.

Demand for T-Birds dropped off a bit. Calendar-year output was 264,451 units. A total of 284,141 T-Birds were produced in the model year. This represented 3.09 percent of the industry total. Of these units, 208,248 were made in Chicago and 75,893 were made in Los Angeles. Calendar-year dealer sales amounted to 215,698 T-Birds, representing 2.6 percent of industry sales.

As might be expected after three years, the down-sized Thunderbird was no longer the newest thing to hit the market and did not benefit from a sales campaign, such as the Diamond Jubilee promotion, to help bring extra buyers into Ford showrooms. As a result, sales declined. In addition, the second Arab oil embargo occurred this year, chasing American car buyers away from V-8-powered cars.

Bobby Allison continued to race a T-Bird for the Bud Moore NASCAR team.

A historical milestone of sorts was marked in 1979 with the firing of Lee Iacocca by Henry Ford II in October 1978. A month later, Iacocca was working for Chrysler Corp. in nearby Highland Park. As things turned out, the "father" of the Ford Mustang would go on to save the No. 3 automaker from doom. Both the creation of the Mustang and the salvation of Chrysler are accomplishments that Mr. Iacocca deserves tremendous credit for, but the fact that nearly a million of his 1977-1979 T-Birds were sold should not be overlooked. Taking a nameplate that was selling 60,000 copies a year up to 300,000 copies a year represented another great automotive marketing achievement.

Ford photo

Ford again offered a midyear special edition in 1980, this time a "Silver Anniversary" model.

1980

Thunderbird

To celebrate its 25th year, the T-Bird had a new size and a new standard engine. It was 17 inches shorter and 700 lbs. lighter than its immediate predecessor. This 'Bird was created by stretching the Ford Fairmont/Mercury Zephyr platform and was identical to the 1980 Mercury Cougar XR-7. For the first time in 15 years, the T-Bird featured unitized body construction. Jack Telnack, who later gained fame for his Taurus, was the head designer of the new T-Bird. William P. Boyer, who had helped create the original two-seat T-Birds, was also assigned to the project. Arthur I. Querfield, another member of the original T-Bird design team, was also involved.

The T-Birds were considered four-passenger models. The base hardtop and Town Landau returned, along with a midyear Silver Anniversary model. The latter featured a Silver Glow exterior highlighted by black accents, a special padded rear-half vinyl roof, a high-gloss roof wrap-over molding and distinctive horizontal coach lamps with Silver Anniversary scripts.

In addition to the featured Anniversary Silver paint color, Black, Light Gray, Red Glow and Midnight Blue Metallic solid exterior finishes could be substituted. There was also a special two-tone combination mating Black with Anniversary Silver. In each case, the color of the roof wrap-over bands, vinyl tops, body-side accent stripes, body-side moldings and bumper rub strips were coordinated with the exterior color selected.

Inside the Silver Anniversary model was a thickly cushioned split-bench front seat upholstered in velvet-like knit-velour and color-keyed 36-oz. carpets. There were burled rosewood wood-tone instrument panel appliqués, a special leather-wrapped steering wheel, and dual illuminated visor-vanity mirrors. The car owner was also sent a bright rhodium nameplate with his or her name engraved on it.

Traditional T-Bird styling trademarks such as hidden headlights and wrap-over roof styling were blended into the T-Bird's new appearance. The body also featured strong sculpturing along the main body-side feature lines, single opera windows to the rear of the wrap-over roof band, and solid-panel roof pillars like the previous Heritage Edition. The grille was again neo-classic in shape, but had a new egg-crate pattern insert. Some of the grille texture showed below the bumper. Soft, color-keyed urethene-clad bumpers were used up front and in the rear. Bumper guards were optional. The large rectangular headlight covers were integral with the huge signal/parking lights that wrapped around the body corners to double as side marker lights.

Ford very wisely used many T-Bird hallmarks to give

BODY COLOR INFORMATION

Color Name	Code	Color Name	Code
Black ++	1C	Pastel Sand	6D
Polar White	9D	Dark Cordovan Metallic	8N
Candyapple Red	2K	Medium Blue Glow (Opt.)	3H
Silver Metallic	1G	Chamois Glow (Opt.)	8W
Light Grey ++	12	Bittersweet Glow (Opt.)	8D
Midnight Blue Metallic ++	3L	Red Glow (Opt.) ++	2H
Dark Pine Metallic	7M	Anniversary Silver Glow (Opt.)	14
Dark Chamois Metallic	8A		

++ Indicates colors that Silver Anniversary models came in.
Silver Anniversary models featured a Silver wrap-over band, except in two combinations: Anniversary Silver Glow paint with Anniversary Silver vinyl top, and Black paint stripe, and Black paint with Anniversary Silver vinyl top and Silver paint stripe. Both of these combinations use a Black wrap-over band.

VINYL TOP COLOR INFORMATION

Color Name	Code	Color Name	Code
Black Valino grain	A	Midnight Blue Valino grain	Q
Bittersweet Valino grain	C	Pastel Sand Valino grain	Y
Medium Red Valino grain	D	White Valino grain	W
Silver Valino grain	P	Anniversary Silver Valino grain	6
Caramel pigskin grain	T		

Vinyl top codes: F=half vinyl top, E=luxury half-vinyl top, V or W=full vinyl top

PAINT STRIPE COLOR INFORMATION

Color Name	Code	Color Name	Code
Black	1	Light Chamois	6
White	2	Bright Bittersweet	8
Candyapple Red	3	Dark Cordovan	10
Silver	4	Brown	7
Medium Blue	5		

INTERIOR TRIM INFORMATION

Seat Type	Material	Dove Grey	Red	Blue	Caramel	Bittersweet
Flight Bench	Cloth & Vinyl	AS	AD	AB	AT	—
Flight Bench	All-Vinyl	BS	BD	BB	BT	—
Bucket	All-Vinyl	DS	DD	DB	DT	—
T-Bird Interior Décor						
Split-Bench	Cloth & Vinyl	ES	ED	EB	ET	EC
Split-Split Bench	SS Vinyl	FS	FD	FB	FT	FC
Bucket	All-Vinyl	GS	GD	GB	GT	GC
Recaro Buckets	Cloth & Vinyl	NS(a)	ND	—	NT	NC
Interior Luxury & T. Landau						
Split-Bench	Cloth	JS	JD	JB	JT	JC
Split-Bench	U-Soft Leather	KS	KD	KB	KT	KC
Recaro Buckets	Cloth & Vinyl	PS (a)	PD		PT	PC
Silver Anniversary						
Split-Bench	Cloth	LS	—	—	—	—
Split Bench	U-Soft Leather	MS	—	—	—	—

TU-TONE INTERIOR TRIM INFORMATION

Seat Type	Material	White/ Red	White/ Blue	White/ Caramel	White/ Bittersweet
T-Bird					
Bucket	All-Vinyl	DN	DQ	D2	D7
T-Bird Interior Décor					
Split-Split Bench	SS Vinyl	FN	FQ	F2	F7
Bucket	All-Vinyl	GN	GQ	G2	G7
Interior Luxury & Town Landau					
Split-Bench	U-Soft Leather	KN	KQ	K2	K7

Legend: (a) Black cloth inserts with Dove Gray facings on door panels and carpets, SS Vinyl means Super-Soft Vinyl, U-Soft Leather means Ultra-Soft Leather

THUNDERBIRD PRODUCTION

Model Number	Body/Style Number	Body Type & Seating	Factory Price	Shipping Weight	Production Total
THUNDERBIRD - (6-CYL/V-8)					
87	66D	2d Hardtop-4P	$6,432	3,118 lbs.	Note 1
THUNDERBIRD TOWN LANDAU - (6-CYL/V-8)					
87/607	66D	2d Hardtop-4P	$10,036	3,357 lbs.	Note 1
THUNDERBIRD SILVER ANNIVERSARY - (6-CYL/V-8)					
87/603	66D	2d Hardtop-4P	$11,679	3,225 lbs.	Note 1

NOTE 1: Production of the three models combined was 156,803.

this new model a strong identity that loyal buyers would recognize. At the rear of the body, wraparound wall-to-wall taillights returned. The general shape was like an upside-down telephone receiver. At each end, the red lens had a white back-up light lens in its center, and these carried a stylized winged T-Bird logo. The entire unit followed the forward slant of the rear deck lid and the lenses wrapped around the rear body corners to function as side markers. Above the right-hand lens was T-Bird lettering. A modified McPherson strut front suspension was used, with four-bar-link coil springs at the rear. Along with the 700-lb. weight loss came higher axle ratios for better fuel economy. Power-assisted, variable-ratio rack-and-pinion steering was another technological advance.

A new 255-cid V-8 was known as the 4.2-liter and was considered standard equipment. It carried the same stroke as the 302-cid (5.0-liter) V-8, but had a smaller bore. The 5.0-liter V-8 was optional. The 4.2-liter V-8 typically delivered 17 to 20 mpg and the 5.0-liter V-8 was good for 16 to 19 mpg. Late in the year, a new in-line six-cylinder was made available as a delete option. It was the first time a six-cylinder engine was ever offered in a T-Bird. A new four-speed overdrive automatic transmission was available with the 5.0-liter V-8.

STANDARD EQUIPMENT

All standard FoMoCo safety, anti-theft, convenience items, and emissions control equipment, 4.2-liter (255-cid) two-barrel V-8, automatic transmission, variable-ratio power rack-and-pinion steering, power front disc/rear drum brakes, DuraSpark ignition system, maintenance-free battery, coolant recovery system, modified McPherson strut front suspension, four-bar link-type rear suspension, front and rear stabilizer bars, three-speed heater and defroster, concealed rectangular headlights, wraparound parking lamps, soft urethane covered bumpers, chrome-plated egg-crate grille, quarter windows, moldings on wheel lips, hood, rocker panels, windshield, drip rail, and door belt, full wheel covers, Flight Bench seating with cloth and vinyl trim, 10-oz. color-keyed cut-pile carpeting, and vinyl door trim with wood-tone accents, push-button AM radio, four-spoke deluxe steering wheel, trip odometer, self-regulating illuminated electric clock, cigar lighter, day-night rearview mirror, glove box and ashtray lights, inertia seatback releases, continuous loop belts, luggage compartment map, mini spare tire, and P185/75R14 black sidewall tires. **Town Landau standard equipment adds or substitutes:** Air conditioning, tinted glass, power side windows, 6-way power driver's seat, power lock group, tilt steering wheel, interval windshield wipers, TR-type white sidewall radial tires, auto lamp on and off delay system, electronic instrument cluster, front cornering lamps, padded rear half-vinyl roof with wrap-over band and coach lamps, wide door belt moldings, color-keyed rear window moldings, striping on hood, body sides and rear deck lid, dual remote-control mirrors, color-keyed vinyl insert body-side moldings with partial wheel lip moldings, cast-aluminum wheels, split-bench seats with dual recliners, velour seat trim, luxury door panel trim with cloth or vinyl inserts, courtesy lamps in quarter trim panels, and front door armrests, electronic AM/FM search stereo radio, illuminated visor-vanity mirror (passenger side), 18-oz. cut-pile luxury carpeting, wood-tone instrument panel appliqués, luxury steering wheel, color-keyed deluxe seat belts, luxury luggage compartment trim, light group with dual-beam lights, map light, instrument panel courtesy lights, engine compartment light, and luggage compartment light.

I.D. NUMBERS

VIN stamped on aluminum tab riveted to the dashboard on passenger side and observable through the windshield from outside the car. First symbol denotes model-year: 0=1980. Second symbol denotes the assembly plant: G=Chicago, Illinois and H=Lorain, Ohio. Third symbol denotes the car-line: 8=T-Bird. Fourth symbol denotes body type: 7=two-door pillared hardtop. Fifth symbol denotes engine: B=200-cid (3.3L) 6-cyl, D=255-cid (4.2L)/115-hp V-8, F = 302-cid (5.0L)/131-hp V-8, G=351-cid V-8. Sixth thru 11th symbols denote sequential production number of specific vehicle starting at 100001. Vehicle certification label located on rear face of driver's door. The top part of the label indicates that the Thunderbird was manufactured by Ford Motor Company. Directly below this is the month and year of manufacture, plus a statement that the car conforms to federal motor vehicle safety standards in effect on the indicated date of manufacture. VIN: The VIN appears first on the first line of encoded information. It matches the 1st to 11th symbols on VIN tag. Some other codes also appear. TYPE: On left side of label, indicates PASSENGER. EXT. COLOR: This line carries the exterior paint color(s) code. DSO: The District Special Order code now appears above "DSO" to the right of the exterior paint color code. BODY: The body style code appears to the extreme left of the bottom line. The only Thunderbird code for this model year is: 66D=2-door pillared hardtop. VR: The vinyl roof type/color code is to the right of the body code. MLDG: The molding code is to the right of the vinyl roof code. INT. TRIM: The interior trim code is to the right of the molding code. A/C: The air conditioning code is to the right of the interior trim code. Cars with air conditioning have "A" stamped here. R: The radio code is to the right of the A/C code. S: The sunroof code appears to the right of the radio code. AX: The axle code appears to the right of the sunroof code. TR: The transmission code appears to the right of the axle code. (Note: The terms and abbreviations shown in capitals appear on the line above the actual codes.)

ENGINE

THUNDERBIRD BASE V-8: 90-degree. Overhead valve. Cast-iron block and head. Displacement: 255 cid (4.2 liters). Bore and stroke: 3.68 x 3.00 in. Compression ratio: 8.8:1. Brake hp: 115 at 3800. Torque: 194 lbs.-ft. at 2200. Five main bearings. Hydraulic valve lifters. Carburetor: Motorcraft 2150 two-barrel. Serial number code: D.

THUNDERBIRD DELETE OPTION IN-LINE 6-CYL (USED

Ford photo

The trimmed-down 1980 Thunderbird was 700 lbs. lighter and 17 inches shorter than the previous year's model.

IN A LIMITED NUMBER OF LATE-IN-THE-YEAR T-BIRDS): 90-degree. Overhead valve. Cast-iron block and head. Displacement: 200 cid (3.3 liters). Bore and stroke: 3.68 x 3.13 in. Compression ratio: 8.6:1. Brake hp: 88 at 3800. Torque: 154 lbs.-ft. at 1400. Seven main bearings. Hydraulic valve lifters. Carburetor: Holley one-barrel. Serial number code: B.

THUNDERBIRD OPTIONAL V-8: 90-degree. Overhead valve V-8. Cast-iron block and head. Displacement: 302 cid (5.0 liters). Bore and stroke: 4.00 x 3.00 in. Compression ratio: 8.4:1. Brake horsepower: 131 at 3600 rpm. Torque: 231 lbs.-ft. at 1600 rpm. Five main bearings. Hydraulic valve lifters. Carburetor: Motorcraft 2150 or 2700VV two-barrel. Serial number code: F.

THUNDERBIRD OPTIONAL V-8: 90-degree. Overhead valve. Cast-iron block and head. Displacement: 351 cid (5.8 liters). Bore and stroke: 4.00 x 3.50 in. Compression ratio: 8.3:1. Brake hp: 140 at 3400 rpm. Torque: 265 lbs.-ft. at 2000 rpm. Five main bearings. Hydraulic valve lifters. Carburetor: Motorcraft 7200VV two-barrel. Windsor engine. Serial number code: G.

CHASSIS

Wheelbase: 108.4 in. Overall length: 200.4. Overall width: 74.1. Overall height: 53 in. Front headroom: 37.1 in. Front legroom: 41.6 in. Rear headroom: 36.3 in. Rear legroom: 36.5 in. Trunk capacity: 17.7 cu. ft. Front tread: 58.1 in. Rear tread: 57.2 in. Ground clearance: 6 in. Tires: P185/75R14 steel-belted radial. Steering: Integral with power-assist. Turning diameter: 40.1 ft. Turns lock-to-lock: 3.4. Front suspension: Modified McPherson strut. Rear suspension: Four-link-bar with coil springs. Steering: Variable-ratio power rack-and-pinion. Standard rear axle: 2.79:1. Front brakes: 10-inch power vented disc. Rear brakes: 9-inch power assisted drums. Fuel tank capacity: 21 gal.

OPTIONS

5.0-liter (302-cid) two-barrel V-8 ($150). 351-cid V-8 engine. Inline six-cylinder engine. Automatic overdrive transmission ($138). Automatic temperature control air conditioner in hardtop ($634). Automatic temperature control air conditioner in Town Landau or Silver Anniversary models ($63). Manual temperature control air conditioner ($571). Auto lamp on and off delay system ($63). Heavy-duty battery ($20). Color-keyed deluxe seat belts ($23). Lower body-side protection with rocker panel moldings ($34). Lower body-side protection on models without rocker panel moldings ($46). Front license plate bracket (no charge). Electronic digital clock ($38). Front cornering lamps ($50). Exterior décor group ($359). Interior décor group ($348). Mud and stone deflectors ($25). Electric rear window defroster ($101). Diagnostic warning lights ($50). California emissions system ($238). High-altitude emissions system ($36). Garage door opener with illuminated visor and vanity mirror in Town Landau or models with interior luxury group ($130). Garage door opener with illuminated visor and vanity mirror in models with interior décor group ($165). Garage door opener with illuminated visor and vanity mirror in all other models ($171). Tinted glass ($71). Engine block immersion heater ($15). Dual-note horn ($9). Illuminated entry system ($58). Electronic instrument cluster in hardtop with interior luxury group ($275). Electronic instrument cluster in all

other models ($313). Keyless entry system with Recaro bucket seats ($106). Keyless entry system without Recaro bucket seats ($119). Light group ($35). Power lock group ($113). Luggage compartment trim ($44). Exterior luxury group ($489). Interior luxury group ($975). Passenger side illuminated visor and vanity mirror with interior décor group ($35). Passenger-side illuminated visor and vanity mirror without interior décor group ($41). Left-hand remote-control OSRV mirror ($18). Dual remote-control mirrors ($69). Rocker panel moldings ($30). Wide door belt moldings with interior luxury group ($31). Wide door belt moldings without interior luxury group ($44). Wide vinyl insert body-side moldings ($54). Metallic Glow paint ($60). Tu-Tone paint and striping treatment on Town Landau ($106). Tu-Tone paint and striping treatment on hardtop with exterior luxury or exterior luxury groups ($123). Tu-Tone paint and striping treatment on base hardtop ($163). Automatic parking brake release ($10). Protection group on models with front license plate bracket ($43). Protection group on models without front license plate bracket ($39). Power radio antenna ($49). AM radio delete ($81 credit). AM/FM monaural radio ($53). AM/FM stereo radio ($90). AM/FM stereo radio with 8-track tape player ($166). AM/FM stereo radio with cassette tape player ($179). Electronic AM/FM stereo search radio ($240). Electronic AM/FM stereo search radio with 8-track tape player in hardtop ($316). Electronic AM/FM stereo search radio with 8-track tape player in Town Landau or Silver Anniversary hardtops ($76). 40-channel CB radio ($316). Electronic AM/FM stereo search radio with cassette tape player and Dolby noise reduction system in hardtop ($329). Electronic AM/FM stereo search radio with cassette tape player and Dolby noise reduction system in Town Landau or Silver Anniversary hardtops ($89). Radio flexibility package ($66). Flip-up open air roof ($219). Vinyl rear half roof ($133). 6-way power driver's seat ($166). 4-way full-width power seat ($111). Bucket seats and console with interior luxury group (no charge). Bucket seats and console without interior luxury group ($176). Recaro bucket seats and console in Town Landau (no charge). Recaro bucket seats and console in hardtop with interior luxury group ($166). Recaro bucket seats and console in hardtop without interior luxury group ($254). Premium sound system, with conventional radio ($119). Premium sound system with electronic radio ($150). Conventional spare tire ($37). Dual rear seat speakers ($38). Fingertip speed control in Town Landau or hardtop with interior luxury group ($116). Fingertip speed control in base hardtop ($129). Leather-wrapped steering wheel ($44). Tilt steering wheel ($78). Dual accent body-side stripes ($40). Hood and body-side accent stripes with Exterior décor or Exterior luxury groups ($16). Hood and body-side accent stripes without Exterior décor or Exterior luxury groups ($56). Heavy-duty handling suspension ($23). All-vinyl seat trim ($26). Ultra-soft leather seat trim in Silver Anniversary model ($318). Ultra-soft leather seat trim in all models except Silver Anniversary ($349). Luxury wheel covers ($88). Simulated wire wheel covers with Exterior luxury group ($50). Simulated wire wheel covers without Exterior luxury group ($138). Power side windows ($136). Interval windshield wipers ($39). P195/75R x 14 steel-belted radial-ply black sidewall tires on base hardtop ($26). P195/75R x 14 steel-belted radial-ply white sidewall tires on base hardtop ($59). TR type radial whitewall tires with exterior décor and including aluminum wheels on Town Landau and Silver Anniversary models ($441). TR type radial whitewall tires without exterior décor ($528). Front floor mats ($19) Luggage compartment light ($29). Electronic instrument cluster delete on Town Landau or Silver Anniversary only ($275 credit).

EQUIPMENT INSTALLATION RATES

Automatic transmission (100 percent). V-8 engine (96.1 percent). Six-cyl engine (3.9 percent). AM radio (15.7 percent). AM/FM Mono. Radio (3.4 percent). AM/FM stereo (37.4 percent). AM/FM with 8-Track tape player (7.7 percent). AM/FM stereo cassette (9.5 percent). AM/FM stereo with CB radio (0.3 percent). AM/FM stereo with 8-track tape player and CB (0.2 percent). AM/FM stereo cassette and CB (0.6 percent). AM/FM Quadratrack 8-track (5.2 percent). AM/FM Quadratrack 8-track with CB (0.5 percent). Power steering (100 percent). Power front disc brakes (100 percent). Power door locks: (30.5 percent). Power seat (27.8 percent). Power windows (39.4 percent). Adjustable steering column (49.3 percent). Tinted windshield only (1 percent). All tinted glass (93.9 percent). Vinyl top (81.4 percent). Sun roof (6.2 percent). Automatic air conditioning (8.1 percent). Manual air conditioning (86 percent). Standard steel-belted radial tires (100 percent). Electric rear window defogger (40.7 percent). Wheel covers (83.8 percent). Aluminum styled wheels 16.2 percent). Speed control (57.5 percent). Remote-control left-hand rearview mirror (88.4 percent). Remote-control right-hand rearview mirror (79.7 percent). Reclining front seats (28 percent). Bucket seats (1.1 percent). Analog clock (68 percent). Digital clock (32 percent). (Note: Based on 138,101 units produced in the model year for the U.S. market only.)

HISTORICAL FOOTNOTES

The 1980 T-Bird was introduced on October 12, 1979. Phillip Caldwell became chairman of the board of Ford Motor Company in 1980. Donald E. Petersen was president. Harold A. Poling was executive vice president of North American Automotive Operations. Philip E. Benton Jr. was Ford Division's vice president and general manager. Bernard L. Crumpton remained general sales manager for the division.

Demand for T-Birds continued to drop. Calendar-year output was 117,856 units. A total of 156,803 T-Birds were produced in the model year. This represented 2.31 percent of the industry total. Of these units, 93,634 were made in Chicago and 63,169 were made in Lorain, Ohio. Calendar-year dealer sales amounted to 127,248 T-Birds, representing 1.9 percent of industry sales.

The new T-Bird had some teething problems. It guzzled more gas than some other cars in its class and was not as agile as some of its competitors. The new unit-body made the car slightly noisier. Ford also wrestled with claims that the T-Bird's automatic transmission slipped gears. The company made an out-of-court settlement of those claims. It also recalled some 1980 T-Birds that were built with Mustang brakes, which were too small. In addition to the brakes, electrical and body integrity problems were other shortcomings of the new car. Cars with the 5.0-liter V-8 using a variable-venturi carburetor were also trouble-prone.

Motor Trend put two 1980 T-Birds on the cover of its September 1979 issue. One was a monotone Red Glow car with no vinyl roof, white stripe tires, and spoke-style wheel covers. The second was a Chamois and Bittersweet Glow two-toned version with a luxury half-vinyl roof and simulated wire wheel covers. "All-New ... Split Personality: Performance, Luxury," read the cover blurb. Peter Frey's article about the new car was a positive review subtitled, "A living legend rises from the ashes of obesity to reclaim its heritage." The article gave specifications for the 1980 model, but no performance numbers.

In its third "Country Wide Test" in June 1980, *Motor Trend* tried out a T-Bird with the 5.0-liter V-8, four-speed overdrive transmission, Luxury exterior group, Recaro bucket seats, electronic instrumentation and Bittersweet Glow Metallic finish. This car was driven on both coasts and made two cross-country trips in the course of four months. Nearly 15,000 miles were driven during the evaluation. Various editors took stints behind the wheel. "Down-sizing has unquestionably improved the breed," said associate editor Bob Nagy. "The fact that, in not many more years, no one will produce a car like this makes me sad," Washington editor Ted Orme noted. However, executive editor Jim McGraw felt differently. "We'd rather spend $11,000 buying an original Thunderbird restoration," said the headline on his report that criticized the car's exterior and interior designs. (Unfortunately, two-seat T-Birds were selling for $15,000 to $18,000 at the time, so McGraw would have had a hard time getting one on his budget.) Associate editor Peter Frey said the T-Bird made him smile, and engineering editor Chuck Nerpel — who had road tested a '55 model for *Motor Trend* — said, "It has better handling than any T-Bird of the past."

Though popular with most magazine editors, the 1980 T-Bird had the misfortune of bowing at a time when Americans were rethinking what they needed and wanted in automobiles. It's true that the automobile industry, as well as the national economy, was in a slump at this time. However, even in a weakened market, the T-Bird's slice of the smaller pie was shrinking. The nameplate owned 3.09 percent of the total market in 1979, but only 2.31 percent in 1980. Records show that 18,702 U.S.-built T-Birds were made for the export market and many of these were shipped to Canada.

By looking at optional equipment installations, it was easy to tell the type of transition the T-Bird had gone through in its 25 years. What had started out as a fancy two-seat sporty car had become an ostentatious luxury coupe. On the track, there were big questions about the future of Grand National stock car racing at this time. The new downsized cars coming out of Detroit were too small for the Grand National wheelbase and size specifications. Nevertheless, the October 1979 issue of *Motor Trend* featured a sketch of Bobby Allison's proposed 1980 T-Bird stock car, saying in the caption that it was unclear if the new model would be approved by NASCAR. A few of these cars did eventually race, but without the much-needed factory backing.

1980 THUNDERBIRD PERFORMANCE		
Model	**CID/HP**	**Performance**
0-60 mph		
Hardtop	302/131	11.10 seconds
1/4-Mile		
Hardtop	302/131	18.01 seconds @ 75.70 mph

Ford photo

The T-Bird didn't change much for 1981. Perhaps the biggest news was that the inline six-cylinder engine became standard. Two V-8's were optional, and few buyers went with the six.

1981
Thunderbird

The 1981 T-Bird looked like the 1980, except the grille texture no longer showed below the bumper. The license plate sat in a recessed opening low on the bumper. Huge full-width taillights again had T-Bird emblems on each side. The deck lid protruded halfway between each taillight half.

New options included a Carriage Roof that made the car look like a convertible, a Traction-Lok axle, pivoting front vent windows, a convex remote-control left-hand rearview mirror and self-sealing puncture-resistant tires. The inline six-cylinder engine that was a delete-option in a small number of late-1980 T-Birds became the base engine for the 1981 series. It was attached to the conventional SelectShift automatic transmission. The 4.2-liter and 5.0-liter V-8s were both extra-cost items.

The base hardtop had more standard equipment and upgraded trimmings. Some of the ingredients had formerly been part of the exterior luxury group package. A Flight Bench front seat was standard with a choice of all-vinyl or cloth and vinyl upholstery.

The Town Landau had "Town Landau" fender scripts. Its Valino grain vinyl roof came in half and luxury half styles with a choice of seven colors. The Town Landau interior offered standard split-bench seat with dual recliners and knit-cloth fabric upholstery. Town Landaus came in seven colors: Black, White, Midnight Blue, Fawn, Medium Red, Bittersweet and Silver with color-coordinated roof wrap-over moldings and specific color (Black or Silver) accent tape on the opera windows.

The top T-Bird was the Heritage Edition hardtop with its padded rear half vinyl roof with brushed aluminum wrap-over band, coach lamps, a "Frenched" backlight, distinctive "arrowheads" at the forward end of the body stripes, a unique hood ornament with a "cut-glass" look and a split-bench seat with velour cloth trim.

BODY COLOR INFORMATION

Color Name	Code	Color Name	Code
Black	1C	Midnight Blue Metallic	3L
Light Grey	12	Dark Cordovan Metallic	8N
Silver Metallic	1G	Fawn	89
Medium Grey Metallic	1P	Medium Blue Glow (Opt.)	3H
Polar White	9D	Light Fawn Glow (Opt.)	5H
Red	24	Medium Fawn Glow (Opt.)	55
Light Medium Blue	3F	Bittersweet Glow (Opt.)	8D

VINYL TOP COLOR INFORMATION

Color Name	Code	Color Name	Code
Black Valino grain	A	Midnight Blue Valino grain	Q
Bittersweet Valino grain	C	Fawn Valino grain	U
Medium Red Valino grain	D	White Valino grain	W
Silver Valino grain	P		

Vinyl top codes: Y=half vinyl top, E=luxury half-vinyl top.

CARRIAGE ROOF COLOR INFORMATION

Color Name	Code	Color Name	Code
Midnight Blue Diamond grain	Q	White Diamond grain	W
Fawn Diamond grain	U		

PAINT STRIPE COLOR INFORMATION

Color Name	Code	Color Name	Code
Black	a	Silver	p
Midnight Blue	b	Dark Champagne	u
Bittersweet	c	Light Champagne	u
Bright Red	e	White	w
Dark Cordovan	f		

TOWN LANDAU WRAPOVER & PAINT STRIPE INFORMATION

Vinyl Roof Color	Wrap-over Color	Opera Window Accent Tape
Black	Black	Silver
White	White	Black
Midnight Blue	Midnight Blue	Silver
Fawn	Fawn	Black
Medium Red	Medium Red	Silver
Bittersweet	Bittersweet	Black
Silver	Medium Grey Metallic	Black

INTERIOR TRIM INFORMATION

Seat Type	Material	Med. Fawn	Dark Red	MW Blue	Dove Grey	Vaquero
Flight Bench	Cloth & Vinyl	AL	AD	AB	AS	—
Flight Bench	All-Vinyl	BL	BD	BB	BS	—
Bucket	All-Vinyl	DL	DD	DB	DS	—
Interior Décor & Town Landau						
Split-Bench	Cloth & Vinyl	EL	ED	EB	ES	EZ
Split-Bench	SS Vinyl	FL	FD	FB	FS	FZ
Bucket	All-Vinyl	GL	GD	GB	GS	GZ
Recaro Buckets	Cloth & Vinyl	—	ND	NB	NS	NZ
Interior Luxury & Heritage						
Split-Bench	Cloth	JL	JD	JB	TS	TZ
Split Bench	U-Soft Leather	KL	KD	KB	KS	KZ
Recaro Buckets	Cloth & Vinyl	—	PD	PB	PS	PZ

TU-TONE INTERIOR TRIM INFORMATION

Seat Type	Material	White/ M. Fawn	White/ D. Red	White/ MWB	White/ Vaquero
Split-Bench	All-Vinyl	B3	BN	BQ	—
Bucket	All-Vinyl	D3	DN	DQ	—
T-Bird Interior Décor & Town Landau					
Split-Split Bench	SS Vinyl	F3	FN	FQ	F9
Bucket	All-Vinyl	G3	GN	GQ	G9

Interior Luxury & Town Landau

Split-Bench	U-Soft Leather	K3	KN	KQ	K9

Legend: Med. is medium, D. Red is Dark Red, MWB or MW Blue is Medium Wedgewood Blue, SS Vinyl is Super-soft vinyl, U-Soft Leather means Ultra-Soft Leather

THUNDERBIRD PRODUCTION

Model Number	Body/Style Number	Body Type & Seating	Factory Price	Shipping Weight	Production Total
THUNDERBIRD - (6-CYL)					
42	66D	2d Hardtop-4P	$7,551	3,004 lbs.	Note 1
THUNDERBIRD - (V-8)					
42	66D	2d Hardtop-4P	$7,601	3,124 lbs.	Note 1
THUNDERBIRD TOWN LANDAU - (6-CYL)					
42/60T	66D	2d Hardtop-4P	$8,689	3,067 lbs.	Note 1
THUNDERBIRD TOWN LANDAU - (V-8)					
42/60T	66D	2d Hardtop-4P	$8,739	3,187 lbs.	Note 1
THUNDERBIRD HERITAGE EDITION - (V-8)					
42/607	66D	2d Hardtop-4P	$11,355	3,303 lbs.	Note 1

NOTE 1: Production of the three models combined was 86,693.

STANDARD EQUIPMENT

All standard FoMoCo safety, anti-theft, convenience items, and emissions control equipment, 3.3-liter (200-cid) one-barrel six-cylinder engine, three-speed automatic transmission, variable-ratio power rack and pinion steering, power front disc/rear drum brakes, DuraSpark ignition system, halogen headlights, maintenance-free 36AH battery, coolant recovery system, modified McPherson strut front suspension with stabilizer bar, four-bar link-type rear suspension with stabilizer bar, three-speed heater and defroster, concealed rectangular headlights, inside hood release, power ventilation system, dual-note horn, chrome-plated egg-crate grille, hood ornament, soft color-keyed urethane covered bumpers with bright bumper rub strips, bright moldings on rear of hood, windshield, drip rail, door belt, and rear window, wide vinyl insert body-side moldings with integral partial wheel lip moldings, quarter windows, full wheel covers, electric clock, cigar lighter, locking glove box, push-button AM radio, four-spoke deluxe steering wheel, inside day-night rearview mirror, Flight Bench seat with adjustable head restraints, color-keyed seat belts with reminder chime, anti-theft door locks, 10-oz. color-keyed cut-pile carpeting, luggage compartment light, mini spare, and P195/75R14 white sidewall steel-belted radial tires. **1981 Thunderbird Town Landau Standard Equipment additions or substitutes:** Padded half-vinyl roof with color-coordinated wrap-over band and coach lamps, hood and body-side accent stripes, right-hand remote-control OSRV mirror, luxury wheel covers, wide door belt moldings, split-bench seats with dual fold-down armrests, 18-oz. luxury color-keyed cut-pile carpets, Coco Bola wood-tone appliqué around instrument panel, light group, tilt steering wheel, interval wipers, and diagnostic warning light system. **1981 Thunderbird Heritage Edition Standard Equipment additions or substitutes:** Padded rear half-vinyl roof with brushed aluminum wrap-over band and coach lamps, "Frenched" vinyl roof treatment around rear window, dual body-side stripes, deck lid accent stripes, bright rocker panel moldings, wire wheel covers, electronic AM/FM stereo search radio, bright rhodium engraved owner's nameplate, luxury steering wheel with wood-tone insert, illuminated passenger side visor and vanity mirror, velour cloth seat trim in luxury sew style, luxury door trim panels with cloth inserts, burled rosewood wood-tone instrument panel appliqués, luxury luggage compartment trim, 4.2-liter (255-cid) V-8 engine, air conditioning with manual temperature control, tinted glass, power side windows, 6-way power driver's seat, power door locks, remote control deck lid release, auto lamp on and off delay system, electronic instrument cluster, and front cornering lamps.

I.D. NUMBERS

VIN Stamped on aluminum tab riveted to dashboard on passenger side and observable through the windshield from outside the car. First symbol 1 denotes built in the United States. Second symbol F denotes Ford. Third symbol A denotes Ford passenger vehicle. Fourth symbol denotes type of restraint system. Fifth symbol P denotes passenger-type vehicle. Sixth symbol 4 denotes Thunderbird. Seventh symbol 2 denotes two-door coupe. Eighth symbol denote engine: B=200-cid (3.3L)/115-hp six-cylinder, D=255-cid (4.2L)/115-hp V-8, F=302-cid (5.0L)/131-hp V-8. Ninth symbol is the check digit. 10th symbol B=1981 model year. 11th symbol denotes assembly plant, all T-Birds made at plant H in Lorain, Ohio. Twelfth through 17th symbols denote sequential production number of specific vehicle starting at 100001. Vehicle certification label located on rear face of driver's door. The top part of the label indicates that the Thunderbird was manufactured by Ford Motor Company. Directly below this is the month and year of manufacture, plus a statement that the car conforms to federal motor vehicle safety standards in effect on the indicated date of manufacture. VIN: The VIN appears first on the first line of encoded information. It matches the 1st to 11th symbols on VIN tag. Some other codes also appear. TYPE: On left side of label, indicates PASSENGER. EXT. COLOR: This line carries the exterior paint color(s) code. DSO: The District Special Order code now appears above "DSO" to the right of the exterior paint color code. BODY: The body style code appears to the extreme left of the bottom line. The only Thunderbird code for this model year is: 66D=Two-door pillared hardtop. VR: The vinyl roof type/color code is to the right of the body code. MLDG: The molding code is to the right of the vinyl roof code. INT. TRIM: The interior trim code is to the right of the molding code. A/C: The air conditioning code is to the right of the interior trim code. Cars with air conditioning have "A" stamped here. R: The radio code is to the right of the A/C code. S: The sunroof code appears to the right of the radio code. AX: The axle code appears to the right of the sunroof code. TR: The transmission code appears to the right of the axle code. (Note: The terms and abbreviations shown in capitals appear on the line above the actual codes.)

ENGINE

THUNDERBIRD BASE SIX-CYL: Inline. Cast-iron block and head. Displacement: 200 cid (3.3 liters). Bore and stroke: 3.68 x 3.13 in. Compression ratio: 8.6:1. Brake hp: 88 at 3800. Torque: 154 lbs.-ft. at 1400. Seven main bearings. Hydraulic valve lifters. Carburetor: Holley 1946 one-barrel. Serial number code: B.

THUNDERBIRD BASE V-8: 90-degree. Overhead valve. Cast-iron block and head. Displacement: 255 cid (4.2 liters). Bore and stroke: 3.68 x 3.00 in. Compression ratio: 8.2:1. Brake hp: 115 at 3400. Torque: 195 lbs.-ft. at 2200. Five main bearings. Hydraulic valve lifters. Carburetor: Motorcraft 2150 or 7200VV two-barrel. Serial number code: D.

THUNDERBIRD OPTIONAL V-8: 90-degree. Overhead valve. Cast-iron block and head. Displacement: 302 cid (5.0 liters). Bore and stroke: 4.00 x 3.00 in. Compression ratio: 8.4:1. Brake hp: 130 at 3400 rpm. Torque: 235 lbs.-ft. at 1600 rpm. Five main bearings. Hydraulic valve lifters. Carburetor: Motorcraft 2150 or 7200VV two-barrel. Serial number code: F.

CHASSIS

Wheelbase: 108.4 in. Overall length: 200.4. Overall width: 74.1. Overall height: 53 in. Front headroom: 37.1 in. Front legroom: 41.6 in. Rear headroom: 36.3 in. Rear legroom: 36.5 in. Trunk capacity: 17.7 cu. ft. Front tread: 58.2 in. Rear tread: 57.0 in. Ground clearance: 6 in. Tires: P185/75R14 steel-belted radial. Steering: Integral with power-assist. Turning diameter: 40.1 ft. Turns lock-to-lock: 3.4. Front suspension: Modified McPherson strut. Rear suspension: Four-link-bar with coil springs. Steering: Variable-ratio power rack and pinion. Standard rear axle: 2.79:1. Front brakes: 10-inch power vented disc. Rear brakes: 9-inch power assisted drums. Fuel tank capacity: 18 gal.

OPTIONS

4.2-liter (255-cid) two-barrel V-8, but standard in Heritage Edition ($50). 5.0-liter (302-cid) two-barrel V-8 in Heritage Edition ($41). 5.0-liter (302-cid) two-barrel V-8 in all except Heritage Edition ($91). Four-speed automatic overdrive transmission ($162). Traction-Lok rear axle ($67). Automatic temperature control air conditioner in Hardtop and Town Landau ($652). Automatic temperature control air conditioner in Heritage Edition ($67). Manual temperature control air conditioner ($585). Auto lamp on and off delay system ($65). Heavy-duty battery ($20). Lower body-side protection on Heritage Edition ($34). Lower body-side protection on other models ($48). Front license plate bracket (no charge). Electronic digital clock ($40). Front cornering lamps ($51). Mud and stone deflectors ($26). Electric rear window defroster ($107). Diagnostic warning lights ($51). California emissions system ($46). High-altitude emissions system ($38). Exterior décor group ($341). Garage door opener with illuminated visor and vanity mirror in Heritage Edition or models with interior luxury group ($134). Garage door opener with illuminated visor and vanity mirror in all other models ($177). Tinted glass ($76). Engine block immersion heater ($16). Illuminated entry system ($60). Electronic instrument cluster in Hardtop with interior luxury group ($282). Electronic instrument cluster in all other models ($322). Electronic instrument cluster delete ($282 credit). Interior décor group ($349). Interior luxury group in Town Landau ($584). Interior Luxury group in other models ($1,039). Keyless entry system ($122). Light group ($30). Power lock group ($120). Luggage compartment trim ($44). Passenger side illuminated visor and vanity mirror ($41). Right-hand remote-control OSRV mirror ($52). Rocker panel moldings ($30). Wide door belt moldings ($45). Tu-Tone paint and striping treatment on Heritage Edition ($111). Tu-Tone paint and striping treatment on hardtop with exterior décor group ($139). Tu-Tone paint and striping treatment on base hardtop ($180). Automatic parking brake release ($10). Protection group ($45). Power radio antenna ($48). AM radio delete ($61 credit). Dual rear speakers with AM radio ($37). AM/FM monaural radio ($51). Dual rear speakers with AM/FM monaural radio ($37). AM/FM stereo radio ($88). AM/FM stereo radio with

8-track tape player in Town Landau ($74). AM/FM stereo radio with 8-track tape player in base hardtop ($162) AM/FM stereo radio with cassette tape player in Town Landau ($87). AM/FM stereo radio with cassette tape player in other models ($174). Electronic AM/FM stereo search radio in Town Landau ($146). Electronic AM/FM stereo search radio in other models ($234). Electronic AM/FM stereo search radio with 8-track tape player in Heritage Edition ($74). Electronic AM/FM stereo search radio with 8-track tape player in Town Landau ($221). Electronic AM/FM stereo search radio with 8-track tape player in other models than Town Landau ($309). Electronic AM/FM stereo search radio with cassette tape player and Dolby noise reduction system in Heritage Edition ($87). Electronic AM/FM stereo search radio with cassette tape player and Dolby noise reduction system in Town Landau ($233). Electronic AM/FM stereo search radio with cassette tape player and Dolby noise reduction system in models other than Town Landau or Heritage Edition ($321). Radio flexibility package ($65). Flip-up open air roof ($228). 6-way power driver's seat ($173). 4-way full-width power seat ($122). Premium sound system, with conventional radio ($116). Premium sound system with electronic radio ($146). Fingertip speed control ($132). Leather-wrapped luxury steering wheel ($45). Tilt steering wheel ($80). Dual accent body-side stripes ($41). Hood and body-side accent stripes

The 1981 Thunderbird Heritage Edition.

Ford photo

with exterior décor group ($16). Hood and body-side accent stripes without exterior décor groups ($57). Heavy-duty handling suspension ($23). Pivoting front vent windows ($55). Luxury wheel covers ($98). Simulated wire wheel covers with Town Landau or exterior décor group ($38). Simulated wire wheel covers without exterior décor group ($135). Power side windows ($140). Interval windshield wipers ($41). P195/75R x 14 puncture-resistant self-sealing steel-belted radial-ply black sidewall tires ($85). TR type radial whitewall tires with exterior décor and including aluminum wheels on Heritage Edition model ($428). TR type radial whitewall tires with exterior décor, includes aluminum wheels on Town Landau model ($466). TR type radial whitewall tires without Exterior décor ($563). Metallic Glow paint ($70). Color-keyed and carpeted front floor mats ($20). Vinyl front floor mats ($13). Bucket seats and console with Town Landau and Interior décor group (no charge). Bucket seats and console without Town Landau or Interior décor group ($182). Recaro bucket seats and console in Heritage Edition ($213). Recaro bucket seats and console in hardtop with interior luxury group ($376). Recaro bucket seats and console in Town Landau and hardtop with interior décor group ($461). All-vinyl seat trim ($28). Ultra-soft leather seat trim ($309). Carriage roof ($902). Rear half-vinyl roof ($130). Tinted windshield ($29).

EQUIPMENT INSTALLATION RATES

Automatic transmission (100 percent). V-8 engine (83.6 percent). Six-cylinder engine (16.4 percent). AM radio (11.9 percent). AM/FM Mono. Radio (1.7 percent). AM/FM stereo (51.3 percent). AM/FM with 8-Track tape player (6.4 percent). AM/FM stereo cassette (7.8 percent). AM/FM Quadratrack 8-track (2.9 percent). AM/FM Quadratrack 8-track with cassette (5.7 percent). Power steering (100 percent). Power front disc brakes (100 percent). Power door locks (33.5 percent). Power seat (33 percent). Power windows (46.5 percent). Adjustable steering column (66.8 percent). Tinted windshield only (0.8 percent). All tinted glass (97.5 percent). Vinyl top: (84.2 percent). Sunroof (5.3 percent). Automatic air conditioning (6.5 percent). Manual air conditioning (90.2 percent). Standard steel-belted radial tires (100 percent). Electric rear window defogger (47.1 percent). Wheel covers (94.1 percent). Aluminum styled wheels (5.9 percent). Speed control (71.8 percent). Remote-control left-hand rearview mirror (100 percent). Remote-control right-hand rearview mirror (75.1 percent). Reclining front seats (73.3 percent). Bucket seats (3.4 percent). Analog clock (65.5 percent). Digital clock (34.5 percent). Limited-slip rear axle (0.8 percent). (Note: Based on 76,979 units produced in the model year for the U.S. market only.)

HISTORICAL FOOTNOTES

The 1981 T-Bird was introduced on October 3, 1980. Phillip Caldwell was chairman of the board of Ford Motor Company. William Clay Ford was vice chairman and Donald E. Petersen was president. Louis E. Lataif was Ford Division's general manager. Bernard L. Crumpton remained general sales manager for the division.

Calendar-year output was 64,328 units. A total of 86,693 T-Birds were produced in the model year. This represented 1.30 percent of the industry total. Of these units, all were made in Lorain, Ohio. Calendar-year dealer sales amounted to 69,775 T-Birds, representing 1.1 percent of industry sales.

The T-Bird's share of market continued to decline in 1981. This year the number of cars with luxury features went up across the board, while sporty options like bucket seats and sunroofs continued to lose favor with those who were still purchasing T-Birds. A larger 16.4 percent of those purchasing 1981 models opted for the inline six.

Neil Bonnett drove the Wood Brother's 1981 T-Bird during the year's NASCAR Winston Cup stock car racing series. Without factory help, there were very few 'Birds of this vintage on the circuit.

1981 THUNDERBIRD PERFORMANCE		
Model	CID/HP	Performance
0-60 mph		
Hardtop	302/131	11.10 seconds
1/4-Mile		
Hardtop	302/131	18.01 seconds @ 75.70 mph

The stylish 1982 Thunderbird Town Landau came standard with an inline six-cylinder engine, but it could be had with an optional V-6 or V-8.

1982

Thunderbird

The 1982 T-Bird had carryover front and rear end styling. The cross-hatched grille had an 8 x 6 pattern of wide holes. Lettered into the grille header was the T-Bird name. A wide see-through hood ornament held a T-Bird insignia. That insignia also highlighted the roof sail panels and the taillight lenses. The same models were offered: Base T-Bird, Town Landau and Heritage.

Technical changes in 1982 models started with engines. The 3.3-liter in-line six was the base power plant in the base 'Bird and Town Landau. A 3.8-liter V-6 was now standard equipment in the Heritage. Buyers of any of the models could get the V-6 or 4.2-liter V-8 installed under the hood at extra cost. SelectShift automatic was standard in the base T-Bird and Town Landau, while automatic overdrive transmission was standard in the Heritage edition. The three-speed SelectShift transmission used this year had noticeable improvements for smoother, more efficient operation, but the four-speed automatic overdrive gave much better fuel economy. It was optional in the base 'Bird and the Town Landau. The gas tank was also enlarged to 21-gal.

A new option was a Tripminder computer that showed time and speed and calculated elapsed time, distance traveled, fuel used, average speed and current or average mpg. Also, a new luxury vinyl roof treatment was standard on the Town Landau. The Carriage Roof was not available on the Town Landau teamed with the flip-up sunroof, keyless entry system, or wide door belt molding packages.

The base type rear half-vinyl roof was standard with the exterior décor group, but not available on Town Landau or Heritage models. When used on the base 'Bird, wide door belt moldings were required, too.

STANDARD EQUIPMENT

All standard FoMoCo safety, anti-theft, convenience items, and emissions control equipment, 3.3-liter (200-cid) one-barrel six-cylinder engine, electronic ignition, maintenance-free battery, coolant recovery system, automatic transmission, variable-ratio power rack and pinion steering, power front disc/rear drum brakes, P195/75R14 white sidewall steel-belted radial tires, three-speed heater and defroster, modified McPherson strut front suspension with stabilizer bar, four-bar link-type rear suspension with stabilizer bar, left-hand remote-control OSRV mirror, chrome-plated egg-crate grille, concealed rectangular halogen headlights, soft color-keyed urethane covered bumpers with black bumper rub strips with white accent stripes, black door window frames, bright moldings on windshield, drip rail, door belt, and rear window, black vinyl insert body moldings with partial wheel lip moldings, full wheel covers, illuminated quartz electric sweep hand clock, cigarette lighter, locking glove box, AM radio with dual front speakers, deluxe four-spoke deluxe steering wheel, inside day-night rearview mirror, Flight Bench seat, 10-oz. color-keyed cut-pile carpeting, luggage compartment light, and mini spare tire.

BODY COLOR INFORMATION

Color Name	Code	Color Name	Code
Black (Tu-Tone avail.)	1C	Pastel Vanilla (Tu-Tone avail.)	6Z
Light Pewter Metallic	1T	Vanilla Metallic	68
Medium Pewter Metallic	17	Dark Cordovan Metallic (Tu-Tone avail.)	8N
Red	24	Polar White	9D
Midnight Blue Metallic (Tu-Tone avail.)	3L	Medium Blue Glow (Opt.)	3H
Dark Brown Metallic (Tu-Tone avail.)	5V	Light Fawn Glow (Opt.)	5H
Medium Vanilla	6V	Medium Vaquero Glow (Opt., Tu-Tone avail.)	5W

ROOF COLOR INFORMATION

Color	Carriage Roof	Base Rear Half-top (Type Y)	Luxury Rear Half-top
Black (A)		YA	EA
Medium Red (D)		YD	ED
Dark Cordovan (F)		YF	EF
Vanilla (L)		YL	EL
Midnight Blue (Q)	AQ	YQ	EQ
Fawn (U)	AU		
White (W)	AW	YW	EW
Dark Brown (Z)		YZ	EZ
Light Pewter (4)		Y4	E4

Note: Carriage Roof not available on Town Landau, Heritage, or with flip-up roof, keyless entry, or wide body moldings. Base rear half-roof standard with Exterior décor group, not available on Town Landau or Heritage, wide belt moldings required with base model. Luxury rear half-roof standard on Town Landau and Heritage.

PAINT STRIPE COLOR INFORMATION

Color Name	Code	Color Name	Code
Black	a	Dark Cordovan	f
Medium Blue	b	Gold	q
Terra Cotta	c	Dark Champagne	q
Medium Red	d	Light Champagne	u
White	w		

INTERIOR TRIM INFORMATION

Seat Type	Material	MN Blue	Dark Red	Med. Fawn	Vanilla	Vaquero
T-Bird						
Flight Bench	Cloth & Vinyl	AB	AD	AL	AZ	—
Flight Bench	All-Vinyl	BB	BD	BL	BZ	—
Bucket	All-Vinyl	CB	CD	CL	CZ	—
Split-Bench	Cloth & Vinyl	EB	ED	EL	EV	EZ
Split-Split Bench	All-Vinyl	FB	FD	FL	FV	FZ
T-Bird Interior Décor & Town Landau						
Split-Bench	Cloth & Vinyl	EB	ED	EL	EV	EZ
Split-Split Bench	All-Vinyl	FB	FD	FL	FV	FZ
Split-Bench	Luxury Cloth	JB	JD	JL	JV	JZ
Split-Split Bench	U-Soft Leather	KB	KD	KL	KV	KZ
Bucket	All-Vinyl	CB	CD	CL	—	CZ
Recaro Bucket	Cloth & Vinyl	NB	ND	—	—	NZ
Interior Luxury & Heritage						
Split-Bench	Luxury Cloth	JB	JD	JL	JV	JZ
Split-Bench	U-Soft Leather	KB	KD	KL	KV	KZ
Recaro Bucket	Cloth & Vinyl	NB	ND	—	—	NZ

TU-TONE INTERIOR TRIM INFORMATION

Seat Type	Material	Opal/ D. Red	Opal/ M. Blue	Opal/ M. Fawn	Opal/ Pewter	Opal/ Vaquero
T-Bird						
Flight Bench	All-Vinyl	BN	BQ	B3	B6	B9
Bucket	All-Vinyl	CN	CQ	C3	C6	C9
Split-Split Bench	All-Vinyl	FN	FQ	F5	F6	F9
T-Bird Interior Décor & Town Landau						
Split-Split Bench	SS-Vinyl	FN	FQ	F3	F6	F9
Split-Split Bench	Luxury Cloth	—	—	J6	—	
Split-Split Bench	U-Soft Leather	—	—	K6	—	
Bucket	All-Vinyl	CN	CQ	C3	C6	C9
Interior Luxury & Heritage						
Split-Split Bench	Luxury Cloth	—	—	J6	—	
Split-Bench	U-Soft Leather	—	—	K6	—	

Legend: MN blue is Midnight Blue, Med. is Medium, U-Soft Leather is Ultra-Soft leather, D. is Dark Red, M. is Medium Blue, SS-Vinyl is Super-Soft Vinyl.

THUNDERBIRD PRODUCTION

Model Number	Body/Style Number	Body Type & Seating	Factory Price	Shipping Weight	Production Total
THUNDERBIRD - (6-CYL)					
42	66D	2d Hardtop-4P	$8,492	3,000 lbs.	Note 1
THUNDERBIRD - (V-8)					
42	66D	2d Hardtop-4P	$8,733	3,137 lbs.	Note 1
THUNDERBIRD TOWN LANDAU - (6-CYL)					
42/60T	66D	2d Hardtop-4P	$9,703	3,063 lbs.	Note 1
THUNDERBIRD TOWN LANDAU - (V-8)					
42/60T	66D	2d Hardtop-4P	$9,944	3,200 lbs.	Note 1
THUNDERBIRD HERITAGE - (V-6)					
42/607	66D	2d Hardtop-4P	$12,742	3,235 lbs.	Note 1
THUNDERBIRD HERITAGE - (V-8)					
42/607	66D	2d Hardtop-4P	$12,742	3,361 lbs.	Note 1

NOTE 1: Production of the three models combined was 45,142.

1982 Thunderbird Town Landau Standard Equipment adds or substitutes: Tilt steering wheel, interval windshield wipers, diagnostic warning light system, luxury padded vinyl roof with color-keyed wrap-over molding and coach lights, hood and body-side accent stripes, right-hand remote-control OSRV mirror, luxury wheel covers, wide door belt moldings, split-bench seats with fold-down armrests, adjustable head restraints, and dual recliners, décor door trim panels, AM/FM stereo radio, 18-oz. luxury color-keyed cut-pile carpets, and light group. **1982 Thunderbird Heritage Edition Standard Equipment adds or substitutes:** 3.8-liter (232-cid) two-barrel V-6 engine, automatic overdrive transmission, air conditioning with manual temperature control, tinted glass, power side windows, 6-way power driver's seat, power door locks, remote-control deck lid, auto lamp on and off delay system, electronic instrument cluster with digital read-out, front cornering lamps, automatic parking brake release, padded rear half-vinyl top with brushed aluminum wrap-over appliqué and coach lamps, deck lid accent stripes, bright rocker panel moldings, wire wheel covers, special "cut-glass" look hood ornament, electronic AM/FM stereo search radio, bright rhodium engraved owner's nameplate, luxury level steering wheel with wood-tone insert, dual illuminated visor and vanity mirrors, velour cloth seat trim in luxury sew style, luxury door trim panels with cloth and burled rosewood wood-tone inserts, burled rosewood wood-tone instrument panel appliqués, and luxury luggage compartment trim.

I.D. NUMBERS

VIN stamped on aluminum tab riveted to the dashboard on passenger side and observable through the windshield from outside the car. First symbol 1 denotes built in the United

States. Second symbol F denotes Ford. Third symbol A denotes Ford passenger vehicle. Fourth symbol denotes type of restraint system. Fifth symbol P denotes passenger-type vehicle. Sixth symbol 4 denotes Thunderbird. Seventh symbol 2 denotes two-door coupe. Eighth symbol denotes engine: B=200-cid (3.3L)/115-hp six-cylinder, 3=232-cid (3.8L)/115-hp V-6, D=255-cid (4.2L)/131-hp V-8. Ninth symbol is the check digit. 10th symbol C=1982 model year. 11th symbol denotes assembly plant, all T-Birds made at plant H in Lorain, Ohio. Twelfth through 17th symbols denote sequential production number of specific vehicle starting at 100001. Vehicle certification label located on rear face of driver's door. The top part of the label indicates that the Thunderbird was manufactured by Ford Motor Company. Directly below this is the month and year of manufacture, plus a statement that the car conforms to federal motor vehicle safety standards in effect on the indicated date of manufacture. VIN: The VIN appears first on the first line of encoded information. It matches the 1st to 11th symbols on VIN tag. Some other codes also appear. TYPE: On left side of label, indicates PASSENGER. EXT. COLOR: This line carries the exterior paint color(s) code. DSO: The District Special Order code now appears above "DSO" to the right of the exterior paint color code. BODY: The body style code appears to the extreme left of the bottom line. The only Thunderbird code for this model-year is: 66D=two-door pillared hardtop. VR: The vinyl roof type/color code is to the right of the body code. MLDG: The molding code is to the right of the vinyl roof code. INT. TRIM: The interior trim code is to the right of the molding code. A/C: The air conditioning code is to the right of the interior trim code. Cars with air conditioning have "A" stamped here. R: The radio code is to the right of the A/C code. S: The sunroof code appears to the right of the radio code. AX: The axle code appears to the right of the sunroof code. TR: The transmission code appears to the right of the axle code. (Note: The terms and abbreviations shown in capitals appear on the line above the actual codes.)

ENGINE

THUNDERBIRD BASE SIX-CYL (EXCEPT HERITAGE EDITION THUNDERBIRD): Inline. Cast-iron block and head. Displacement: 200 cid (3.3 liters). Bore and stroke: 3.68 x 3.13 in. Compression ratio: 8.6:1. Brake hp: 88 at 3800. Torque: 154 lbs.-ft. at 1400. Seven main bearings. Hydraulic valve lifters. Carburetor: Holley 1946 one-barrel. Serial number code: B.

THUNDERBIRD BASE V-6 (HERITAGE EDITION THUNDERBIRD): 90-degree. Overhead valve. Cast-iron block and aluminum head. Displacement: 232 cid (3.8 liters). Bore and stroke: 3.80 x 3.40 in. Compression ratio: 8.65:1. Brake hp: 112 at 4000. Torque: 175 lbs.-ft. at 2000. Four main bearings. Hydraulic valve lifters. Carburetor: Motorcraft 2150 two-barrel. Serial number code: 3.

THUNDERBIRD BASE V-8: 90-degree. Overhead valve V-8. Cast-iron block and head. Displacement: 255 cid (4.2 liters). Bore and stroke: 3.68 x 3.00 in. Compression ratio: 8.2:1. Brake hp: 120 at 3400. Torque: 205 lbs.-ft. at 1600. Five main bearings. Hydraulic valve lifters. Carburetor: Motorcraft 2150 or 7200VV two-barrel. Serial number code: D.

CHASSIS

Wheelbase: 108.4 in. Overall length: 200.4. Overall width:

74.1. Overall height: 53.3 in. Front headroom: 37.1 in. Front legroom: 41.6 in. Rear headroom: 36.3 in. Rear legroom: 36.5 in. Trunk capacity: 17.7 cu. ft. Front tread: 58.1 in. Rear tread: 57 in. Ground clearance: 6 in. Tires: P195/75R14 steel-belted radial. Steering: Integral with power-assist. Turning diameter: 40.1 ft. Turns lock-to-lock: 3.4. Front suspension: Modified McPherson strut. Rear suspension: Four-link-bar with coil springs. Steering: Variable-ratio power rack and pinion. Standard rear axle: 2.73:1. Front brakes: 10-in. power vented disc. Rear brakes: 9-in. power assisted drums. Fuel tank capacity: 21 gal.

OPTIONS

3.8-liter (232-cid) two-barrel V-6 engine, except standard on Heritage Edition ($241). 4.2-liter (255-cid) two-barrel V-8, no charge in Heritage Edition, in other models ($241). Traction-Lok rear axle ($76). Automatic temperature control air conditioner in hardtop and Town Landau ($754). Automatic temperature control air conditioner in Heritage Edition ($78). Manual temperature control air conditioner ($676). Auto lamp on and off delay system ($73). Heavy-duty battery ($24). Lower body-side protection on Heritage Edition ($39). Lower body-side protection on other models ($54). Front license plate bracket (no charge). Electronic digital clock ($46). Front cornering lamps ($59). Electric rear window defroster ($126). Diagnostic warning lights ($59). California emissions system ($46). High-altitude emissions system (no charge). Exterior décor group ($385). Tinted glass ($88). Engine block immersion heater ($17). Illuminated entry system ($68). Electronic instrument cluster with interior luxury group ($321). Electronic instrument cluster without interior luxury group ($367). Electronic instrument cluster delete ($321 credit). Interior décor group ($372). Interior luxury group in Town Landau ($683). Interior luxury group in other models ($1,204). Keyless entry system ($139). Light group ($35). Power lock group ($138). Luxury luggage compartment trim ($48). Dual illuminated visor and vanity mirrors in Heritage or with interior luxury group ($46). Dual illuminated visor and vanity mirrors without interior luxury group ($91). Right-hand remote-control OSRV mirror ($60). Rocker panel moldings ($33). Wide door belt moldings ($51). Tu-Tone paint and striping treatment on Heritage Edition ($128). Tu-Tone paint and striping treatment on hardtop with exterior décor group ($157). Tu-Tone paint and striping treatment on base hardtop ($206). Automatic parking brake release ($12). Appearance protection group ($51). Power radio antenna ($55). AM radio delete ($61 credit). AM radio with rear speakers ($39). AM/FM monaural radio ($54). Dual rear speakers with AM/FM monaural radio ($39). AM/FM stereo radio ($85). AM/FM stereo radio with 8-track tape player in Town Landau ($87). AM/FM stereo radio with 8-track tape player in base hardtop ($172). AM/FM stereo radio with cassette tape player in Town Landau ($87). AM/FM stereo radio with cassette tape player in other models ($172). Electronic AM/FM stereo search radio in Town Landau ($146). Electronic AM/FM stereo search radio in other models ($232). Electronic AM/FM stereo search radio with 8-track tape player in Heritage Edition ($87). Electronic AM/FM stereo search radio with 8-track tape player in Town Landau ($233). Electronic AM/FM stereo search radio with 8-track tape player in other models than Town Landau ($318). Electronic AM/FM stereo search radio with cassette tape player and Dolby noise reduction system in Heritage Edition ($87). Electronic AM/FM stereo search radio with cassette tape player and Dolby noise reduction system in Town Landau ($233). Electronic AM/FM stereo search radio with cassette tape player and Dolby noise reduction system in models other than Town Landau or Heritage Edition ($318). Premium sound system, with conventional radio ($133). Premium sound system with electronic radio ($167). Flip-up open air roof ($276). 6-way power driver's seat ($198). Fingertip speed control ($155). Leather-wrapped luxury steering wheel ($51). Tilt steering wheel ($95). Dual accent body-side stripes ($49). Hood and body-side accent stripes with exterior décor group ($16). Hood and body-side accent stripes without exterior décor groups ($65). Heavy-duty handling suspension ($26). TripMinder computer with Heritage, Interior luxury group or electronic instrument cluster ($215). TripMinder computer without Heritage, Interior luxury group, or electronic instrument cluster ($261). Pivoting front vent windows ($63). Luxury wheel covers ($107). Simulated wire wheel covers with Town Landau or Exterior décor group ($45). Simulated wire wheel covers without Exterior décor group ($152). Power side windows ($165). Interval windshield wipers ($48). P195/75R x 14 puncture-resistant self-sealing steel-belted radial-ply black sidewall tires ($106). TR type radial whitewall tires including aluminum wheels on Heritage Edition model ($490). TR type radial whitewall tires with Exterior décor and Town Landau model ($535).TR type radial whitewall tires without exterior décor ($643). Metallic Glow paint ($80). Color-keyed and carpeted front floor mats ($22). Bucket seats and console with Town Landau and Interior décor group (no charge). Bucket seats and console without Town Landau or interior décor group ($211). Recaro bucket seats and console in Heritage Edition ($222). Recaro bucket seats and console in hardtop with interior luxury group ($405). Recaro bucket seats and console in Town Landau and hardtop with interior décor group ($523). Split-bench seat ($216). Luxury split-bench seat ($124). All-vinyl seat trim ($28). Super-soft vinyl split-bench seat trim ($30). Ultra-soft leather seat trim ($409). Carriage roof with Exterior décor group ($766). Carriage roof without Exterior décor group ($973). Rear half-vinyl roof with Exterior décor group ($163). Rear half-vinyl roof without Exterior décor group ($320). Tinted windshield ($32). Electronic digital clock ($38). Front cornering lamps.

EQUIPMENT INSTALLATION RATES

Automatic transmission (100 percent). V-8 engine (61.4 percent). Six-cylinder engine (38.6 percent). AM radio (6.5 percent). AM/FM Mono. Radio (0.8 percent). AM/FM stereo (49.7 percent). AM/FM with 8-track tape player (3.3 percent). AM/FM stereo cassette (16.3 percent). Electronic AM/FM stereo (1.5 percent). Electronic AM/FM Stereo 8-track (1.6 percent). Electronic AM/FM stereo cassette (12.5 percent). Power steering (100 percent). Power front disc brakes (100 percent). Power door locks (43.8 percent). Power seat (43.3 percent). Power windows (59.4 percent). Adjustable steering column (77.5 percent). All tinted glass (97.8 percent). Vinyl top (89.5 percent). Sunroof (7.3 percent). Automatic air conditioning (6.6 percent). Manual air conditioning (91.3 percent). Standard steel-belted radial tires (100 percent). Electric rear window defogger (66.2 percent). Aluminum styled wheels (6 percent). Speed control (82 percent). Remote-control left-hand rearview mirror (100 percent). Remote-control right-hand rearview mirror (80 percent). Reclining front seats (85.6 percent). Bucket seats (1.6 percent). Analog clock (55.2 percent). Digital clock (44.8 percent). Limited-slip rear axle (1.7 percent). (Note: Based on 41,795 units produced in the model year for the U.S. market only.)

HISTORICAL FOOTNOTES

The 1982 T-Bird was introduced on September 24, 1981. Phillip Caldwell remained as chairman of the board of Ford Motor Co. Once again, William Clay Ford was vice chairman and Donald E. Petersen was president. Louis E. Lataif continued as Ford Division's general manager. Bernard L. Crumpton remained general sales manager for the division.

Calendar-year output was 29,336 units. A total of 45,142 T-Birds were produced in the model year. This represented 0.88 percent of the industry total. All T-Bird were made in Lorain, Ohio. Calendar-year dealer sales amounted to 47,903 T-Birds, representing 0.9 percent of industry sales.

For 1982 T-Birds, Ford recommended an engine oil change every 7,500 miles, a spark plug change every 30,000 miles, air filter replacement every 30,000 miles and engine coolant replacement at 52,500 miles or every three years. *Consumer Report's* overall trouble index rated the T-Bird a "good" car, although it was slightly costlier than average to fix when repairs were required. *Consumer Reports* also found the seats extremely comfortable, the car quiet and smooth riding, the comfort control system excellent, the power adequate and the brakes impressive.

With the 3.8-liter V-6, the car used 675 gallons of fuel in 15,000 miles. It averaged 16 mpg in the city and 29 mpg on the highway. "These rear-wheel-drive Ford products are our models of choice in the domestic specialty coupe field," said the magazine. "Primarily because of their relatively good overall repair records."

Dale Earnhardt, the NASCAR driver better known as "Mr. Chevrolet," piloted a 1982 T-Bird this year. He drove the Bud Moore car to victory in events like the Rebel 500 at Darlington, which was his first checkered flag since winning the 1980 Winston Cup Championship. Bill Elliott, who would play a bigger role in racing the next generation of 'Birds against Earnhardt's Monte Carlo, also raced a 1982 T-Bird.

Ford photo

The unique 1983 Thunderbird received a lukewarm reception at first, but it ultimately proved to be much more successful than its immediate predecessors.

1983

Thunderbird

The all-new 10th-generation Thunderbird had a slick aero look. Although downsized again, the T-Bird was only 3 inches shorter and narrower than the 1982 model, with a 2.8 inches shorter wheelbase. The front compartment was larger, the rear compartment was tighter-fitting and cargo volume dropped from 17.7 cu. ft. to 14.6 cu. ft.

At first, some traditional T-Bird buyers had a negative reaction to the new "Dearborn jelly bean" and preferred the 1982 model, but the new "Aero 'Bird" ultimately tripled the popularity of T-Birds. Much curvier than before, the new T-Birds looked very radical. Exposed quad rectangular halogen headlights flanked a small, bright, neo-classic egg-crate grille with an 8 x 6 pattern. A T-Bird insignia was stamped on the header bar. The grille and headlight surrounds sloped backwards, as did the cornering lamps (which doubled as side markers). The center of the hood had a tapered bulge. A curved, urethane-clad front bumper held slit-like rectangular parking lights. The windshield slanted back at a rakish angle. It was a very slippery-looking car with a low 0.35 coefficient of drag.

Decorative trim was minimal. Wide, color-keyed moldings were optional on the base model and standard on others. They continued the bumper line around the smooth, curving body sides. Full-width wraparound taillights met the recessed rear license plate housing in a sloping back panel. T-Bird insignias and back-up lights were in the center of each taillight lens.

Three distinct models were merchandised, the base Thunderbird coupe, the Heritage coupe, and a midyear

Turbo Coupe with a high-tech 2.3-liter (140-cid) turbocharged four-cylinder MPEFI engine. A Garrett AIResearch T-03 turbocharger helped it produce 145 hp at 5000 rpm. A unique front fascia with an air dam and Marchal fog lamps gave the Turbo Coupe instant recognition. It wore unique 14-inch aluminum wheels and P205/70HR14 performance tires. Bumper rub strip extensions, wide body-side moldings, and striping on the body-side and deck lid were also included.

Turbo Coupes were offered in Black, Pastel Charcoal, Bright Red, Desert Tan, Silver Metallic Clearcoat, Dark Charcoal Metallic Clearcoat, and Medium Red Metallic Clearcoat. The clearcoat paint colors were optional. A special Turbo Coupe paint scheme featured Dark Charcoal accents around the entire lower body perimeter. It was available with all Turbo Coupe colors except Black, Light Desert Tan, and Dark Charcoal Clearcoat Metallic. A five-speed manual transmission, special handling suspension and Traction-Lok axle were included. Inside were special Lear-Siegler articulated bucket seats with back rest and bolster adjustments, a leather-clad floor shifter, fishnet map pockets on the door panels, a few other goodies and some exclusive options.

The T-Bird Turbo Coupe was the darling of the automotive press at the time. Other 1983 Thunderbirds came in a choice of 13 exterior finishes. Five were extra-cost metallic clearcoat colors. Base interiors featured individually reclining bucket seats with knit cloth-and-vinyl trim, plus a padded console with a flocked and illuminated interior and a removable trash bin. The standard all-vinyl

149

NON-TURBO COUPE BODY COLOR INFORMATION (U.S. AS OF 12/10/82)

Color Name	Code	Color Name	Code
Black (Tu-Tone avail.)	1C	Optional Glamor Colors	
Pastel Charcoal	1M	Dark Charcoal Clearcoat Met. (Tu-Tone avail.)	92
Red (Tu-Tone avail.)	24	Silver Clearcoat Metallic (Tu-Tone avail.)	1Q
Light Academy Blue (Tu-Tone avail.)	38	Medium Red Clearcoat Metallic	2U
Pastel Vanilla	6Z	Walnut Clearcoat Metallic (Tu-Tone avail.)	9S
Desert Tan	9P	Midnight Academy Blue Clearcoat Met. (Tu-Tone)	9Z
Light Desert Tan (Tu-Tone avail.)	9Q		

TURBO COUPE BODY COLOR INFORMATION (U.S. AS OF 12/10/82)

Color Name	Code	Color Name	Code
Black	1C	Silver Clearcoat Metallic (Tu-Tone avail.)	1Q
Pastel Charcoal	1M	Dark Charcoal Clearcoat Metallic	92
Bright Red	27	Medium Red Clearcoat Metallic	2U
Desert Tan	9P		

PAINT STRIPE COLOR INFORMATION (U.S.)

Color Name	Code	Color Name	Code
Black (except Turbo Coupe)	a	Tan (except Turbo Coupe)	u
White (except Turbo Coupe)	w	Copper (except Turbo Coupe)	c
Light Grey (except Turbo Coupe)	p	Medium Grey (Turbo only)	1
Medium Red (except Turbo Coupe)	d	Maroon (Turbo only)	2
Light Academy Blue (except Turbo Coupe)	b	Dark Tan (Turbo only)	3
Dark Academy Blue (except Turbo Coupe)	q		

NON-TURBO COUPE BODY COLOR INFORMATION (CANADA AS OF 5/1/83)

Color Name	Code	Color Name	Code
Black	1C	Light Desert Tan	9Q
Polar White	9D	Dark Charcoal*	92
Pastel Charcoal	1M	Silver*	1Q
Red	24	Medium Red*	2U
Light Academy Blue	38	Midnight Academy Blue*	9Z
Pastel Vanilla	6Z	Walnut*	9S
Desert Tan	9P		

*Indicates optional clearcoat metallic colors.

TURBO COUPE BODY COLOR INFORMATION (CANADA AS OF 5/1/83)

Color Name	Code	Color Name	Code
Black	1C	Silver*	1Q
Pastel Charcoal	1M	Dark Charcoal*	92
Bright Red	27	Medium Red*	2U
Desert Tan	9P		

*Indicates optional clearcoat metallic colors.

PAINT STRIPE COLORS (CANADA)

Color Name	Code	Color Name	Code
Black (except Turbo Coupe)	A	Tan (except Turbo Coupe)	U
White (except Turbo Coupe)	W	Copper (except Turbo Coupe)	C
Light Grey (except Turbo Coupe)	P	Medium Grey (Turbo only)	1
Medium Red (except Turbo Coupe)	D	Maroon (Turbo only)	2
Light Academy Blue (ex. Turbo Coupe)	B	Dark Tan (Turbo only)	3
Dark Academy Blue (except Turbo Coupe)	Q		

INTERIOR TRIM INFORMATION (U.S. & CANADA)

Seat Type	Material	Med. Charcoal	Acad. Red	Blue	Desert Walnut	Tan
Base T-Bird						
40/40 Buckets	Cloth & Vinyl	AA	AD	AB	AE	AH
40/40 Buckets	SS-Vinyl	CA	CD	CB	CE	CH
Base/Interior Luxury Group						
Articulated Buckets	Cloth & Vinyl	BA	BD	—	—	BH
Articulated Buckets	U Soft Leather	FA	FD	—	—	FH
Interior Luxury Group/Heritage						
40/40 Buckets	Velour Cloth	DA	DD	DB	DE	DH
40/40 Buckets	U Soft Leather	EA	ED	EB	EE	EH

TU-TONE INTERIOR TRIM INFORMATION (U.S. & CANADA)

Seat Type	Material	Opal/ Char	Opal/ Red	Opal/ Blue	Opal/ Tan
T-Bird					
40/40 Buckets	S-Soft Vinyl	CW	CN	CQ	C3

Legend: Med. is Medium; Acad. Blue is Academy Blue; U Soft Leather is Ultra-Soft leather; SS-Vinyl is Super-Soft Vinyl, Char is Charcoal.

THUNDERBIRD PRODUCTON

Model Number	Body/Style Number	Body Type & Seating	Factory Price	Shipping Weight	Production Total
THUNDERBIRD - (V-6)					
46	66D	2d Coupe-4P	$9,197	2,905	Note 1
THUNDERBIRD - (V-8)					
46	66D	2d Coupe-4P	$9,485	2,936	Note 1
THUNDERBIRD HERITAGE - (V-6)					
46/607	66D	2d Coupe-4P	$12,228	3,027	Note 1
THUNDERBIRD HERITAGE - (V-8)					
46/607	66D	2d Coupe-4P	$12,516	—	Note 1
THUNDERBIRD TURBO COUPE - (4-CYL)					
46/934	66D	2d Coupe-4P	$11,790	—	Note 1

NOTE 1: Production of the all models combined was 121,999.

door trim panels had assist straps and storage bins. The fancier Heritage model had the Interior Luxury group, a wood-grained steering wheel, and clock and sound system upgrades. The basic 1983 T-Bird had a modified McPherson strut front suspension with gas-filled struts. At the rear was a four-bar-link suspension with gas-filled shock absorbers. Steering was again rack-and-pinion type with power-assist. The base and Heritage models used a variable-ratio system, while the Turbo Coupe featured increased power steering effort and a 15.1:1 non-variable ratio.

STANDARD EQUIPMENT

3.8-liter (232-cid) V-6 engine, three-speed automatic transmission, power brakes, power steering, electronic ignition and voltage regulator, dual-note horn, halogen headlights, left-hand remote-control OSRV mirror, vinyl insert body-side moldings, deluxe wheel covers, seat belt reminder chimes, analog quartz clock, center console, vinyl door panels, full carpeting including trunk, AM radio with dual front speakers, individual reclining front seats, four-spoke luxury steering wheel, cloth and vinyl upholstery, trip odometer. **1983 Thunderbird Heritage Edition Standard Equipment adds or substitutes:** Auto lamp on and off delay system, tinted glass, illuminated entry system, power lock group, automatic parking brake release, diagnostic warning light display, power door windows, interval wipers, electroluminescent coach lamps, front cornering lamps, dual electric remote-control door mirrors, wide body-side moldings, accent tape stripes, wire wheel covers, luxury floor carpeting, carpeted seat cushion side facings, cloth insert door panel trim, wood-tone instrument cluster appliqués, electronic instrument cluster, quarter panel courtesy lights, light group, seatback map pockets, dual illuminated visor-vanity mirrors, premium sound system with AM/FM electronic stereo search radio, and velour cloth upholstery. **1983 Thunderbird Turbo Coupe Standard Equipment adds or substitutes:** 2.3-liter (140-cid) turbocharged four-cylinder engine with fuel-injection, five-speed overdrive manual transmission, and special handling suspension.

I.D. NUMBERS

VIN stamped on aluminum tab riveted the to dashboard on passenger side and observable through the windshield from outside the car. First symbol 1 denotes built in the United States. Second symbol F denotes Ford. Third symbol A denotes Ford passenger vehicle. Fourth symbol denotes type of restraint system. Fifth symbol P denotes passenger-type vehicle. Sixth symbol 4 denotes Thunderbird. Seventh symbol 6 denotes two-door coupe. Eighth symbol denotes engine: D=140-cid (2.3L)/142-hp turbocharged four-cylinder, 3=232-cid (3.8L)/110-hp V-6, F=302 cid (5.0L)/130-hp V-8. Ninth symbol is the check digit. 10th symbol D=1983 model year. 11th symbol denotes assembly plant: A=Atlanta, Georgia or H=Lorain, Ohio. Twelfth through 17th symbols denote sequential production number of specific vehicle starting at 100001. Vehicle certification label located on rear face of driver's door. The top part of the label indicates that the Thunderbird was manufactured by Ford Motor Company. Directly below this is the month and year of manufacture, plus a statement that the car conforms to federal motor vehicle safety standards in effect on the indicated date of manufacture. VIN: The VIN appears first on the first line of encoded information. It matches the first to 11th symbols on VIN tag. Some other codes also appear. TYPE: On left side of label, indicates PASSENGER. EXT. COLOR: This line carries the exterior paint color(s) code. DSO: The District Special Order code now appears above "DSO" to the right of the exterior paint color code. BODY: The body style code appears to the extreme left of the bottom line. The only Thunderbird code for this model-year is: 66D=two-door pillared hardtop. VR: The vinyl roof type/color code is to the right of the body code. MLDG: The molding code is to the right of the vinyl roof code. INT. TRIM: The interior trim code is to the right of the molding code. A/C: The air conditioning code is to the right of the interior trim code. Cars with air conditioning have "A" stamped here. R: The radio code is to the right of the A/C code. S: The sunroof code appears to the right of the radio code. AX: The axle code appears to the right of the sunroof code. TR: The transmission code appears to the right of the axle code. (Note: The terms and abbreviations shown in capitals appear on the line above the actual codes.)

ENGINE

THUNDERBIRD BASE V-6: 90-degree. Overhead valve. Cast-iron block and aluminum head. Displacement: 232 cid (3.8 liters). Bore and stroke: 3.80 x 3.40 in. Compression ratio: 8.65:1. Brake hp: 114 at 4000. Torque: 175 lbs.-ft. at 2200. Four main bearings. Hydraulic valve lifters. Carburetor: Motorcraft 2150 or 7200VV two-barrel. Serial number code: 3.

THUNDERBIRD TURBO COUPE BASE FOUR-CYL TURBO: Inline. Overhead valve. Cast-iron block and head. Displacement: 140 cid (2.3 liters). Bore and stroke: 3.78 x 3.13 in. Compression ratio: 8.0:1. Brake hp: 142 at 5000. Torque: 172 lbs.-ft. at 3800. Five main bearings. Hydraulic valve lifters. Induction: Multi-Port Electronic Fuel injection. Garrett AIResearch T-03 turbocharger. Serial number code: D.

THUNDERBIRD OPTIONAL V-8: 90-degree. Overhead valve. Cast-iron block and head. Displacement: 302 cid (5.0 liters). Bore and stroke: 4.00 x 3.00 in. Compression ratio: 8.4:1. Brake hp: 130 at 3200 rpm. Torque: 240 lbs.-ft. at 2000 rpm. Five main bearings. Hydraulic valve lifters. Induction: Electronic Fuel injection. Serial number code: F.

CHASSIS

Wheelbase: 104 in. Overall length: 197.6. Overall width:

Ford photo

The significant 1983 redesign gave the T-Bird a less prominent rear end and subtracted about 3 cubic feet from the trunk.

Mike Mueller photo

Ford's bold styling moves on the 1983 Thunderbird paid off after some initial public skepticism. The "Aero Birds" were certainly more sleek and plane-like than their boxy predecessors.

71.1. Overall height: 53.2 in. Front headroom: 37.7 in. Front legroom: 42 in. Front shoulder room: 55.2 in. Rear headroom: 36.7 in. Rear legroom: 34.3 in. Trunk capacity: 14.6 cu. ft. Front tread: 58.1 in. Rear tread: 58.5 in. Tires: P195/75R14 steel-belted radial. Steering: Variable-ratio, power, rack-and-pinion. Steering ratio: 15.0-13.0:1. Turning diameter: 38.6 ft. Turns lock-to-lock: 2.5. Front suspension: Modified McPherson strut. Rear suspension: Four-link-bar. Weight distribution: 56/44 percent front/rear. Power to weight ratio: 20.56 lb./hp. Steering: Variable-ratio power rack-and-pinion. Standard rear axle: 2.73:1. Front brakes: Power vented disc. Rear brakes: Power-assisted drums. Brakes Swept/1,000 lb. 275.6 sq. in. Rear axle (with five-speed manual transmission): 3.45:1. Rear axle (with three-speed automatic transmission): 2.47:1. Rear axle (four-speed automatic transmission): 3.08:1. Fuel tank capacity: 18 gal.

OPTIONS

5.0-liter EFI V-8 engine, except in Turbo Coupe ($288). Four-speed overdrive automatic transmission, except in Turbo Coupe ($176). Traction-Lok axle ($95). Exterior accent group ($343). Automatic temperature control air conditioning ($802). Manual control air conditioning ($724). Anti-theft system ($159). Auto lamp on and off delay system, standard in Heritage ($73). Heavy-duty battery ($26). Lower body-side protection on Turbo Coupe ($39). Lower body-side protection, except Turbo Coupe ($54). Bumper rub strip extensions ($52). Electronic digital clock ($61). Front cornering lamps ($60). Electric rear window defroster ($135). Diagnostic warning lights, standard in Heritage ($59). Carpeted front floor mats ($22). Remote locking fuel filler door ($26). Full tinted glass ($105). Engine block immersion heater ($17). Illuminated entry system, standard in Heritage ($76). Electronic instrument cluster with Interior luxury group ($321). Electronic instrument cluster without Interior luxury group ($382). Electronic instrument cluster standard in Heritage, delete option ($321 credit). Keyless entry system in Heritage ($88). Keyless entry system, except in Heritage ($163). Light group, standard in Heritage ($35). Power lock group, standard on Heritage ($160). Luxury carpet group in Turbo Coupe ($48). Luxury carpet group except in Turbo Coupe ($72). Interior luxury group ($1,170). Electronic dimming rearview mirror ($77). Dual illuminated visor-vanity mirrors, standard in Heritage ($100). Dual electric remote-control door mirrors, standard on Heritage ($94). Bright rocker panel moldings ($33). Wide body-side moldings, standard on Heritage ($51). Two-tone paint and tape treatment on Heritage ($148). Two-tone paint and tape treatment with exterior accent group ($163). Two-tone paint and tape treatment without exterior accent group ($218). Automatic parking brake release, standard in Heritage ($12). Power antenna ($60). AM radio delete ($61 credit). AM/FM stereo radio ($109). AM/FM stereo with 8-track or cassette tape in Turbo Coupe ($90). AM/FM stereo with 8-track or cassette tape except in Turbo Coupe and Heritage ($199). AM/FM stereo electronic search radio, in base coupe ($252). AM/FM stereo electronic search radio, in

The 1983 Thunderbird in Black.

Turbo Coupe ($144). (Note: Previous radio standard in Heritage Edition.) AM/FM stereo electronic search radio and cassette, in base coupe ($396). AM/FM stereo electronic search radio and cassette, in Turbo Coupe ($288). AM/FM stereo electronic search radio and cassette, in Heritage Coupe ($144). Premium sound system ($179). Flip-up open-air roof ($310). 6-way power driver's seat ($210). Dual-control power seat ($420). Fingertip speed control ($170). Leather-wrapped luxury steering wheel ($59). Tilt steering wheel ($105). Dual accent body-side striping and deck lid stripes ($55). Hood, body-side and deck lid stripes ($71). Hood stripe ($16). Heavy-duty suspension, except not available in Turbo Coupe ($26). Medium-duty trailer tow package ($251). Traveler's assistance kit ($65). TripMinder computer with Heritage, Luxury interior group, or electronic instrument cluster ($215). TripMinder computer except with Heritage, Luxury interior group, or electronic instrument cluster ($276). Pivoting front vent windows ($76). Electronic voice alert ($67). Luxury wheel covers ($113). Locking wire wheel covers with Heritage ($20). Locking wire wheel covers with Exterior accent group ($84). Locking wire wheel covers with all others ($198). Wire wheel covers with Exterior accent group ($45). Wire wheel covers without Exterior accent group ($159). Styled road wheels with Exterior accent group ($65). Styled road wheels without Exterior accent group ($178). Power side windows, standard in Heritage ($180). Interval wipers ($49). Articulated seats with Interior luxury group ($183). Articulated seats without interior luxury group ($427). Vinyl seat trim ($37). Ultra-soft leather trim with Turbo Coupe or with articulated seats ($659). Ultra-soft leather trim without articulated seats or Turbo Coupe ($415).

EQUIPMENT INSTALLATION RATES

Automatic transmission (89.7 percent). Five-speed manual transmission (10.3 percent). V-8 engine (31.9 percent). Six-cylinder engine (57.8 percent). Four-cylinder turbocharged engine (10.3 percent). AM radio (6.1 percent). AM/FM stereo (37.6 percent). AM/FM with 8-track tape player (0.3 percent). AM/FM stereo cassette (14.2 percent). Electronic AM/FM stereo (4.2 percent). Electronic AM/FM Stereo Cassette (31 percent). Power steering (100 percent). Power

front disc brakes (100 percent). Power door locks (49.4 percent). Power seat (58.6 percent). Power windows (67.2 percent). Adjustable steering column (81.3 percent). All tinted glass (97.9 percent). Sun roof (2.2 percent). Automatic air conditioning (8.7 percent). Manual air conditioning (87.8 percent). Standard steel-belted radial tires (100 percent). Electric rear window defogger (80.5 percent). Steel styled wheels (30.6 percent). Aluminum styled wheels (15 percent). Speed control (80.2 percent). Remote-control left-hand rearview mirror (100 percent). Remote-control right-hand rearview mirror (87.3 percent). Reclining front seats (100 percent). Analog clock (49.4 percent). Digital clock (50.6 percent). Limited-slip rear axle: (12.8 percent). (Note: Based on 113,676 units produced in the model year for the U.S. market only.)

HISTORICAL FOOTNOTES

The 1983 T-Bird was introduced on February 17, 1983, and the Thunderbird Turbo was introduced on April 1, 1983. Phillip Caldwell remained as chairman of the board of Ford Motor Co. Once again, William Clay Ford was vice chairman and Donald E. Petersen was president. Louis E. Lataif continued as Ford Division's general manager. Bernard L. Crumpton remained general sales manager for the division.

The new aerodynamically styled T-Bird rose 107 percent in sales to a respectable 99,176 units, up from 47,903 in 1982. A Ford official said: "Thunderbird did all we could have expected of it." He pointed out that T-Bird sales were even strong in the traditionally import-intensive coastal regions. Calendar-year output was 186,566 units. A total of 121,999 T-Birds were produced in the model year. This represented 2.14 percent of the industry total. Of these units, 45,994 were made in Atlanta, Georgia, and 76,005 were made in Lorain, Ohio. Calendar-year dealer sales amounted to 134,710 T-Birds, representing 6 percent of industry sales.

Seven cars competed for *Motor Trend* magazine's "Car of the Year Award" in 1983 and the new T-Bird was among them. Each of the cars was rated in eight categories: including styling and design, comfort and convenience, ride and drive, quality control, instrumented performance, fuel economy, handling and value. The Thunderbird V-6 placed third overall, but came in first in handling and second in the appearance, quality and value categories. The car did 0 to 60 mph in 13.07 seconds and the quarter-mile in 19.04 seconds at 72.90 mph. *Motor Trend* featured the T-Bird Turbo Coupe in its June 1983 issue. "Three decades later, the T-Bird finally becomes what it started out to be," crowed writer Ron Grable, who loved both the form and functioning of the Turbo Coupe. His test car had the five-speed manual gearbox (the sole Turbo option) and a 3.45:1 rear axle. With a curb weight of 2,982 lb., it did 0 to 60 in 8.56 seconds. The standing quarter-mile took 16.45 seconds at 81 mph. Top speed was 142 mph.

It didn't take long for race car builders to realize the competition potential of the powerful, great-handling, wind-cheating Aero 'Birds. In stock car racing, Dale Earnhardt, Buddy Baker, and Bill Elliott were among the drivers who got new T-Birds to campaign during the 1983 season. The cars did handle well and got plenty of factory support, but some developmental problems and bad racing luck worked against them. By summer, *Motor Trend* was referring to the cars as "a group of promising but still teething T-Birds."

At midyear, NASCAR made some rules changes, outlawing certain valve train modifications that worked to the advantage of cars with Chevrolet V-8s. Then the tides started to turn. Driving the Wood Brothers' T-Bird, Buddy Baker took first place in Daytona's Firecracker 400. A week later, Dale Earnhardt was victorious at Nashville in the 'Bird that Bud Moore built for him. Earnhardt also took his T-Bird to a checkered flag at Talladega two races later. The final race of the season was the Winston Western 500 (km) at Riverside, California. It was in this event that driver Bill Elliott collected his first Winston Cup win with the Melling Ford T-Bird.

1983 THUNDERBIRD PERFORMANCE

Model	CID/HP	Performance
0-60 mph		
Base Coupe	232/114	13.07 seconds
Turbo Coupe (manual)	140/145	8.56 seconds
Turbo Coupe (automatic)	140/145	10 seconds
1/4-Mile		
Base Coupe	232/114	19.04 seconds @ 72.90 mph
Turbo Coupe	140/190	16.45 seconds @ 81 mph

Ford photo

The 1983 "Aero Bird" found more than twice as many buyers as the 1982 model, and became instantly attractive to racers.

Ford photo

The Elan model replaced the Heritage Edition in the 1984 T-Bird lineup.

1984

Thunderbird

New T-Bird features for 1984 included electronic controls and fuel injection on all engines, an automatic transmission for Turbo Coupes, and new Elan and FILA models. All models now had bumper rub strip extensions as standard equipment. A slightly curved 8 x 6-hole cross-hatched grille with a T-Bird insignia on the header characterized the front end. Staggered, exposed and recessed dual headlights flanked side of the grille. Set into the bumper were new, clear plastic parking lights. Small amber wraparound marker light lenses were used at each front body corner. T-Bird insignias dressed up the roof sail panels. Wraparound wall-to-wall taillights again lit the rear of the T-Bird. The T-Bird insignias on the taillight lenses had a new molded appearance.

The model lineup was revised. The Heritage became the Elan name. It had the same 3.8-liter EFI V-6 as the base 'Bird. The 5.0-liter V-8 was optional. A new FILA model was developed in conjunction with FILA Sports, Inc., an Italian manufacturer of apparel for active leisure sports such as skiing and tennis. The FILA model had exclusive Pastel Charcoal paint with Dark Charcoal Metallic lower accents and unique red and blue tape stripes like the company logo. Bright trim was minimal. Instead of chrome, the grille and wheels had distinctive body-color finish. Charcoal windshield and backlight moldings were also featured. Inside, the FILA edition had Charcoal trim components. Its articulated bucket seats were done in Oxford White leather with perforated leather inserts or in Oxford Gray luxury cloth with perforated cloth inserts.

Turbo Coupes added Charcoal greenhouse moldings and a new viscous clutch fan, as well as a starter/clutch interlock system and oil temperature warning switch. The Turbo Coupe now came with automatic transmission, as well as the five-speed manual gearbox. The Turbo Coupe used a non-variable ratio to increase power steering effort for better high-speed control.

NON-TURBO COUPE BODY COLOR INFORMATION

Color Name	Code	Color Name	Code
Black+	1C	Silver Clearcoat Metallic+	1Q
Bright Canyon Red	2E	Dark Charcoal Clearcoat Metallic+	1Y
Midnight Canyon Red	2J	Medium Red Clearcoat Metallic	2U
Light Wheat+	6C	Midnight Academy Blue Clearcoat Metal.	3A
Wheat+	6D	Medium Desert Tan Clearcoat Metallic	83
Oxford White+	9L	Walnut Clearcoat Metallic	9S
		Pastel Academy Blue Clearcoat Metallic	91

+ Indicates available as a Tu-Tone color, clearcoat metallic colors optional at extra cost.

TURBO COUPE BODY COLOR INFORMATION

Color Name	Code	Color Name	Code
Black	1C	Dark Charcoal Clearcoat Metallic	1Y
Bright Canyon Red*	2E	Medium Red Clearcoat Metallic*	2U
Oxford White*	9L	Medium Desert Tan Clearcoat Metallic*	83
Silver Clearcoat Metallic*	1Q	Pastel Academy Blue Clearcoat Metallic*	91

* Indicates available with Dark Charcoal lower accent treatment, clearcoat metallic colors optional at extra cost.

PAINT STRIPE COLOR INFORMATION

Color Name	Code	Color Name	Code
Light Academy Blue (except Turbo Coupe)	B	Tan (except Turbo Coupe)	U
Medium Dark Canyon Red (except Turbo Coupe)	D	White (except Turbo Coupe)	W
Bright Bittersweet (Except Turbo Coupe)	E	Brown (Except Turbo Coupe)	Z
Dark Gold (Except Turbo Coupe)	G	Medium Grey (Turbo Coupe)	1
Light Grey (Except Turbo Coupe)	P	Maroon (Turbo Coupe)	2
Dark Academy Blue (Except Turbo Coupe)	Q	Dark Tan (Turbo Coupe)	3
		Med. Light Academy Blue (Turbo Coupe)	4

STANDARD EQUIPMENT

3.8-liter two-barrel EFI V-6 engine, SelectShift automatic transmission with locking torque converter, variable-ratio rack and pinion steering, power front disc/rear drum brakes, DuraSpark electronic ignition, electronic voltage regulator, maintenance-free battery, McPherson strut front suspension with gas-filled struts, four-bar-link rear suspension with gas-filled shocks, dual fluidic windshield washer system, P195/75R15 all-season white sidewall tires, concealed drip moldings, quad rectangular halogen headlights, left-hand remote-control OSRV mirror, soft urethane-covered front and rear bumpers, charcoal bumper rub strips with extensions, deluxe wheel covers, individually reclining seats, padded console with illuminated interior and removable litter bin, 10-oz. color-keyed cut-pile carpeting, all-vinyl door trim panels with assist straps and storage bins, luxury steering wheel with center horn blow, trip odometer, quartz electric (sweep-hand) clock, glove box and ashtray lights, color-keyed cloth headlining and sun visors, utility strap on driver's visor, visor-vanity mirror on passenger visor, inertia seatback releases, color-keyed deluxe seat belts with comfort regulator feature and reminder chime, and AM radio (may be deleted for credit). **1984 Thunderbird Elan Equipment adds or substitutes the following over base T-Bird:** Automatic parking brake release, dual electric remote-control OSRV mirrors, wide body-side moldings, front cornering lamps, hood stripes, body-side and deck lid accent stripes, styled road wheels, luxury carpet group, quarter panel courtesy lights, electronic digital clock, electronic AM/FM stereo search radio, premium sound system, power lock group, interval windshield wipers, power windows, complete tinted glass, tilt steering wheel, Autolamp on and off delay system, illuminated entry system, electronic instrument cluster, diagnostic warning lights, and light group. **1984 Thunderbird FILA Equipment adds or substitutes the following over base T-Bird:** Automatic overdrive transmission, special handling package, P205/70HR14 black sidewall performance tires,

INTERIOR TRIM INFORMATION

Seat Type	Material	Charcoal	Oxford Gray	Can Red	Aca Blue	Desert Tan	Wheat	Oxford White
Base T-Bird								
40/40 Buckets	Cloth & Vinyl	AA	AJ	AD	AB	AH	AR	—
40/40 Buckets	SS-Vinyl	CA	CJ	CD	CB	CH	CR	—
Base/Interior Luxury Group/Turbo Coupe								
Articulated Buckets	Cloth & Vinyl	BA	—	BD	—	BH	—	—
Articulated Buckets	U-Soft Leather	FA	—	FD	—	FH	—	—
Interior Luxury Group/Elan								
40/40 Buckets	Velour Cloth	DA	DJ	DD	DB	DH	DR	—
40/40 Buckets	U-Soft Leather	EA	EJ	ED	EB	EH	ER	—
FILA								
Articulated Buckets	Cloth	—	MJ	—	—	—	—	—
Articulated Buckets	Leather	—	—	—	—	—	—	GW

Legend: First letter denotes seat type, second letter denotes color. Can Red means Canyon Red. Aca Blue means Academy Blue. SS-Vinyl means Super-Soft Vinyl. U Soft Leather means Ultra Soft Leather.

THUNDERBIRD PRODUCTION

Model Number	Body/Style Number	Body Type & Seating	Factory Price	Shipping Weight	Production Total
THUNDERBIRD - (V-6)					
46	66D	2d Coupe-4P	$9,633	2,890 lbs.	Note 1
THUNDERBIRD - (V-8)					
46	66D	2d Coupe-4P	$10,253	3,097 lbs.	Note 1
THUNDERBIRD ELAN - (V-6)					
46/607	66D	2d Coupe-4P	$12,661	2,956 lbs.	Note 1
THUNDERBIRD ELAN - (V-8)					
46/607	66D	2d Coupe-4P	$13,281	3,163 lbs.	Note 1
THUNDERBIRD FILA - (V-6)					
46/606	66D	2d Coupe-4P	$14,471	3,061 lbs.	Note 1
THUNDERBIRD FILA - (V-8)					
46/606	66D	2d Coupe-4P	$14,854	3,268 lbs.	Note 1
THUNDERBIRD TURBO COUPE - (4-CYL)					
46/934	66D	2d Coupe-4P	$12,330	2,938 lbs.	Note 1

NOTE 1: Production of the all models combined was 170,533.

automatic parking brake release, dual electric remote-control mirrors, wide body-side moldings, front cornering lamps, 14-inch aluminum wheels, articulated seats, luxury carpet group, quarter panel courtesy lights, leather-wrapped steering wheel, electronic digital clock, electronic AM/FM stereo search radio with cassette player and Dolby noise reduction system, premium sound system, power lock group, 6-way power driver's seat, complete tinted glass, tilt steering wheel, fingertip speed control, Autolamp on and off delay system, illuminated entry system, diagnostic warning lights, and light group. **1984 Thunderbird Turbo Coupe Equipment adds or substitutes the following over base T-Bird:** 2.3-liter overhead-cam EFI turbocharged four-cylinder engine, five-speed manual overdrive transmission, special handling package, tachometer with boost and over-boost lights, Traction-Lok rear axle, P205/70HR14 black sidewall performance tires, dual electric remote-control mirrors, wide body-side moldings, body-side and deck lid accent stripes, unique front fascia with air dam and fog lights, 14-inch aluminum wheels, articulated seats, luxury carpet group, leather-wrapped sports steering wheel, electronic digital clock, AM/FM stereo radio, diagnostic warning lights, and light group.

The 1984 Thunderbird lineup (from top): base T-Bird, Turbo Coupe, Elan, and FILA.

The sleek and swift 1984 Turbo Coupe.

I.D. NUMBERS

VIN stamped on aluminum tab riveted to the dashboard on passenger side and observable through the windshield from outside the car. First symbol 1 denotes built in the United States. Second symbol F denotes Ford. Third symbol A denotes Ford passenger vehicle. Fourth symbol denotes type of restraint system. Fifth symbol P denotes passenger-type vehicle. Sixth symbol 4 denotes Thunderbird. Seventh symbol 6 denotes two-door coupe. Eighth symbol denotes engine: W=140-cid (2.3L)/145 hp turbocharged four-cylinder, 3=232-cid (3.8L)/120-hp V-6, F=302-cid (5.0L)/140-hp V-8. Ninth symbol is the check digit. 10th symbol E=1984 model year. Eleventh symbol denotes assembly plant: A=Atlanta, Georgia or H=Lorain, Ohio. Twelfth through 17th symbols denote sequential production number of specific vehicle starting at 100001. Vehicle certification label located on rear face of driver's door. The top part of the label indicates that the Thunderbird was manufactured by Ford Motor Company. Directly below this is the month and year of manufacture, plus a statement that the car conforms to federal motor vehicle safety standards in effect on the indicated date of manufacture. VIN: The VIN appears first on the first line of encoded information. It matches the first to 11th symbols on VIN tag. Some other codes also appear. TYPE: On left side of label, indicates PASSENGER. EXT. COLOR: This line carries the exterior paint color(s) code. DSO: The District Special Order code now appears above "DSO" to the right of the exterior paint color code. BODY: The body style code appears to the extreme left of the bottom line. The only Thunderbird code for this model year is: 66D=two-door pillared hardtop. VR: The vinyl roof type/color code is to the right of the body code. MLDG: The molding code is to the right of the vinyl roof code. INT. TRIM: The interior trim code is to the right of the molding code. A/C: The air conditioning code is to the right of the interior trim code. Cars with air conditioning have "A" stamped here. R: The radio code is to the right of the A/C code. S: The sunroof code appears to the right of the radio code. AX: The axle code appears to the right of the sunroof code. TR: The transmission code appears to the right of the axle code. (Note: The terms and abbreviations shown in capitals appear on the line above the actual codes.)

ENGINE

THUNDERBIRD BASE V-6: 90-degree. Overhead valve. Cast-iron block and aluminum head. Displacement: 232 cid (3.8 liters). Bore and stroke: 3.80 x 3.40 in. Compression ratio: 8.7:1. Brake hp: 120 at 3600. Torque: 205 lbs.-ft. at 1600. Four main bearings. Hydraulic valve lifters. Induction: Throttle Body Injection. Serial number code: 3.

THUNDERBIRD TURBO COUPE BASE FOUR-CYL TURBO: Inline. Overhead valve. Cast-iron block and head. Displacement: 140 cid (2.3 liters). Bore and stroke: 3.78 x 3.13 in. Compression ratio: 8.0:1. Brake hp: 145 at 4600. Torque: 180 lbs.-ft. at 3600. Five main bearings. Hydraulic valve lifters. Induction: Multi-point electronic fuel injection. Garrett AIResearch T-03 turbocharger. Serial number code: W.

THUNDERBIRD OPTIONAL V-8: 90-degree. Overhead valve. Cast-iron block and head. Displacement: 302 cid (5.0 liters). Bore and stroke: 4.00 x 3.00 in. Compression ratio: 8.4:1. Brake hp: 140 at 3200 rpm. Torque: 250 lbs.-ft. at 1600 rpm. Five main bearings. Hydraulic valve lifters. Induction: Throttle Body Injection. Serial number code: F.

CHASSIS

Wheelbase: 104 in. Overall length: 197.6. Overall width: 71.1. Overall height: 53.2 in. Front headroom: 37.7 in. Front legroom: 42 in. Front shoulder room: 55.2 in. Rear headroom: 36.7 in. Rear legroom: 34.3 in. Trunk capacity: 14.6 cu. ft. Front tread: 58.1 in. Rear tread: 58.5 in. Tires: P195/75R14 white sidewall steel-belted radial. Steering: Variable-ratio, power, rack-and-pinion. Steering ratio: 15.0-13.0:1. Turning diameter: 38.6 ft. Turns lock-to-lock: 2.5. Front suspension: Modified McPherson strut. Rear suspension: Four-link-bar. Weight distribution: 56/44 percent front/rear. Power-to-weight ratio: 20.56 lb./hp. Steering: Variable-ratio power rack and pinion. Standard rear axle: 2.73:1. Front brakes: Power disc. Rear brakes: Power drum. Brakes Swept/1000 lb.275.1 sq. in. Rear axle (with five-speed manual transmission): 3.45:1. Rear Axle (with three-speed automatic transmission): 2.47:1. Rear axle (four-speed automatic transmission): 3.08:1. Fuel tank capacity: 21 gal.

OPTIONS

AM/FM stereo radio ($98). AM/FM stereo radio with cassette tape player. Electronic AM/FM stereo search radio, Electronic AM/FM stereo search radio with cassette tape player and Dolby noise reduction system, Premium sound system (stereo radios only). Wide body-side moldings. Exterior accent group. Luxury carpet group. Dual body-side and deck lid tape stripes. Tu-Tone paint/tape treatments. Charcoal lower accent treatment. Charcoal Metallic paint. Electroluminescent coach lamps. Autolamp on and off delay system. Diagnostic warning lights. Electronic instrument cluster. TripMinder computer. Electronic voice alert. Traveler's assistance kit. Front cornering lamps. Electric rear window defroster ($126). Remote-control locking fuel door. Dual electric remote-control mirrors ($86). Pivoting front vent windows. Keyless entry system including illuminated entry system. Illuminated entry system. Interval windshield wipers ($45). Flip-up Open-Air roof ($284). SelectAire conditioner with automatic control ($669). SelectAire conditioner with manual control. Automatic parking brake release. Electronic digital clock. Complete tinted glass ($99). Light group. Fingertip speed control ($158). Electronic dimming day/night rearview mirror. Leather-wrapped luxury steering wheel. Tilt steering wheel ($99). Interior luxury group. Articulated seats. Ultrasoft leather trim. Anti-theft system. Lower body-sides

protection. Bright rocker panel moldings. Front floor mats. Front license plate bracket. License plate frames. Power lock group ($159). Power radio antenna. 6-way power driver's seat. Dual 6-way power seats. Power side windows ($178). Luxury wheel covers. Locking wire wheel style wheel covers. Styled road wheel covers. TRX aluminum wheels, including Michelin TRX tires. 5.0-liter V-8 with EFI optional in all models, except Super Coupe. SelectShift automatic transmission with locking torque converter, standard in T-Bird and Elan, optional in Super Coupe ($284). Automatic overdrive transmission, optional in T-Bird and Elan, standard in FILA, not available in Super coupe. Traction-Lok differential, standard in Super Coupe. Medium-duty trailer towing package. Heavy-duty battery. Heavy-duty suspension. Special handling package (standard in FILA and Super Coupe). Engine block immersion heater. California emissions system. Note: Incomplete options pricing data at time of publiations.

EQUIPMENT INSTALLATION RATES

Automatic transmission (93.3 percent). Five-speed manual transmission (6.7 percent). V-8 engine (33 percent). Six-cylinder engine (57.9 percent). Four-cylinder turbocharged engine (9.1 percent). AM radio (6.6 percent). AM/FM stereo (28.8 percent). AM/FM stereo cassette (32.2 percent). Electronic AM/FM stereo (2.3 percent). Electronic AM/FM Stereo cassette (24.9 percent). Power steering (100 percent). Power front disc brakes (100 percent). Power door locks (59.1 percent). Power seat (57.1 percent). Power windows (74.2 percent). Adjustable steering column (81.8 percent). All tinted glass (97.2 percent). Sunroof (8.7 percent). Automatic air conditioning (12.7 percent). Manual air conditioning (84.1 percent). Standard steel-belted radial tires (100 percent). Electric rear window defogger (65.1 percent). Steel styled wheels (35.2 percent). Aluminum styled wheels: (24.1 percent). Speed control (78.1 percent). Remote-control left-hand rearview mirror (100 percent). Remote-control right-hand rearview mirror (84.3 percent). Reclining front seats (100 percent). Analog clock (37.7 percent). Digital clock (62.3 percent). Limited-slip rear axle (11.3 percent). (Note: Based on 162,024 units produced in the model year for the U.S. market only.)

HISTORICAL FOOTNOTES

The 1984 T-Bird was introduced on September 22, 1983. Phillip Caldwell remained as chairman of the board of Ford Motor Co. Once again, William Clay Ford was vice chairman and Donald E. Petersen was president. Louis E. Lataif continued as Ford Division's general manager. Bernard L. Crumpton remained general sales manager for the division. Some reshuffling of the executive staff would occur by the start of 1985.

Calendar-year output was 146,186 units. A total of 170,551 T-Birds were produced in the model year. This represented 2.10 percent of the industry total. Of these units, 34,250 were made in Atlanta, Georgia, and 136,301 were made in Lorain, Ohio. Calendar-year dealer sales amounted to 156,583 T-Birds, representing 2 percent of industry sales.

This year the Turbo Coupe was merchandised heavily in both the U.S. and Canada. Starting on March 16, 1984, three Special Value Packages with a discount were available. Each package included the same 11 basic extras. Collectors are likely to find many well-loaded 1984 Turbo Coupes

Ford photo

The 1984 Turbo Coupe was identifiable by its fog lights and lower front fascia.

today because of this promotion. *Motor Trend* (April 1984) tested the Turbo Coupe, describing it as a "show and go that you can afford to keep on the road." The car traveled from 0 to 60 mph in 8.98 seconds and ran the quarter-mile in 16.73 seconds at 80.9 mph. Writer Jim Hall focused on its economy of operation. In 13,257.3 miles of long-term use, the Silver T-Bird cost $987.65 (7.4 cents per mile) to operate. The total included $55.45 in maintenance costs

and $932.20 worth of gas.

Surging upon acceleration and pinging on climbing steep hills were two problems. After 1,000 miles of use, the surging went away. The pinging was minimized by use of unleaded premium fuel. An air conditioning compressor was also replaced under the factory warranty. The T-Bird was summarized as a "good looking performance car that won't cost the driver an arm and a leg during the first year of ownership."

In an interesting comparison report, *Motor Trend's* long-term Turbo test car was later (July 1984 issue) compared to a Turbo 'Bird modified by Creative Car Products (CCP) of Hawthorne, California. The CCP Thunderbird featured a front air dam, side skirts, rear valance panel, rear spoiler, and a Turbo Auto intercooler atop its engine. Additional upgrades included chrome-silicon coil springs front and rear, larger anti-roll bars, and Koni adjustable shocks, plus special Hayashi wheels and Goodyear tires. The magazine described the car's overall look as "reminiscent of the NASCAR Grand National cars." At Sears Point Raceway, the CCP Thunderbird took 9.11 seconds to do 0 to 60, and covered the quarter-mile in 16.86 seconds at 80.4 mph. Although it was slower accelerating than the stock Turbo because of its "stickier" tires, the sleek CCP 'Bird performed better in braking and handling tests.

In addition to street-performance modifications, the new-generation Aero 'Birds were also gaining the attention of the racecar set. In stock car racing, Ford's Special Vehicle Operations (SVO) parts pipeline was funneling hardware to racecar builders that made the T-Birds even more competitive in 1984. Bill Elliott took his Coors Melling T-Bird to the first back-to-back victories in the 1984 NASCAR Winston Cup Series in October. Other stock car drivers racing T-Birds this year included Benny Parsons in the number 55 Copenhagen car, Ricky Rudd in the Wrangler T-Bird, Dick Brooks in the Chameleon Sunglasses T-Bird, Kyle Petty's 7-Eleven car, Kenny Schrader in the Sunny King/Honda Bird, and Buddy Baker in the Valvoline T-Bird. In sports car racing, John Bauer campaigned his number 77 T-Bird. The blue and white car, with Ford/Motorcraft sponsorship, dominated GTO competition. At Pikes Peak, Leonard Vahsholtz and Larry Overholser raced T-Birds up the mountain with mixed success. They were competitive in the event, but wound up in second and fourth place, respectively. Finally, in drag racing, Chief Auto Parts announced its principal sponsorship of Bob Glidden's Pro Stock T-Bird.

The 30th anniversary of the T-Bird's introduction was celebrated in the fall of 1984, and by the end of the year, there would be more to celebrate as model-year production in the U.S. leaped to 170,551, a gain of nearly 50,000 over 1983.

1984 THUNDERBIRD PERFORMANCE		
Model	CID/HP	Performance
0-60 mph		
Turbo Coupe	140/142	8.98 seconds
CCP/Turbo Coupe	140/142	9.11 seconds
1/4-Mile		
Turbo Coupe	140/142	16.73 seconds @ 80.9 mph
CCP/Turbo Coupe	140/142	16.86 seconds @ 80.4 mph

This FILA T-Bird is shown with optional pivoting front vent windows.

Ford photo

The Turbo Coupe sported a blacked-out lower body and was devoid of chrome for 1985.

1985 *Thunderbird*

Ford celebrated the 30th Anniversary of the T-Bird with a special limited-edition commemorative model with unique exterior and interior trim. Regular T-Birds got a new color-keyed grille and full-width taillights with inboard back-up lights. There was also a new T-Bird emblem on the taillight lenses, the "C" pillars and the grille header bar. The base coupe, the Elan Coupe and the FILA Coupe returned. The 1985 Turbo Coupe was "dechromed" to give it a more purposeful look. It also got larger tires on aluminum wheels.

Ford offered 14 colors for the exterior of T-Birds. Seven were standard colors and seven were Clearcoat Metallics. Seven color-coordinated paint stripe colors were used. The Turbo Coupe first came in three standard colors and five clearcoats, all with a Dark Charcoal lower accent treatment. However a 1985-1/2 running change offered three of the same exterior colors (Bright Canyon Red, Oxford White, or Medium Regatta Blue Clearcoat Metallic) in a monotone

treatment without Dark Charcoal lower accenting. The FILA model again offered a Pastel Charcoal exterior with Dark Charcoal lower accent treatment. However, the Red and Blue tape stripes of 1984 were changed to Red Orange and Dark Blue. Three other Monotone color options were added: Black, Bright Canyon Red, and Medium Charcoal Metallic Clearcoat. All three also came with the same FILA tape stripes.

The most collectible car of the year was the 30th Anniversary Limited-Edition T-Bird. It came exclusively with Medium Regatta Blue Metallic exterior finish highlighted with Silver Metallic graduated paint stripes. Interior changes included a new instrument panel with a digital speedometer and analog gauges. Also revised were the door trim panels. The front center console was shortened and a third seat belt was added in the rear for five-passenger seating. A total of 33 interior trim options

NON-TURBO COUPE BODY COLOR INFORMATION (AS OF 2/1/85)

Color Name	Code	Color Name	Code
Black+	1C	Silver Clearcoat Metallic+	1Q
Bright Canyon Red	2E	Medium Dark Charcoal Clearcoat Met.+	1Z
Midnight Regatta Blue	3U	Medium Canyon Red Clearcoat Metallic	2M
Dark Sage	4E	Pastel Regatta Blue Clearcoat Metallic	3S
Sand Beige	8L	Medium Regatta Blue Clearcoat Metallic	3Y
Dark Clove Brown	81	Light Sage Clearcoat Metallic	4B
Oxford White	9L	Medium Sand Beige Clearcoat Metallic	8U

+ Indicates available as a Tu-Tone color, clearcoat metallic colors optional at extra cost.

PAINT STRIPE COLOR INFORMATION

Color Name	Code	Color Name	Code
Charcoal	a	Medium Regatta Blue	q
Light Blue	b	Copper	t
Bright Canyon Red	e	Beige	y
Light Grey	p		

TURBO COUPE BODY COLOR INFORMATION

Color Name	Code	Color Name	Code
Black*	1C	Medium Charcoal Clearcoat Metallic*	1Z
Bright Canyon Red+	2E	Medium Canyon Red Clearcoat Metallic*	2M
Oxford White+	9L	Pastel Regatta Blue Clearcoat Met.*	3S
Silver Clearcoat Metallic*	1Q	Medium Regatta Blue Clearcoat Met.+	3Y

+Indicates Turbo Coupe monotone exterior colors — 1985 1/2 running change, early production included Dark Charcoal lower accent treatment. Clearcoat Metallic colors optional at extra cost.
*Indicates that color includes Dark Charcoal lower accent treatment, clearcoat metallic colors optional at extra cost.

FILA COUPE BODY COLOR INFORMATION

Color Name	Code	Color Name	Code
Black	1C	Medium Charcoal Clearcoat Metallic*	1Z
Pastel Charcoal*	1M	Bright Canyon Red	2E

* Indicates that color includes Dark Charcoal lower accent treatment, Clearcoat Metallic colors optional at extra cost.
All FILA models include Red-Orange and Dark Blue paint stripes.

30TH ANNIVERSARY LIMITED-EDITION COUPE BODY COLOR INFORMATION

Color Name	Code
Medium Regatta Blue Clearcoat Metallic+	3Y

Includes Silver Metallic graduated paint stripe and Regatta Blue (Code SB) interior trim color.

INTERIOR TRIM INFORMATION (U.S. & CANADA)

Seat Type	Material	Charcoal	Oxford Gray	Can Red	Rega Blue	Sand Beige	Oxford White
Base T-Bird							
Split-Bench	All-Cloth	HA	HD	HB	HY	—	—
Split Bench	SS-Vinyl	JA	JD	JB	JY	—	—
Individual	All-Cloth	AA	AD	AB	AY	—	—
Individual	SS-Vinyl	CA	CD	CB	CY	—	—
Base/Elan/Turbo							
Articulated Buckets	All-Cloth	BA	—	BD	—	BY	—
Articulated Buckets	Leather	FA	—	FD	—	FY	—
Elan							
Split-Bench	Luxury Cloth	KA	KJ	KD	KB	KY	—
Split-Bench	Leather	LA	—	LD	—	LY	—
FILA							
Articulated Buckets	Cloth Surfaces	—	MJ	—	—	—	—
Articulated Buckets	Leather	—	—	—	—	—	GW
30th Anniversary Limited Edition							
Split-Bench	Luxury Cloth	—	—	—	—	SB	—

Legend: First letter denotes seat type, second letter denotes color. Can Red means Canyon Red. Rega Blue means Regatta Blue. SS-Vinyl means Super-Soft Vinyl. U-Leather means leather seating surfaces.

THUNDERBIRD PRODUCTION

Model Number	Body/Style Number	Body Type & Seating	Factory Price	Shipping Weight	Production Total
THUNDERBIRD - (V-6)					
46	66D	2d Coupe-4P	$10,249	2,890 lbs.	Note 1
THUNDERBIRD - (V-8)					
46	66D	2d Coupe-4P	$10,884	3,097 lbs.	Note 1
THUNDERBIRD ELAN - (V-6)					
46/607	66D	2d Coupe-4P	$11,916	2,956 lbs.	Note 1
THUNDERBIRD ELAN - (V-8)					
46/607	66D	2d Coupe-4P	$12,551	3,163 lbs.	Note 1
THUNDERBIRD FILA - (V-6)					
46/606	66D	2d Coupe-4P	$14,974	3,061 lbs.	Note 1
THUNDERBIRD FILA - (V-8)					
46/606	66D	2d Coupe-4P	$15,609	3,268 lbs.	Note 1
THUNDERBIRD TURBO COUPE - (4-CYL)					
46/934	66D	2d Coupe-4P	$13,365	2,938 lbs.	Note 1

NOTE 1: Production of the all models combined was 151,852.

were listed in 1985. They included a special Regatta Blue luxury cloth split-bench seat interior for the 30th Anniversary T-Bird.

The Turbo Coupe received a modified 2.3-liter four-cylinder engine with electronic boost control and higher flow-rate fuel injectors to increase power. The improvements were the result of research and development done for the Merkur XR4Ti, built by Ford of Germany, which used the same engine. There was also a new five-speed manual transmission with new gear ratios, plus an automatic transmission designed to handle the Turbo Coupe's high-revving capabilities. When the driver accelerated quickly, it stayed in low gear right through the power curve, not shifting until higher performance could be gained by going to a higher gear.

STANDARD EQUIPMENT

3.8-liter two-barrel EFI V-6 engine, SelectShift automatic transmission with locking torque converter, variable-ratio rack and pinion steering, power front disc/rear drum brakes, electronic voltage regulator, McPherson strut front suspension with gas-filled struts, four-bar-link rear suspension with gas-filled shocks, P205/70R14 all-season black sidewall tires, concealed drip moldings, halogen headlights, luxury wheel covers, individually reclining split-bench seats with cloth seating surfaces and consolette, 16-oz. color-keyed cut-pile carpeting, luxury steering wheel

with center horn blow, quartz electric (sweep-hand) clock, AM radio (may be deleted for credit). **1985 Thunderbird Elan Equipment adds or substitutes the following over base T-Bird:** Automatic parking brake release, dual electric remote-control OSRV mirrors, wide body-side moldings, body-side and deck lid accent stripes, rear seat center folding armrest, luxury door and quarter panel trim, quarter panel courtesy lights, electronic digital clock, AM/FM stereo cassette tape player, interval windshield wipers, power windows, complete tinted glass, diagnostic warning lights, light group, and remote-locking fuel door. **1985 Thunderbird FILA Equipment adds or substitutes the following over base T-Bird:** Automatic overdrive transmission, automatic parking brake release, dual electric remote-control mirrors, wide body-side moldings, body-side and deck lid striping, cornering lamps, 14-in. aluminum wheels, articulated seats, rear seat center folding armrest, luxury door and quarter trim panels, quarter panel courtesy lights, leather-wrapped steering wheel, electronic digital clock, electronic AM/FM stereo search radio with cassette player and Dolby noise reduction system, premium sound system, power lock group, interval wipers, 6-way power driver's seat, complete tinted glass, tilt steering wheel, speed control, Autolamp on and off delay system, illuminated entry system, diagnostic warning lights, light group, and remote locking fuel door. **1985 Thunderbird Super Coupe Equipment adds or substitutes the following over base T-Bird:** 2.3-liter overhead-cam EFI turbocharged four-cylinder engine, five-speed manual overdrive transmission, full analog instrumentation with tachometer with boost and over-boost lights, Traction-Lok rear axle, P225/60VR15 black sidewall performance tires, dual electric remote-control mirrors, wide body-side moldings, cornering lamps, unique front fascia with air dam and Marchal fog lights, 15-in. aluminum wheels, articulated seats, rear seat center folding armrest, performance instrumentation, luxury door and quarter trim panels, quarter panel courtesy lights, leather-wrapped steering wheel, electronic digital clock, AM/FM stereo radio, interval wipers, tinted glass complete, diagnostic warning lights, light group, and remote locking fuel door.

I.D. NUMBERS

VIN stamped on aluminum tab riveted to the dashboard on passenger side and observable through the windshield from outside the car. First symbol 1 denotes built in the United States. Second symbol F denotes Ford. Third symbol A denotes Ford passenger vehicle. Fourth symbol denotes type of restraint system. Fifth symbol P denotes passenger-type vehicle. Sixth symbol 4 denotes Thunderbird. Seventh symbol 6 denotes two-door coupe. Eighth symbol denotes engine: W=140 cid (2.3L) 155 hp turbocharged four-cylinder, 3=232-cid (3.8L)/120-hp V-6, F=302-cid (5.0L)/140-hp V-8. Ninth symbol is the check digit. 10th symbol F=1985 model year. 11th symbol denotes assembly plant: A=Atlanta, Georgia or H=Lorain, Ohio. Twelfth through 17th symbols denote sequential production number of specific vehicle starting at 100001. Vehicle certification label located on rear face of driver's door. The top part of the label indicates that the Thunderbird was manufactured by Ford Motor Company. Directly below this is the month and year of manufacture, plus a statement that the car conforms to federal motor vehicle safety standard in effect on the indicated date of manufacture. VIN: The VIN appears first on the first line of encoded information. It matches the 1st to 11th symbols on VIN tag. Some other codes also appear. TYPE: On left side of label, indicates PASSENGER. EXT. COLOR: This line carries the exterior paint color(s) code. See table below. DSO: The District Special Order code now appears above "DSO" to the right of the exterior paint color code. BODY: The body style code appears to the extreme left of the bottom line. The only Thunderbird code for this model-year is: 66D=two-door pillared hardtop. VR: The vinyl roof type/color code is to the right of the body code. MLDG: The molding code is to the right of the vinyl roof code. INT. TRIM: The interior trim code is to the right of the molding code. See table below. A/C: The air conditioning code is to the right of the interior trim code. Cars with air conditioning have "A" stamped here. R: The radio code is to the right of the A/C code. S: The sunroof code appears to the right of the radio code. AX: The axle code appears to the right of the sunroof code. TR: The transmission code appears to the right of the axle code. Note: The terms and abbreviations shown in capitals appear on the line above the actual codes. Note:

ENGINE

THUNDERBIRD BASE V-6: 90-degree. Overhead valve. Cast-iron block and aluminum head. Displacement: 232 cid (3.8 liters). Bore and stroke: 3.80 x 3.40 in. Compression ratio: 8.7:1. Brake hp: 120 at 3600. Torque: 205 lbs.-ft. at 1600. Four main bearings. Hydraulic valve lifters. Induction: Throttle Body Injection. Serial number code: 3.

THUNDERBIRD TURBO COUPE BASE 4-CYL TURBO: Inline. Overhead valve. Cast-iron block and head. Displacement: 140 cid (2.3 liters). Bore and stroke: 3.78 x 3.13 in. Compression ratio: 8.0:1. Brake hp: 155 at 4600. Torque: 190 lbs.-ft. at 2800. Five main bearings. Hydraulic valve lifters. Induction: Multi-Point Electronic Fuel injection. Garrett AIResearch T-03 turbocharger. Serial number code: W.

THUNDERBIRD OPTIONAL V-8: 90-degree. Overhead valve. Cast-iron block and head. Displacement: 302 cid (5.0 liters). Bore and stroke: 4.00 x 3.00 in. Compression ratio: 8.4:1. Brake hp: 140 at 3200 rpm. Torque: 250 lbs.-ft. at 1600 rpm. Five main bearings. Hydraulic valve lifters. Induction: Throttle Body Injection. Serial number code: F.

CHASSIS

Wheelbase: 104 in. Overall length: 197.6. Overall width: 71.1. Overall height: 53.2 in. Front headroom: 37.7 in. Front legroom: 42 in. Front shoulder room: 55.2 in. Rear headroom: 36.7 in. Rear legroom: 34.3 in. Trunk capacity: 14.6 cu. ft. Front tread: 58.1 in. Rear tread: 58.5 in. Tires: P195/75R14 white sidewall steel-belted radial. Steering: Variable-ratio, power, rack-and-pinion. Steering ratio: 15.0-13.0:1 (15.1:1 on Turbo Coupe). Turning diameter: 38.6 ft. Turns lock-to-lock: 2.5. Front suspension: Modified McPherson strut. Rear suspension: Four-link-bar (quad shocks on Turbo Coupe). Weight distribution: 56/44 percent front/rear. Power-to-weight ratio: 20.56 lb./hp. Steering: Variable-ratio power rack and pinion. Standard rear axle: 2.73:1. Front brakes: Power disc. Rear brakes: Power drum. Brakes swept area: 275.6 sq. in. Rear axle (with five-speed manual transmission): 3.45:1. Rear axle (with three-speed automatic transmission): 2.47:1. Rear axle (four-speed automatic transmission): 3.08:1. Fuel tank capacity: 21 gal.

OPTIONS

AM/FM stereo radio with cassette tape player ($133). Electronic AM/FM stereo search radio with cassette tape player and Dolby noise reduction system. Premium sound system (stereo radios only). Graphic equalizer. Wide body-side moldings. Dual body-side and deck lid tape stripes. Hood stripes. Tu-Tone paint/tape treatments. Clearcoat Metallic paint. Rear cornering lamps. Rear window defroster. Dual electric remote-control mirrors ($86). Pivoting front vent windows. Keyless entry system including illuminated entry system ($105). Illuminated entry system. Interval windshield wipers. Flip-up Open-Air roof ($284). SelectAire conditioner with electronic control ($686). SelectAire conditioner with manual control. Automatic parking brake release. Electronic digital clock. Complete tinted glass ($104). Light group. Speed control ($158). Electronic dimming day/night rearview mirror. Dual illuminated visor mirrors. Leather-wrapped luxury steering wheel. Tilt steering wheel ($104). Heated driver and passenger seat. Articulated seats. Ultrasoft leather seat trim. Anti-theft system. Bright rocker panel moldings. Front floor mats. Front license plate bracket. License plate frames. Power lock group ($198). Power radio antenna. 6-way power driver's seat ($214). Dual 6-way power seats. Power seat recliners. Power side windows ($186). Locking wire wheel style wheel covers. Styled road wheel covers. Alloy wheels. 5.0-liter V-8 with EFI and automatic overdrive transmission optional in all models, except Super Coupe ($448 engine/$213 transmission). SelectShift automatic transmission with locking torque converter, standard in T-Bird and Elan, optional in Super Coupe ($284). Traction-Lok differential, standard in Super Coupe. Medium-duty trailer towing package. Heavy-duty battery. Heavy-duty suspension. Engine block immersion heater. California emissions system. Note: Incomplete options pricing data at time of publication.

EQUIPMENT INSTALLATION RATES

Automatic transmission (92 percent). Five-speed manual transmission (8 percent). V-8 engine (34.3 percent). Six-cylinder engine (52 percent). Four-cyl turbocharged engine (13.7 percent). AM/FM stereo (22.8 percent). AM/FM stereo cassette (45.9 percent). Electronic AM/FM Stereo Cassette (29 percent). Power steering (100 percent). Power front disc brakes (100 percent). Power door locks (59.9 percent). Power seat (57.8 percent). Power windows (87.1 percent). Adjustable steering column (87.7 percent). All tinted glass (97.9 percent). Sunroof (7.6 percent). Automatic air conditioning (13.4 percent). Manual air conditioning (84.7 percent). Standard steel-belted radial tires (100 percent). Electric rear window defogger (81.4 percent). Steel styled wheels (29.4 percent). Aluminum styled wheels (24.5 percent). Speed control (84.7 percent). Remote-control left-hand rearview mirror (100 percent). Remote-control right-hand rearview mirror (86.8 percent). Reclining front seats (100 percent). Analog clock (41 percent). Digital clock (59

Ford photo

The 1985 Turbo Coupe used a 2.3-liter turbo-charged four-cylinder engine. The base price on the sporty T-Bird was $13,365.

percent). Limited-slip rear axle (15.3 percent). (Note: Based on 144,426 units produced in the model year for the U.S. market only.)

HISTORICAL FOOTNOTES

The 1985 T-Bird was introduced on October 4, 1984. Donald E. Petersen became chairman of the board and CEO of Ford Motor Co. William Clay Ford remained vice chairman and Harold A. Poling was president and chief operating officer. Ford Vice President Robert L. Rewey took over as Ford Division's general manager. Phillip M. Novell was general sales manager for the division.

Calendar-year output was 170,541 units. A total of 151,852 T-Birds were produced in the model year. This represented 1.94 percent of the industry total. Of these units, 20,637 were made in Atlanta, Georgia, and 131,215 were made in Lorain, Ohio. Calendar-year dealer sales amounted to 169,770 T-Birds, representing 2.1 percent of industry sales.

In racing, the T-Birds were flying high this season, with Ricky Rudd's Bud Moore-built Motorcraft T-Bird making him one of the most promising newcomers in NASCAR events. The T-Birds were so dominant that Chevy buff Junior Johnson convinced Winston Cup officials that he should be able to lower his Monte Carlos to the same roof height specs applied to T-Birds (50 in. instead of 51 in.). At midyear, NASCAR established a new uniform minimum roof height dimension of 50 in. It didn't matter. Bill Elliott's Coors-sponsored T-Bird continued to rule NASCAR and set a record qualifying speed in its next outing. That was the Winston 500 at Talladega Superspeedway, a race in which T-Birds finished 1-2-3. Elliott took the checkered flag with a mind-blowing average speed of 186.288 mph. He also won the Daytona 500, the Transouth 500 at Darlington, the Budweiser 500 at Dover, Delaware, the Pocono Summer 500, the Champion Spark Plug 500 at Michigan International, and the Southern 500 at Darlington. His victory in the latter event made Elliott the winner of the new Winston Million series, which earned him a check for $1 million from R.J. Reynolds. Ultimately, Darrell Waltrip would come from behind to take the 1985 points championship, which created a bit of controversy over the way the scoring was handled. Elliott, though, had become the first driver to ever win 11 Winston Cup superspeedway races in a single season. It was still a great year for Bill's pocketbook and the T-Bird's long performance history. Cale Yarborough (Hardees Ranier T-Bird), Kyle Petty (Woods Brothers T-Bird), and Bobby Allison were other T-Bird pilots in NASCAR.

In drag racing, Rickie Smith's Motorcraft T-Bird broke the 180-mph and 8-second barriers in Pro Stock competition. This car was a star on both the NHRA and IHRA circuits in 1985. In a third venue, Darin Brassfield had success with his Brooks Racing T-Bird in the IMSA Camel GT Series.

Ford photo

Most of the 1985 Thunderbird styling cues returned in 1986. Base, Elan, and Turbo Coupe models were offered.

1986
Thunderbird

T-Bird styling was similar to 1985, except for a new high-mounted stop lamp. A new electronic climate control system was announced and an electronically tuned AM/FM stereo became standard equipment in the base model. The T-bird hood had counter-balanced springs to hold it open instead of inconvenient prop rods. Larger 215/70R14 tires and a collapsible spare with an on-board compressor to inflate it were other changes. Added to the options list were a power-operated moonroof and a specially designed Tot-Guard child seat. Ford switched to a three-year unlimited mileage warranty on major power train components.

The base and Elan models returned. Five conventional finishes and eight extra-cost Clearcoat paints were offered for base and Elan models. Five colors were available in two-tone combinations. There were nine color-keyed striping colors. The Turbo Coupe came in three regular colors and five clearcoat metallics. Four (including Black) were available in combination with Dark Charcoal lower-body accents. Five interior colors were listed for base and Elan models. A sixth color, called Raven, was only for Elans with articulated seats. Articulated sports seats were available in the Elan and Turbo Coupe. Turbos came with only three interior colors. A wood-tone instrument panel applique was added to the interior.

The 3.8-liter fuel-injected V-6 hooked to a three-speed SelectShift automatic transmission was standard. New hydraulic engine mounts made the car smoother running. The 5.0-liter V-8 now featured sequential fuel injection, roller tappets, low-tension piston rings, fast-burn combustion chambers and hydraulic engine mounts. A four-speed automatic overdrive transmission and upgraded rear axle were standard with the V-8. The Turbo Coupe featured a standard 2.3-liter turbocharged engine and five-speed manual transmission.

STANDARD EQUIPMENT

3.8-liter (232-cid) TBI V-6 engine, three-speed automatic transmission, power brakes, power steering, dual note horn, halogen headlights, left-hand remote-control door mirror, vinyl insert body-side moldings, deluxe wheel covers, seat belt reminder chimes, analog quartz clock, center console, vinyl door panels, full carpeting including trunk, AM/FM stereo radio, individual reclining front seats, luxury steering wheel, cloth upholstery, trip odometer, P215/70R14 tires. **1986 Thunderbird Elan Coupe Equipment adds or substitutes the following over base T-Bird:** Power windows, folding rear seat armrest, tinted glass, light group, dual electric remote-control OSRV mirrors, wide body-side moldings, AM/FM cassette stereo, intermittent windshield

NON-TURBO COUPE BODY COLOR INFORMATION (AS OF 2/15/86)

Color Name	Code	Color Name	Code
Black+	1C	Silver Clearcoat Metallic+	1Q
Bright Canyon Red	2E	Medium Canyon Red Clearcoat Metallic	2M
Midnight Regatta Blue	3U	Midnight Wine Clearcoat Metallic+	2Y
Sand Beige	8L	Regatta Blue Clearcoat Metallic	3W
Oxford White	9L	Light Taupe Clearcoat Metallic+	5E
Medium Grey Clearcoat Metallic+	1F	Deep Shadow Blue Clearcoat Metallic	7C
Sand Beige Clearcoat Metallic	8M		

+ Indicates available as a Tu-Tone color; Clearcoat Metallic colors optional at extra cost.

TURBO COUPE BODY COLOR INFORMATION (AS OF 2/15/86)

Color Name	Code	Color Name	Code
Black*	1C	Silver Clearcoat Metallic*	1Q
Bright Canyon Red	2E	Medium Canyon Red Clearcoat Metallic*	2M
Oxford White	9L	Regatta Blue Clearcoat Metallic	3W
Medium Grey Clearcoat Metallic*	1F	Sand Beige Clearcoat Metallic*	8M

* Indicates that color includes Dark Charcoal lower accent treatment; Clearcoat Metallic colors optional at extra cost.

PAINT STRIPE COLOR INFORMATION

Color Name	Code	Color Name	Code
Black	a	Light Charcoal	p
Copper	c	Dark Academy Blue	q
Dark Red	d	Medium Sandalwood	t
Bright Canyon Red	e	Medium Champagne	y
Dark Taupe	f		

INTERIOR TRIM INFORMATION (U.S. & CANADA)

Seat Type	Material	Med. Gray	Can. Red	Rega. Blue	Sand Beige	Taupe	Raven
Base T-Bird							
Split-Bench	All-Cloth	HG	HD	HB	HY	HE	—
Split Bench	SS-Vinyl	JG	JD	JB	JY	JE	—
Individual	All-Cloth	AG	AD	AB	AY	AE	—
Elan							
Split-Bench	All-Cloth	KG	KD	KB	KY	KE	—
Split-Bench	Leather	LG	LD	—	LY	LE	—
Turbo/Elan							
Articulated Buckets	All-Cloth	—	BD	—	BY	—	BH
Articulated Buckets	Leather	—	FD	—	FY	—	FH

Legend: First letter denotes seat type; second letter denotes color. Med means Medium; Can Red means Canyon Red; Rega Blue means Regatta Blue; SS-Vinyl means Super-Soft Vinyl. Leather means leather seating surfaces.

THUNDERBIRD PRODUCTION

Model Number	Body/Style Number	Body Type & Seating	Factory Price	Shipping Weight	Production Total
THUNDERBIRD - (V-6)					
46	66D	2d Coupe-4P	$11,020	2,923 lbs.	Note 1
THUNDERBIRD - (V-8)					
46	66D	2d Coupe-4P	$11,805	3,101 lbs.	Note 1
THUNDERBIRD ELAN - (V-6)					
46/607	66D	2d Coupe-4P	$12,554	2,977 lbs.	Note 1
THUNDERBIRD ELAN - (V-8)					
46/607	66D	2d Coupe-4P	$13,339	3,155 lbs.	Note 1
THUNDERBIRD TURBO COUPE - (4-CYL)					
46/934	66D	2d Coupe-4P	$14,143	3,016 lbs.	Note 1

NOTE 1: Production of the all models combined was 163,965.

wipers. **1986 Thunderbird Turbo Coupe Equipment adds or substitutes the following over base T-Bird:** 2.3-liter (140-cid) turbocharged four-cylinder PFI engine, five-speed manual overdrive transmission, and special handling suspension.

I.D. NUMBERS

VIN stamped on aluminum tab riveted to dashboard on passenger side and observable through the windshield from outside the car. First symbol 1 denotes built in the United States. Second symbol F denotes Ford. Third symbol A denotes Ford passenger vehicle. Fourth symbol denotes type of restraint system. Fifth symbol P denotes passenger-type vehicle. Sixth symbol 4 denotes Thunderbird. Seventh symbol 6 denotes two-door coupe. Eighth symbol denotes engine: W=140-cid (2.3L)/145-hp turbocharged four-cylinder/automatic, W=140-cid (2.3L)/155-hp turbocharged four-cylinder/manual, 3=232-cid (3.8L)/120-hp V-6, F=302-cid (5.0L)/150-hp V-8. Ninth symbol is the check digit. 10th symbol G=1986 model year. 11th symbol denotes assembly plant. H=Lorain, Ohio. Twelfth through 17th symbols denote sequential production number of specific vehicle starting at 100001. Vehicle certification label located on rear face of driver's door. The top part of the label indicates that the Thunderbird was manufactured by Ford Motor Company. Directly below this is the month and year of manufacture, plus a statement that the car conforms to federal motor vehicle safety standard in effect on the indicated date of manufacture. VIN: The VIN appears first on the first line of encoded information. It matches the 1st to 11th symbols on VIN tag. Some other codes also appear. TYPE: On left side of label, indicates PASSENGER. EXT. COLOR: This line carries the exterior paint color(s) code. DSO: The District Special Order code now appears above "DSO" to the right of the exterior paint color code. BODY: The body style code appears to the extreme left of the bottom line. The only Thunderbird code for this model-year is: 66D=two-door pillared hardtop. VR: The vinyl roof type/color code is to the right of the body code. No T-Birds had vinyl tops. MLDG: The molding code is to the right of the vinyl roof code. INT. TRIM: The interior trim code is to

the right of the molding code. A/C: The air conditioning code is to the right of the interior trim code. Cars with air conditioning have "A" stamped here. R: The radio code is to the right of the A/C code. S: The sunroof code appears to the right of the radio code. AX: The axle code appears to the right of the sunroof code. TR: The transmission code appears to the right of the axle code. (Note: The terms and abbreviations shown in capitals appear on the line above the actual codes.)

ENGINE

THUNDERBIRD BASE V-6: 90-degree. Overhead valve. Cast-iron block and aluminum head. Displacement: 232 cid (3.8 liters). Bore and stroke: 3.80 x 3.40 in. Compression ratio: 8.7:1. Brake hp: 120 at 3600. Torque: 205 lbs.-ft. at 1600. Four main bearings. Hydraulic valve lifters. Induction: Throttle Body Injection. Serial number code: 3.

THUNDERBIRD TURBO COUPE BASE FOUR-CYL TURBO (AUTOMATIC): Inline. Overhead valve. Cast-iron block and head. Displacement: 140 cid (2.3 liters). Bore and stroke: 3.78 x 3.13 in. Compression ratio: 8.0:1. Brake hp: 145 at 4400. Torque: 180 lbs.-ft. at 3000. Five main bearings. Hydraulic valve lifters. Induction: Multi-Point Electronic Fuel injection. Garrett AIResearch T-03 turbocharger. Serial number code: W.

THUNDERBIRD TURBO COUPE BASE FOUR-CYL TURBO: Inline. Overhead valve. Cast-iron block and head.

Displacement: 140 cid (2.3 liters). Bore and stroke: 3.78 x 3.13 in. Compression ratio: 8.0:1. Brake hp: 155 at 4600. Torque: 190 lbs.-ft. at 2800. Five main bearings. Hydraulic valve lifters. Induction: Multi-Point Electronic Fuel injection. Garrett AIResearch T-03 turbocharger. Serial number code: W.

THUNDERBIRD OPTIONAL V-8: 90-degree. Overhead valve. Cast-iron block and head. Displacement: 302 cid (5.0 liters). Bore and stroke: 4.00 x 3.00 in. Compression ratio: 8.9:1. Brake hp: 150 at 3200 rpm. Torque: 270 lbs.-ft. at 2000 rpm. Five main bearings. Hydraulic valve lifters. Induction: Sequential (port) fuel injection. Serial number code: F.

CHASSIS

Wheelbase: 104 in. Overall length: 197.6. Overall width: 71.1. Overall height: 53.2 in. Front headroom: 37.7 in. Front legroom: 42 in. Front shoulder room: 55.2 in. Rear headroom: 36.7 in. Rear legroom: 34.3 in. Trunk capacity: 14.6 cu. ft. Front tread: 58.1 in. Rear tread: 58.5 in. Tires: P195/70R14 white sidewall steel-belted radial. Steering: Variable-ratio, power, rack-and pinion. Steering ratio: 15.0-13.0:1 (15.1:1 on Turbo Coupe). Turning diameter: 38.6 ft. Turns lock-to-lock: 2.5. Front suspension: Modified McPherson strut. Rear suspension: Four-link-bar (quad shocks on Turbo Coupe). Weight distribution: 56/44 percent front/rear. Power-to-weight ratio: 20.56 lb./hp. Steering: Variable-ratio power rack and pinion. Standard rear axle: 2.73:1. Front brakes: Power disc. Rear brakes: Power drum. Brakes swept area: 275.6 sq. in. Rear axle (with five-speed manual transmission): 3.45:1. Rear Axle (with three-speed automatic transmission): 2.47:1. Rear axle (four-speed automatic transmission): 3.08:1. Fuel tank capacity: 21 gal.

OPTIONS

5.0-liter PFI V-8 ($505). Three-speed automatic transmission in Turbo Coupe ($290). Four-speed automatic transmission in T-Bird and Elan ($220). Traction-Lok axle ($920. Inflatable spare tire ($112). Conventional spare tire ($558). Automatic air conditioning ($850). Air conditioning ($700). Anti-theft system ($145). Autolamp system ($67). Heavy-duty battery ($25). Digital clock ($56). Cornering lamps ($63). Rear defogger ($133). Diagnostic alert lights ($82). Tinted glass ($106). Engine block immersion heater ($17). Illuminated entry system ($75). Electronic instrument cluster in T-Bird ($305). Electronic instrument cluster in T-Bird Elan coupe ($250). Remote keyless entry system ($182). Light group ($32). Power lock group ($200). Front floor mats ($20). Dual illuminated sun visor mirrors ($98). Dual remote-control OSRV mirrors ($88). Wide body-side moldings ($52). Power-operated moonroof ($645). Two-tone exterior paint on T-Bird ($200). Two-tone exterior paint on T-Bird Elan Coupe ($150). Metallic clearcoat paint ($168). Power antenna ($65). AM/FM stereo delete option ($167 credit). AM/FM electronically tuned stereo with cassette tape player ($117). Graphic equalizer ($200). Premium sound system ($155). Articulated sport seats ($168). 6-way power driver's seat ($220). Dual 6-way power seats ($440). Dual power recliners ($174). Speed control ($162). Leather steering wheel ($54). Tilt steering column ($106). Vinyl seat trim ($34). Leather seat trim ($380). TripMinder computer in T-Bird ($255). TripMinder computer in Elan Coupe and Turbo Coupe ($198). Front vent windows ($73). Locking wire wheel covers ($195). Cast-aluminum wheels ($315). Styled road wheels ($164).

Power windows ($190). Intermittent windshield wipers ($46). California emissions system ($81), and tinted windshield ($44).

EQUIPMENT INSTALLATION RATES

Automatic transmission (91.7 percent). Five-speed manual transmission (8.3 percent). V-8 engine (19.2 percent). Six-cylinder engine (67.8 percent). Four-cylinder turbocharged engine (13 percent). Electronic AM/FM stereo cassette (85.9 percent). Power steering (100 percent). Power front disc brakes (100 percent). Power door locks:(69.9 percent). Power seat (47.9 percent). Power windows (93.8 percent). Adjustable steering column (94.9 percent). All tinted glass (98.9 percent). Automatic air conditioning (13.1 percent). Manual air conditioning (85.6 percent). Standard steel-belted radial tires (100 percent). Electric rear window defogger (90.2 percent). Steel styled wheels: (48.9 percent). Aluminum styled wheels: (10.4 percent). Speed control (94.7 percent). Remote-control left-hand rearview mirror (95.5 percent). Remote-control right-hand rearview mirror (95.5 percent). Reclining front seats: (6.7 percent). Digital clock: (85.3 percent). Limited-slip rear axle: (13.9 percent). (Note: Based on 156,461 units produced in the model year for the U.S. market only.)

HISTORICAL FOOTNOTES

The 1986 T-Bird was introduced on October 3, 1985. Donald E. Petersen was again chairman of the board and CEO of Ford Motor Co. William Clay Ford remained vice chairman and Harold A. Poling stayed on as president and chief operating officer of the corporation. Ford Vice President Robert L. Rewey was again the Ford Division's general manager and Phillip M. Novell continued as divisional general sales manager.

Calendar-year output was 131,383 units. A total of 163,965 T-Birds were produced in the model year. This represented 2.07 percent of the industry total. Of these units, all were made in Lorain, Ohio. Calendar-year dealer sales amounted to 144,577 T-Birds, representing 1.8 percent of industry sales.

Motor Trend tested a Turbo and announced, "There is almost nothing to dislike about the Ford Thunderbird Turbo Coupe." Writer Daniel Charles Ross averaged 18.23 mpg with the car during the 2,493 miles he drove it. His test T-Bird had the three-speed automatic transmission, which came with a slightly less powerful engine. It developed 145 hp at 4400 rpm and 180 lbs.-ft. of torque at 3000 rpm. "The car looks like it was designed by someone with an engineering degree from MIT and an art degree from the Sorbonne," Ross wrote. He managed 0 to 60 mph in 9.29 seconds and estimated that times in the 8-second range would be possible with 91 octane gas or premium unleaded fuel. Turbo lag, usually in stop-and-go traffic, was the only problem experienced with the car.

1986 THUNDERBIRD PERFORMANCE		
Model	**CID/HP**	**Performance**
0-60 mph		
Turbo Coupe	140/145	9.29 seconds

Ford photo

The twin hood scoops were distinctive features on the 1987 Thunderbird Turbo Coupe.

1987 *Thunderbird*

Evolutionary styling changes were very apparent on the 1987 T-Bird. The front and rear ends were totally new, along with the hood, roof, rear deck lid, doors and quarter panels. Flush aero-style headlights, notched-in full-width taillights that wrapped around the body corners (to function as side markers) and aerodynamic flush side glass were all new. Antilock brakes and automatic ride control were standard.

Standard in the base coupe and LX were a 3.8-liter fuel-injected V-6 and four-speed automatic overdrive transmission. The fancier LX also featured the V-6. A sequentially injected 5.0-liter V-8 with a four-speed overdrive automatic transmission was optional in these models and standard in a new Sport model.

The Turbo Coupe got an air-to-air intercooler. Four standard exterior colors and a record nine clearcoat metallic colors were offered for non-Turbo models. Specific stripes were used with specific exterior/interior color combinations. Four interior colors were offered in Turbos,

six for other models. Two-tone paint treatments were not available for Turbos. The Turbo Coupe featured a grilleless front end and functional hood scoops. There was a large T-Bird emblem on the car's nose. Its engine upgrades reflected research and development done by Ford's SVO (Special Vehicle Operations) branch. It had a new IHI turbocharger designed to optimize low-end and mid-range response and to minimize turbo lag. Also featured were new higher-flow manifolds and a dual exhaust system. The improvements boosted engine output to 190 hp.

STANDARD EQUIPMENT

Air conditioning, diagnostic alert lights (LX, Turbo). Traction-Lok axle (Turbo), maintenance free battery, power front disc/rear drum brakes (except Turbo), four-wheel disc brakes with ABS (Turbo), electronic ignition, 3.8-liter V-6 (except Sport and Turbo), 5.0-liter V-8 (Sport), 2.3-liter EFI turbocharged four-cylinder engine (Turbo), hydraulic

170

NON-TURBO COUPE BODY COLOR INFORMATION (AS OF 1/15/87)

Color Name	Code	Color Name	Code
Black+	1C	Medium Canyon Red Clearcoat Metallic	26
Light Grey	1K	Silver Blue Clearcoat Metallic+	33
Scarlet Red	2D	Driftwood Clearcoat Metallic	5B
Oxford White	9L	Light Taupe Clearcoat Metallic+	5W
Silver Clearcoat Metallic+	14	Dark Taupe Clearcoat Metallic+	55
Medium Grey Clearcoat Metallic+	18	Dark Shadow Blue Clearcoat Metallic+	77
Sandalwood Clearcoat Metallic	8Z		

+ Indicates available as a Tu-Tone color, clearcoat metallic colors optional at extra cost.

TURBO COUPE BODY COLOR INFORMATION

Color Name	Code	Color Name	Code
Black	1C	Medium Red Clearcoat Metallic	26
Oxford White+	9L	Silver Blue Clearcoat Metallic	33
Silver Clearcoat Metallic	14	Driftwood Clearcoat Metallic	5B
Medium Grey Clearcoat Metallic	18	Dark Shadow Blue Clearcoat Metallic+	77

Clearcoat metallic colors optional at extra cost.

PAINT STRIPE INFORMATION

Color Name	Code	Color Name	Code
Black	a	Light Oxford Grey	h
Copper	c	Light Charcoal	p
Dark Red	d	Dark Blue	q
Medium Red	e	Bright Regatta Blue	s
Dark Taupe	f	Medium Champagne	y
Dark Champagne	z		

INTERIOR TRIM INFORMATION (U.S. & Canada)

Seat Type	Material	Med. Gray	Scar. Red	Shad. Blue	Sand Beige	Taupe	Raven
T-Bird Standard							
Split-Bench	All-Cloth	HG	HD	HB	HY	HE	—
Split Bench	SS-Vinyl	JG	JD	JB	JY	JE	—
Individual	All-Cloth	AG	AD	AB	AY	AE	—
Thunderbird Sport							
Individual	All-Cloth	AG	AD	AB	AY	AE	—
Thunderbird LX							
Split-Bench	Luxury Cloth	KG	KD	KB	KY	KE	—
Split-Bench	Leather	LG	LD	LB	LY	LE	—
Thunderbird Turbo/Thunderbird LX							
Articulated Buckets	All-Cloth	—	BD	BB	BY	—	BH
Articulated Buckets	Leather	—	FD	FB	FY	—	FH

Legend: First letter denotes seat type, second letter denotes color. Med. means Medium, Scar Red means Scarlet Red, Shad Blue means Shadow Blue, SS-Vinyl means Super-Soft Vinyl. Leather means leather seating surfaces.

THUNDERBIRD PRODUCTION

Model Number	Body/Style Number	Body Type & Seating	Factory Price	Shipping Weight	Production Total
THUNDERBIRD - (V-6)					
60	66D	2d Coupe-4P	$12,972	3,133 lbs.	Note 1
THUNDERBIRD - (V-8)					
60	66D	2d Coupe-4P	$13,611	3,272 lbs.	Note 1
THUNDERBIRD SPORT - (V-8)					
61	66D	2d Coupe-4P	$15,079	3,346 lbs.	Note 1
THUNDERBIRD LX - (V-6)					
62	66D	2d Coupe-4P	$15,383	3,176 lbs.	Note 1
THUNDERBIRD LX - (V-8)					
62	66D	2d Coupe-4P	$16,022	3,315 lbs.	Note 1
THUNDERBIRD TURBO COUPE - (4-CYL)					
64	66D	2d Coupe-4P	$16,805	3,380 lbs.	Note 1

NOTE 1: Production of the all models combined was 128,135.

engine mounts, remote-control fuel door (Turbo), tinted glass, three-speed heater and defroster, illuminated entry system (LX), high-mount rear brake light, power lock group (LX), automatic ride control (Turbo), gas pressurized shock absorbers, speed control (LX), power steering, tilt steering wheel (LX), special handling package (Sport and Turbo), P215/70R14 black sidewall tires (Base T-Bird and LX), P215/70HR14 black sidewall tires (Sport), P225/60VR16 black sidewall Goodyear Gatorback tires (Turbo). SelectShift automatic transmission (Base T-Bird and LX), automatic overdrive transmission (Sport), 5-speed manual overdrive transmission (Turbo), windshield washer, two-speed electric windshield wipers, halogen headlights, hood scoops (Turbo), fog lamps (Turbo), left-hand remote-control OSRV mirror (Base T-Bird), dual electric remote-control mirrors (Sport, LX and Turbo), luxury wheel covers (Base T-Bird), cast-aluminum wheels (Turbo), styled road wheels (Sport and LX).

I.D. NUMBERS

VIN stamped on aluminum tab riveted to the dashboard on passenger side and observable through the windshield from outside the car. First symbol 1 denotes built in the United States. Second symbol F denotes Ford. Third symbol A denotes Ford passenger vehicle. Fourth symbol denotes type of restraint system. Fifth symbol P denotes passenger-type vehicle. Sixth symbol 6 denotes Thunderbird. The seventh symbol denotes body type. 0=standard coupe, 1=Sport Coupe, 2=LX Coupe, 4=Turbo Coupe. The eighth symbol denotes the engine: W=140-cid (2.3L)/190-hp turbocharged four-cylinder/manual, W=140-cid (2.3L)/150-hp turbocharged four-cylinder/automatic, 3=232-cid (3.8L)/120-hp V-6, F=302-cid (5.0L)/150-hp V-8. Ninth symbol is the check digit. 10th symbol H=1987 model year. Eleventh symbol denotes assembly plant: H=Lorain, Ohio. Twelfth through 17th symbols denote sequential production number of specific vehicle starting at 100001. Vehicle certification label located on rear face of driver's door. The top part of the label indicates that the Thunderbird was manufactured by Ford Motor Company. Directly below this is the month and year of manufacture, plus a statement that the car conforms to federal motor vehicle safety standards in effect on the indicated date of manufacture. VIN: The VIN appears first on the first line of encoded information. It matches the first to 11th symbols on VIN tag. Some other codes also appear. TYPE: On left side of label, indicates PASSENGER. EXT. COLOR: This line carries the exterior paint color(s) code. See table below. DSO: The District Special Order code now appears above "DSO" to the right of the exterior paint color code. BODY: The body style code appears to the extreme left of the bottom line. The only Thunderbird code for this model-year is: 66D=two-door pillared hardtop. VR: The vinyl roof type/color code is to the right of the body code. No T-Birds had vinyl tops. MLDG: The molding code is to the right of the vinyl roof code. INT. TRIM: The interior trim code is to the right of the molding code. See table below. A/C: The air conditioning code is to the right of the interior trim code. Cars with air conditioning have "A" stamped here. R: The radio code is to the right of the A/C code. S: The sunroof code appears to the right of the radio code. AX: The axle code appears to the right of the sunroof code. TR: The transmission code appears to the right of the axle code. (Note: The terms and abbreviations shown in capitals appear on the line above the actual codes.)

ENGINE

THUNDERBIRD BASE V-6: 90-degree. Overhead valve. Cast-iron block and aluminum head. Displacement: 232 cid (3.8 liters). Bore and stroke: 3.80 x 3.40 in. Compression ratio: 8.7:1. Brake hp: 120 at 3600. Torque: 205 lbs.-ft. at 1600. Four main bearings. Hydraulic valve lifters. Induction: Throttle Body Injection. Serial number code: 3.

THUNDERBIRD TURBO COUPE BASE FOUR-CYL TURBO (AUTOMATIC): Inline. Overhead valve. Cast-iron block and head. Displacement: 140 cid (2.3 liters). Bore and stroke: 3.78 x 3.13 in. Compression ratio: 8.0:1. Brake hp: 150 at 4400. Five main bearings. Hydraulic valve lifters. Induction: Multi-Point Electronic Fuel injection. Garrett AIResearch T-03 turbocharger. Serial number code: W.

THUNDERBIRD TURBO COUPE BASE FOUR-CYL TURBO: Inline. Overhead valve. Cast-iron block and head. Displacement: 140 cid (2.3 liters). Bore and stroke: 3.78 x 3.13 in. Compression ratio: 8.0:1. Brake hp: 190 at 4600. Torque: 240 lbs.-ft. at 3400. Five main bearings. Hydraulic valve lifters. Induction: Multi-Point Electronic Fuel injection. Garrett AIResearch T-03 turbocharger. Serial number code: W.

THUNDERBIRD OPTIONAL V-8: 90-degree. Overhead valve V-8. Cast-iron block and head. Displacement: 302 cid (5.0 liters). Bore and stroke: 4.00 x 3.00 in. Compression ratio: 8.9:1. Brake hp: 150 at 3200 rpm. Torque: 270 lbs.-ft. at 2000 rpm. Five main bearings. Hydraulic valve lifters. Induction: Sequential (port) Fuel injection. Serial number code: F.

CHASSIS

Wheelbase: 104.2 in. Overall length: 202.1. Overall width: 71.1. Overall height: 53.4 in. Front headroom: 37.7 in. Front legroom: 42 in. Front shoulder room: 55.2 in. Rear headroom: 36.7 in. Rear legroom: 34.3 in. Trunk capacity: 14.6 cu. ft. Front tread: 58.1 in. Rear tread: 58.5 in. Tires: P195/75R14 white sidewall steel-belted radial. Steering: Variable-ratio, power, rack-and-pinion. Steering ratio: 15.0-13.0:1 (15.1:1 on Turbo Coupe). Turning diameter: 38.6 ft. Turns lock-to-lock: 2.5. Front suspension: Modified McPherson strut. Rear suspension: Four-link-bar (quad shocks on Turbo Coupe). Weight distribution: 53/47 percent front/rear. Power-to-weight ratio: 20.56 lb./hp. Steering: Variable-ratio power rack and pinion. Standard rear axle: 2.73:1. Front brakes: Power disc. Rear brakes: Power drum. Brakes swept area: 275.6 sq. in. Rear axle (with five-speed manual transmission): 3.45:1. Rear axle (with three-speed automatic transmission): 2.47:1. Rear axle (four-speed automatic transmission): 3.08:1. Fuel tank capacity: 18.2 gal.

OPTIONS

5.0-liter V-8, except standard on Sport ($639). Four-speed automatic overdrive transmission, optional on Turbo ($515). P215/70R14 tires on standard base T-Bird and LX ($72 extra). Conventional spare tire ($73). Heavy-duty 54-amp. battery ($27). Electronic equipment group, on base T-Bird ($634), on Sport and Turbo ($365), on LX ($577). Front floor mats ($30). Luxury light and convenience group, on base T-Bird ($461), on base T-Bird with electronic equipment group ($379), on Sport and Turbo ($426), on

A sleeker front end greeted buyers of the 1987 Thunderbird. The 'Birds received some notable styling changes for the model year, and four models were available in all: base, Sport, LX, and Turbo Coupe.

Ford photo

Sport and Turbo with electronic equipment group ($344), on LX ($244). Dual power seat, on Base T-Bird and LX and Sport ($302), on Turbo or LX with articulated seats ($251). Power antenna ($76). Front license plate bracket (no charge). Electronic digital clock ($61). Rear window defroster ($145). Engine block immersion heater ($18). Power lock group ($249). Dual electric remote-control mirrors ($96). Moonroof, on base T-Bird, Turbo or Sport ($801), on LX or with luxury and lights package ($741). Premium luxury package, standard on models with value option package 151A, on Sport model with 154A ($829), on Turbo with 157A ($717), AM/FM stereo credit ($206). Electronic AM/FM stereo with cassette tape player ($137). Graphic equalizer ($218). Premium sound system ($168). 6-way power driver's seat ($251). Speed control ($176). Leather-wrapped luxury steering wheel ($59). Tilt steering wheel ($124). Body side and deck lid stripes ($55). Locking wire style wheel covers, on LX or with 151A package, above price of road wheels ($90), with standard base T-Bird over price of luxury wheel covers ($212). Cast aluminum wheels, on LX or Sport with 151A package ($89), on base T-Bird ($211). Styled road wheels ($122). Power side windows ($222). California emissions system ($55). High-altitude emissions system ($99). Two-tone paint treatment base T-Bird, cost over body-side and deck lid striping or LX ($218), on LX with 151A package ($163). Clearcoat paint ($183). Articulated Sport seats ($183). Vinyl trim ($37). Leather trim ($415). Base T-Bird Value Option Package 151A ($1,329-$1,402). Sport Value Option Package 154A ($986-$1,009). LX Value Option Package 161A (no charge-$73). Select LX Value Option Package 162A ($807-$830). Turbo Value Option Package 157A (no charge -$72).

EQUIPMENT INSTALLATION RATES

Automatic transmission (88 percent). Five-speed manual transmission (12 percent). V-8 engine (22.2 percent). V-6 engine (59.2 percent). Four-cylinder turbocharged engine (18.6 percent). Electronic AM/FM Stereo cassette (83.2 percent). Electronic AM/FM Stereo (16.8 percent). Power steering (100 percent). Antilock brakes (18.6 percent). Power front disc brakes (81.4 percent). Power door locks (88.6 percent). Power seat (58.9 percent). Power windows (95 percent). Adjustable steering column (96.1 percent). All tinted glass (100 percent). Automatic air conditioning (26.1 percent). Manual air conditioning (73.9 percent). Standard steel-belted radial tires (100 percent). Electric rear window defogger (91.2 percent). Steel styled wheels (30.2 percent). Aluminum styled wheels (19.5 percent). Speed control (94.8 percent). Remote-control left-hand rearview mirror (96.4 percent). Remote-control right-hand rearview mirror (96.4 percent). Sunroof (6.3 percent). Delay windshield wipers (87.3 percent). Reclining front seats (100 percent). Digital clocks: (86.5 percent). Limited-slip rear axle (17 percent). (Note: Based on 122,059 units produced in the model year for the U.S. market only.)

HISTORICAL FOOTNOTES

The 1987 T-Bird was introduced on October 2, 1986. Donald E. Petersen was chairman of the board and CEO of Ford Motor Co. William Clay Ford was vice chairman. Harold A. Poling was president and chief operating officer of the corporation. Ford Vice President Robert L. Rewey was the Ford Division's general manager and Phillip M. Novell

was divisional general sales manager.

Calendar-year output was 157,507 units. A total of 128,135 T-Birds were produced in the model year. This represented 1.74 percent of the industry total. Of these units, all were made in Lorain, Ohio. Calendar-year dealer sales amounted to 126,767 T-Birds, representing 1.7 percent of industry sales.

A "Preview Test" by Gary Witzenberg in the October 1986 issue of *Motor Trend* put the 1987 T-Bird Turbo Coupe through its paces. Witzenberg did some brief measured tests at Ford's proving grounds in Romeo, Michigan and recorded 0 to 60-mph performance at 8.4 seconds. The car did the standing quarter-mile in 16.13 seconds and 81.8 mph. It also exhibited improved handling and braking, as well as an outstanding "high-performance" premium sound system. "We've liked Ford's T-Bird—especially the sleek-looking, smart-handling Turbo Coupe—since its '83 reincarnation," said Witzenberg in his summary. "We like it even better for 1987, and we'll likely go on liking it for some time to come. Think of it as the average man's 635csi and you won't be far wrong." *Motor Trend* gave the 1987 T-Bird Turbo Coupe its "Car of the Year" award.

Road & Track (August 1987) also wrung out the Turbo. The handling and braking abilities of the T-Bird were highly praised and the writer said it had an "attractive shape." The magazine liked the handsome body design, the ABS brakes and the advantage of a large dealer network.

In racing, Bill Elliott and Kyle Petty were two of the leading drivers of T-Bird stock cars. In fact, Ford's ads were still making hay over the records Elliott established during 1985. Davey Allison, driver of the number 28 Havoline T-Bird, was 1987 "Rookie of the Year" and the first driver to ever win more than one Winston Cup event in his first season on the circuit. In drag racing, Ford had the winningest driver in the history of NHRA competition. Bob Glidden's bright red 1987 Pro Stock T-Bird helped him become the only seven-time NHRA World Champion.

Unfortunately, not everyone liked the '87 T-Birds as much as *Motor Trend*, although production totals clearly suggest that the "Car of the Year" honors helped Ford sell more Turbo models that year. Overall output dropped to 128,135 T-Birds and a 1.74 percent share of industry in model-year 1987. The Lorain, Ohio factory accounted for all 128,135 units. Of these, 122,059 were made for sale in the U.S. This total included 59.2 percent with a V-6 and 22.2 percent with a V-8. However, Turbo Coupe output climbed to an all-time high of 23,833 cars or 18.6 percent of all domestic-market T-Birds. Accordingly, a record-high 12 percent had five-speed transmissions this season.

1987 THUNDERBIRD PERFORMANCE		
Model	**CID/HP**	**Performance**
0-60 mph		
Turbo Coupe	140/190	8.40 seconds
Turbo Coupe	140/150	8.5 seconds
1/4-Mile		
Turbo Coupe (manual)	140/190	16.13 seconds @ 81.8 mph
Turbo Coupe (automatic)	140/150	16.3 seconds @ 84.5 mph

Mike Mueller photo

The 1988 LX T-Bird featured body-side and deck lid striping, and was available with either a V-6 or V-8.

1988

Thunderbird

Minor changes, many hidden, separated 1987 and 1988 T-Birds. The 1988 model was available in base coupe and LX (V-6 or V-8), Sport (V-8 only) and Turbo Coupe (four-cylinder turbocharged) models. Sport models now had analog gauges and came with articulated sport seats.

Five regular and nine clearcoat metallic colors were offered for base and LX models and five could be had in two-tone combinations. Eight different color-coordinated stripes were used, but only in specific combinations. There were five monotone interiors. Sport models could only be had in

two of the 14 exterior hues and with four interior shades only. Turbo Coupes came in just two conventional colors and five clearcoat metallics. A Raven-colored interior was exclusive to this model, but the Medium Gray and Cinnabar interiors could not be ordered for the Turbo.

Multi-point fuel injection replaced the former single-point system in the T-Bird's base V-6 engine this year. This boosted horsepower by 20. Inside the engine was a new balance shaft that produced smoother operation. Dual exhausts were now standard with the 5.0-liter V-8, which was standard in the Sport model and optional in the base and LX models.

STANDARD EQUIPMENT

All standard FoMoCo safety, anti-theft, convenience items, and emissions control equipment, 3.8-liter MPEFI V-6, automatic overdrive transmission, power rack-and-pinion steering, front disc/rear drum brakes, modified McPherson strut front suspension with variable rate springs and gas-pressurized struts, four-bar-link rear suspension with variable-rate springs and gas-pressurized shock absorbers, P215/70Rx14 black sidewall all-season tires, dual aerodynamic halogen headlights, wide body-side moldings, luxury wheel covers, bright windshield moldings, bright side window moldings, bright back window moldings, black bumper rub strips and extensions with bright insert, left-hand remote-control mirror, air conditioning, tinted glass, safety belt reminder chimes, deep-well trunk with mini spare tire, luggage compartment light, 16-oz. color-keyed cut-pile carpeting, electronic digital clock, ashtray lights, continuous color-keyed safety belts with comfort regulator feature, LCD speedometer with trip odometer, and electronic AM/FM stereo radio with four speakers (may be deleted for credit. **1988 Thunderbird Sport Standard Equipment adds or substitutes (over base T-Bird):** 5.0-liter EFI V-8 engine, handling suspension including quadra-shock rear suspension, heavy-duty battery, Traction-Lok axle, dual-note Sport-tuned horn, P215/70HRx14 speed-rated handling tires, styled road wheels, black windshield moldings, black side window moldings, black rear window moldings, adjustable articulated sport seats, 24-oz. luxury carpeting, light group with dual beam map light, instrument panel courtesy lights, and engine compartment light, full analog instrumentation, Systems Sentry diagnostic alert lights, leather-wrapped steering wheel, tunnel-mounted shift with leather-wrapped handle, full console with covered storage compartment lid/armrest, and speed control. **1988 Thunderbird LX standard equipment adds or substitutes (over base T-Bird):** Automatic parking brake release, body-side and deck lid accent stripes, dual remote-control electric mirrors, luxury cloth split-bench seats in special sew style with four-way headrests, 24-oz. luxury carpet, light group with dual beam map light, instrument panel courtesy lights, and engine compartment light, luxury door and quarter trim panels, Systems Sentry diagnostic alert lights, leather-wrapped steering wheel, electronic AM/FM stereo radio with four speakers and cassette tape player, illuminated entry system, power side windows, interval windshield wipers, speed control, tilt steering, power lock group with power door locks, remote deck lid release in glove box, and remote fuel filler door release in glove box, and power driver's seat: **1988 Thunderbird Turbo Coupe**

STANDARD AND LX COUPE BODY COLOR INFORMATION (AS OF 6/15/87)

Color Name	Code	Color Name	Code
Black+	1C	Medium Sandalwood Clearcoat Metallic	62
Light Grey	1K	Light Sandalwood Clearcoat Metallic	63
Scarlet Red	2D	Twilight Blue Clearcoat Metallic	7F
Oxford White	9L	Rose Quartz Clearcoat Metallic+	8N
Medium Red Clearcoat Metallic	26	Silver Clearcoat Metallic+	9Z
Light Regatta Blue Clearcoat Metallic	31	Medium Grey Clearcoat Metallic+	91
Dark Cinnabar Clearcoat Metallic+	5C		

+ Indicates available as a Tu-Tone color, clearcoat metallic colors optional at extra cost.

SPORT COUPE BODY COLOR INFORMATION

Color Name	Code	Color Name	Code
Black	1C	Light Regatta Blue Clearcoat Metallic	31
Light Grey	1K	Medium Sandalwood Clearcoat Metallic	62
Scarlet Red	2D	Light sandalwood Clearcoat Metallic	63
Light Sandalwood	8R	Twilight Blue Clearcoat Metallic	7F
Oxford White	9L	Silver Clearcoat Metallic	9Z
Medium Red Clearcoat Metallic	26	Medium Grey Clearcoat Metallic	91

Clearcoat metallic colors optional at extra cost.

TURBO COUPE BODY COLOR INFORMATION

Color Name	Code	Color Name	Code
Black	1C	Twilight Blue Clearcoat Metallic	7F
Oxford White+	9L	Silver Clearcoat Metallic	9Z
Medium Red Clearcoat Metallic	26	Medium Grey Clearcoat Metallic	91
Light Sandalwood Clearcoat Metallic+	63		

Clearcoat metallic colors optional at extra cost.
In some U.S. and Canadian sale catalogs Black, Oxford White, Medium Red Clearcoat Metallic, Light Sandalwood Clearcoat Metallic, and Twilight Blue Clearcoat Metallic are listed as Turbo Coupe colors, while Silver Clearcoat Metallic and Medium Gray Clearcoat Metallic are not listed for the Turbo Coupe.

PAINT STRIPE COLOR INFORMATION

Color Name	Code	Color Name	Code
Black	a	Light Oxford Grey	h
Copper	c	Light Charcoal	p
Dark Red	d	Dark Blue	q
Medium Red	e	Bright Regatta Blue	s
Dark Taupe	f	Medium Champagne	y
Dark Champagne	z		

INTERIOR TRIM INFORMATION (U.S. & CANADA)

Seat Type	Material	Med. Gray	Scar. Red	Shad. Blue	Lt. Sandalwood	Cinnabar	Raven
T-Bird Standard							
Split-Bench	All-Cloth	HG	HD	HB	HP	HK	—
Thunderbird LX							
Split-Bench	Luxury Cloth	KG	KD	KB	KP	KK	
Split-Bench	Leather	LG	LD	LB	LP	LK	—
Thunderbird Sport							
Articulated	All-Cloth	BG	BD	BB	BP	—	—
Articulated	Leather	FG	FD	FB	FP	—	—
Thunderbird Turbo							
Articulated Buckets	All-Cloth	—	BD	BB	BP	—	BH
Articulated Buckets	Leather	—	FD	FB	FP	—	FH

Legend: First letter denotes seat type, second letter denotes color. Med means Medium, Scar Red means Scarlet Red, Shad Blue means Shadow Blue, Lt. means Light, SS-Vinyl means Super-Soft Vinyl. Leather means leather seating surfaces.

THUNDERBIRD PRODUCTION

Model Number	Body/Style Number	Body Type & Seating	Factory Price	Shipping Weight	Production Total
THUNDERBIRD - (V-6)					
60	66D	2d Coupe-4P	$13,599	3,215 lbs.	Note 1
THUNDERBIRD - (V-8)					
60	66D	2d Coupe-4P	$14,320	3,345 lbs.	Note 1
THUNDERBIRD SPORT - (V-8)					
61	66D	2d Coupe-4P	$16,030	3,450 lbs.	Note 1
THUNDERBIRD LX - (V-6)					
62	66D	2d Coupe-4P	$15,885	3,259 lbs.	Note 1
THUNDERBIRD LX - (V-8)					
62	66D	2d Coupe-4P	$16,606	3,389 lbs.	Note 1
THUNDERBIRD TURBO COUPE - (4-CYL)					
64	66D	2d Coupe-4P	$17,250	3,415 lbs.	Note 1

NOTE 1: Production of the all models combined was 147,243.

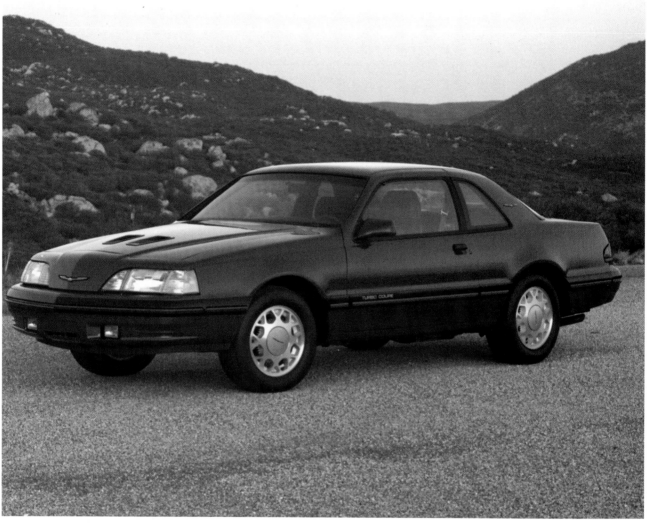

Ford photo

The 190-hp 1988 Thunderbird Turbo Coupe had an estimated top speed of 143 mph.

standard equipment adds or substitutes (over base T-Bird): 2.3-liter overhead-cam turbocharged engine with EFI, air-to-air intercooler, and regular/premium fuel selection, five-speed manual overdrive transmission, power four-wheel disc brakes with electronic antilock system (ABS), special handling package including automatic ride control and quadra-shock rear suspension, heavy-duty battery, Traction-Lok rear axle, remote-control fuel filler door release, dual-note Sport-tuned horn, automatic parking brake release, P225/60VRx16 black sidewall performance tires and unique 16 x 7-in.-diameter aluminum wheels, unique front fascia with Hella fog lights, black windshield, side window and rear window moldings, red insert replacing bright metal insert on black bumper rub strips, dual intercooler hood scoops, dual remote-control electric mirrors, adjustable articulated sport seats, 24-oz. luxury carpet, light group with dual beam map light, instrument panel courtesy lights, and engine compartment light, luxury door and quarter trim panels, full analog instrumentation, Systems Sentry diagnostic alert lights, Soft Feel steering wheel, tunnel-mounted shift with leather-wrapped handle, full console with covered storage compartment lid/armrest, power side windows, and interval windshield wipers.

I.D. NUMBERS

VIN stamped on aluminum tab riveted to the dashboard on passenger side and observable through the windshield from outside the car. First symbol 1 denotes built in the United States. Second symbol F denotes Ford. Third symbol A denotes Ford passenger vehicle. Fourth symbol denotes type of restraint system. Fifth symbol P denotes passenger-type vehicle. Sixth symbol 6 denotes Thunderbird. Seventh symbol denotes body type. 0=standard coupe, 1=Sport Coupe, 2=LX Coupe, 4=Turbo Coupe. Eighth symbol denotes engine: W=140-cid (2.3L)/190-hp turbocharged four-cylinder/manual, W=140-cid (2.3L)/150-hp turbo-charged four-cylinder/automatic, 3=232-cid (3.8L)/140-hp V-6, F=302-cid (5.0L)/155-hp V-8. Ninth symbol is the check digit. Tenth symbol J=1988 model year. Eleventh symbol denotes assembly plant: H=Lorain, Ohio. Twelfth through 17th symbols denote sequential production number of specific vehicle starting at 100001. Vehicle certification label located on rear face of driver's door. The top part of the label indicates that the Thunderbird was manufactured by Ford Motor Company. Directly below this is the month and year of manufacture, plus a statement that the car conforms to federal motor vehicle safety standards in effect on the indicated date of manufacture. VIN: The VIN appears first on the first line of encoded information. It matches the first to 11th symbols on VIN tag. Some other codes also appear. TYPE: On left side of label, indicates PASSENGER. EXT. COLOR: This line carries the exterior paint color(s) code. DSO: The District Special Order code now appears above "DSO" to the right of the exterior paint color code. BODY: The body style code appears to the extreme left of the bottom line. The only Thunderbird code for this model-year is: 66D=two-door pillared hardtop. VR: The vinyl roof-type/color code is to the right of the body code. No T-Birds had vinyl tops. MLDG: The molding code is to the right of the vinyl roof code. INT. TRIM: The interior trim code is to the right of the molding code. A/C: The air conditioning code is to the right of the interior trim code. Cars with air conditioning have "A" stamped here. R: The radio code is to the right of the A/C code. S: The sunroof code appears to the right of the radio code. AX: The axle code appears to the right of the sunroof code. TR: The transmission code appears to the right of the axle code. (Note: The terms and abbreviations shown in capitals appear on the line above the actual codes.)

ENGINE

THUNDERBIRD BASE V-6: 90-degree. Overhead-valve V-6. Cast-iron block and aluminum head. Displacement: 232 cid (3.8 liters). Bore and stroke: 3.80 x 3.40 in. Compression ratio: 9.0:1. Brake hp: 140 at 3800. Torque: 215 lbs.-ft. at 2400. Four main bearings. Hydraulic valve lifters. Induction: Throttle Body Injection. Serial number code: 3.

THUNDERBIRD TURBO COUPE BASE FOUR-CYL TURBO (AUTOMATIC): Inline. Overhead valve. Cast-iron block and head. Displacement: 140 cid (2.3 liters). Bore and stroke: 3.78 x 3.13 in. Compression ratio: 8.0:1. Brake hp: 150 at 4400. Five main bearings. Hydraulic valve lifters. Induction: Multi-Point Electronic Fuel injection. Garrett AIResearch T-03 turbocharger. Serial number code: W.

THUNDERBIRD TURBO COUPE BASE FOUR-CYL TURBO: Inline. Overhead valve. Cast-iron block and head. Displacement: 140 cid (2.3 liters). Bore and stroke: 3.78 x 3.13 in. Compression ratio: 8.0:1. Brake hp: 190 at 4600. Torque: 240 lbs.-ft. at 3400. Five main bearings. Hydraulic valve lifters. Induction: Multi-Point Electronic Fuel injection. Garrett AIResearch T-03 turbocharger. Serial number code: W.

THUNDERBIRD OPTIONAL V-8: 90-degree. Overhead valve. Cast-iron block and head. Displacement: 302 cid (5.0 liters). Bore and stroke: 4.00 x 3.00 in. Compression ratio: 8.9:1. Brake hp: 155 at 3400 rpm. Torque: 265 lbs.-ft. at 2200 rpm. Five main bearings. Roller cam. Induction: Sequential (port) fuel injection. Serial number code F.

CHASSIS

Wheelbase: 104.2 in. Overall length: 202.1. Overall width: 71.1. Overall height: 53.4 in. Front headroom: 37.7 in. Front legroom: 42 in. Front shoulder room: 55.2 in. Rear headroom: 36.7 in. Rear legroom: 34.3 in. Trunk capacity: 14.6 cu. ft. Front tread: 58.1 in. Rear tread: 58.5 in. Tires: P195/75R14 white sidewall steel-belted radial. Steering: Variable-ratio, power, rack-and-pinion. Steering ratio: 15.0-13.0:1 (15.1:1 on Turbo Coupe). Turning diameter: 38.6 ft. Turns lock-to-lock: 2.5. Front suspension: Modified McPherson strut. Rear suspension: Four-link-bar (quad

shocks on Turbo Coupe). Weight distribution: 53/47 percent front/rear. Power-to-weight ratio: 20.56 lb./hp. Steering: Variable-ratio power rack-and-pinion. Standard rear axle: 2.73:1. Front brakes: Power disc. Rear brakes: Power drum. Brakes swept area: 275.6 sq. in. Rear axle (with five-speed manual transmission): 3.45:1, Rear axle (with three-speed automatic transmission): 2.47:1. Rear axle (four-speed automatic transmission): 3.08:1. Fuel tank capacity: 21 gal.

OPTIONS

5.0-liter V-8, except standard in Sport and Turbo Coupe ($639). Four-speed automatic overdrive transmission, optional on Turbo ($515). Heavy-duty battery in base T-Bird and LX ($27). Styled road wheels on base T-Bird ($122). Cast-aluminum wheels, on LX or Sport with 151A package ($89), on base T-Bird ($211). Locking wire style wheel covers, on LX or base T-Bird with 151A package, above price of road wheels ($90), with standard base T-Bird over price of luxury wheel covers ($212). Body side and deck lid stripes on base T-Bird or Sport models ($55). Two-tone paint treatment on base T-Bird, cost over body-side and deck lid striping or LX ($218), on LX with 151A package ($163). Dual electric remote-control mirrors on base T-Bird or Sport ($96). Moon roof, on base T-Bird, Turbo or Sport ($801), on LX or with luxury and lights package ($741). Leather trim, except base T-Bird ($415). Light group, on base T-Bird (N/A). Systems Sentry diagnostic alert lights, on base T-Bird (N/A). Electronic AM/FM stereo with cassette tape player, on all except LX ($137). Premium sound system, optional all models ($168). Graphic equalizer, optional all models ($218). Illuminated entry system, except LX (N/A). Power side windows in base T-Bird and Sport ($222). Interval windshield wipers, in base T-Bird or Sport (N/A). Speed control on base T-Bird or Turbo Coupe ($176). Tilt steering wheel, except LX ($124). Power lock group, except LX ($249). 6-way power driver's seat, except LX ($251). Power antenna, all ($76). Luxury light and convenience group, on Base T-Bird ($461), on base T-Bird with electronic equipment group ($379), on Sport and Turbo ($426), on Sport and Turbo with electronic equipment group ($344), on LX ($244). Electronic equipment group, on base T-Bird ($634), on Sport and Turbo ($365), on LX ($577). Dual power seat, on base T-Bird and LX and Sport ($302), on Turbo or LX with articulated seats ($251). Front floor mats ($30). PEP 140A includes P215/70R14 tires, automatic overdrive transmission, and dual electric mirrors for base T-Bird (N/A). PEP 141A includes P215/70R14 tires, automatic overdrive transmission, dual electric mirrors, light group, electronic AM/FM stereo with cassette, interval wipers, premium sound system, front floor mats, and styled road wheels for base T-Bird (N/A). PEP 142A includes: P215/70R14 tires, automatic overdrive transmission, dual electric mirrors, light group, electronic AM/FM stereo with cassette, interval wipers, premium sound system, front floor mats, styled road wheels, and manual temperature control air conditioning for base T-Bird (N/A). PEP 145A includes P215/70HRx14 handling tires, automatic overdrive transmission, dual electric mirrors, light group, electronic AM/FM stereo with cassette, interval windshield wipers, styled road wheels, manual air conditioning, power lock group, power side windows, tilt steering, speed control, and 6-way power driver's seat for Sport T-bird (N/A). PEP 150A includes: P215/70Rx14 all-season tires, automatic overdrive transmission, dual electric mirrors, light group, electronic AM/FM stereo with cassette, interval windshield wipers, styled road wheels, power lock group, power side windows,

Ford photo

The flashy T-Bird Turbo Coupe was again the high-performance version of the Thunderbird for 1988.

tilt steering, speed control, and 6-way power driver's seat for LX T-bird (N/A). Extra Value Package 151A includes: P215/70Rx14 all-season tires, automatic overdrive transmission, dual electric mirrors, light group, electronic AM/FM stereo with cassette, interval windshield wipers, front floor mats, manual air conditioning, power lock group, power side windows, tilt steering, speed control, dual power seats with recliners, power radio antenna, keyless entry system, luxury light and convenience group, graphic equalizer, and wire wheel covers for LX T-bird (N/A). Extra Value Package 155A includes: five-speed manual overdrive transmission, P225/60VRx16 black sidewall tires, power side windows, dual electric mirrors, interval wipers, manual air conditioning, light group, power lock group, electronic AM/FM stereo with cassette, speed control, tilt steering, and power driver's seat for T-Bird Turbo Coupe (N/A). Extra Value Package 156A includes five-speed manual overdrive transmission, P225/60VRx16 black sidewall tires, power side windows, dual electric mirrors, interval wipers, manual air conditioning, light group, front floor mats, luxury light and convenience group, premium sound system, power radio antenna, power lock group, electronic AM/FM stereo with cassette, speed control, tilt steering, and power driver's seat for T-Bird Turbo Coupe (N/A).

EQUIPMENT INSTALLATION RATES

Automatic transmission (84.6 percent). Five-speed manual transmission (15.4 percent). V-8 engine (28.4 percent). V-6 engine (46.3 percent). Four-cylinder turbocharged engine (25.3 percent). Electronic AM/FM stereo cassette (83.6 percent). Electronic AM/FM stereo (16.1 percent). Premium speaker system (28.5 percent). Premium amplifiers (18.3 percent). Power steering (100 percent). Antilock brakes (25.3 percent). Power front disc brakes (74.7 percent). Power door locks (95.8 percent). Power seat (82.3 percent). Power windows (96.9 percent). Adjustable steering column (97.6 percent). All tinted glass (100 percent). Automatic air conditioning (33.2 percent). Manual air conditioning (66.8 percent). Standard steel-belted radial tires (100 percent). Electric rear window defogger (95.5 percent). Steel styled wheels (29.5 percent). Aluminum styled wheels (24.4 percent). Speed control (97.9 percent). Remote-control left-hand rearview mirror (97.6 percent). Remote-control right-hand rearview mirror (97.6 percent). Sunroof (12.9 percent). Delay windshield wipers (84.9 percent). Reclining front seats (100 percent). Digital clock (100 percent). Limited-slip rear axle (20 percent). (Note: Based on 139,411 units produced in the model year for the U.S. market only.)

HISTORICAL FOOTNOTES

The 1987 T-Bird was introduced on October 1, 1987. Donald E. Petersen was chairman of the board and CEO of Ford Motor Co. William Clay Ford was vice chairman. Harold A. Poling was president and chief operating officer of the corporation. Ford Vice Thomas J. Wagner was the Ford Division's new general manager and Richard L. Fenstermacher was divisional general sales manager.

Calendar-year output was 111,760 units. A total of 147,243 T-Birds were produced in the model year. This represented 2.11 percent of the industry total. Of these units, all were made in Lorain, Ohio. Calendar year dealer sales amounted to 117,866 T-Birds, representing 5.8 percent of industry sales.

Motor Trend's December 1987 issue was a special issue devoted to Ford and included a "Retrospect" on the 1955 T-Bird. Included in the issue was a road test of the T-Bird Turbo Coupe. The article written by Don Fuller carried a Ford-friendly title: "Thunderbird Turbo Coupe: Redefining the American high-tech performance car." Fuller described the Turbo as "the dream of every enthusiast who has waited for all the positive elements of the modern age to be wrapped up in one American roadburner." One of the highlights of the article was a fabulous, two-page three-quarter front view phantom illustration of the 1988 Turbo Coupe drawn by David Kimble.

Ford's factory racing efforts were also covered. In NASCAR racing Bill Elliott won the 1988 Winston Cup with his Coors/Melling T-Bird. Other 1988 Ford drivers included Davey Allison, Kyle Petty, Ralph Jones, Derrike Cope, Benny Parsons, Brett Bodine, Phil Barkdoll, Mark Martin, and Alan Kulwicki. Kulwicki won his first Winston Cup race during 1988. Another name associated with Ford was that of IHRA driver Floyd Cheek. His drag-racing T-Bird was champion in the 8.90-second class.

1988 THUNDERBIRD PERFORMANCE		
Model	CID/HP	Performance
0-60 mph		
Turbo Coupe	140/190	8.59 seconds
1/4-Mile		
Turbo Coupe	140/190	16.48 seconds @ 85.1 mph
Top Speed		
Turbo Coupe	140/190	143 mph

Ford photo

The new Super Coupe replaced the Turbo Coupe in 1989. The "SC" logo was imprinted on the front bumper between twin air intakes near the headlights.

1989 *Thunderbird*

The 1989 T-Bird was a completely redesigned rear-drive model with a longer wheelbase and lower profile. A "grille-less" front end emphasized lowness and width. New flush-fitting headlights were of low-profile, composite design. The parking lamps swept around the body corners to function as side marker lights. The hood dipped between the headlights and carried a T-Bird emblem on its center. A unique trapezoid-shaped greenhouse featured increased glass area. Thin rear roof pillars minimized blind spots. The full-width taillights had a T-Bird insignia on each side.

A new Super Coupe (replacing the Turbo Coupe) featured a different frontal treatment with a large horizontal air intake below each headlight and "SC" embossed in the bumper. It also had a front spoiler, narrow body-side skirting, a lower rear valance incorporating an air extractor and a supercharged 3.8-liter V-6 coupled to a five-speed manual gearbox. A four-speed automatic transmission was extra. The base Coupe came loaded and the LX added fancier trim, electronic instrumentation, power locks, a cassette player and styled road wheel covers. The Super Coupe had 16-in. cast aluminum wheels, fat performance

STANDARD AND LX COUPE BODY COLOR INFORMATION (AS OF 6/15/88)			
Color Name	Code	Color Name	Code
Black	1C	Light Crystal Blue Clearcoat Metallic	3Q
Bright Red	21	Deep Titanium Clearcoat Metallic	4S
Almond	6V	Medium Sandalwood Clearcoat Metallic	62
Oxford White	9L	Crystal Blue Clearcoat Metallic	7E
Light Titanium Clearcoat Metallic	11	Twilight Blue Clearcoat Metallic	7F
Currant Red Clearcoat Metallic	2S		
Clearcoat Metallic colors optional at extra cost.			

SUPER COUPE BODY COLOR INFORMATION			
Color Name	Code	Color Name	Code
Black	1C	Light Titanium Clearcoat Metallic	11
Bright Red	21	Twilight Blue Clearcoat Metallic	7F
Oxford White	9L		
Clearcoat Metallic colors optional at extra cost.			

INTERIOR TRIM INFORMATION (U.S.)					
Seat Type	Material	Currant Titanium	Shadow Red	Lt. Blue	Sandalwood
Standard					
Buckets	Cloth Surface	CA	CF	CB	CP
LX					
Bucket Seats	Cloth Surface	DA	DF	DB	DP
Bucket Seats	Leather Surface	FA	FF	FB	FP
Super Coupe					
Articulated Buckets	Cloth Surface	EA	EF	EB	—
Articulated Buckets	Leather Surface	GA	GF	GB	—
Legend: Lt. mean Light					

THUNDERBIRD PRODUCTION					
Model Number	Body/Style Number	Body Type & Seating	Factory Price	Shipping Weight	Production Total
THUNDERBIRD - (V-6)					
60	66D	2d Coupe-4P	$14,612	3,542 lbs.	Note 1
THUNDERBIRD LX (V-6)					
62	66D	2d Coupe-4P	$16,817	3,554 lbs.	Note 1
THUNDERBIRD SUPER COUPE - (V-6)					
64	66D	2d Coupe-4P	$19,823	3,701 lbs.	Note 1
NOTE 1: Production of the all models combined was 122,909.					

tires and front fog lights.

A new T-Bird interior featured reclining bucket seats, a floor-length console, a floor shift and new motorized front seat belts Cloth seating surfaces and vinyl trim was standard. The LX included luxury cloth seat trim, a leather-wrapped steering wheel and a six-way power driver's seat. The articulated seats used in the Super Coupe had power lumbar and seatback bolster adjustments. A total of 11 exterior finishes (seven metallic clearcoats) and four different color-keyed interiors were offered on base and LX models. Three regular and two metallic clearcoat colors were available for the Super Coupe, which also had three interior color options.

The 3.8-liter V-6 received friction-reducing roller tappets, light-weight magnesium rocker covers, and an aluminum-hub crankshaft damper. Sequential operation of the multi-port EFI system enhanced the precision of fuel delivery system. A new "distributorless" ignition system used electronic engine controls. For exceptionally smooth operation, Ford used hydraulic engine mounts and isolation in the third cross member. The Super Coupe engine used a custom-made Roots-type positive displacement supercharger for its power boost. The engine crankshaft drove the 90-cid supercharger via a poly v-belt running at 2.6 times crankshaft speed. This produced a maximum boost of 12 psi at 4000 rpm. Twin three-lobe helical rotors helped the blower do its work more smoothly and quietly. It also had an engine oil cooler and an intercooler to lower intake air temperature.

T-Birds had a new four-wheel independent suspension. On standard and LX models, a long-spindle short and long arm (SLA) setup was used in front, along with variable-rate coil springs, double-acting gas-pressurized shocks, and a .27-mm diameter stabilizer bar. At the rear there was also an SLA setup with toe control link, plus variable-rate springs, gas shocks and a .25-mm diameter stabilizer. The Super Coupe added Automatic Ride Control to the front and rear suspensions, plus beefier stabilizer bars at both ends. Power rack-and-pinion steering with a 14.1:1 ratio on center was standard. It was speed-sensitive on the LX and Super Coupe.

STANDARD EQUIPMENT

All standard FoMoCo safety, anti-theft, convenience items and emissions control equipment, 3.8-liter V-6, automatic overdrive transmission, power-assisted antilock braking system, four-wheel disc brakes, 15 x 6-in. stamped steel wheels, P205/70R15 black sidewall tires, air conditioning, tinted glass, power steering, power brakes, power windows, side window defoggers, interval windshield wipers, front automatic seat belt restraint system, full-length console with floor-mounted shifter, vinyl door trim with storage bins, cloth bucket seats with recliners, analog instrumentation, electronic AM/FM stereo search radio with digital clock (may be deleted for credit), left-hand remote-control OSRV mirror, wide body-side protection moldings, deluxe wheel covers, all-season radial tires and 5-mph color-keyed bumpers. **1989 Thunderbird LX standard equipment adds or substitutes:** Luxury cloth seats with recliners, six-way power driver's seat, luxury door trim and carpeting, electronic instrument cluster, instrument panel upper storage compartment, illuminated entry system and convenience lights, speed control and tilt steering wheel, speed-sensitive power steering, leather-wrapped luxury steering wheel, illuminated visor mirrors, power lock group, electronic AM/FM stereo search radio with cassette and digital clock, rear seat center armrest, vehicle maintenance monitor, remote release fuel door, dual electric remote-control mirrors, bright window moldings and styled road wheel covers. **1989 Thunderbird Super Coupe standard equipment adds or substitutes (over standard):** 3.8-liter supercharged and inter-cooled V-6 with dual exhausts, five-speed manual transmission, automatic ride control system, heavier front and rear stabilizer bars, Traction-Lok differential, 16 x 7-in. cast-aluminum wheels, Goodyear Eagle P225/60VR16 performance tires, articulated sports seats with power lumbar and power seatback bolster adjustments, Sport soft-feel steering wheel, luxury door trim and carpeting, instrument panel upper storage compartment, performance instrumentation, vehicle maintenance monitor, fog lamps, narrow body-side moldings and lower body-side cladding, anti-lock braking system with four-wheel disc brakes, Traction-Lok differential, speed-sensitive power steering, dual electric remote-control mirrors, heavy-duty battery and heavy-duty alternator.

Ford photo

The Super Coupe of 1989 was loaded. It had a supercharged 3.8-liter V-6 with intercooler, sequential multiport fuel injection, and anti-lock brakes with four-wheel discs.

I.D. NUMBERS

Stamped on aluminum tab riveted to the dashboard on passenger side and observable through the windshield from outside the car. First symbol 1 denotes built in the United States. Second symbol F denotes Ford. Third symbol A denotes Ford passenger vehicle. Fourth symbol denotes type of restraint system. Fifth symbol P denotes passenger-type vehicle. Sixth symbol 6 denotes Thunderbird. Seventh symbol denotes body type. 0=standard coupe, 2=LX Coupe, 4=Super Coupe. Eighth symbol denotes engine: 4=232-cid (3.8L)/140 hp V-6, R=232-cid (3.6L)/210 hp supercharged V-6. Ninth symbol is the check digit. Tenth symbol K=1989 model year. Eleventh symbol denotes assembly plant: H=Lorain, Ohio. Twelfth through 17th symbols denote sequential production number of specific vehicle starting at 100001. Vehicle certification label located on rear face of driver's door. The top part of the label indicates that the Thunderbird was manufactured by Ford Motor Company. Directly below this is the month and year of manufacture, plus a statement that the car conforms to federal motor vehicle safety standards in effect on the indicated date of manufacture. VIN: The VIN appears first on the first line of encoded information. It matches the first to 11th symbols on VIN tag. Some other codes also appear. TYPE: On left side of label, indicates PASSENGER. EXT. COLOR: This line carries the exterior paint color(s) code. See table below. DSO: The District Special Order code now appears above "DSO" to the right of the exterior paint color code. BODY: The body style code appears to the extreme left of the bottom line. The only Thunderbird code for this model-year is: BS2=two-door pillared hardtop. VR: The vinyl roof type/color code is to the right of the body code. No T-Birds had vinyl tops. MLDG: The molding code is to the right of the vinyl roof code. INT. TRIM: The interior trim code is to the right of the molding code. A/C: The air conditioning code is to the right of the interior trim code. Cars with air conditioning have "A" stamped here. R: The radio code is to the right of the A/C code. S: The sunroof code appears to the right of the radio code. AX: The axle code appears to the right of the sunroof code. TR: The transmission code

appears to the right of the axle code. (Note: The terms and abbreviations shown in capitals appear on the line above the actual codes.)

ENGINE

THUNDERBIRD BASE V-6: 90-degree. Overhead valve. Cast-iron block and aluminum head. Displacement: 232 cid (3.8 liters). Bore and stroke: 3.80 x 3.40 in. Compression ratio: 9.0:1. Brake hp: 140 at 3800. Torque: 215 lbs.-ft. at 2400. Four main bearings. Hydraulic valve lifters. Induction: Throttle Body Injection. Serial number code: 4.

THUNDERBIRD SUPER COUPE SUPERCHARGED V-6: 90-degree. Overhead valve. Cast-iron block and aluminum head. Displacement: 232 cid (3.8 liters). Bore and stroke: 3.80 x 3.40 in. Compression ratio: 8.3:1. Brake hp: 210 at 4000. Torque: 315 lbs.-ft. at 2600. Four main bearings. Hydraulic valve lifters. Induction: Sequential Electronic Fuel Injection (Supercharged). Serial number code: R.

CHASSIS

Wheelbase: 113 in. Overall length: 198.7. Overall width: 72.7. Overall height: 52.7 in. Front tread: 61.6 in. Rear tread: 60.2 in. Tires: P205/70R14 white sidewall steel-belted radial. Steering ratio: 14.1:1. Turning diameter: 38.6 ft. Turns lock-to-lock: 2.5. Front suspension: Independent, upper and lower control arms, coil springs, tubular shocks and anti-roll bar. Rear suspension: Live axle, four-link control arms, coil springs, adjustable tubular shocks and anti-roll bar. Weight distribution: 53/47 percent front/rear. Power-to-weight ratio: 20.56 lb./hp. Front brakes: Power vented disc. Rear brakes: Power drum. Fuel tank capacity: 19 gal.

OPTIONS

Four-speed overdrive transmission on Super Coupe ($539). P205/75R15 white sidewall tires ($73). Eagle GT + 4 P225/60VR16 black sidewall all-season performance tires,

Super Coupe only ($73). Conventional spare tire in base T-Bird and LX ($73). Traction-Lok axle for base T-Bird and LX ($100). Optional 3.27:1 axle ratio for Super Coupe ($21). Premium luxury group for base T-Bird ($420), for Super Coupe with 157A ($761). Antilock braking system, except standard on Super Coupe ($1,085). Anti-theft system ($183). Moonroof ($741-$841 depending on options teamed with). Clearcoat paint system ($183). Ford JBL audio system ($488). Compact disc player ($491). Radio-delete credits ($245-$382). Locking wire wheel covers, on base T-Bird ($212), as option on others ($127). Cast-aluminum wheels on base T-Bird ($299), as option on others ($213). California emissions ($100). High-altitude emissions (no charge). LX leather trim ($489). Super Coupe leather trim ($622). Front license plate bracket (no charge). Cold weather group on Super Coupe ($18), on others ($45). Preferred equipment package 151B ($1,235). Preferred equipment package 162A ($735). Luxury group ($735). Preferred equipment group 157B for Super Coupe (no charge).

EQUIPMENT INSTALLATION RATES

Automatic transmission (93 percent). Five-speed manual transmission (7 percent). Fuel-injected V-6 engine (88.7 percent). Supercharged V-6 engine (11.3 percent). Electronic AM/FM Stereo Cassette (74.4 percent). Bose/JBL stereo (15.9). Bose/JBL stereo with CD (7.6 percent). Electronic AM/FM Stereo (2.1 percent). Premium amplifiers (30 percent). Power steering (100 percent). Antilock brakes (17 percent). Power front disc brakes (83 percent). Power seat (100 percent). Power windows (100 percent). Adjustable steering column (100 percent). All tinted glass (100 percent). Manual air conditioning (100 percent). Standard steel-belted radial tires (100 percent). Electric rear window defogger (100 percent. Aluminum styled wheels (43.5 percent). Speed control (100 percent). Remote-control left-hand rearview mirror (100 percent). Remote-control right-hand rearview mirror (100 percent). Sunroof (15 percent). Delay windshield wipers (100 percent). Reclining front seats (100 percent). Digital clock (100 percent). Limited-slip rear axle (20 percent). (Note: Based on 107,996 units produced in the model year for the U.S. market only.)

HISTORICAL FOOTNOTES

The 1989 Fords were introduced on October 6, 1987, but the all-new 1989 Thunderbird did not bow until the day after Christmas. Donald E. Petersen was chairman of the

Ford photo

The Super Coupe came with a starting sticker price of $19,823. Bright Red was one of five exterior color choices.

board and CEO of Ford Motor Co. William Clay Ford was vice chairman. Harold A. Poling was president and chief operating officer of the corporation. Ford Vice Thomas J. Wagner was the Ford Division's new General Manager and Richard L. Fenstermacher was divisional general sales manager.

Calendar-year output was 137,326 units. A total of 114,868 T-Birds were produced in the model year. This represented 1.61 percent of the industry total. Of these units, all were made in Lorain, Ohio. Calendar-year dealer sales amounted to 120,645 T-Birds.

The T-Bird was one of the year's most outstanding new vehicles and took "Car of the Year" honors from *Motor Trend* magazine. Ford Chairman Donald Petersen received lots of credit for turning the T-Bird into a world-class "image" car for his company and was promoted by year's end. Over $1 billion was spent to develop the new body, chassis, suspension, engine and interior package. By January 1989, Ford had 20,000 orders for the new Super Coupe, which had been appearing on the cover of (and inside) enthusiasts magazines since the middle of the previous summer.

The Super Coupe's introduction was delayed due to durability problems with production versions of the original Duracast crankshaft. Duracast metal—actually a kind of cast iron—had tested fine in pre-production prototype engines. However, Ford found out later that the manufacturer had custom-selected the cranks used in the prototypes. The metal in production versions, which were manufactured for an engine that had been considerably upgraded, did turn out to be too porous to stand up in severe use and Ford decided to use a forged crankshaft. This change in plan was accomplished in near-record time and the supercharged V-6 entered production on January 30, 1989 at a FoMoCo plant in Essex, Ontario, Canada. Ford then announced that it would build 300 engines daily (up from a planned 200-per-day schedule) and ship 600 by the end of February. Ford actually tested some of the earliest production supercharged engines by installing 15 of them in fleet vehicles and police cars. The cop cars were 1988 Thunderbird LXs. Three belonged to the police department in Dearborn, Michigan, where Ford has its headquarters.

This allowed the automaker to monitor the engine's performance in a cold environment. Seven more were installed in Arizona Highway Patrol cars for the opposite reason. A Dallas, Texas courier service also got five engines.

AutoWeek magazine got to try out two of the Dearborn Police Department cars and did a report in its February 20, 1989 issue. Myron Stokes' sidebar story revealed that two cars had also been given to a testing service in Flint, Michigan, and three were assigned to Ford's Arizona Proving Grounds. *Motor Trend* gave the Super Coupe preliminary coverage in its October 1988 issue. The report, by Daniel Charles Ross, called it "a remarkable step forward for a car that was already impressively potent." A spy report, by *Car and Driver's* Rich Ceppos (July 1988), hinted that the Super Coupe would do 0 to 60 mph in the low-7-second bracket and hit 145 mph at top end. New T-Bird racecars came out of the gate running strong, though not ahead of the entire pack. Davey Allison put his Robert Yates/Havoline T-Bird across the finish line second at Daytona. Ford stock cars had their longest winning streak in 20 years and Ford driver Mark Martin ultimately took third in the standings, with two other Fords in the top 10. In NHRA Funny Car competition, Tom Heney's T-Bird racked up 7,774 points to earn him an eighth place national ranking. At Pike's Peak, Leonard Vasholtz pushed his T-Bird up the 12.42-mile, 156-turn course in 12:23:31 to win the Stock Cars class. Also, in October 1988, a specially prepared 1989 T-Bird circled Alabama International Motor Speedway with Lyn St. James at the wheel and set 21 new records.

1989 THUNDERBIRD PERFORMANCE		
Model	CID/HP	Performance
0-60 mph		
Super Coupe (manual)	232/210	7.5 seconds
Super Coupe (manual)	232/210	7.84 seconds
1/4-Mile		
Super Coupe (manual)	232/210	15.3 seconds @ 88 mph
Super Coupe (manual)	232/210	16.24 seconds @ 88.7 mph
Top Speed		
Super Coupe	232/210	145 mph

After it was named Motor Trend's "Car of the Year" in 1989, the Thunderbird changed very little for 1990. This Super Coupe is shown in Oxford White.

After its dramatic restyling, *Motor Trend's* 1989 "Car of the Year" changed very little. Two new option groups were offered in 1990: the Power Equipment Group and the Luxury Group. To celebrate the Thunderbird's 35th birthday, a limited-edition 35th Anniversary commemorative package was made available in January for the Super Coupe and 5,000 copies were planned. Anniversary models used the same supercharged 3.8-liter V-6 as the standard Super Coupe. They featured unique Black and Titanium two-tone paint, blue accent stripes, black road wheels and commemorative fender badges. A special interior trim featured suede-and-leather bucket seats, a split fold-down rear seat and commemorative badges on the interior door panels. Also standard was an anti-lock brake system, a handling package with automatic ride control and a Traction-Lok axle. The 35th Anniversary package (option no. 563) carried a dealer cost of $1,584. Its factory-suggested retail price added $1,863 to the regular cost of a Super Coupe.

Two new exterior colors were offered for 1990 T-Birds, Alabaster and Sandalwood Frost Clearcoat Metallic. The regular Super Coupe came in the same five colors as last season, three of which were extra-cost Clearcoat Metallic finishes. Interiors were color-coordinated with the exterior finishes. On base Coupes and LXs, as a total of four colors was offered: Crystal Blue, Currant Red, Black and Light Sandalwood. There were 18 different interior trims.

STANDARD EQUIPMENT

All standard FoMoCo safety, anti-theft, convenience items, and emissions control equipment, 3.8-liter V-6, four-speed automatic overdrive transmission, daytime running lights, rear window defroster, 72-amp battery, 65-amp alternator, wide body-side protection moldings, deluxe wheel covers, full-length console with floor-mounted shift, vinyl door trim with storage bins, cloth bucket seats with recliners, air conditioning, tinted glass, analog instrumentation, electronic AM/FM search radio with digital clock (may be deleted for credit), power steering, all-season radial tires, power windows and interval windshield wipers. **Thunderbird LX standard equipment adds or substitutes (over standard):** Power lock group, dual electric remote-control mirrors, bright window moldings, electronic AM/FM stereo radio with cassette and clock, speed control system, tilt steering wheel, styled road wheel covers, illuminated entry system, fog lamps, luxury-level door trim and carpeting, convenience lights, instrument panel upper storage compartment, illuminated visor mirrors, luxury cloth bucket seats with recliners, rear seat center armrest, leather-wrapped luxury steering wheel, vehicle maintenance monitor, remote-release fuel door, electronic instrument cluster and speed-sensitive power steering. **Thunderbird Super Coupe standard equipment adds or substitutes (over standard):** 3.8-liter EFI supercharged V-6 engine, five-speed manual overdrive transmission, power lock group, dual electric remote-control mirrors, electronic AM/FM stereo radio with cassette and clock, speed control system, tilt steering wheel, fog lamps, narrow body-side moldings, lower body-side cladding, 16-in. cast aluminum wheels, P255/60R16 black sidewall performance tires, luxury door trim and carpeting, articulated sports seat with power lumbar and power seatback bolster adjustments, Sport soft-feel steering wheel, heavy-duty alternator, automatic ride control adjustable suspension and performance instrumentation.

185

STANDARD AND LX COUPE BODY COLOR INFORMATION

Color Name	Code	Color Name	Code
Alabaster	AH	Bright Red Non-metallic Clearcoat	E4
Black	YC	Light Crystal Blue Clearcoat Metallic	KA
Oxford White	YO	Twilight Blue Clearcoat Metallic	MK
Sandalwood Frost Clearcoat Metallic	AP	Light Titanium Clearcoat Metallic	YF
Medium Sandalwood Clearcoat Metallic	AW	Deep Titanium Clearcoat Metallic	YU
Currant Red	ED		

Clearcoat metallic colors optional at extra cost.

SUPER COUPE BODY COLOR INFORMATION

Color Name	Code	Color Name	Code
Black	YC	Twilight Blue Clearcoat Metallic	MK
Oxford White	YO	Light Titanium Clearcoat Metallic	YF
Bright Red Non-metallic Clearcoat	E4		

Clearcoat metallic colors optional at extra cost.

INTERIOR TRIM CODE INFORMATION (U.S.)

Seat Type	Material	Cry. Blue	Cur Red	Black	Lt. Sandalwood
Standard					
Buckets	Cloth & Vinyl	QB	QF	QJ	QP
LX					
Bucket Seats	Luxury Cloth	RB	RF	RJ	RP
Bucket Seats	Leather	SB	SF	SJ	SP
Super Coupe					
Articulated Buckets	Cloth	TB	TF	TJ	—
Articulated Buckets	Leather	UB	UF	UJ	—

Legend: Cry Blue means Crystal Blue; Cur Red means Currant Red; Lt. means Light; Leather means leather seating surfaces.

THUNDERBIRD PRODUCTION

Model Number	Body/Style Number	Body Type & Seating	Factory Price	Shipping Weight	Production Total
THUNDERBIRD - (V-6)					
60	66D	2d Coupe-4P	$14,980	3,581 lbs.	Note 1
THUNDERBIRD LX - (V-6)					
62	66D	2d Coupe-4P	$17,263	3,618 lbs.	Note 1
THUNDERBIRD SUPER COUPE - (V-6)					
64	66D	2d Coupe-4P	$20,390	3,809 lbs.	Note 1

NOTE 1: Production of the all models combined was 113,957.

I.D. NUMBERS

VIN Stamped on aluminum tab riveted to the dashboard on passenger side and observable through the windshield from outside the car. First symbol 1 denotes built in the United States. Second symbol F denotes Ford. Third symbol A denotes Ford passenger vehicle. Fourth symbol denotes type of restraint system. Fifth symbol P denotes passenger-type vehicle. Sixth symbol 6 denotes Thunderbird. Seventh symbol denotes body type. 0=standard coupe, 2=LX Coupe, 4=Super Coupe. Eighth symbol denotes engine: 4=232-cid (3.8L)/140-hp V-6, R=232-cid (3.6L)/210-hp supercharged V-6. Ninth symbol is the check digit. Tenth symbol L=1990 model year. Eleventh symbol denotes assembly plant: H=Lorain, Ohio. Twelfth through 17th symbols denote sequential production number of specific vehicle starting at 100001. Vehicle certification label located on rear face of driver's door. The top part of the label indicates that the Thunderbird was manufactured by Ford Motor Company. Directly below this is the month and year of manufacture, plus a statement that the car conforms to federal motor vehicle safety standards in effect on the indicated date of manufacture. VIN: The VIN appears two lines above UPC. It matches the first to 11th symbols on VIN tag. Some other codes also appear. TYPE: Appears on left side of label on line above UPC; indicates PASSENGER. UPC: A scannable bar code carries the UPC. EXT. COLOR: This line carries the exterior paint color(s) code. DSO: The District Special Order code now appears above "DSO" to the right of the exterior paint color code. BODY: The body style code appears to the extreme left of the bottom line. The only Thunderbird code for this model-year is: BS2=two-door pillared hardtop. VR: The vinyl roof type/color code is to the right of the body code. No T-Birds had vinyl tops. MLDG: The molding code is to the right of the vinyl roof code. INT. TRIM: The interior trim code is to the right of the molding code. TAPE: The tape treatment code appears to right of the interior trim code. R: The radio code is to the right of the A/C code. S: The sunroof code is to the right of the radio code. AX: The axle code appears to the right of the sunroof code. TR: The transmission code appears to the right of the axle code. Note: The terms and abbreviations shown in capitals appear on the line above the actual codes

ENGINE

THUNDERBIRD BASE V-6: 90-degree. Overhead valve. Cast-iron block and aluminum head. Displacement: 232 cid (3.8 liters). Bore and stroke: 3.80 x 3.40 in. Compression ratio: 9.0:1. Brake hp: 140 at 3800. Torque: 215 lbs.-ft. at 2400. Four main bearings. Hydraulic valve lifters. Induction: Throttle Body Injection. Serial number code: 4.

THUNDERBIRD SUPER COUPE SUPERCHARGED V-6: 90-degree. Overhead valve. Cast-iron block and aluminum head. Displacement: 232 cid (3.8 liters). Bore and stroke: 3.80 x 3.40 in. Compression ratio: 8.3:1. Brake hp: 210 at 4000. Torque: 315 lbs.-ft. at 2600. Four main bearings. Hydraulic valve lifters. Induction: Sequential Electronic Fuel Injection (Supercharged). Serial number code: R.

CHASSIS

Wheelbase: 113 in. Overall length: 198.7. Overall width: 72.7. Overall height: 52.7 in. Front tread: 61.6 in. Rear tread: 60.2 in. Front suspension: Independent, upper and lower control arms, coil springs, tubular shocks and anti-roll bar. Rear suspension Live axle, four-link control arms, coil springs, adjustable tubular shocks and anti-roll bar. Steering: Power rack-and-pinion, speed-sensitive on LX. Front brakes: Power vented disc. Rear brakes: Power drum. Fuel tank capacity: 19 gal. Seating capacity: Five (5). Fuel economy: 17-24 mpg. Transmission: four-speed automatic. Wheels: 16 in. Tires: P225/60VR16.

OPTIONS

Four-speed overdrive transmission on Super Coupe ($539). P205/75R15 white sidewall tires ($73). Eagle GT + 4 P225/60VR16 black sidewall all-season performance tires, Super Coupe only ($73). Conventional spare tire in base T-Bird and LX ($73). Traction-Lok axle for base T-Bird and LX ($100). Optional 3.27:1 axle ratio for Super Coupe ($21). Premium luxury group for base T-Bird ($420), for Super Coupe with 157A ($761). Antilock braking system, except standard on Super Coupe ($1,085). Anti-theft system ($183). Keyless entry system for base T-Bird ($219), for others ($137). Front carpeted floor mats ($33) Luxury and lights convenience group ($26). Moonroof ($741-$841 depending on options teamed with). Clearcoat paint system ($188). Electronic premium cassette radio ($305-$442).

Ford JBL audio system ($488). Compact disc player ($491). Radio-delete credits ($245). Power antenna ($76). Locking wire wheel covers, on base T-Bird ($228), as option on others ($143). Cast-aluminum wheels on base T-Bird ($298), as option on others ($213). California emissions ($100). High-altitude emissions (no charge). LX leather trim ($489). Super Coupe leather trim ($622). Front license plate bracket (no charge). Cold weather group on most ($168-$195), on others ($18-$45). Preferred equipment package 151A ($1,288). Preferred equipment package 155A ($819). Preferred equipment group 157B for Super Coupe (no charge).

EQUIPMENT INSTALLATION RATES

Automatic transmission (94.2 percent). Five-speed manual transmission (5.8 percent). Fuel-injected V-6 engine (79 percent). Supercharged V-6 engine (21 percent). Electronic AM/FM Stereo Cassette (62.5 percent). Bose/JBL stereo (19 percent). Bose/JBL stereo with CD (10.6 percent). Electronic AM/FM Stereo (7.9 percent). Power steering (100 percent). Antilock brakes (23.2 percent). Power front disc brakes (76.8 percent). Power seat (100 percent). Power windows (100 percent). Adjustable steering column (99.6 percent). All tinted glass (100 percent). Manual air conditioning (100 percent). Power door locks (85.6 percent). Standard steel-belted radial tires (100 percent). Electric rear window defogger (99.7 percent). Aluminum styled wheels (85.2 percent). Speed control (99.6 percent). Manual remote-control left-hand rearview mirror (0.3 percent). Power remote-control left-hand rearview mirror (99.7 percent). Power remote-control right-hand rearview mirror (97.6 percent). Sunroof (19.6 percent). Delay windshield wipers (100 percent). Reclining front seats (100 percent). Limited-slip rear axle (26.4 percent). (Note: Based on 104,602 units produced in the model year for the U.S. market only.)

HISTORICAL FOOTNOTES

Harold A. Poling was chairman of the board and CEO of Ford Motor Co. Phillip E. Benton, Jr. was president and chief operating officer of the corporation. Allan D. Gilmour was executive vice president and president of the Ford Automotive Group. Thomas J. Wagner continued as the Ford Division's general manager and Phillip M. Novell was divisional general sales manager.

Calendar-year output was 107,430 units. A total of 113,957 T-Birds was produced in the model year. This represented 1.82 percent of the industry total. Of these units, all were made in Lorain, Ohio. Calendar-year dealer sales amounted to 106,124 for a 12.1 percent share of the domestic Large Specialty class.

Motor Trend magazine road tested the 1990 T-Bird Super Coupe in its September 1990 issue. The car moved from 0 to 60 mph in 7.4 seconds and covered the quarter-mile in 15.8 seconds at 90.8 mph. During lateral acceleration the car pulled .82g. It took 136 ft. to come to a complete halt from 60 mph. Its average EPA city mileage rating was 17 mpg.

In racing, it was a good year for Thunderbirds, with five Fords in NASCAR's top 10 Winston Cup standings. Dale Earnhardt's nine victories gave Chevrolet its eighth manufacturer's title in a row. However, the T-Birds were really nipping at the heels of his number 3 Lumina. Earnhardt had only a 26-point margin over Mark Martin's Folgers Coffee Ford. Martin took checkered flags at Richmond, Michigan, and North Wilkesboro.

1990 THUNDERBIRD PERFORMANCE		
Model	**CID/HP**	**Performance**
0-60 mph		
Super Coupe	232/210	7.4 seconds
1/4-Mile		
Super Coupe	232/210	15.8 seconds @ 90.8 mph

The Super Coupe was still somewhat reserved in its styling and profile in 1990, but its supercharged 210-hp V-6 gave it solid performance.

Ford photo

The base Thunderbird and the LX (above) could both be ordered with a 200-hp V-8 in 1991. The supercharged V-6 remained the power plant for the Super Coupe.

1991

Thunderbird

Very few revisions were made to 1991 T-Birds. The biggest change was the reinstatement of a V-8 engine. A new 200-hp version of the 5.0-liter Mustang V-8 was made optional in standard and LX models.

The standard T-Bird also received some interior upgrades. Leather seat facings and cloth-and-vinyl door panel inserts were added on the LX model. The LX also had bright window moldings, dual electric remote control mirrors, styled road wheel covers, luxury level door trim and carpeting, an illuminated entry system with convenience lights, an upper storage compartment for the instrument panel, illuminated visor mirrors, luxury cloth bucket seats with recliners, a front seat center armrest, a leather-wrapped luxury steering wheel, a power lock group, speed control, tilt steering, and speed-sensitive power steering. The top-of-the-line Super Coupe had seats with a T-Bird insignia embroidered into them and under its hood

was the 210-hp supercharged V-6.

STANDARD EQUIPMENT

All standard FoMoCo safety, anti-theft, convenience items and emissions control equipment, 3.8-liter V-6, four-speed automatic overdrive transmission, daytime running lights, rear window defroster, 72-amp battery, 65-amp alternator, wide body-side protection moldings, deluxe wheel covers, full-length console with floor-mounted shift, vinyl door trim with storage bins, cloth bucket seats with recliners, air conditioning, tinted glass, analog instrumentation, electronic AM/FM search radio with digital clock (may be deleted for credit), power steering, all-season radial tires, power windows, and interval windshield wipers. **Thunderbird LX standard equipment adds or substitutes (over standard):** Power lock group, dual electric remote-control mirrors, bright window moldings, electronic AM/FM

STANDARD AND LX COUPE BODY COLOR INFORMATION

Color Name	Code	Color Name	Code
Oxford White	YO	Crystal Blue Frost Clearcoat Metallic	MD
Mocha Frost Clearcoat Metallic	DD	Twilight Blue Clearcoat Metallic	MK
Medium Mocha Clearcoat Metallic	DC	Black Non-Metallic Clearcoat	UA
Electric Red Clearcoat Metallic	EG	Medium Titanium Clearcoat Metallic	YG
Bright Red Non-metallic Clearcoat	E4	Titanium Frost Clearcoat Metallic	YX
Steel Blue Frost Clearcoat Metallic	MB		

Clearcoat Metallic colors optional at extra cost.

SUPER COUPE BODY COLOR INFORMATION

Color Name	Code	Color Name	Code
Black Non-metallic Clearcoat	UA	Twilight Blue Clearcoat Metallic	MK
Oxford White	YO	Titanium Frost Clearcoat Metallic	YX
Bright Red Non-metallic Clearcoat	E4		

Clearcoat metallic colors optional at extra cost.

INTERIOR TRIM CODE INFORMATION (U.S. & CANADA)

Seat Type	Material	Crys Titanium Blue		Cur Red	Mocha	Black
Standard						
Buckets	Cloth	WA	WB	WF	WH	WJ
LX						
Bucket Seats	Luxury Cloth	5A	5B	5F	5H	5J
Bucket Seats	Leather	4A	4B	4F	4H	4J
Super Coupe						
Articulated Buckets	Cloth	3A	3B	3F	—	3J
Articulated Buckets	Leather	UA	UB	UF	—	UJ

Legend: Cry Blue means Crystal Blue, Cur Red means Currant Red, Luxury Cloth interior includes leather and vinyl components.

THUNDERBIRD PRODUCTION

Model Number	Body/Style Number	Body Type & Seating	Factory Price	Shipping Weight	Production Total
THUNDERBIRD - (V-6)					
60	66D	2d Coupe-4P	$15,318	3,550 lbs.	Note 1
THUNDERBIRD - (V-8)					
60	66D	2d Coupe-4P	$16,398	3,732 lbs.	Note 1
THUNDERBIRD LX - (V-6)					
62	66D	2d Coupe-4P	$17,734	3,572 lbs.	Note 1
THUNDERBIRD LX - (V-8)					
62	66D	2d Coupe-4P	$18,814	3,742 lbs.	Note 1
THUNDERBIRD SUPER COUPE - (V-6)					
64	66D	2d Coupe-4P	20,999	3,767 lbs.	Note 1

NOTE 1: Production of the all models combined was 82,973.

stereo radio with cassette and clock, speed control system, tilt steering wheel, styled road wheel covers, illuminated entry system, fog lamps, luxury-level door trim and carpeting, convenience lights, instrument panel upper storage compartment, illuminated visor mirrors, luxury cloth bucket seats with recliners, rear seat center armrest, leather-wrapped luxury steering wheel, vehicle maintenance monitor, remote-release fuel door, electronic instrument cluster, and speed-sensitive power steering. **1991 Thunderbird Super Coupe standard equipment adds or substitutes (over standard):** 3.8-liter EFI supercharged V-6 engine, five-speed manual overdrive transmission, power lock group, dual electric remote-control mirrors, electronic AM/FM stereo radio with cassette and clock, speed control system, tilt steering wheel, fog lamps, narrow body-side moldings, lower body-side cladding, 16-inch cast-aluminum wheels, P255/60R16 black sidewall performance tires, luxury door trim and carpeting, articulated sports seat

with power lumbar and power seatback bolster adjustments, Sport soft-feel steering wheel, heavy-duty alternator, automatic ride control adjustable suspension, and performance instrumentation.

I.D. NUMBERS

VIN stamped on aluminum tab riveted to the dashboard on passenger side and observable through the windshield from outside the car. First symbol 1 denotes built in the United States. Second symbol F denotes Ford. Third symbol A denotes Ford passenger vehicle. Fourth symbol denotes type of restraint system. Fifth symbol P denotes passenger-type vehicle. Sixth symbol 6 denotes Thunderbird. Seventh symbol denotes body type. 0=Standard Coupe, 2=LX Coupe, 4=Super Coupe. Eighth symbol denotes engine: 4=232-cid (3.8L)/140-hp V-6, R=232-cid (3.6L)/210-hp supercharged V-6, T=302-cid (5.0L)/200-hp V-6. Ninth symbol is the check digit. Tenth symbol M=1991 model year. Eleventh symbol denotes assembly plant: H=Lorain, Ohio. Twelfth through 17th symbols denote sequential production number of specific vehicle starting at 100001. Vehicle certification label located on rear face of driver's door. The top part of the label indicates that the Thunderbird was manufactured by Ford Motor Company. Directly below this is the month and year of manufacture, plus a statement that the car conforms to federal motor vehicle safety standards in effect on the indicated date of manufacture. VIN: The VIN appears two lines above UPC. It matches the 1st to 11th symbols on VIN tag. Some other codes also appear. TYPE: Appears on left side of label on line above UPC, indicates PASSENGER. UPC: A scannable bar code carries the UPC. EXT. COLOR: This line carries the exterior paint color(s) code. DSO: The District Special Order code now appears above "DSO" to the right of the exterior paint color code. BODY: The body style code appears to the extreme left of the bottom line. The only Thunderbird code for this model-year is: BS2=two-door pillared hardtop. VR: The vinyl roof type/color code is to the right of the body code. No T-Birds had vinyl tops. MLDG: The molding code is to the right of the vinyl roof code. INT. TRIM: The interior trim code is to the right of the molding code. TAPE: The tape treatment code appears to right of the interior trim code. R: The radio code is to the right of the A/C code. S: The sunroof code is to the right of the radio code. AX: The axle code appears to the right of the sunroof code. TR: The transmission code appears to the right of the axle code. (Note: The terms and abbreviations shown in capitals appear on the line above the actual codes.)

ENGINE

THUNDERBIRD BASE V-6: 90-degree. Overhead valve. Cast-iron block and aluminum head. Displacement: 232 cid (3.8 liters). Bore and stroke: 3.80 x 3.40 in. Compression ratio: 9.0:1. Brake hp: 140 at 3800. Torque: 215 lbs.-ft. at 2400. Four main bearings. Hydraulic valve lifters. Induction: Throttle Body Injection. Serial number code: 4.

THUNDERBIRD SUPER COUPE SUPERCHARGED V-6: 90-degree. Overhead valve. Cast-iron block and aluminum head. Displacement: 232 cid (3.8 liters). Bore and stroke: 3.80 x 3.40 in. Compression ratio: 8.3:1. Brake hp: 210 at 4000. Torque: 315 lbs.-ft. at 2600. Four main bearings. Hydraulic valve lifters. Induction: Sequential Electronic Fuel Injection (Supercharged). Serial number code: R.

Ford photo

While they were probably still known best for their looks and amenities, the 1991 T-Birds performed well when put through their paces by magazine testers, and they were also successful on the NASCAR track.

THUNDERBIRD, THUNDERBIRD LX OPTIONAL V-8: 90-degree. Overhead valve. Cast-iron block and head. Displacement: 302 cid (5.0 liters). Bore and stroke: 4.00 x 3.00 in. Compression ratio: 8.9:1. Brake hp: 200 at 4000 rpm. Torque: 275 lbs.-ft. at 3000 rpm. Five main bearings. Roller cam. Induction: Sequential fuel injection.

CHASSIS

Wheelbase: 113 in. Overall length: 198.7. Overall width: 72.7. Overall height: 52.7 in. Trunk capacity: 14.7 cu. ft. Front tread: 61.6 in. Rear tread: 60.2 in. Front suspension: Independent, upper and lower control arms, coil springs, tubular shocks and anti-roll bar. Rear suspension Live axle, four-link control arms, coil springs, adjustable tubular shocks and anti-roll bar. Steering: Power rack-and-pinion, speed-sensitive on LX. Front brakes: Power vented disc. Rear brakes: Power drum. Fuel tank capacity: 18 gal. Seating capacity: Five. Fuel Economy: 17-24 mpg. Transmission: four-speed automatic. Wheels: 15 in. Tires: P215/70R15. Fuel economy: Base V-6: 19 mpg city/27 mpg highway; Supercharged V-6: 17 mpg city/24 mpg highway; and V-8: 15 mpg city/23 mpg highway.

OPTIONS

5.0-liter V-8 in base T-Bird and LX ($1,080). Four-speed overdrive transmission on Super Coupe ($595). P205/75R15 white sidewall tires ($73). Eagle GT + 4 P225/60VR16 black sidewall all-season performance tires, Super Coupe only ($73). Conventional spare tire in base T-Bird and LX ($73). Traction-Lok axle for base T-Bird and LX ($100). Premium Luxury group for base T-Bird ($420), for Super Coupe with 157A ($761). Antilock braking system including Traction-Lok axle, except standard on Super Coupe ($1,085). Anti-theft system ($245). Auto lamp group ($176). Keyless entry system for base T-Bird ($219), for others ($137). Front carpeted floor mats ($33). Luxury group ($345-$627)). Moonroof ($776-$876 depending on options teamed with). Cornering lamps ($68). Rear window defroster ($160). Electronic auto temperature control ($162). Electronic premium cassette radio ($305-$460). Ford JBL audio system ($488). Illuminated entry system ($82). Compact disc player ($491). Radio-delete credits ($245). Power lock group ($245). Light convenience group ($100-$146). Luxury group ($345-$627). Power antenna ($82). 6-way power driver's seat ($290). 6-way power passenger seat ($290). Speed control and tilt steering ($345). Vehicle maintenance monitor ($89). Locking wire wheel covers, on base T-Bird ($228), as option on others

($143). Cast aluminum wheels on base T-Bird ($299), as option on others ($214). LX leather trim ($489). Super Coupe leather trim ($622). Front license plate bracket (no charge). Cold weather group on most ($178-$205), on others ($18-$45). Preferred equipment package 151A ($796). Preferred equipment package 155A ($977). Preferred equipment group 157A for Super Coupe ($739).

EQUIPMENT INSTALLATION RATES

Automatic transmission (97.7 percent). Five-speed manual transmission (2.3 percent). Fuel-injected V-6 engine (71.9 percent). Supercharged V-6 engine (8.5 percent). V-8 engine (19.6 percent). Electronic AM/FM stereo cassette (19.3 percent). Bose/JBL stereo (9.6 percent). Bose/JBL stereo with CD (5.6 percent). Premium speakers (26.9 percent). Electronic AM/FM Stereo (65.5 percent). Power steering (100 percent). Antilock brakes (11.6 percent). Power front disc brakes (88.4 percent). Power seat (100 percent). Power windows (100 percent). Adjustable steering column (99.2 percent). All tinted glass (100 percent). Manual air conditioning (79.5 percent). Automatic air conditioning (20.5 percent). Power door locks (89.2 percent). Standard steel-belted radial tires (100 percent). Electric rear window defogger (99.2 percent). Aluminum styled wheels (73.7 percent). Speed control (99.2 percent). Manual remote-control left-hand rearview mirror (0.9 percent). Manual remote-control right-hand rearview mirror (0.9 percent). Power remote-control left-hand rearview mirror (99.1 percent). Power remote-control right-hand rearview mirror (99.1 percent). Sunroof (12.2 percent). (Note: Based on 77,688 units produced in the model year for the U.S. market only.)

HISTORICAL FOOTNOTES

The new T-Birds were released on September 17, 1990. Harold A. Poling was chairman of the board and CEO of Ford Motor Co. Phillip E. Benton, Jr. was president and chief operating officer of the corporation. Allan D. Gilmour was executive vice president and president of the Ford Automotive Group. Ford Vice Thomas J. Wagner continued as the Ford Division's general manager and Phillip M. Novell was divisional general sales manager.

Calendar-year output was 71,395 units. A total of 82,973 T-Birds was produced in the model year. This represented 1.43 percent of the industry total. Of these units, all were made in Lorain, Ohio. Calendar-year dealer sales amounted to 74,189 for a 11 percent share of the domestic Large Specialty class.

T-Bird enthusiasts helped bring the V-8 engine back in 1991 by asking Ford dealers for the type of engine that was traditional in their favorite car. The company stuffed the 5.0-liter Mustang engine into the T-Bird's smaller engine bay and created an optional hood with a "power bulge." This appeared in an *Autoweek* spy photo as early as May 1, 1989, and didn't look bad, but designer Jack Telnack didn't like it. He killed the idea of putting a bulge on the hood, so Ford redesigned the 5.0-liter V-8. Its length was shortened by 2 1/2 inches and its height was lowered by redesigning the intake manifold.

Road & Track road tested the 1991 T-Bird LX Coupe and published the results in its April 1991 issue. The car, as tested, priced out at $23,181. It was equipped with the four-speed automatic transmission. In the acceleration category, the car did 0 to 60 mph in 9.0 seconds. The quarter-mile took 16.7 seconds. The car's top speed was 140 mph. Braking performance was also good, with 255 feet required to stop the car from 80 mph. It averaged 60.3 mph through the slalom.

T-Birds also turned in impressive performances in various types of racing events during 1991. Hot-driving NASCAR competitors running Fords included Davey Allison, Mark Martin, and Sterling Marlin. Ford was a close second to Chevrolet in the battle for the Manufacturer's Cup. Also, for the first time since 1988, Ford managed a superspeedway triumph in ARCA stock car racing when Greg Trammell put his Melling-Elliott T-Bird across the finish line first in the March 16 race at Atlanta Motor Speedway. He averaged a blistering 131.532 mph to set an event record. Bobby Bowsher placed third in his Don Thompson Excavating T-Bird. In NHRA drag racing, Bob Glidden's Pro Stock T-Bird struggled to a fifth place finish.

Ford photo

The 1992 Thunderbird Sport came with a few upgrades: black sidewall tires, aluminum wheels, speed-sensitive power steering and an upgraded suspension, and interior amenities like a leather-wrapped steering wheel.

1992 *Thunderbird*

Minor changes were seen on 1992 T-Birds. The LX and Sport models now had the same aggressive front fascia used on the Super Coupe, but without the "SC" initials embossed in the bumper. Four colors—Cayman Green Clearcoat Metallic, Dark Plum Clearcoat Metallic, Opal Grey and Silver—were new for 1992.

STANDARD EQUIPMENT

All standard FoMoCo safety, anti-theft, convenience items, and emissions control equipment, 3.8-liter 140-hp MPEFI V-6, automatic overdrive transmission, long-spindle SLA front suspension with variable-rate coil springs, double-acting gas-pressurized shock absorbers and 1.1-inch diameter stabilizer bar, independent H-arm rear suspension with toe control link, variable-rate springs, double-acting gas-pressurized shocks, and 1.04-inch diameter stabilizer bar, power rack and pinion steering with 14.1:1 ratio on center, power front disc/rear drum brakes, 15 x 6-inch stamped steel wheels, deluxe wheel covers, P205/70R15 steel-belted black sidewall all-season radial tires, new long-lasting LED taillights, body-side protection moldings with bright insert, (U.S.) fully automatic shoulder belt restraint system with manual lap belt, full-length console with floor-mounted

STANDARD AND LX COUPE BODY COLOR INFORMATION

Color Name	Code	Color Name	Code
Oxford White	YO	Crystal Blue Frost Clearcoat Metallic	MD
Cayman Green Clearcoat Metallic	DA	Twilight Blue Clearcoat Metallic	MK
Mocha Frost Clearcoat Metallic	DD	Black Non-metallic Clearcoat	UA
Electric Red Clearcoat Metallic	EG	Opal Gray Clearcoat Metallic	WC
Bright Red Non-metallic Clearcoat	E4	Silver Clearcoat Metallic	YN
Dark Plum Clearcoat Metallic	G4		

Clearcoat Metallic colors optional at extra cost

SUPER COUPE BODY COLOR INFORMATION

Color Name	Code	Color Name	Code
Bright Red Non-metallic Clearcoat	E4	Black Non-metallic Clearcoat	UA
Twilight Blue Clearcoat Metallic	MK	Silver Clearcoat Metallic	YN

INTERIOR TRIM INFORMATION (U.S. & CANADA)

Seat Type	Material	Crys Titanium Blue	Cur Red	Mocha	Black
(Standard & Sport)					
Buckets	Cloth	WA WB	WF	WH	WJ
(LX)					
Bucket Seats	Luxury Cloth	5A 5B	5F	5H	5J
Bucket Seats	Leather	4A 4B	4F	4H	4J
(Super Coupe)					
Articulated Buckets	Cloth	3A 3B	3F	—	3J
Articulated Buckets	Leather	PA PB	PF	—	PJ

Legend: Cry Blue means Crystal Blue, Cur Red means Currant Red, Luxury Cloth interior includes leather and vinyl components.

THUNDERBIRD PRODUCTION

Model Number	Body/Style Number	Body Type & Seating	Factory Price	Shipping Weight	Production Total
THUNDERBIRD - (V-6)					
60	66D	2d Coupe-4P	$16,345	3,514 lbs.	Note 1
THUNDERBIRD - (V-8)					
60	66D	2d Coupe-4P	$17,425	3,772 lbs.	Note 1
THUNDERBIRD - (V-8)					
60	66D	2d Spt Cpe-4P	$18,611	3,686 lbs.	Note 1
THUNDERBIRD LX - (V-6)					
62	66D	2d Coupe-4P	$18,783	3,566 lbs.	Note 1
THUNDERBIRD LX - (V-8)					
62	66D	2d Coupe-4P	$19,863	3,719 lbs.	Note 1
THUNDERBIRD SUPER COUPE - (V-6)					
64	66D	2d Coupe-4P	$22,046	3,768 lbs.	Note 1

NOTE 1: Production of the all models combined was 77,789.

shifter, vinyl door trim with storage bins, cloth bucket seats with recliners, map and dome lights, luggage compartment light, ashtray light, driver's foot well light, air conditioning, tinted glass, analog instruments, electronic AM/FM stereo search radio with digital clock (may be deleted for credit), power windows, interval windshield wipers, (Canada) heavy-duty battery, and (Canada) electric rear window defroster. **T-Bird LX major standard equipment (over standard T-Bird equipment):** Speed-sensitive variable-assist power steering with 14.1:1 ratio on center, styled road wheel covers, dual electric remote-control OSRV mirrors, luxury level door trim and carpeting, power lock group with power door locks, remote deck lid release, and remote-control for fuel filler door in glove box, analog performance instrumentation with tachometer, fog lamps, illuminated entry system and convenience lights, illuminated visor mirrors, luxury cloth/leather/vinyl bucket seats with recliners and 6-way power driver's seat, rear seat center armrest, leather-wrapped luxury steering wheel, electronic

AM/FM stereo search radio with cassette and digital clock and speed control with tilt steering wheel. **T-Bird Sport major standard equipment (over standard T-Bird equipment):** 5.0-liter EFI V-8, automatic overdrive transmission, cast-aluminum wheels, P215/70R15 black sidewall tires, speed-sensitive variable-assisted power steering with 14.1:1 ratio on center, handling suspension, performance analog instrument cluster and leather-wrapped steering wheel. **T-Bird Super Coupe major standard equipment (over standard T-Bird equipment):** 3.8-liter 210-hp supercharged and intercooled SMPEFI, 5-speed manual overdrive transmission, automatic ride control suspension in addition to standard suspension (includes 1.12-inch diameter front stabilizer bar and .9-inch diameter solid rear stabilizer bar), Traction-Lok rear axle, speed-sensitive variable-assist power steering with 14.1:1 ratio on center, four-wheel power disc brakes with anti-lock braking system, cast-aluminum 16 x 7.0-inch wheels and P225/60 performance tires, fog lamps, narrow body-side moldings and lower body-side cladding, dual electric remote-control mirrors, luxury door trim and carpeting, articulated sport seats with power lumbar and seatback bolster adjustments, Sport soft-feel steering wheel, heavy-duty battery and alternator and analog performance instrumentation with tachometer.

I.D. NUMBERS

VIN stamped on aluminum tab riveted to dashboard on passenger side and observable through the windshield from outside the car. First symbol 1 denotes built in the United States. Second symbol F denotes Ford. Third symbol A denotes Ford passenger vehicle. Fourth symbol denotes type of restraint system. Fifth symbol P denotes passenger-type vehicle. Sixth symbol 6 denotes Thunderbird. Seventh symbol denotes body type. 0=standard coupe, 2=LX Coupe, 4=Super Coupe. Eighth symbol denotes engine: 4=232-cid (3.8L)/140-hp V-6, R=232-cid (3.6L)/210-hp supercharged V-6, T=302 cid (5.0L) 200-hp V-6. Ninth symbol is the check digit. Tenth symbol N=1992 model year. Eleventh symbol denotes assembly plant: H=Lorain, Ohio. Twelfth through 17th symbols denote sequential production number of specific vehicle starting at 100001. Vehicle certification label located on rear face of driver's door. The top part of the label indicates that the Thunderbird was manufactured by Ford Motor Company. Directly below this is the month and year of manufacture, plus a statement that the car conforms to federal motor vehicle safety standards in effect on the indicated date of manufacture. VIN: The VIN appears two lines above UPC. It matches the first to 11th symbols on VIN tag. Some other codes also appear. TYPE: Appears on left side of label on line above UPC, indicates PASSENGER. UPC: A scannable bar code carries the UPC. EXT. COLOR: This line carries the exterior paint color(s) code. DSO: The District Special Order code now appears above "DSO" to the right of the exterior paint color code. BODY: The body style code appears to the extreme left of the bottom line. The only Thunderbird code for this model-year is: Thunderbird code for this model-year is: BS2=two-door base coupe, LX2=two-door LX Coupe, SC2=two-door Super Coupe. VR: The vinyl roof type/color code is to the right of the body code. No T-Birds had vinyl tops. MLDG: The molding code is to the right of the vinyl roof code. INT. TRIM: The interior trim code is to the right of the molding code. TAPE: The tape treatment code appears to right of the interior trim code. R: The radio code is to the right of the A/C code. S: The sunroof code is to the right of the radio code. AX: The axle code appears to the

Ford photo

The 1992 Super Coupe's supercharged 3.8-liter V-6 produced 210 hp.

right of the sunroof code. TR: The transmission code appears to the right of the axle code. (Note: The terms and abbreviations shown in capitals appear on the line above the actual codes.)

ENGINE

THUNDERBIRD BASE V-6: 90-degree. Overhead valve. Cast-iron block and aluminum head. Displacement: 232 cid (3.8 liters). Bore and stroke: 3.80 x 3.40 in. Compression ratio: 9.0:1. Brake hp: 140 at 3800. Torque: 215 lbs.-ft. at 2400. Four main bearings. Hydraulic valve lifters. Induction: Throttle Body Injection. Serial number code: 4.

THUNDERBIRD SUPER COUPE SUPERCHARGED V-6: 90-degree. Overhead valve. Cast-iron block and aluminum head. Displacement: 232 cid (3.8 liters). Bore and stroke: 3.80 x 3.40 in. Compression ratio: 8.3:1. Brake hp: 210 at 4000. Torque: 315 lbs.-ft. at 2600. Four main bearings. Hydraulic valve lifters. Induction: Sequential Electronic Fuel Injection (Supercharged). Serial number code: R.

THUNDERBIRD, THUNDERBIRD LX OPTIONAL V-8: 90-degree. Overhead valve. Cast-iron block and head. Displacement: 302 cid (5.0 liters). Bore and stroke: 4.00 x 3.00 in. Compression ratio: 8.9:1. Brake hp: 200 at 4000 rpm. Torque: 275 lbs.-ft. at 3000 rpm. Five main bearings. Roller cam. Induction: Sequential fuel injection.

CHASSIS

Wheelbase: 113 in. Overall length: 198.7. Overall width: 72.7. Overall height: 52.7 in. Front legroom: 41.5 in. Trunk capacity: 14.7 cu. ft. Front tread: 61.6 in. Rear tread: 60.2 in. Front suspension: Independent, upper and lower control arms, coil springs, tubular shocks and anti-roll bar. Rear suspension: Live axle, four-link control arms, coil springs, adjustable tubular shocks and anti-roll bar. Steering: Power rack-and-pinion, speed-sensitive on LX. Turning circle: 37.5 ft. Front brakes: Power vented disc. Rear brakes: Power drum. Fuel tank capacity: 18 gal. Seating capacity: Five (5). Fuel Economy: 17-24 mpg. Transmission: four-speed automatic. Wheels: 15 in. Tires: P215/70R15. Fuel economy: Base V-6 19 mpg city/27 mpg highway, Supercharged V-6 20 mpg city/27 mpg highway, and [V-8]

15 mpg city/23 mpg highway. Weight distribution: 57/43 percent.

OPTIONS

5.0-liter HO V-8 in base T-Bird and Sport ($1,080). Four-speed overdrive transmission on in T-Bird and Sport ($595). California emissions ($100). P225/60ZR16 black sidewall all-season performance tires, Super Coupe only ($73). Conventional spare tire in base T-Bird and LX ($73). Leather bucket seating surfaces in LX ($515). Leather bucket seating surfaces in Super Coupe ($648). Anti-lock braking system, includes Traction-Lok axle ($695). Anti-theft system ($245). Autolamp group ($193). Traction-Lok axle for base T-Bird, Sport and LX ($100). CD player, requires premium cassette radio ($491). Cornering lights ($68). Rear window defroster ($170). Automatic air conditioning for LX and Super Coupe ($162). Electronic instrument cluster for LX ($270). Electronic premium cassette radio ($305-$460). AM/FM ETR (stereo) with cassette in base T-Bird and LX ($155). Ford JBL audio system ($526). Radio-delete credits ($245). Keyless entry, including illuminated entry system and power lock group ($146-$228). Light convenience group ($100-$146). Power lock group ($311). Luxury group ($311-$561). Moon roof ($776-$876 depending on options teamed with). Power antenna ($85). 6-way power driver's seat ($305). 6-way power passenger seat ($305). Vehicle maintenance monitor ($89). Cast-aluminum wheels on base T-Bird ($306), as option on others ($221). Front license plate bracket (no charge). Cold weather group on most ($178-$205), on others ($18-$45). Preferred equipment package 151A ($762). Preferred equipment package 155A ($1,038). Preferred equipment group 157A for Super Coupe ($858).

EQUIPMENT INSTALLATION RATES

Three-speed automatic transmission (1.7 percent). Four-speed automatic transmission (98.3 percent). V-6 engine (83 percent). V-8 engine (17 percent). Electronic AM/FM stereo cassette (89.7 percent). Bose/JBL stereo (4.1 percent). Bose/JBL stereo with CD (6 percent). Premium speakers (19.5 percent). Electronic AM/FM Stereo (0.2 percent). Power steering (100 percent). Antilock brakes (14.3 percent). Power front disc brakes (85.7 percent).

Ford photo

The 1992 Thunderbird LX had a new front fascia and, like the base T-Bird, was available in V-6 and V-8 varieties.

Power seat (100 percent). Power windows (100 percent). Adjustable steering column (100 percent). All tinted glass (100 percent). Manual air conditioning (63.6 percent). Automatic air conditioning (36.4 percent). Power door locks (93.4 percent). Standard steel-belted radial tires (100 percent). Electric rear window defogger (99.8 percent). Aluminum styled wheels (99.5 percent). Speed control (99.8 percent). Power remote-control left-hand rearview mirror (99.8 percent). Power remote-control right-hand rearview mirror (99.8 percent). Delay windshield wipers (100 percent). Limited-slip differential (18.7 percent). Sun roof (12.2 percent). (Note: Based on 73,892 units produced in the model year for the U.S. market only.)

HISTORICAL FOOTNOTES

Harold A. Poling was chairman of the board and CEO of Ford Motor Co. Phillip E. Benton, Jr. was president and chief operating officer of the corporation. Allan D. Gilmour was executive vice president and president of the Ford Automotive Group. Ross Roberts became the Ford Division's general manager and Phillip M. Novell remained divisional general sales manager.

Calendar-year output was 97,822 units. A total of 77,789 T-Birds was produced in the model year. This represented 1.38 percent of the industry total. Of these units, all were made in Lorain, Ohio. Calendar-year dealer sales amounted to 84,186 for an 11.2 percent share of the domestic large specialty class.

"For some of us who love cars, the most intriguing models are not racing cars or sports cars, but big coupes. Grand Touring Cars. Cars with powerful engines, good road manners, style, and grace," said *Road & Track's Complete '92 Car Buying Guide*. "A gentleman's car like the Jensen Interceptor III, Facel-Vega HK 500. Aston Martin DB4. If there is a modern successor to these machines, it is the Ford T-Bird."

In racing, the 1992 T-Birds proved more reliable. They came out of the gate strong in 1992 NASCAR Winston Cup racing, earning consecutive wins in the first nine races. Between the Charlotte race in the fall of 1991, and the spring 1992 Winston Cup event at the same track, Ford drivers netted 14 checkered flags. Still, the season wound up being another cliff-hanger. Back-to-back Geoff Bodine victories finally clinched the Winston Cup Manufacturer's Championship for Ford. Bodine's number 15 Bud Moore/Motorcraft T-Bird racecar crossed the line first at Martinsville and North Wilkesboro, taking both events on Mondays after Sunday rain-outs. It was the first time in nine years that the blue oval cars wrestled the Manufacturer's Cup away from Chevrolet. The coup de grace came at season's end, when Bill Elliott put his T-Bird across the line first in the Hooters 500 at Atlanta Motor Speedway in Ford's 400th NASCAR victory, and Ford pilot Alan Kulwicki captured the Winston Cup Championship with his Hooters T-Bird. That gave Kulwicki, Elliott and Davey Allison the top three places in the point standings. In all, the Fords had 16 wins on the season, led the most laps, took a dominating 57 top-five finishes, and ran in the top 10 places 142 times. Another flock of 'Bird jockeys—led by title-winner Bobby Bowsher—performed nearly as well in 1992 ARCA competition. A win by another Ford in the last race of the season settled the title bout between Bowsher and Chrysler LeBaron driver Bob Keselowski. This came in the Motorcraft 500k race at Atlanta, which Loy Allen, Jr. won with his Robert Yates-built number 2 Hooters T-Bird. Ford drivers struggled in NHRA drag racing, with Bob Glidden's Pro Stock T-Bird placing only third at the Keystone Nationals and second at Topeka. Glidden managed to pull out a late-season win at Dallas and finished fifth in the point standings again. In IHRA competition, Glen May's "Cranberry Connection" T-Bird did become the first "door-slammer" car to break the 220-mph barrier.

The Super Coupe (above) and LX were the only Thunderbirds offered in 1993.

1993

Thunderbird

The standard T-Bird coupe and the Sport Coupe disappeared from the T-Bird model lineup. Prices on some of the remaining models were slightly lowered. The 1993 retail prices ranged from $16,292 to $22,525 and compared to the 1992 price range of $16,763 to $22,457.

STANDARD EQUIPMENT

All standard FoMoCo safety, anti-theft, convenience items and emissions control equipment, 3.8-liter 140-hp SMPEFI V-6, automatic overdrive transmission, long-spindle SLA front suspension with variable-rate coil springs, double-acting gas-pressurized shock absorbers and 1.1-inch diameter stabilizer bar, independent H-arm rear suspension with toe control link, variable-rate springs, double-acting gas-pressurized shocks and 1.04-inch diameter stabilizer bar, speed-sensitive variable-assist power steering, power front disc/rear drum brakes, 15 x 6-inch stamped steel wheels, styled road wheel covers, P205/70R15 steel-belted black sidewall radial tires, long-lasting LED taillights, body color body-side protection moldings, full-length console with floor-mounted leather-wrapped shifter, map/dome, luggage compartment, ashtray and driver's foot well lights,

air conditioning and tinted glass, power windows, power door locks, remote deck lid, remote fuel filler door release, interval windshield wipers, dual electric remote-control mirrors, luxury level door trim and carpeting, analog performance instrumentation with tachometer, integral fog lamps in front fascia, illuminated entry system, rear seat courtesy lights, luxury cloth/leather/vinyl bucket seats with recliners and 6-way power for driver, rear seat center armrest, leather-wrapped luxury steering wheel, electronic AM/FM stereo search radio with cassette tape player and digital clock, and speed control with tilt steering wheel. **T-Bird Super Coupe major standard equipment (over standard T-Bird LX equipment):** 3.8-liter 210-hp supercharged and intercooled SMPEFI V-6 with dual exhausts, five-speed manual overdrive transmission, supercharger boost gauge in instrument cluster, automatic ride control suspension in addition to standard suspension, Handling components including 1.10-inch (28 mm) diameter solid front stabilizer bar and 0.90-inch (23 mm) diameter solid rear stabilizer bar, Traction-Lok rear axle, four-wheel power disc brakes with anti-lock system, directional cast-aluminum 16 x 7.0-in. wheels and P225/60ZR black sidewall performance tires, narrow black

LX COUPE BODY COLOR INFORMATION

Color Name	Code	Color Name	Code
Oxford White	YO	Twilight Blue Clearcoat Metallic	MK
Mocha Frost Clearcoat Metallic	DD	Teal Clearcoat Metallic*	RD
Black Non-metallic Clearcoat	UA	Black Non-metallic Clearcoat	UA
Electric Red Clearcoat Metallic	EG	Midnight Opal Clearcoat Metallic*	WL
Sunrise Red Clearcoat Metallic*	FC	Silver Clearcoat Metallic	YN
Crystal Blue Frost Clearcoat Metallic	MD		

Clearcoat Metallic colors optional at extra cost.
* Indicates color used only on "feature" car.
The 1992 colors Cayman Green (code DA) and Dark Plum (code GA) were used, but deleted during 1993. Crimson Clearcoat (code WH) was changed to code YN. Sunrise Red Clearcoat (code FC) and Teal Clearcoat (code RD) were two colors added for a Super Coupe "feature car." White Opalescent Gray (Code PX) was also added.

SUPER COUPE BODY COLOR INFORMATION

Color Name	Code	Color Name	Code
Sunrise Red Clearcoat Metallic*	FC	Black Non-metallic Clearcoat	UA
Twilight Blue Clearcoat Metallic	MK	Crimson Non-Metallic Clearcoat *	WH
Teal Clearcoat Metallic*	RD	Silver Clearcoat Metallic	YN

Clearcoat Metallic colors optional at extra cost.
* Indicates color used only on "feature" car.

EARLY INTERIOR TRIM INFORMATION

EXTERIOR COLOR   INTERIOR TRIM COLORS

Thunderbird LX	Opal Grey	Crystal Blue	Ruby Red	Mocha	Black
Oxford White (C)	X	X	X	X	X
Cayman Green (CM)	X	—	—	X	X
Mocha Frost (CM)	—	—	—	X	X
Electric Red (CM)	X	—	X	X	X
Dark Plum (CM)	X	—	—	X	X
Crystal Blue Frost (CM)	X	—	—	X	X
Twilight Blue (CM)	X	—	—	X	X
Black (NC)	X	X	X	X	X
Midnight Opal (CM)	X	—	X	—	X
Silver (CM)	X	X	X	—	X
Super Coupe					
Oxford White (C)	X	X	X	—	X
Crimson (NC)	X	—	X	—	X
Black (NC)	X	X	X	—	X
Twilight Blue (CM)	X	X	—	—	X
Silver (CM)	X	X	X	—	X

Legend: C means conventional paint, CM means clearcoat metallic, NC means non-metallic clearcoat, CM means clearcoat metallic.

LATE INTERIOR TRIM INFORMATION

EXTERIOR COLORS   INTERIOR TRIM COLORS

Thunderbird LX	Titanium	Crystal Blue	Currant Red	Mocha	Black
Oxford White (C)	X	X	X	X	X
Cayman Green (CM)	—	—	—	X	X
Mocha Frost (CM)	—	—	—	X	X
Electric Red (CM)	X	—	X	X	X
Bright Red (NC)	X	—	—	X	X
Dark Plum (CM)	X	—	—	X	X
Crystal Blue Frost (CM)	X	X	—	—	X
Twilight Blue (CM)	X	X	—	—	X
Black (NC)	X	X	X	X	X
Opal Grey (CM)	X	—	X	—	X
Silver (CM)	X	X	X	—	X
Super Coupe					
Oxford White (C)	X	X	X	—	X
Bright Red (NC)	X	—	—	—	X
Twilight Blue (CM)	X	X	—	—	X
Black (NC)	X	X	X	—	X
Silver (CM)	X	X	X	—	X

Legend: C means conventional paint, NC means non-metallic Clearcoat, CM means Clearcoat metallic

INTERIOR TRIM INFORMATION

Seat Type	Material	Opal Grey	Crys Blue	Mocha	Black	Ruby Red	Opal Grey & White (*)
LX							
Bucket Seats	Luxury Cloth	56	5B	5H	5J	5R	—
Bucket Seats	Leather	46	—	4H	4J	—	4X
Super Coupe							
Articulated Buckets	Cloth	36	3B	—	3J	3R	—
Articulated Buckets	Leather	P6	—	—	PJ	—	PX

Legend: Luxury Cloth interior includes leather and vinyl components, Crys Blue means Crystal Blue.

THUNDERBIRD PRODUCTION

Model Number	Body/Style Number	Body Type & Seating	Factory Price	Shipping Weight	Production Total
THUNDERBIRD LX - (V-6)					
62	66D	2d Coupe-4P	$15,797	3,536 lbs.	Note 1
THUNDERBIRD LX - (V-8)					
62	66D	2d Coupe-4P	$16,883	3,673 lbs.	Note 1
THUNDERBIRD SUPER COUPE - (V-6)					
64	66D	2d Coupe-4P	$22,030	3,760 lbs.	Note 1

NOTE 1: Production of the all models combined was 134,111.

body-side moldings, lower body-side cladding, unique rear fascia, sport soft-feel steering wheel, light convenience group with instrument panel courtesy light and engine compartment light, all-cloth articulated sport seats with power lumbar and seatback bolster adjustments, plus four-way adjustable head restraints (up/down/forward/back).

I.D. NUMBERS

VIN stamped on aluminum tab riveted to the dashboard on passenger side and observable through the windshield from outside the car. First symbol 1 denotes built in the United States. Second symbol F denotes Ford. Third symbol A denotes Ford passenger vehicle. Fourth symbol denotes type of restraint system. Fifth symbol P denotes passenger-type vehicle. Sixth symbol 6 denotes Thunderbird. Seventh symbol denotes body type. 2=LX Coupe, 4=Super Coupe. Eighth symbol denotes engine: 4=232-cid (3.8L)/140-hp V-6, R=232-cid (3.6L)/210-hp supercharged V-6, T=302-cid (5.0L)/200 hp V-8. Ninth symbol is the check digit. Tenth symbol P=1993 model year. Eleventh symbol denotes assembly plant: H=Lorain, Ohio. Twelfth through 17th symbols denote sequential production number of specific vehicle starting at 100001. Vehicle certification label located on rear face of driver's door. The top part of the label indicates that the Thunderbird was manufactured by Ford Motor Company. Directly below this is the month and year of manufacture, plus a statement that the car conforms to federal motor vehicle safety standards in effect on the indicated date of manufacture. VIN: The VIN appears two lines above UPC. It matches the first to 11th symbols on VIN tag. Some other codes also appear. TYPE: Appears on left side of label on line above UPC, indicates PASSENGER. UPC: A scannable bar code carries the UPC. EXT. COLOR: This line carries the exterior paint color(s) code. DSO: The District Special Order code now appears above "DSO" to the right of the exterior paint color code. BODY: The body style code appears to the extreme left of the bottom line. The only Thunderbird code for this model-year is: Thunderbird code for this model-year is: LX2=two-door LX Coupe, SC2=two-door Super Coupe. VR: The vinyl roof type/color code is to the right of the body code. No T-Birds had vinyl tops. MLDG: The molding code is to the right of the vinyl roof code. INT. TRIM: The interior trim code is to the right of the molding code. TAPE: The tape treatment code appears to right of the interior trim code. R: The radio code is to the right of the A/C code. S: The sunroof code is to the right of the radio code. AX: The axle code appears to the right of the sunroof code. TR: The transmission code appears to the right of the axle code. (Note: The terms and abbreviations shown in capitals appear on the line above the actual codes.)

ENGINE

THUNDERBIRD BASE V-6: 90-degree. Overhead valve. Cast-iron block and aluminum head. Displacement: 232 cid (3.8 liters). Bore and stroke: 3.80 x 3.40 in. Compression ratio: 9.0:1. Brake hp: 140 at 3800. Torque: 215 lbs.-ft. at 2400. Four main bearings. Hydraulic valve lifters. Induction: Throttle Body Injection. Serial number code: 4.

THUNDERBIRD SUPER COUPE SUPERCHARGED V-6: 90-degree. Overhead valve. Cast-iron block and aluminum head. Displacement: 232 cid (3.8 liters). Bore and stroke: 3.80 x 3.40 in. Compression ratio: 8.3:1. Brake hp: 210 at 4400. Torque: 315 lbs.-ft. at 2500. Four main bearings. Hydraulic valve lifters. Induction: Sequential Electronic Fuel Injection (Supercharged). Serial number code: R.

THUNDERBIRD, THUNDERBIRD LX OPTIONAL V-8: 90-degree. Overhead valve. Cast-iron block and head. Displacement: 302 cid (5.0 liters). Bore and stroke: 4.00 x 3.00 in. Compression ratio: 8.9:1. Brake hp: 200 at 4000 rpm. Torque: 275 lbs.-ft. at 3000 rpm. Five main bearings. Roller cam. Induction: Sequential fuel injection.

CHASSIS

Wheelbase: 113 in. Overall length: 198.7. Overall width: 72.7. Overall height: 52.5 in. Front headroom: 38.1 in. Rear headroom: 37.5 in. Front legroom: 42.5 in. Rear legroom: 35.8 in. Front shoulder room: 59 in. Rear shoulder room: 58.9 in. Trunk capacity: 15.1 cu. ft. Front tread: 61.6 in. Rear tread: 60.2 in. Front suspension: Long spindle SLA type, variable-rate coil springs, tubular gas shocks and stabilizer bar. Rear suspension: Independent, H-arm design with toe control link, variable-rate coil springs, gas shocks and stabilizer bar. Steering: Power rack-and-pinion. Turning circle: 39 ft. Brakes: Power front disc/rear drum on LX, power four-wheel disc with ABS on Super Coupe. Fuel tank capacity: 18 gal. Seating capacity: Five (5). Transmission: four-speed automatic. Wheels: 15 in. Tires: (LX) P205/70R15 black sidewall, (Super Coupe) P225/60ZR16 black sidewall. Fuel economy: Base V-6: 19 mpg city/27 mpg highway; Supercharged V-6: 20 mpg city/27 mpg highway; and V-8: 15 mpg city/23 mpg highway. Weight distribution: 57/43 percent.

OPTIONS

5.0-liter HO V-8 in T-Bird LX only ($1,086). Four-speed overdrive transmission in T-Bird Super Coupe ($595). Power lock group ($311). Moonroof (($776-$876 depending on options teamed with). 6-way power driver's seat ($305). 6-way power passenger seat ($305). CD player, requires premium cassette radio ($491). Electronic premium cassette radio with premium sound system ($305). Ford JBL audio system ($526). Power antenna ($85). Radio-delete credits ($400). Automatic air conditioning for LX and Super Coupe ($162). Anti-lock braking system, includes Traction-Lok axle ($695). Anti-theft system ($245). Autolamp group ($193). Traction-Lok axle for base T-Bird LX ($100). Front license plate bracket (no charge). Cold weather group on LX and Super Coupe ($18-$5-$178-$205 depending on transmission and if car has PEP 157A). Rear window defroster included in PEPs and cold weather group and required in New York state ($170). California emissions ($100). High-altitude emissions (no charge). Front carpeted floor mats ($33). Illuminated entry system in Super Coupe ($82). Electronic instrument cluster in LX ($270). Keyless entry, including illuminated entry system and power lock group in LX ($196), in Super Coupe ($278). Light convenience group with instrument panel courtesy light and engine compartment light, standard in Super Coupe ($46). Dual illuminated visor-vanity mirrors ($100). Speed control and tilt steering ($369). Leather seating surfaces in LX ($515). Leather seating surfaces in Super Coupe, includes fold-down rear seat and requires power seats and locks ($648). Vehicle maintenance monitor ($89). Directional cast-aluminum wheels with up-size P215/70R15 black sidewall tires on T-Bird LX ($221). P225/60ZR16 black sidewall all-season performance tires on Super Coupe ($73 extra). Preferred equipment package 155A ($1,086).

EQUIPMENT INSTALLATION RATES

Five-speed manual transmission (0.8 percent). Four-speed automatic transmission (99.2 percent). Traction control (14.6 percent). Fuel-injected V-6 engine (81.9 percent). Supercharged V-6 engine (3 percent). V-8 engine (15.1 percent). Electronic AM/FM stereo cassette (83 percent). Bose/JBL stereo (2.7 percent). Bose/JBL stereo with CD (2.5 percent). Premium sound (11.8 percent). Power steering (100 percent). Antilock brakes (14.6 percent). Power front disc brakes (85.4 percent). Power seat (100 percent). Power windows (100 percent). Adjustable steering column (100 percent). All tinted glass (100 percent). Manual air conditioning (97.5 percent). Automatic air conditioning (2.5 percent). Power door locks (100 percent). Standard steel-belted radial tires (100 percent). Electric rear window defogger (100 percent). Aluminum styled wheels (99.9 percent). Speed control (100 percent). Power remote-control left-hand rearview mirror (100 percent). Power remote-control right-hand rearview mirror (100 percent). Delay windshield wipers (100 percent). Limited-slip differential (19.4 percent). Sunroof (14.2 percent). (Note: Based on 129,712 units produced in the model year for the U.S. market only.)

HISTORICAL FOOTNOTES

Harold A. Poling was chairman of the board and CEO of Ford Motor Co. Allan D. Gilmour was vice chairman of the corporation. Alexander J. Trotman was president and chief operating officer of the corporation. Louis R. Ross was vice chairman and chief technical officer of the Ford Automotive Group. Ross Roberts was again Ford Division's general manager and Phillip M. Novell remained divisional general sales manager.

Calendar-year output was 125,659 units. A total of 134,111 T-Birds was produced in the model year. This represented 2.24 percent of the industry total. Of these units, all were made in Lorain, Ohio. Calendar-year dealer sales amounted to 122,415.

The five-year-old Thunderbird lineup was restyled for 1994. A new front end featured more prominent air intake ports under the bumpers, and aerodynamics were improved with some new streamlined sheet metal. This car is a Super Coupe model.

1994

Thunderbird

The first major T-Bird styling changes in five years were seen in 1994. The LX and Super Coupe both had more rounded front and rear ends. More pronounced air intake slots characterized the frontal appearance. A T-Bird badge "floated" in the slot between the new Aero-design halogen headlights. Engine cooling air was now taken from under the bumper, rather than through a grille. Integrated flush bumpers enhanced the streamlined appearance. An all-new hood was shorter and the front fenders curved into the hood line to enhance aerodynamics. The doors merged into the roofline and the drip rails were fully concealed. New aero-designed rearview mirrors completed the sleek-looking body package. Fine-tuning the body surface directed airflow to create more down-force to improve handling.

The totally restyled "organic" interior featured an aircraft-inspired look with twin "pods" for driver and front passenger. Analog gauges were standard. The console swept up into the instrument panel and its curved feature line continued smoothly through to the door panel. A large glove box and dual cup holders in the console were new. Easy-twist round knobs controlled many driving functions. Back-lit instrument panel switches, dual air bags and a CPC-free manual air conditioner were standard.

A new Electronic Traction Assist system that linked to the 4-wheel anti-lock brakes was optional. Minor electronic improvements were made to the base V-6 used in LXs, but the big news was Ford's new 4.6-liter Modular V-8 becoming an option. This single-overhead-cam engine developed 205 hp. It came attached to an electronically controlled four-speed automatic transmission that provided "seamless" part-throttle shifts and positive full-throttle gear-shifting. In addition to being more refined than the previous 5.0-liter push rod engine, the new V-8 was also cleaner burning and more fuel efficient. It increased gas mileage by 1 to 2 mpg. The 1994 Super Coupe also had a couple of engine refinements. A new Eaton supercharger with low-drag Teflon-coated rotors was used. In addition to being quieter, it upped output by 10 percent to 230 hp. Torque also

199

LX COUPE BODY COLOR INFORMATION

Color Name	Code	Color Name	Code
Champagne Clearcoat Metallic	DK	Teal Clearcoat Metallic	RD
Electric Red Clearcoat Metallic	EG	Black Clearcoat	UA
Light Evergreen Frost Clearcoat Metallic	FA	Vibrant White	WB
Indigo Clearcoat Metallic	KK	Opal Frost Clearcoat Metallic	WJ
Moonlight Blue Clearcoat Metallic	KM	White Opalescent Clearcoat	PX
Deep Emerald Green Clearcoat Metallic	PA		WR

Clearcoat metallic colors optional at extra cost.

SUPER COUPE BODY COLOR INFORMATION

Color Name	Code	Color Name	Code
Moonlight Blue Clearcoat Metallic	KM	Crimson Clearcoat	WH
Teal Clearcoat Metallic	RD	Opal Frost Clearcoat Metallic	WJ
Black Clearcoat	UA	White Opalescent Clearcoat	WR
Vibrant White	WB		

Clearcoat Metallic colors optional at extra cost.

INTERIOR TRIM INFORMATION

EXTERIOR COLORS	Opal Grey	Portofino Evergreen	Ruby Mocha	Blue	Red
Thunderbird LX					
Champagne (CM)	X	X	X	—	—
Electric Red (CM)	X	—	X	—	X
Lt. Evergreen Frost (CM)	X	X	X	—	—
Indigo (CM)	X	—	—	X	—
Midnight Blue (CM)	X	—	X	X	—
Deep Emerald Green (CM)	X	X	X	—	—
Teal (CM)	X	—	X	—	—
Black (NC)	X	X	X	X	X
Vibrant White (C)	X	X	X	X	X
Opal Frost (CM)	X	X	X	X	X
White Opalescent (NC)	X	X	X	X	X
Super Coupe					
Midnight Blue (C)	X	—	X	X	—
Teal (CM)	X	—	X	X	X
Black (NC)	X	—	X	X	X
Vibrant White (C)	X	—	X	X	X
Crimson (NC)	X	—	X	—	X
Opal Frost (CM)	X	—	X	X	X
White Opalescent (NC)	X	—	X	X	X

Legend: C means conventional paint. CM means clearcoat metallic. NC means non-metallic clearcoat. Lt. means light

THUNDERBIRD PRODUCTION

Model Number	Body/Style Number	Body Type & Seating	Factory Price	Shipping Weight	Production Total
THUNDERBIRD LX - (V-6)					
62	66D	2d Coupe-4P	$16,830	3,570 lbs.	Note 1
THUNDERBIRD LX - (V-8)					
62	66D	2d Coupe-4P	$17,860	3,711 lbs.	Note 1
THUNDERBIRD SUPER COUPE - (V-6)					
64	66D	2d Coupe-4P	$22,240	3,758 lbs.	Note 1

NOTE 1: Production of the all models combined was 123,757.

increased by 5 percent. Also new were an improved camshaft, a cam-over-cable throttle linkage and heftier pistons, rods, and cylinder heads to complement the harder-working motor. A five-speed manual gearbox remained standard fare, but the electronic four-speed automatic overdrive transmission was optional.

STANDARD EQUIPMENT

All standard FoMoCo safety, anti-theft, convenience items

and emissions control equipment, 3.8-liter 140-hp SMPEFI V-6, EEC IV electronic engine controls, automatic overdrive transmission, long-spindle SLA front suspension with variable-rate coil springs, double-acting gas-pressurized shock absorbers and 1.1-inch diameter stabilizer bar, independent H-arm rear suspension with toe control link, variable-rate springs, double-acting gas-pressurized shocks and 1.04-inch diameter stabilizer bar, speed-sensitive variable-assist power steering, power front disc/rear drum brakes, 15 x 6-inch stamped steel wheels, styled road wheel covers, P205/70R15 steel-belted black sidewall all-season radial tires, mini spare tire, long-lasting LED taillights, full-length console with floor-mounted leather-wrapped shifter, dual cup holders, manual air conditioning and tinted glass, power windows, power door lock group (LX only), 130-amp alternator, remote deck lid, remote fuel filler door release, interval windshield wipers, dual electric remote-control mirrors, luxury level door trim with courtesy lights and door bins, 24-oz. cut-pile luxury carpeting, analog performance instrumentation with trip odometer, oil pressure gauge, fuel gauge, temperature gauge and voltmeter, integral fog lamps in front fascia, illuminated entry system, rear seat courtesy lights, luxury cloth bucket seats with 6-way power for driver, rear seat center armrest, leather-wrapped luxury steering wheel, electronic AM/FM ETR stereo search radio with cassette tape player and digital clock, tilt steering wheel, speed control (LX only), dual-note horn, illuminated entry system (LX only), dome, map, luggage compartment, ashtray, driver's side footwell and glove box lights, rear seat courtesy lights, carpeted low liftover luggage compartment, dual supplemental airbags restraint system, 3-point passive restraint system with active front lap belt and three-point active restraints in rear outboard position and center rear lap belt, seat belt reminder chime, black moldings on windshield, side windows and rear window, side window defoggers, soft color-keyed front and rear bumpers, integral fog lamps in front fascia, double-spear-shaped body color body-side protection moldings, aerodynamic halogen headlights and parking lights, dual covered visor mirrors with headliner pocket and styled road wheel covers. **1994 T-Bird Super Coupe major standard equipment (over standard T-Bird LX equipment):** 3.8-liter 210-hp supercharged and intercooled SMPEFI V-6 engine with dual exhaust, five-speed manual overdrive transmission, four-wheel disc brakes with ABS, hand-operated console-mounted parking brake, indicator light and supercharger boost gauge in instrument cluster, automatic ride control suspension in addition to standard suspension, Handling components including 1.10-inch (28 mm) diameter solid front stabilizer bar and 0.90-inch (23 mm) diameter solid rear stabilizer bar, Traction-Lok rear axle, 110-amp heavy-duty alternator, 58-amp maintenance-free battery (72-amp with automatic overdrive), directional cast-aluminum 16 x 7.0-inch wheels with locking lug nuts and P225/60ZR16 black sidewall performance tires, lower body-side cladding, unique rear fascia, sport soft-feel steering wheel, light convenience group with instrument panel courtesy light and engine compartment light, all-cloth articulated sport seats with seatback pockets and power lumbar and seatback bolster adjustments, plus 4-way adjustable head restraints (up/down/forward/back), electronic semi-automatic temperature control, driver's foot rest and adjustable suspension with "firm ride" indicator light.

I.D. NUMBERS

Stamped on aluminum tab riveted to the dashboard on

passenger side and observable through the windshield from outside the car. First symbol 1 denotes built in the United States. Second symbol F denotes Ford. Third symbol A denotes Ford passenger vehicle. Fourth symbol denotes type of restraint system. Fifth symbol P denotes passenger-type vehicle. Sixth symbol 6 denotes Thunderbird. Seventh symbol denotes body type. 2=LX Coupe, 4=Super Coupe. Eighth symbol denotes engine: 4=232-cid (3.8L)/140 hp V-6, R=232-cid (3.6L)/230-hp supercharged V-6, W=281-cid (4.6L) 205-hp V-8. Ninth symbol is the check digit. Tenth symbol Q=1994 model year. Eleventh symbol denotes assembly plant: H=Lorain, Ohio. Twelfth through 17th symbols denote sequential production number of specific vehicle starting at 100001. Vehicle certification label located on rear face of driver's door. The top part of the label indicates that the Thunderbird was manufactured by Ford Motor Company. Directly below this is the month and year of manufacture, plus a statement that the car conforms to federal motor vehicle safety standards in effect on the indicated date of manufacture. VIN: The VIN appears two lines above UPC. It matches the first to 11th symbols on VIN tag. Some other codes also appear. TYPE: Appears on left side of label on line above UPC, indicates PASSENGER. UPC: A scannable bar code carries the UPC. EXT. COLOR: This line carries the exterior paint color(s) code. See table below. DSO: The District Special Order code now appears above "DSO" to the right of the exterior paint color code. BODY: The body style code appears to the extreme left of the bottom line. Thunderbird code for this model-year is:

LX2=two-door LX coupe, SC2=two-door Super Coupe. VR: The vinyl roof type/color code is to the right of the body code. No T-Birds had vinyl tops. MLDG: The molding code is to the right of the vinyl roof code. INT. TRIM: The interior trim code is to the right of the molding code. See table below. TAPE: The tape treatment code appears to right of the interior trim code. R: The radio code is to the right of the A/C code. S: The sunroof code is to the right of the radio code. AX: The axle code appears to the right of the sunroof code. TR: The transmission code appears to the right of the axle code. (Note: The terms and abbreviations shown in capitals appear on the line above the actual codes.)

ENGINE

THUNDERBIRD BASE V-6: 90-degree. Overhead valve . Cast-iron block and aluminum head. Displacement: 232 cid (3.8 liters). Bore and stroke: 3.80 x 3.40 in. Compression ratio: 9.0:1. Brake hp: 140 at 3800. Torque: 215 lbs.-ft. at 2400. Four main bearings. Hydraulic valve lifters. Induction: Throttle Body Injection. Serial number code: 4.

THUNDERBIRD SUPER COUPE SUPERCHARGED V-6: 90-degree. Overhead valve. Cast-iron block and aluminum head. Displacement: 232 cid (3.8 liters). Bore and stroke: 3.80 x 3.40 in. Compression ratio: 8.3:1. Brake hp: 210 at 4400. Torque: 315 lbs.-ft. at 2500. Four main bearings. Hydraulic valve lifters. Induction: Sequential Electronic Fuel Injection (Supercharged). Serial number code: R.

(Ford photo)

The Super Coupe again featured the supercharged V-6 and checked in at $22,240 for a base model. LX models with either a V-6 or V-8 were also offered.

THUNDERBIRD, THUNDERBIRD LX OPTIONAL V-8: Modular, overhead cam V-8. Single overhead cam. Displacement: 281 cid (4.6 liters). Bore and stroke: 3.60 x 3.60. Compression ratio: 9.0:1. Brake hp: 205 at 4500 rpm. Torque: 265 lbs.-ft. at 3200 rpm. Hydraulic valve lifters. Induction: Sequential fuel injection.

CHASSIS

Wheelbase: 113 in. Overall length: 200.3. Overall width: 72.7. Overall height: 52.5 in. Front headroom: 38.1 in. Rear headroom: 37.5 in. Front legroom: 42.5 in. Rear legroom: 35.8 in. Front shoulder room: 59 in. Rear shoulder room: 58.9 in. Trunk capacity: 15.1 cu. ft. Front tread: 61.6 in. Rear tread: 60.2 in. Front suspension: Long spindle SLA type, variable-rate coil springs, tubular gas shocks and stabilizer bar. Rear suspension Independent, H-arm design with toe control link, variable-rate coil springs, gas shocks and stabilizer bar. Steering: Power rack-and-pinion. Turning circle: 39 ft. Brakes: Power front disc/rear drum on LX, Power four-wheel disc with ABS on Super Coupe. Fuel tank capacity: 18 gal. Seating capacity: Five (5). Fuel Economy: 17-24 mpg. Transmission: Four-speed automatic. Wheels: 15 in. Tires: (LX) P205/70R15 black sidewall, (Super Coupe) P225/60ZR16 black sidewall. Fuel economy: Base V-6: 19 mpg city/27 mpg highway; Supercharged V-6: 20 mpg city/27 mpg highway; and V-8: 15 mpg city/23 mpg highway. Weight distribution: 57/43 percent.

OPTIONS

4.6-liter V-8 ($515 net). Four-speed overdrive transmission in T-Bird Super Coupe ($790). California emissions ($85). High-altitude emissions (no charge). P225/60ZR16 black sidewall all-season performance tires on Super Coupe ($70 extra). Leather seating surfaces in LX ($490). Leather seating surfaces in Super Coupe, includes fold-down rear seat and requires power seats and locks ($615). Anti-lock braking system, includes Traction-Lok axle ($565). Anti-theft system ($245). Cold weather group on LX and Super Coupe, including engine block heater, 72-amp battery, rear window defroster and 3.27:1 Traction-Lok rear axle ($18-$20-$300, depending on transmission and if car has PEPs 155A or 157A). Front floor mats ($30). Keyless entry, including illuminated entry system and power lock group in LX or Super Coupe with luxury group ($215), in Super Coupe ($295). Power moonroof ($740). Hands-free cellular telephone ($530). Traction assist in LX only ($210). Tri-coat paint ($225). Electronic premium cassette radio with premium sound system and power antenna ($370). Ford JBL audio system ($500). Trunk mounted compact disc changer ($785). Group 2 (RPO 411) includes: lock group, power group, speed control and 6-way power driver's seat for Super Coupe only ($800). Group 2 (RPO 432) includes semi-automatic temperature control and rear window defroster ($160 for Super Coupe and $315 for LX). Group 3 includes: cast-aluminum wheels, P215/70RX15 tires for LX only, plus dual illuminated vanity mirrors ($95 for Super Coupe or $305 for LX). Luxury group includes: Autolamp on and off delay, illuminated entry system for Super Coupe only, light group for LX only, 6-way power passenger seat and Integrated warning lamp module for LX only ($580 for LX and $555 for Super Coupe). Preferred equipment package 155A for LX ($620, but no charge with applicable Group 2 discounts). Preferred equipment package 157A for Super Coupe ($1,055, but no charge with applicable Group 2 discounts).

EQUIPMENT INSTALLATION RATES

Five-speed manual transmission (0.6 percent). Four-speed automatic transmission (99.4 percent). Traction control (29.3 percent). Fuel-injected V-6 engine (42.4 percent). Supercharged V-6 engine (2.2 percent). V-8 engine (55.4 percent). Electronic AM/FM stereo cassette (97.1 percent). Bose/JBL stereo (1.3 percent). Bose/JBL stereo with CD (1.6 percent). Mobile phone (0.6 percent). Power steering (100 percent). Antilock brakes (27 percent). Power front disc brakes (73 percent). Dual airbags (100 percent). Power seat (100 percent). Power windows (100 percent). Adjustable steering column (100 percent). All tinted glass (100 percent). Manual air conditioning (97.7 percent). Automatic air conditioning (2.3 percent). Power door locks (100 percent). Standard steel-belted radial tires (100 percent). Electric rear window defogger (100 percent). Aluminum styled wheels (100 percent). Speed control (100 percent). Power remote-control left-hand rearview mirror (100 percent). Power remote-control right-hand rearview mirror (100 percent). Delay windshield wipers (100 percent). Limited-slip differential (5 percent). Sunroof (21.7 percent). (Note: Based on 120,320 units produced in the model year for the U.S. market only.)

HISTORICAL FOOTNOTES

Alexander J. Trotman was chairman of the board and CEO of Ford Motor Co. Allan D. Gilmour was vice chairman of the corporation. Louis R. Ross was vice chairman and chief technical officer of the Ford Automotive Group. Ross Roberts was again Ford Division's general manager and Phillip M. Novell remained divisional general sales manager.

Calendar-year output was 146,846 units. A total of 123,757 T-Birds was produced in the model year. This represented 2.05 percent of the industry total. Of these units, all were made in Lorain, Ohio. Calendar-year dealer sales amounted to 130,713.

Motor Trend road tested the V-8-optioned LX. It moved from 0 to 60 mph in 8.5 seconds and did the quarter-mile in 16.4 seconds at 87.6 mph. It braked from 60 to 0 mph in 139 feet.

In stock car racing, T-Birds had a super year in 1993, led by Rusty Wallace in his number 2 Miller Genuine Draft Ford. Wallace took 10 victories. Geoff Bodine (three wins) and Mark Martin and Jimmy Spencer (two wins each) also put in strong performances all year long. Bill Elliott and Ricky Rudd both had a win apiece. In 31 contests, Fords sat on the pole 25 times and won 20 checkered flags. They also established 17 new track records. However, it became a clear case of winning the battles and losing the war, as Chevy pilot Dale Earnhardt nailed his seventh Winston Cup points championship with his consistent high-place finishes. One thing that hurt the blue oval effort was Ernie Irvan's wreck of his Texaco T-Bird. The car was a hot contender, with three victories during the first half of '94, but the wreck put Irvan out for the season and longer. Ford did capture NASCAR's Manufacturer's Cup.

By 1995, horsepower for the Super Coupe had grown to 230, about 35 hp better than the original 'Bird.

1995

Thunderbird

The 1995 T-Birds had few changes from the 1994 models. The LX and the Super Coupe returned. Both models had modest weight changes. The LX continued to utilize the 3.8-liter/140-hp V-6 as its standard power plant, with the Modular V-8 as an option. The Super Coupe included a 230-hp supercharged version of the V-6, plus a standard five-speed manual transmission and anti-lock brakes. Dual air bags are standard in both models and a Traction Control system was optional with both. Conventional power steering was standard in the LX. Variable-assist steering was standard in LXs with the optional V-8 and in Super Coupes. An anti-theft alarm, an engine block heater, a Traction-Lok axle and a heavy-duty battery were no longer offered.

STANDARD EQUIPMENT

Front and rear soft color-keyed 5-mph bumpers, flush windshield, door quarter window and backlight glass, aerodynamic halogen headlights and parking lamps, dual color-keyed remote-control electric mirrors, black windshield, window, door quarter window and backlight moldings, body-color double-spear-shaped body-side protection moldings, Bolfon design road wheel styled wheel covers, air bag supplemental restraint system, three-point safety belts with active-restraints in all outboard positions and center rear belt and reminder chime, foot-operated parking brake, 24-oz. cut-pile carpeting, full-length console with floor-mounted leather-wrapped gear shift handle and storage compartment, dual console-mounted cup holders, luxury level door trim with courtesy lights and illuminated switches, front floor mats, driver's side footwell lights, illuminated entry system, map/dome, luggage compartment, front ashtray, glove box and rear seat courtesy lights, low lift-over design carpeted luggage compartment, dual visor mirrors, luxury cloth bucket seats with 6-way power driver's seat, luxury leather-wrapped tilt steering wheel, manual air conditioner with rotary controls, 130-amp alternator, 58-amp maintenance-free battery, power front disc/rear drum brakes, digital clock, EEC-IV electronic engine controls system, 3.8-liter SMPEFI V-6 engine, 18-gallon fuel tank, tethered gas filler cap, complete tinted glass and dual note horn. **1995 T-Bird Super Coupe Major Standard Equipment (over standard T-Bird LX equipment):** Unique rear bumper treatment, lower body-side cladding, integral fog lamps in front fascia, 16 x 7-in. directional cast-aluminum wheels with locking lug nuts, console-mounted hand-operated parking brake with leather-wrapped handle, driver's foot rest, integrated warning lamp module, light group including right-hand panel courtesy light and engine compartment light, articulated bucket seats in cloth/leather/vinyl trim with power adjustable lumbar support and seatback bolsters, rear seat headrests, electronic air conditioner with semi-automatic temperature

LX COUPE BODY COLOR INFORMATION

Color Name	Code	Color Name	Code
Champagne Clearcoat Metallic	DK	Chameleon Clearcoat Metallic	TA
Electric Red Clearcoat Metallic	EG	Black Clearcoat	UA
Light Evergreen Frost Clearcoat Metallic	FA	Vibrant White	WT
Rose Mist Clearcoat Metallic	GK	Silver Frost Clearcoat Metallic	TS
Moonlight Blue Clearcoat Metallic	KM	White Opalescent Clearcoat	WR
Deep Emerald Green Clearcoat Metallic	PA	Silver Blue Mist Clearcoat	ZU

SUPER COUPE BODY COLOR INFORMATION

Color Name	Code	Color Name	Code
Electric Red Clearcoat Metallic	EG	Black Clearcoat	UA
Moonlight Blue Clearcoat Metallic	KM	White Opalescent Clearcoat	WR
Chameleon Clearcoat Metallic	TA	Silver Blue Mist Clearcoat	ZU

THUNDERBIRD THUNDERBIRD

Model Number	Body/Style Number	Body Type & Seating	Factory Price	Shipping Weight	Production Total
THUNDERBIRD LX - (V-6)					
62	66D	2d Coupe-4P	$17,225	3,536 lbs.	Note 1
THUNDERBIRD LX - (V-8)					
62	66D	2d Coupe-4P	$18,355	3,673 lbs.	Note 1
THUNDERBIRD SUPER COUPE - (V-6)					
64	66D	2d Coupe-4P	$22,735	3,758 lbs.	Note 1

NOTE 1: Production of the all models combined was 116,069.

control, 110-amp alternator, Traction-Lok rear axle, 58-amp (72-amp with automatic overdrive) maintenance-free battery, antilock braking system with four-wheel disc brakes, 3.8-liter SMPEFI supercharged and intercooled V-6 with dual exhausts and speed control deletion.

I.D. NUMBERS

VIN Stamped on aluminum tab riveted to the dashboard on passenger side and observable through the windshield from outside the car. First symbol 1 denotes built in the United States. Second symbol F denotes Ford. Third symbol A denotes Ford passenger vehicle. Fourth symbol denotes type of restraint system. Fifth symbol P denotes passenger-type vehicle. Sixth symbol 6 denotes Thunderbird. Seventh symbol denotes body type. 2=LX Coupe, 4=Super Coupe. Eighth symbol denotes engine: 4=232-cid (3.8L)/140 hp V-6, R=232-cid (3.6L)/230-hp supercharged V-6, W=281-cid (4.6L) 205 hp V-8. Ninth symbol is the check digit. Tenth symbol R=1995 model year. 11th symbol denotes assembly plant: H=Lorain, Ohio. Twelfth through 17th symbols denote sequential production number of specific vehicle starting at 100001. Vehicle certification label located on rear face of driver's door. The top part of the label indicates that the Thunderbird was manufactured by Ford Motor Company. Directly below this is the month and year of manufacture, plus a statement that the car conforms to federal motor vehicle safety standards in effect on the indicated date of manufacture. VIN: The VIN appears two lines above UPC. It matches the first to 11th symbols on VIN tag. Some other codes also appear. TYPE: Appears on left side of label on line above UPC, indicates PASSENGER. UPC: A scannable bar code carries the UPC. EXT. COLOR: This line carries the exterior paint color(s) code. DSO: The District Special Order code now appears above "DSO" to the right of the exterior paint color code. BODY: The body style code appears to the extreme left of the bottom line. The only Thunderbird code for this model-year is: Thunderbird code for this model year is: LX2=two-door LX

Ford photo

It was a stretch to say that the 1995 Thunderbird resembled its 40-year-old relative, the 1955 T-Bird. For starters, the 1995 model was more than 700 lbs. heavier.

Mike Mueller photo

Thunderbird buyers could get their 'Birds with a standard V-6, an optional V-8, or a supercharged 230-hp V-6 in the Super Coupe (above).

Coupe, SC2=two-door Super Coupe. VR: The vinyl roof type/color code is to the right of the body code. No T-Birds had vinyl tops. MLDG: The molding code is to the right of the vinyl roof code. INT. TRIM: The interior trim code is to the right of the molding code. TAPE: The tape treatment code appears to right of the interior trim code. R: The radio code is to the right of the A/C code. S: The sunroof code is to the right of the radio code. AX: The axle code appears to the right of the sunroof code. TR: The transmission code appears to the right of the axle code. (Note: The terms and abbreviations shown in capitals appear on the line above the actual codes.)

ENGINE

THUNDERBIRD BASE V-6: 90-degree. Overhead valve. Cast-iron block and aluminum head. Displacement: 232 cid (3.8 liters). Bore and stroke: 3.80 x 3.40 in. Compression ratio: 9.0:1. Brake hp: 140 at 3800. Torque: 215 lbs.-ft. at 2400. Four main bearings. Hydraulic valve lifters. Induction: Throttle Body Injection. Serial number code: 4.

THUNDERBIRD SUPER COUPE SUPERCHARGED V-6: 90-degree. Overhead valve. Cast-iron block and aluminum head. Displacement: 232 cid (3.8 liters). Bore and stroke: 3.80 x 3.40 in. Compression ratio: 8.3:1. Brake hp: 230 at 4400. Torque: 330 lbs.-ft. at 2500. Four main bearings. Hydraulic valve lifters. Induction: Sequential Electronic Fuel Injection (Supercharged). Serial number code: R.

THUNDERBIRD, THUNDERBIRD LX OPTIONAL V-8: Modular. Overhead cam. Single overhead cam. Displacement: 281 cid (4.6 liters). Bore and stroke: 3.60 x 3.60. Compression ratio: 9.0:1. Brake hp: 205 at 4500 rpm. Torque: 265 lbs.-ft. at 3200 rpm. Hydraulic valve lifters. Induction: Sequential fuel injection.

CHASSIS

Wheelbase: 113 in. Overall length: 200.3. Overall width: 72.7. Overall height: 52.5 in. Front headroom: 38.1 in. Rear headroom: 37.5 in. Front legroom: 42.5 in. Rear legroom: 35.8 in. Front shoulder room: 59.1 in. Rear shoulder room: 58.9 in. Trunk capacity: 15.1 cu. ft. Front tread: 61.6 in. Rear tread: 60.2 in. Front suspension: Long spindle SLA type, variable-rate coil springs, tubular gas shocks and stabilizer bar. Rear suspension Independent, H-arm design with toe control link, variable-rate coil springs, gas shocks and stabilizer bar. Steering: Power rack-and-pinion. Turning circle: 39 ft. Brakes: Power front disc/rear drum on LX, Power four-wheel disc with ABS on Super Coupe. Fuel tank capacity: 18 gal. Seating capacity: Five. Transmission: four-speed automatic. Wheels: 15 in. Tires: (LX) P205/70R15 black sidewall, (Super Coupe) P225/60ZR16 black sidewall. Fuel Economy: Base V-6: 19 mpg city/27 mpg highway; Supercharged V-6: 20 mpg city/27 mpg highway; and V-8: 15 mpg city/23 mpg highway. Weight distribution: 57/43 percent.

OPTIONS

4.6-liter V-8, including heavy-duty battery and speed-sensitive power steering for LX only ($615 net). Four-speed overdrive transmission in T-Bird Super Coupe ($790).

California emissions ($95). High-altitude emissions (no charge). P225/60ZR16 black sidewall all-season performance tires on Super Coupe ($70 extra). Leather seating surfaces in LX ($490). Leather seating surfaces in Super Coupe, includes fold-down rear seat and requires power seats and locks ($615). Option Group 1 includes: power lock group, speed control, and 6-way power driver's seat for Super Coupe ($800). Option Group 2 includes: rear window defroster for both models and semi-automatic temperature control for LX ($160 for Super Coupe and $315 for LX). Option Group 3 includes: cast-aluminum wheels and P21570R15 black sidewall tires ($210). Anti-lock braking system, includes Traction-Lok axle ($565). Traction-Lok rear axle (standard on Super Coupe with five-speed, otherwise $95). Front license plate bracket (no charge). Front floor mats ($30). Remote keyless entry, including illuminated entry system two remotes LX or Super Coupe with luxury group ($215), in Super Coupe ($295). Luxury group includes Autolamp on and off delay,

power antenna, illuminated entry system for Super Coupe only, light group for LX only and dual illuminated visor mirrors and integrated warning lamp module for LX only ($350 for LX and $325 for Super Coupe). Power-operated moonroof, requires luxury group and PEP 155A or PEP 157A ($740). 6-way power passenger seat, requires Option Group 1 ($290). Hands free cellular telephone ($530). Traction-Assist, requires ABS and luxury group and not available for Super Coupe with 5-speed (standard for Super Coupe with automatic transmission, otherwise $210). Tri-Coat paint ($225). AM/FM stereo ETR with cassette and premium sound system ($290). AM/FM stereo ETR with compact disc player and premium sound system ($430). Heavy-duty 72-amp battery ($25). Engine block heater ($20). 155A for LX ($620, but no charge with applicable Group 2 discounts). Preferred equipment package 157A for Super Coupe ($1,055, but no charge with applicable Group 2 discounts).

The trademark round headlights, bumper "bullets," hood scoop, and chrome grille of the 1955 Thunderbird were nowhere to be found on the 1995 model.

Mike Mueller photo

EQUIPMENT INSTALLATION RATES

Five-speed manual transmission (0.5 percent). Four-speed automatic transmission (99.5 percent). Traction control (21.6 percent). Fuel-injected V-6 engine (17 percent). Supercharged V-6 engine (0.5 percent). V-8 engine (82.5 percent). Electronic AM/FM stereo cassette (76.2 percent). Premium sound system (16 percent). Other CD changer (7.8 percent). Mobile phone (0.6 percent). Keyless remote entry (35.1 percent). Power steering (100 percent). Leather seats (21.8 percent). Antilock brakes (39.7 percent). Power front disc brakes (60.3 percent). Dual airbags (100 percent). Power seat (97 percent). Power windows (100 percent). Adjustable steering column (100 percent). All tinted glass (100 percent). Manual air conditioning (95 percent). Automatic air conditioning (5 percent). Power door locks (100 percent). Standard steel-belted radial tires (100 percent). Electric rear window defogger (100 percent). Aluminum styled wheels (100 percent). Speed control (100 percent). Power remote-control left-hand rearview mirror (100 percent). Power remote-control right-hand rearview mirror (100 percent). Delay windshield wipers (100 percent). Limited-slip differential (5.0 percent). Sunroof (21.2 percent). (Note: Based on 114,823 units produced in the model year for the U.S. market only.)

HISTORICAL FOOTNOTES

Alexander J. Trotman was chairman of the board and CEO of Ford Motor Co. Louis R. Ross was vice chairman and chief technical officer. Ross Roberts was again Ford Division's general manager and Phillip M. Novell remained divisional general sales manager.

Calendar-year output was 94,027 units. A total of 116,069 T-Birds was produced in the model year. This represented 1.72 percent of the industry total. Of these units, all were made in Lorain, Ohio. Calendar-year dealer sales amounted to 104,254.

After capturing its second NASCAR Manufacturer's Cup in a row, Ford entered 1995 with a dramatic television ad promoting its latest stock cars as the most ominous thing to come from "bird-dom" since Alfred Hitchcock's classic thriller film "The Birds." It was a fitting throwback to the era in which the first T-Birds was created and a reminder to many of the marque's continuing vitality on its 40th birthday. As the '95 Ford sales catalog asked, "How many cars on the road today can you identify at a glance, whose badges elicit instant recognition and admiration? There certainly aren't many, but one should readily come to mind. It's the familiar Thunderbird wide wingspan."

The 1995 Thunderbird LX in Champagne Clearcoat Metallic (top) and Thunderbird Super Coupe in Silver Blue Mist Clearcoat Metallic.

Ford photo

The LX was the lone remaining Thunderbird model in 1996. It could be had in either V-6 or V-8 versions.

1996 *Thunderbird*

With the discontinuation of the Super Coupe for 1996, T-Bird was reduced to a one-model series. Remaining was the LX coupe. It didn't take a genius to read the writing on the wall. Ford was taking at hard look at the future of the T-Bird in a changing marketplace.

The T-Bird received a mild facelift for the 1996 model year, but remained one of Ford's best chassis. The T-Bird handled well when leaned on for a big (16.7-feet.-long) car. It was larger than the Contour four-door sedan. The 1996 LX received a mild restyling in the hood, grille, headlight and bumper cover areas. Wide body cladding and now door handles were color-keyed to match the exterior paint for what Ford called "a sporty, monochromatic look." The standard 3.8-liter V-6 was upgraded and was now rated at 145 hp. Optional at no cost was a package consisting of rear window defroster, P215/70R15 tires and cast aluminum wheels. An anti-theft system and traction control system returned to the optional equipment list after not being offered the year previous. A four-speed automatic overdrive transmission was standard.

STANDARD EQUIPMENT

Dual front air bags, manual air conditioning, 130-amp alternator, rear seat center armrest, 58-amp maintenance-free battery, power front disc/rear drum brakes, soft, color-keyed front and rear bumpers, 18-oz. cut-pile carpeting, lower body-side cladding with integral body-color body-side molding, digital clock, full-length console with floor-mounted shift, storage and dual cupholders, power remote deck lid release, power door locks with illuminated switches, luxury level door trim with courtesy lights, stowage bins and illuminated door switches, 145-hp, 3.8-liter SMPEFI V-6 engine, EEC-IV electronic engine control system, 18-gallon fuel tank with tethered cap, solar-tinted glass, aerodynamic halogen complex-reflector head- and parking lamps, rear seat heating ducts, analog instrument cluster with speedometer, trip odometer, voltmeter, oil pressure gauge, fuel gauge and temperature gauge, interior lights—dome/map, luggage compartment, ashtray, driver's side foot well, glove box and engine compartment, low lift-over carpeted luggage compartment, dual electric remote-controlled color-keyed mirrors, black moldings on windshield, backlight, door and quarter windows, foot-operated parking brake, three-point seat belts with front and rear outboard positions, center lap belt and reminder chime, rear-wheel drive, luxury cloth bucket seats, leather shift knob, mini spare tire, speed control, AM/FM/stereo/cassette ETR sound system with four speakers, power steering, tilt steering wheel, long-spindle SLA front suspension with stabilizer bar, variable rate

BODY COLOR INFORMATION

Color Name	Code	Color Name	Code
Light Saddle Clearcoat Metallic	DZ	Silver Frost Clearcoat Metallic	TS
Bright Red Clearcoat	E4	Black Clearcoat	UA
Laser Red Tinted Clearcoat	E9	White Opalescent Clearcoat*	WR
Moonlight Blue Clearcoat Metallic	KM	Vibrant White Clearcoat`	WT
Pacific Green Clearcoat Metallic	PS	Silver Blue Mist Clearcoat Metallic	ZU
Alpine Green Clearcoat Metallic	SR		

*Extra cost tri-coat paint.

THUNDERBIRD PRODUCTION

Model Number	Body/Style Number	Body Type & Seating	Factory Price	Shipping Weight	Production Total
THUNDERBIRD LX - (V-6)					
62	66D	2d Coupe-4P	$17,485	3,561 lbs.	Note 1
THUNDERBIRD LX - (V-8)					
62	66D	2d Coupe-4P	$18,615	3,689 lbs.	Note 1

NOTE 1: Production of the all models combined was 82,010.

springs, lower control arm and tension strut, independent H-arm rear suspension with variable rate springs and stabilizer bar, full-width taillights, P205/70R15 black sidewall all-season radial tires, four-speed ECT automatic transmission with overdrive and overdrive lockout, styled road wheel covers, power windows with illuminated switches, and variable interval windshield wipers.

I.D. NUMBERS

VIN stamped on aluminum tab riveted to the dashboard on passenger side and observable through the windshield from outside the car. First symbol 1 denotes built in the United States. Second symbol F denotes Ford. Third symbol A denotes Ford passenger vehicle. Fourth symbol denotes type of restraint system. Fifth symbol P denotes passenger-type vehicle. Sixth symbol 6 denotes Thunderbird. Seventh symbol denotes body type. 2=LX coupe. Eighth symbol denotes engine: 4=232-cid (3.8L)/145-hp V-6, W=281-cid (4.6L)/205-hp V-8. Ninth symbol is the check digit. Tenth symbol T=1996 model year. Eleventh symbol denotes assembly plant: H=Lorain, Ohio. Twelfth through 17th symbols denote sequential production number of specific vehicle starting at 100001. Vehicle certification label located on rear face of driver's door. The top part of the label indicates that the Thunderbird was manufactured by Ford Motor Company. Directly below this is the month and year of manufacture, plus a statement that the car conforms to federal motor vehicle safety standards in effect on the indicated date of manufacture. VIN: The VIN appears two lines above UPC. It matches the first to 11th symbols on VIN tag. Some other codes also appear. TYPE: Appears on left side of label on line above UPC, indicates PASSENGER. UPC: A scannable bar code carries the UPC. EXT. COLOR: This line carries the exterior paint color(s) code. DSO: The

All T-Birds came with a four-speed automatic for 1996. Sales were almost equally split between the V-6 and the V-8, with the V-8 only slightly more popular.

Ford photo

District Special Order code now appears above "DSO" to the right of the exterior paint color code. BODY: The body style code appears to the extreme left of the bottom line. The only Thunderbird code for this model-year is: Thunderbird code for this model-year is: LX2=2-door LX coupe. VR: The vinyl roof type/color code is to the right of the body code. No T-Birds had vinyl tops. MLDG: The molding code is to the right of the vinyl roof code. INT. TRIM: The interior trim code is to the right of the molding code. TAPE: The tape treatment code appears to right of the interior trim code. R: The radio code is to the right of the A/C code. S: The sunroof code is to the right of the radio code. AX: The axle code appears to the right of the sunroof code. TR: The transmission code appears to the right of the axle code. Note: The terms and abbreviations shown in capitals appear on the line above the actual codes.

ENGINE

THUNDERBIRD BASE V-6: 90-degree. Overhead valve. Cast-iron block and aluminum head. Displacement: 232 cid (3.8 liters). Bore and stroke: 3.80 x 3.40 in. Compression ratio: 9.0:1. Brake hp: 140 at 3800. Torque: 215 lbs.-ft. at 2400. Four main bearings. Hydraulic valve lifters. Induction: Throttle Body Injection. Serial number code: 4.

THUNDERBIRD, THUNDERBIRD LX OPTIONAL V-8: Modular. Single overhead cam. Displacement: 281 cid (4.6 liters). Bore and stroke: 3.60 x 3.60. Compression ratio: 9.0:1. Brake hp: 205 at 4500 rpm. Torque: 265 lbs.-ft. at 3200 rpm. Hydraulic valve lifters. Induction: Sequential fuel injection.

CHASSIS

Wheelbase: 113 in. Overall length: 200.3. Overall width: 72.7. Overall height: 52.5 in. Front headroom: 38.1 in. Rear headroom: 37.5 in. Front legroom: 42.5 in. Rear legroom: 35.8 in. Front shoulder room: 59.1 in. Rear shoulder room: 58.9 in. Trunk capacity: 15.1 cu. ft. Front tread: 61.6 in. Rear tread: 60.2 in. Front suspension: Long spindle SLA type, variable-rate coil springs, tubular gas shocks and stabilizer bar. Rear suspension Independent, H-arm design with toe control link, variable-rate coil springs, gas shocks and stabilizer bar. Steering: Power rack-and-pinion. Turning circle: 39 ft. Brakes: Power front disc/rear drum on LX, Power four-wheel disc with ABS on Super Coupe. Fuel tank capacity: 18 gal. Seating capacity: Five (5). Transmission: four-speed automatic. Wheels: 15 in. Tires: (LX) P205/70R15 black sidewall. Fuel tank: 18 gal. Fuel Economy: (Base V-6) 19 mpg city/27 mpg highway, (V-8) 15 mpg city/23 mpg highway. Weight distribution: 57/43 percent.

OPTIONS

Preferred Equipment Packages: (155A) rear window defroster, P215/70R15 tires and cast-aluminum wheels (NC). (157A) 4.6-liter SOHC V-8, including: speed-sensitive power steering, heavy-duty battery, 6-way power driver's seat, illuminated entry system and leather-wrapped steering wheel ($835 net). California emissions system ($100).

Leather-faced bucket seats ($490). Remote keyless entry ($270). Front floor mats ($30). Electronic AM/FM stereo radio with cassette and premium sound ($290). Electronic AM/FM stereo radio with CD player and premium sound ($430). Anti-lock brakes ($570). Anti-theft system ($145). Power moonroof ($740). Sport Option, includes: 16-inch aluminum wheels, P225/65R16 BSW tires, modified stabilizer bars and revised spring rates ($210). Tri-coat paint ($225). Traction assist ($210). Traction-Lok axle ($95). Power driver's seat ($290). Luxury Group, includes: electronic semi-automatic temperature control air conditioning, dual illuminated visor mirrors, light group, integrated warning lamp module and power antenna ($495). 15-inch chrome wheels ($580).

EQUIPMENT INSTALLATION RATES

Four-speed automatic transmission (100 percent). Traction control (19.7 percent). Fuel-injected V-6 engine (49.2 percent). V-8 engine (50.8 percent). Electronic AM/FM stereo cassette (63.2 percent). Premium sound system (24.8 percent). Other CD changer (12 percent). Keyless remote entry (39.4 percent). Power steering (100 percent). Leather seats (22.2 percent). Antilock brakes (34.6 percent). Power front disc brakes (65.4 percent). Dual airbags (100 percent). Power seat (72.8 percent). Power windows (100 percent). Adjustable steering column (100 percent). All tinted glass (100 percent). Manual air conditioning (57.3 percent). Automatic air conditioning (42.7 percent). Power door locks (100 percent). Standard steel-belted radial tires (100 percent). Electric rear window defogger (100 percent). Aluminum styled wheels (100 percent). Speed control (100 percent). Power remote-control left-hand rearview mirror (100 percent). Power remote-control right-hand rearview mirror (100 percent). Delay windshield wipers (100 percent). Limited-slip differential (14.8 percent). Sunroof (21.9 percent). (Note: Based on 85,029 units produced in the model year for the U.S. market only.)

HISTORICAL FOOTNOTES

Alexander J. Trotman was chairman of the board and CEO of Ford Motor Co. Ross Roberts was again Ford Division's general manager and Phillip M. Novell remained divisional general sales manager.

Calendar-year output was 77,094 units. A total of 82,010 T-Birds was produced in the model year. This represented 1.60 percent of the industry total. Of these units, all were made in Lorain, Ohio. Calendar-year dealer sales amounted to 79,721. Ford Motor Company's board of directors asked Alex Trotman to stay on as chairman of the board for a year and a half past his 60th birthday, but Jacques A. Nasser, a native of Lebanon raised in Australia, emerged in 1995 as Trotman's successor. Nasser was promoted to the position of president of Ford Automotive Operations in October 1996. Nasser immediately initiated a product review that concluded that the Thunderbird should be dropped from the model lineup. This was done following the 1997 model year.

A total of 79,180 Thunderbirds were were produced for 1997 before the model was discontinued. The T-Bird was again available only in LX form with either a standard V-6 or an optional V-8.

1997

Thunderbird

The 1997 T-Bird came only in LX coupe format. Under the hood buyers could order the standard 3.8-liter/145-bhp V-6 or the extra-cost 4.6-liter 205-hp V-8. Aggressive and sporty, the T-Bird offered a new Sport package with 16-inch wheels and an upgraded suspension. The standard 4R70W four-speed electronically controlled automatic overdrive transmission was upgraded for better quality and corrosion protection. A new instrument cluster prominently arranged key functions in three separate displays and a new console provided easy-access dual cup holders, a larger ashtray and a coin holder.

The 4.6-liter SOHC V-8 was again part of an option package—this time priced at $840—that also included speed-sensitive power steering, battery upgrade, six-way power driver's seat, illuminated entry system, and leather-wrapped steering wheel. Optional at no cost was a package consisting of rear window defroster, P215/70RX5 tires, and cast aluminum wheels. An anti-theft system and traction control returned as optional equipment. Also offered were leather-faced seats, chrome-plated wheels, power-operated moonroof, and rear deck lid spoiler.

Drivers of a more adventurous bent could opt for the Sport package, which consisted of 16-inch, nine-spoke aluminum wheels wearing P225/60R16 touring tires, a larger rear stabilizer bar, larger front disc brake rotors,

revised spring rates, revised front lower arm bushings, revised shock absorber valving, and the rear deck lid spoiler with integral stop lamp. The four-speed automatic overdrive transmission was standard. In addition to the new Sport package, other options geared to T-Bird's free-sprited buyers included a power sliding moonroof with a one-touch open feature and 15-inch, seven-spoke chrome aluminum wheels. A decklid spoiler with integrated stoplight became available in late 1996.

Three new exterior color selections included Light Prairie Tan, Light Denim Blue, and Arctic Green. Prairie Tan was also a new interior color.

STANDARD EQUIPMENT

Dual front air bags, manual air conditioning, 130-amp alternator, rear seat center armrest, 58-amp maintenance-free battery, power four-wheel-disc brakes, soft color-keyed front and rear bumpers, 18-oz. cut-pile carpeting, lower body-side cladding with integral body-color body-side molding, digital clock, full-length console with floor-mounted shift, storage and dual cupholders, power remote deck lid release, power door locks with illuminated switches, luxury level door trim with courtesy lights, stowage bins and illuminated door switches, side window

BODY COLOR INFORMATION

Color Name	Code	Color Name	Code
Light Prairie Tan Clearcoat Metallic	BA	Alpine Green Clearcoat Metallic	SR
Arctic Green Clearcoat Metallic	D8	Silver Frost Clearcoat Metallic	TS
Laser Red Tinted Clearcoat	E9	Black Clearcoat	UA
Light Denim Blue Clearcoat Metallic	K1	White Opalescent Clearcoat*	WR
Moonlight Blue Clearcoat Metallic	KM	Vibrant White Clearcoat	WT
Pacific Green Clearcoat Metallic	PS		

*Extra cost tri-coat paint.

THUNDERBIRD PRODUCTION

Model Number	Body/Style Number	Body Type & Seating	Factory Price	Shipping Weight	Production Total
THUNDERBIRD LX - (V-6)					
62	66D	2d Coupe-4P	$17,885	3,561 lbs.	Note 1
THUNDERBIRD LX - (V-8)					
62	66D	2d Coupe-4P	$19,015	3,644 lbs.	Note 1

NOTE 1: Production of the all models combined was 79,180.

speedometer, trip odometer, tachometer, fuel gauge, temperature gauge and indicators for low fuel, low washer fluid, low coolant and door ajar, shift-knob-mounted overdrive lockout with cluster indicator light, tap up/tap down speed control with cluster indicator light, interior lights - dome/map, luggage compartment, ashtray, driver's side foot well, glove box and engine compartment, low lift-over carpeted luggage compartment, dual electric remote-controlled color-keyed mirrors, black moldings on windshield, backlight, door and quarter windows, foot-operated parking brake, three-point seat belts with front and rear outboard positions, center lap belt and reminder chime, rear-wheel drive, luxury cloth bucket seats, leather shift knob, mini spare tire, AM/FM/stereo/cassette sound system with four speakers, power steering, tilt steering wheel, long-spindle SLA front suspension with stabilizer bar, variable rate springs, lower control arm and tension strut, independent H-arm rear suspension with variable rate springs and stabilizer bar, full-width taillights, P205/70R15 black sidewall all-season radial tires, four-speed ECT automatic transmission with overdrive and overdrive lockout, bolt-on design styled road wheel covers, power windows with illuminated switches and variable interval windshield wipers.

defoggers, 145-hp/3.8-liter SMPEFI V-6 engine with hydraulic engine mounts and single exhaust, 18-gallon fuel tank with tethered cap, solar-tinted glass, aerodynamic halogen complex-reflector head- and parking lamps, rear seat heating ducts, analog instrument cluster with

Mike Mueller photo

Although it was living on borrowed time, the Thunderbird remained an attractive driving machine in 1997.

Mike Mueller photo

The old and the young: The 1957 and 1997 Thunderbirds.

I.D. NUMBERS

VIN stamped on aluminum tab riveted to the dashboard on passenger side and observable through the windshield from outside the car. First symbol 1 denotes built in the United States. Second symbol F denotes Ford. Third symbol A denotes Ford passenger vehicle. Fourth symbol denotes type of restraint system. Fifth symbol P denotes passenger-type vehicle. Sixth symbol 6 denotes Thunderbird. Seventh symbol denotes body type: 2=LX Coupe. Eighth symbol denotes engine: 4=232 cid (3.8L) 145 hp V-6, W = 281 cid (4..6L) 205 hp V-8. Ninth symbol is the check digit. Tenth symbol V=1997 model year. Eleventh symbol denotes assembly plant: H=Lorain, Ohio. Twelfth through 17th symbols denote sequential production number of specific vehicle starting at 100001. Vehicle certification label located on rear face of driver's door. The top part of the label indicates that the Thunderbird was manufactured by Ford Motor Company. Directly below this is the month and year of manufacture, plus a statement that the car conforms to federal motor vehicle safety standards in effect on the indicated date of manufacture. VIN: The VIN appears two lines above UPC. It matches the first to 11th symbols on VIN tag. Some other codes also appear. TYPE: Appears on left side of label on line above UPC, indicates PASSENGER. UPC: A scannable bar code carries the UPC. EXT. COLOR:

This line carries the exterior paint color(s) code. DSO: The District Special Order code now appears above "DSO" to the right of the exterior paint color code. BODY: The body style code appears to the extreme left of the bottom line. The only Thunderbird code for this model-year is: Thunderbird code for this model-year is: LX2=2-door LX coupe. VR: The vinyl roof type/color code is to the right of the body code. No T-Birds had vinyl tops. MLDG: The molding code is to the right of the vinyl roof code. INT. TRIM: The interior trim code is to the right of the molding code. TAPE: The tape treatment code appears to right of the interior trim code. R: The radio code is to the right of the A/C code. S: The sunroof code is to the right of the radio code. AX: The axle code appears to the right of the sunroof code. TR: The transmission code appears to the right of the axle code. Note: The terms and abbreviations shown in capitals appear on the line above the actual codes.

ENGINE

THUNDERBIRD BASE V-6: 90-degree. Overhead valve. Cast-iron block and aluminum head. Displacement: 232 cid (3.8 liters). Bore and stroke: 3.80 x 3.40 in. Compression ratio: 9.0:1. Brake hp: 145 at 4000. Torque: 215 lbs.-ft. at 2750. Four main bearings. Hydraulic valve lifters. Induction: Sequential Electronic Fuel Injection (SEFI). Serial number code: 4.

Mike Mueller photo

The V-8 T-Bird could be had for about $19,000 in its final year before a five-year hiatus. The V-6 version went for less than $18,000.

THUNDERBIRD, THUNDERBIRD LX OPTIONAL V-8: Modular. Single overhead cam. Displacement: 281 cid (4.6 liters). Bore and stroke: 3.60 x 3.60. Compression ratio: 9.0:1. Brake hp: 205 at 4500 rpm. Torque: 280 lbs.-ft. at 3000 rpm. Hydraulic valve lifters. Induction: Sequential fuel injection.

CHASSIS

Wheelbase: 113 in. Overall length: 200.3. Overall width: 72.7. Overall height: 52.5 in. Front headroom: 38.1 in. Rear headroom: 37.5 in. Front legroom: 42.5 in. Rear legroom: 35.8 in. Front shoulder room: 59.1 in. Rear shoulder room: 58.9 in. Trunk capacity: 15.1 cu. ft. Front tread: 61.6 in. Rear tread: 60.2 in. Front suspension: Long spindle SLA type, variable-rate coil springs, tubular gas shocks and stabilizer bar. Rear suspension Independent, H-arm design with toe control link, variable-rate coil springs, gas shocks and stabilizer bar. Steering: Power rack-and-pinion. Turning circle: 39 ft. Brakes: Power front disc/rear drum on LX, power four-wheel disc with ABS on Super Coupe. Fuel tank capacity: 18 gal. Seating capacity: Five (5). Transmission: four-speed automatic. Wheels: 15 in. Tires: (LX) P205/70R15 black sidewall. Fuel tank: 18 gal. Fuel economy: (base V-6) 19 mpg city/27 mpg highway, (V-8) 15 mpg city/23 mpg highway. Weight distribution: 57/43 percent.

OPTIONS

Preferred Equipment Packages: (155A) rear window defroster, P215/70R15 tires and cast-aluminum wheels (NC). (157A) includes 155A plus 4.6-liter SOHC V-8, speed-sensitive power steering, heavy-duty battery, 6-way power driver's seat, illuminated entry system and leather-wrapped steering wheel/shift knob ($840 net). (99W) includes 4.6-liter SOHC V-8 plus speed-sensitive power steering and heavy-duty battery ($1130). Engine block heater ($20). California emissions system ($170). Leather-faced bucket seats ($490). Remote keyless entry ($270). Front floor mats ($30). Electronic AM/FM stereo radio with cassette and premium sound ($290). Electronic AM/FM stereo radio with CD player and premium sound ($430). Anti-lock brakes ($570). Anti-theft system ($145). Power moonroof ($740). Sport Option: includes 16-inch aluminum wheels, P225/60R16 BSW tires, modified stabilizer bars, larger front disc brake rotors, revised spring rates and rear decklid spoiler ($450). Rear decklid spoiler ($250). Leather-wrapped steering wheel and shift knob ($90). Tri-coat paint ($225). Traction assist ($210). Traction-Lok axle ($95). Power driver's seat ($290). Luxury Group: includes electronic semi-automatic temperature control air conditioning, dual illuminated visor mirrors, Autolamp and power antenna ($395). 15-inch chrome wheels ($580).

EQUIPMENT INSTALLATION RATES

Four-speed automatic transmission (100 percent). Traction control (23.3 percent). Fuel-injected V-6 engine (43.5 percent). V-8 engine (56.5 percent). Electronic AM/FM stereo cassette (43.2 percent). Premium sound system (28.2 percent). Name brand stereo (12.5 percent). Power steering (100 percent). Remote keyless entry (46.2 percent). Leather seats (26.7 percent). Antitheft device (14.1 percent). Antilock brakes (32 percent). Power front disc brakes (68 percent). Dual airbags (100 percent). Power seat (78.7 percent). Automatic headlights (49.3 percent). Power windows (100 percent). Adjustable steering column (100 percent). All tinted glass (100 percent). Manual air conditioning (50.7 percent). Automatic air conditioning (49.3 percent). Power door locks (100 percent). Standard steel-belted radial tires (100 percent). Electric rear window defogger (100 percent). Chrome styled wheels (9 percent). Aluminum styled wheels (91 percent). Speed control (100 percent). Power remote-control left-hand rearview mirror (100 percent). Power remote-control right-hand rearview mirror (100 percent). Delay windshield wipers (100 percent). Limited-slip differential (15.8 percent). Sunroof (25.6 percent). (Note: Based on 73,814 units produced in the model year for the U.S. market only.)

HISTORICAL FOOTNOTES

Alexander J. Trotman was chairman of the board and CEO of Ford Motor Co. W. Wayne Booker and Edward E. Hagenlocker were vice chairmen of the corporation. Ross Roberts was again Ford Division's general manager and Phillip M. Novell remained divisional general sales manager.

Calendar-year output was 47,073 units. A total of 79,180 T-Birds was produced in the model year. This represented 1.29 percent of the industry total. Of these units, all were made in Lorain, Ohio. Calendar-year dealer sales amounted to 66,334, which was 5.9 percent of total Ford passenger car sales.

T-Bird sales continued to slide. *Car and Driver*, October 1996, pointed out that, "Last year a major styling makeover didn't cure the T-Bird's slipping sales, but Ford is leaving the big two-door alone for 1997." The editors of *Automobile* magazine noted, "The new T-Bird will arrive early in the next decade, it's time Ford gave it a new flight plan." When the 1997 model year ended, sales were at their lowest level in six years and the plug was temporarily pulled on one of the best-known American automobile nameplates in history. *Car and Driver* magazine, commenting in its "Charting the Changes for '98" section (October 1997), delivered a rather abrupt and unceremonious obituary when it pronounced, "The Aerostar, the Aspire, the Probe and the T-Bird are dead."

Ford photo

The 2001 Thunderbird concept car.

2001
Thunderbird

An automotive legend was re-born when the T-Bird made its return as an all-new concept car at the North American International Auto Show on January 3, 1999. The all-new Thunderbird concept drew on the T-Bird's rich heritage in introducing a modern interpretation of an automotive legend. It incorporated the trademark design cues that set the original T-Bird apart from a crowd of 1955 sports cars and made it an American cultural icon. "The Ford Thunderbird has an emotional hold on the American public that spans decades and generations," said Jac Nasser, Ford's president and chief executive officer at the time. "This timeless classic is an important part of Ford Motor Company's heritage and, indeed, this country's automotive history. The new concept car is an indication of where we're headed with the Thunderbird when it goes back into production for the new millennium."

The new concept car featured design elements from T-Birds of 1955-1957 and 1961-1962 simplified into contemporary forms. Its design cues included porthole windows, aluminum-finished chevrons, a hood scoop and a trademark Thunderbird badge. "The design of the Thunderbird concept reflects the attitude of a simpler

time," J Mays—Ford's vice president of design—stated at the show in Detroit, Michigan. "The unbridled optimism and the confident attitude of the 1950s comes through in an absolutely modern design."

The Thunderbird concept's stance was designed to be relaxed and confident. Mays achieved this attitude via a negative-wedge design in which the front of the vehicle appears to be set slightly higher than the rear. The 18-inch, eight-spoke aluminum wheels and P245R50-18 tires gave the Sunmist Yellow show car a sporty stance. A circular design theme ran throughout the vehicle, starting with the round headlights and fog lamps and back to the round taillights. The removable hardtop, with its porthole windows, was the signature cue from the original Thunderbird. "This is an aspirational design," Mays told the press. "Simple shapes combined with timeless materials and textures conveys a relaxed, confident look and a feel that is the true essence of the original Thunderbird." The oval grille opening remained true to the original with an aluminum finished eggcrate design. Two large fog lamps were set into the front bumper, with a secondary grille opening below them. The scoop was integrated into the

216

Ford photo

The 2001 T-Bird prototype was unveiled at the 1999 Chicago Auto Show and displayed some definite retro styling.

Ford photo

The leather bucket seats were part of a two-tone interior on the 2001 concept T-Bird.

Ford photo

The T-Bird achieved a classic sports car look with its hardtop removed.

hood design — rather than serving merely as a prominent addition. The porthole windows were functional, allowing additional light to enter the vehicle and providing better rearward visibility when the top is on. The chrome slash marks decorating the show car's front quarter panels were cut into the sheet metal and represented a modern interpretation of the chrome chevrons on the original car.

The concept car also featured cues from 1961-1962 Thunderbirds, which were more equally proportioned than their predecessors. The show car's interior continued the design theme by combining modern materials and a two-tone color combination. Two, black leather-wrapped bucket seats were specially stitched with a washboard-like pattern. The interior door panels were covered in black leather with yellow leather inserts and brushed aluminum accents. The instrument panel sported white gauges with turquoise pointers. The upper instrument panel, steering wheel and floor-mounted shifter were covered in black leather. The lower instrument panel and glove box were accented in yellow leather, matching the car's Sunmist Yellow exterior. A black leather wrapped tonneau cover was visible when the show car's hardtop was removed. Aluminum-finished Thunderbird body badges featured a turquoise insert across the wings. They appeared prominently on the vehicle's nose, rear and across the front seatbacks. An aluminum finished Thunderbird script stretched across both rear quarter panels.

STANDARD EQUIPMENT

Undetermined for concept car, but very similar to 2002 Premium production version.

I.D. NUMBERS

Undetermined for concept car, but probably around 1FAHP60A11Y100001.

THUNDERBIRD PRODUCTION				
Model Number	Body Type & Seating	Factory Price	Shipping Weight	Production Total
PREMIUM THUNDERBIRD - (V-8)				
60	2d Roadster-2P	—	—	Note 1

NOTE 1: Calendar 2001 production of 5,177 T-Birds did not include the concept car. These cars were early 2002 production models.

ENGINE

THUNDERBIRD V-8: Double overhead cam. 32 valve. Aluminum block and heads. Displacement: 240 cid (3.9 liters). Bore and stroke: 3.39 x 3.35 in. Compression ratio: 10.55:1. Brake hp: 252 at 6100 rpm. Torque: 261 lbs.-ft. at 4300 rpm. Sequential multiport electronic fuel injection.

CHASSIS

Wheelbase: 107.2 in. Overall length: 186.3. Overall width: 72. Overall height: 52.1 in. Front headroom: 37.2 in. Front legroom: 43.7 in. Front hip room: 53.7. Front shoulder room: 57.3 in. Luggage capacity: 8.5 cu. ft. Front tread: 61.6 in. Rear tread: 60.2 in. Front suspension: short and long arm type with aircraft-grade forged or cast aluminum control arms and stabilizer bar. Rear Suspension short and long arm type with stabilizer bar. Steering: Power rack-and-pinion. Brakes: Power four-wheel disc with ABS. Fuel tank capacity: 18 gal. Transmission: five-speed automatic. Wheels: 17 x 7.5-in. alloy rims. Tires: P235/50VR17. Fuel tank: 18 gal.

HISTORICAL FOOTNOTES

The new Ford Thunderbird concept vehicle was a modern interpretation of a classic American icon – a phenomenon that Ford labeled "modern-heritage" in its first press kit for the all-new T-Bird. "Styling heritage comes from the soul of a great automotive nameplate," stated J Mays, Ford's vice president of design. "There are only a select few nameplates that have earned their way into the hearts of the motoring public by establishing a true heritage. Thunderbird is

The T-Bird logo was about the only reminder of the last Thunderbird from 1997—the year the model was discontinued.

Ford photo

certainly one of them." Styling elements of the Thunderbird concept car had meaning beyond mere sheet metal. With the Thunderbird concept, Ford designers had a wealth of styling cues to call upon. The project direction was to recreate the enthusiasm of the original car by building a two-seat roadster with Thunderbird elements in a distinctly modern interpretation. The modern Thunderbird concept saluted the original, but also symbolized turn-of-the-millennium automotive styling. Mays insisted, "It's not retro; while the Thunderbird concept is loaded with heritage cues, it is a decidedly modern machine. This hints at the direction we plan to take when we bring back the production car early in the next century."

The instrument panel featured white gauges with turquoise pointers, and it was wrapped in black leather with yellow leather accents.

Ford photo

Mike Mueller photo

The Thunderbird flew back on the scene in 2001 with a brilliant new 2002 model that was named *Motor Trend's* "Car of the Year."

2002 *Thunderbird*

After a four-year absence, the T-Bird returned in 2001 as an all-new 2002 "retro" model. It was a throwback to the original roadster-convertible that wore the T-Bird name.

The new car came only as a two-seat roadster with a modern interpretation of the styling themes of the original 1955 Thunderbird. The car was built on the Lincoln LS platform and powered by Lincoln's 3.9-liter double-overhead camshaft V-8. It had a fully independent suspension, four-wheel disc brakes and an antilock braking system.

The styling was characterized by a machined egg-crate grille, aluminum finished decorative chevrons, a scooped hood, rounded headlights, large round taillights, fog lamps and porthole windows in the optional removable hardtop.

Traditional-looking turquoise blue Thunderbird emblems identified the car. The wraparound windshield was set at a rakish 64-degree angle and surrounded by a wide band of chrome. The doors were set to the center, rather than to the rear, and a crisp feature line runs from the headlights straight back to the taillights creating the hint of a '50s-style tail fin. The T-Bird interior continued the back-to-the-'50s design theme by combining modern materials and finishes with the flair of the past and two-tone upholstery options. The standard black leather-wrapped bucket seats had a "Thunderbird tuck-and-roll" look. With the two-tone interior the door panels were covered in black leather with colored leather inserts and brushed aluminum accents. The upper instrument panel, steering wheel and floor-mounted shifter were black leather. The lower instrument panel and glove box carried color accents. When the package was

BODY COLOR INFORMATION

Color Name	Code	Color Name	Code
Evening Black	UA	Torch Red	D3
Whisper White	W5	Thunderbird Blue	LY
Inspiration Yellow	C5		

*Extra cost tri-coat paint.

THUNDERBIRD PRODUCTION

Model Number	Body Type & Seating	Factory Price	Shipping Weight	Production Total
DELUXE THUNDERBIRD - (V-8)				
60	2d Roadster-2P	$34,965	3,775 lbs.	Note 1
DELUXE THUNDERBIRD - (V-8)				
60	2d w/Hardtop-2P	$35,965	3,863 lbs.	Note 1
NIEMAN MARCUS EDITION THUNDERBIRD - (V-8)				
60	2d w/Hardtop-2P	$41,995	3,863 lbs.	Note 1
PREMIUM THUNDERBIRD - (V-8)				
60	2d Roadster-2P	$38,465	3,775 lbs.	Note 1
PREMIUM THUNDERBIRD - (V-8)				
60	2d w/Hardtop-2P	$41,465	3,863 lbs.	Note 1

NOTE 1: Calendar 2001 production of the all models combined was 5,177.
NOTE 2: Model-year production for 2002 models was 31,121 units. This included 8,686 cars in Evening Black (including Neiman Marcus editions), 7,353 in Thunderbird Blue, 7,184 in Torch Red, 4,149 in Whisper White and 3,749 in Inspiration Yellow.

ordered for Yellow, Red or Blue cars, the color accents matched. In Black or White cars, the color accents were red. A black leather tonneau cover was visible when the hardtop was removed.

STANDARD EQUIPMENT

(Deluxe) 3.9-liter DOHC V-8, a new-generation power train electronic controller (PTEC), a specially-engineered close-ratio five-speed automatic transmission, 17 x 7.5 cast-aluminum rims, P235/50VR17 all-season tires, a space saver spare tire, four-wheel independent suspension, front and rear stabilizer bars, front and rear ventilated disc brakes, antilock braking system with electronic brake force distribution, vented rotors and dual-piston calipers, an airbag deactivation switch, child seat anchors, emergency release in trunk, leather upholstery, front bucket seats with headrests, 6-way power driver's seat with adjustable lumbar support, 2-way power passenger seat, remote vehicle anti-theft system, auto-delay-off headlights, variable intermittent windshield wipers, power-operated convertible top, glass rear window, rear window defogger, remote power door locks, one-touch power windows, dual power outside rearview mirrors, AM/FM cassette 6-CD stereo, multi-CD

Mike Mueller photo

Evening Black was one of five colors available on the new Thunderbird, which had a base price of $34,965 for the Deluxe Roadster.

changer located in dash, 180-watt stereo output, eight speakers, element antenna, cruise control, power steering, tilt-and-telescopic steering wheel with built-in cruise and audio controls, front cupholders, front door pockets, front seat console with storage provisions, retained accessory power, dual-zone climate control system, front reading lights, dual visor-vanity mirrors, leather-wrapped steering wheel, front floor mats, trunk light, tachometer, trip computer, clock and low-fuel warning. **(Premium)** In addition to or instead of deluxe equipment, the Premium model includes chrome alloy wheel rims and traction control. **(Nieman Marcus)** In addition to or instead of premium equipment, this model included a special Black-and-Silver paint scheme, a removable hardtop, an element antenna, Neiman Marcus emblems on the instrument panel, front floor mats with Neiman Marcus emblems and a special vehicle identification number as a guarantee of authenticity.

I.D. NUMBERS

VIN stamped on aluminum tab riveted to dashboard on passenger side and observable through the windshield from outside the car. First symbol 1 denotes built in the United States. Second symbol F denotes Ford. Third symbol A denotes Ford passenger vehicle. Fourth symbol denotes type of restraint system: B=Active belts, F=Driver and passenger airbags and side airbags and active belts and H=Driver and passenger airbags and side airbags, curtains or canopies and active belts. Fifth symbol P denotes passenger-type vehicle. Sixth and seventh symbols denote body style: 60=Thunderbird base convertible and 64=Neiman Marcus Thunderbird convertible. Eighth symbol denotes engine: A=3.9-liter EFI double overhead

The 2002 'Birds could be had without the optional hardtop, which featured the throwback "porthole" window.

Daniel B. Lyons photo

Ford photo

The reincarnated Thunderbird had some retro styling themes, but it was all modern in the handling and performance departments, with a 3.9-liter V-8, independent suspension, four-wheel disc breaks, ABS, and electronically controlled five-speed automatic transmission.

cam V-8. Ninth symbol is the check digit. Tenth symbol 2=2002 model year. Eleventh symbol denotes assembly plant: Y=Wixom, Michigan. Twelfth through 17th symbols denote sequential production number of specific vehicle starting at 100001.

ENGINE

THUNDERBIRD V-8: Double overhead cam. 32 valve. Aluminum block and heads. Displacement: 240 cid (3.9 liters). Bore and stroke: 3.39 x 3.35 in. Compression ratio: 10.55:1. Brake hp: 252 cid at 6100 rpm. Torque: 261 lbs-ft. at 4300 rpm. Sequential multiport electronic fuel injection. VIN code A.

CHASSIS

Wheelbase: 107.2 in. Overall length: 186.3. Overall width: 72. Overall height: 52.1 in. Front headroom: 37.2 in. Front legroom: 43.7 in. Front hip room: 53.7. Front shoulder room: 57.3 in. Luggage capacity: 8.5 cu. ft. Front tread: 60.5 in. Rear tread: 60.2 in. Front suspension: Independent, unequal-length control arms made of aircraft-grade forged or cast aluminum, coil springs, shock absorbers and stabilizer bar. Rear suspension: Independent, unequal-length control arms with anti-lift design, coil springs, shock absorbers and stabilizer bar. Steering: Power, speed-sensitive, variable-assist rack-and-pinion with 18.0:1 overall ratio and 35.2-ft. curb-to-curb turn circle. Turns lock-to-lock: 3. Frame: Cross-car beam and three bolted-on X-

braces. Front brakes: Power disc with ABS, outside rotor diameter 11.8 in., inside rotor diameter 7.17 in., total swept area 277 sq. in. Rear brakes: Power disc with ABS, outside rotor diameter 11.3 in., inside rotor diameter 7.83 in., total swept area 211.1 sq. in. Fuel tank capacity: 18 gal. Transmission: Special close-ratio five-speed automatic with overdrive. Wheels: 17 x 7.5-in. alloy rims. Tires: P235/50VR17. Fuel tank: 18 gal.

OPTIONS

153 front license plate bracket (no cost). 422 California emissions requirements (no cost). 428 high-altitude principal use (no cost). 51P supplemental parking lamps (no cost). 553 traction control ($230). 68B black accent package, includes black accent on steering wheel and shift handle, not available with 68C or 68D ($295). 68C full-color interior package, not available with 68A or 68D ($800). 68D partial interior color accent package, not available with 68A or 68C ($595).

HISTORICAL FOOTNOTES

Dressed in a formal design for a very special occasion, The Thunderbird Custom made its official debut at the 50th Annual Concours d'Elegance in Pebble Beach in August 2000. This one-of-a-kind project car brought a new look to the roadster through subtle design changes.

The Custom was designed to be a contemporary

interpretation of the customizing and hot rod movement of the 1950s. It started as a 2002 Ford Thunderbird. Ford designers were asked to develop design renderings of new styling possibilities for future years. One sketch featured several unique elements, including a blacked-out grille, a more pronounced belt line, and big chrome wheels with knock-off hubs. The sketch looked so good, Ford decided to build it. Changes included doubling the size of the recesses for the characteristic chevrons on the T-Bird's front fenders and adding a black mesh insert behind them to accentuate their presence.

The Custom was painted with several coats of Dark Shadow Gray Metallic lacquer for a deep, glossy finish. The iconic egg-crate grille was recessed slightly and painted the same color as the body. It was further accentuated with a chrome bezel surrounding the grille. To achieve a longer, more relaxed exterior appearance for the project car, the design team lowered the coil-spring suspension one-inch front and rear, making it look higher in front and lower in the rear. The exhaust system was re-tuned to give it a low "barritone burble" at idle and a more aggressive performance tone during acceleration. Chrome tailpipe extensions were prominent in the side view.

Halibrand created a unique interpretation of its classic

Mike Mueller photo

A total of 31,121 2002 Thunderbirds were produced, including 4,149 in Whisper White.

The 2002 Thunderbird and its 45-year-old ancestor, the 1957 T-Bird roadster.

Mike Mueller photo

"Kidney Bean 5" polished chrome wheel featuring five spokes with kidney-bean-shaped "windows" that created a strobing effect when the car was in motion. The wheel hubs were set off with three-arm knock-offs, a classic customizing touch. Aggressively treaded Michelin Pilot Sport Z-rated 18-in. tires finished the look, virtually filling the project car's wheel wells.

The Thunderbird Custom had a black convertible top that was stored below a removable two-piece, Ebony-leather-wrapped tonneau cover. The interior featured a two-tone theme with Sienna and Ebony leather set off by engine-turned aluminum accent panels. The door sill plate was wrapped in a thin layer of Sienna leather with an opening in the middle displaying the Thunderbird logo etched in aluminum. The door panels featured Sienna leather armrests and upper sills with engine-turned aluminum accents. The bucket seats were covered in Sienna leather and featured plush side bolsters and adjustable head restraints. The seating surfaces were covered with perforated Sienna leather in the familiar Thunderbird tuck-and-roll style. The steering wheel and shift knob were tightly wrapped and stitched in Sienna leather. The shifter bezel featured an engine-turned aluminum background. The center stack was finished in Dark Shadow Gray matching the exterior. It flowed into a one-of-a-kind White-on-Black Thunderbird instrument cluster that was precision stitched in Ebony leather.

At Pebble Beach, Ford announced that it would offer 200 uniquely designed Neiman Marcus Edition Thunderbirds exclusively through the specialty retailer's "Christmas Book," which came out in September 2000. The Neiman Marcus Edition Thunderbird featured Black–and-Silver finish with a removable Silver top. The removable top was highlighted with the Thunderbird insignia etched into the porthole glass. Chrome 17-inch wheels matched the A-

Daniel B. Lyons photo

With a hood scoop and "bullets" that were lights rather than bumper guards, the 2002 T-Bird had some definite nods to the early years.

Ford photo

The Nieman Marcus Thunderbirds were bought up quickly by the public.

pillars. The hood scoop was adorned with trim accents and a chrome bezel. The Black-and-Silver theme was carried through to the interior. The steering wheel and shift knob were painted silver to match the exterior roof and accent colors. The lower door panel was silver to match the aluminum molding and inserts on the padded instrument panel. The seats contained a perforated, silver leather insert surrounded by black leather. The Neiman Marcus Thunderbird was made available exclusively through the *Neiman Marcus Christmas Book* beginning on September 25th at a price of $41,995. All 200 copies sold in 2 hours and 15 minutes. The cars were not delivered until production actually started in the summer of 2001.

Ford officially opened the order banks for the 2002 Thunderbird on Monday, January 8, 2001, the day that the car made its regular-production debut at the North American International Auto Show in Detroit, Michigan. The regular-production "new" T-Bird was originally slated to go on sale in June of 2001 as a 2002 model, but the first real sales were not concluded and counted until August of the year 2001. Sales for calendar-year 2001 still amounted to 5,177 units. This included 243 cars sold in August 2001, 340 cars sold in September, 1,315 cars sold in October, 1,421 cars sold in November and 1,858 cars sold in December 2001. Calendar-year 2001 output of 2002 T-Birds was 7,955 units. Of these units, all were made in Wixom, Michigan.

By the end of 2002, Jacques Nasser's rein at Ford ended abruptly with his dismissal for failure to control financial losses. William Clay Ford, Jr., took over as chief excutive officer and Nick Scheele assumed the role of president and chief operating officer. Alan Gilmour was chief financial officer.

The January 1, 2001, issue of *Automotive News* had a picture of a Red Thunderbird with a White interior to promote the Detroit Auto Show. This show car had a matching Torch Red tonneau cover. It was themed after the '60s T-Bird Sport Roadster and used the same name. A Nieman Marcus Thunderbird was shown at the 2001 Los Angeles Auto Show. On November 12, 2001, at the SEMA Show in Las Vegas, *Motor Trend* announced that it had picked the 2002 Thunderbird as "Car of the Year." It was the fourth time that *Motor Trend* had bestowed this honor on the T-Bird. "We're especially honored that the Ford Thunderbird was chosen *Motor Trend's* 'Car of the Year' for the fourth time," said Ford Division President Jim O'Connor. "The all-new Thunderbird celebrates Ford's heritage of innovation and reaffirms our goal to build the best cars on the planet—cars that evoke passion and touch people's hearts and souls." "Motor Week" later selected the Thunderbird as "Best Convertible for 2002," Women Journalists picked it as their "Favorite Car of the Year" and *Auto Interiors* selected it for "Best Interior" honors.

Ford photo

The beautiful Nieman Marcus T-Bird of 2002 was outfitted with a special black paint scheme and removable hardtop.

Ford photo

The Nieman Marcus interior of the 2002 T-Bird.

Daniel B. Lyons photo

A fabulous 2003 Thunderbird, dressed in Desert Sky Blue.

2003

Thunderbird

BODY COLOR INFORMATION

Color Name	Code	Color Name	Code
Evening Black	UA	Torch Red	D3
Whisper White	W5	Desert Sky Blue	CZ
Mountain Shadow Gray	CX	007 (Coral)	CQ

THUNDERBIRD PRODUCTION

Model Number	Body Type & Seating	Factory Price	Shipping Weight	Production Total
DELUXE THUNDERBIRD - (V-8)				
60	2d Convertible-2P	$37,550	3,775 lbs.	Note 2
DELUXE THUNDERBIRD - (V-8)				
60	2d with Hardtop-2P	$40,045	3,863 lbs.	Note 2
PREMIUM THUNDERBIRD - (V-8)				
60	2d Convertible-2P	$38,590	3,863 lbs.	Note 2
PREMIUM THUNDERBIRD - (V-8)				
60	2d with Hardtop-2P	$41,090	3,863 lbs.	Note 2
007 EDITION THUNDERBIRD - (V-8)				
60	2d Convertible-2P	$44,600	3,775 lbs.	Note 2

NOTE 1: Prices include $605 dealer destination charges.
NOTE 2: Production total 14,506

PRODUCTION BY BODY COLOR

Color	Total	Color	Total
Evening Black	3,047	Torch Red	3,472
Whisper White	2,431	Desert Sky Blue	1,728
Mountain Shadow Gray	3,134	007 (Coral)	694

The T-Bird's rounded, retro styling continued to be characterized by a machined egg-crate grille, aluminum-finished decorative chevrons, a scooped hood, rounded headlights, large round taillights, fog lamps and port hole windows in the optional removable hardtop. Traditional-looking turquoise blue Thunderbird emblems identified the car. The wraparound windshield had the same 64-degree setback and was surrounded by a wide band of chrome. The standard bucket seats had the "Thunderbird tuck-and-roll" look. A black leather tonneau cover was used when the hardtop was removed.

Thanks to a new electronic throttle control system and new variable-cam timing, there was more horsepower and torque below the hood. All-speed traction control was standard and heated seats were a new option. The instrument cluster was revised and there were new body colors of Desert Sky Blue and Mountain Shadow Grey. A Saddle leather interior package was also added.

STANDARD EQUIPMENT

(Deluxe) 17-in. painted cast-aluminum wheels, dual exhausts with bright tips, dual power outside rearview mirrors, perimeter alarm system, power retractable convertible top with black boot, two-speed variable-intermittent windshield wipers, air conditioning with dual-zone automatic temperature control, AM/FM stereo with 6-disc in-dash changer, clock and Audiophile sound system, analog instrument cluster with tachometer, auto headlamps with on/off delay, center console with storage and leather-wrapped armrest, delayed accessory power shutoff, dual vanity mirrors, illuminated entry with theater-dimming feature, leather-wrapped steering wheel with audio and speed controls, power 6-way driver's seat, power 2-way passenger seat, power tilt/telescoping steering column, power windows, power door locks, premium leather-trimmed seats with recliners, rear window defroster, remote

keyless entry, 3.9-liter 32-valve aluminum DOHC V-8 with 280 hp, four-wheel anti-lock braking system, five-speed automatic transmission with overdrive, all-speed traction control, power four-wheel ventilated disc brakes, Belt-Minder safety belt reminder, front and side airbags for driver and passenger with passenger side deactivation switch, lower and top anchors for child safety seat, SecuriLock passive anti-theft system and side intrusion door beams. (Premium) In addition to or instead of deluxe equipment, the Premium model includes chrome alloy wheel rims and traction control. (007 Edition) In addition to or instead of premium equipment, this model included a special Coral exterior, chrome wheels, a Performance White interior, aluminum appliqués and a special limited-edition numbering plate to identify the car as one of only 700 built to commemorate the James Bond movie "Die Another Day."

I.D. NUMBERS

VIN stamped on aluminum tab riveted to the dashboard on passenger side and observable through the windshield from outside the car. First symbol 1 denotes built in the United States. Second symbol F denotes Ford. Third symbol A denotes Ford passenger vehicle. Fourth symbol denotes type of restraint system: F=Driver and passenger airbags and side airbags and active belts and H=Driver and passenger airbags and side airbags, curtains or canopies and active belts. Fifth symbol P denotes passenger-type vehicle. Sixth and seventh symbols denote body style: 60=Thunderbird base convertible and 62=007 Edition Thunderbird convertible. Eighth symbol denotes engine: A=3.9-liter EFI double overhead cam V-8. Ninth symbol is the check digit. Tenth symbol 3=2003 model year. Eleventh symbol denotes assembly plant: Y=Wixom, Michigan. Twelfth through 17th symbols denote sequential production number of specific vehicle starting at 100001.

ENGINE

THUNDERBIRD V-8: Double overhead cam. 32 valve. Aluminum block and heads. Displacement: 240 cid (3.9 liters). Bore and stroke: 3.39 x 3.35 in. Compression ratio: 10.75:1. Brake hp: 280 at 6000 rpm. Torque: 286 lbs.-ft. at 4000 rpm. Sequential multiport electronic fuel injection. VIN code A.

CHASSIS

Wheelbase: 107.2-in. Overall length: 186.3. Overall width: 72. Overall height: 52.1 in. Front headroom: 37.2 in. Front legroom: 42.7 in. Front hip room: 53.7. Front shoulder room: 57.3 in. Luggage capacity: 8.5 cu. ft. Front tread: 60.5 in. Rear tread: 60.2 in. Front suspension: Independent, short-and-long control arms made of aircraft-grade forged or cast aluminum, dual taper coil springs, twin tube-type shock absorbers with integral rebound springs and 1.22-in. tubular steel stabilizer bar. Rear suspension: Independent, short-and-long control arms with anti-lift coil springs over shock absorbers design, dual taper coil springs, twin tube-type shock absorbers and 0.73-in. solid steel rear stabilizer bar. Steering: Power, speed-sensitive, variable-assist rack-and-pinion with 18.0:1 overall ratio and 35.2-ft. curb-to-curb turn circle. Turns lock-to-lock: 3. Frame: Cross-car beam and three bolted-on X-braces. Front brakes: Power disc with ABS, outside rotor diameter 11.8 in., inside rotor diameter 7.17 in., total swept area 277 sq. in. Rear brakes: Power disc with ABS, outside rotor diameter 11.3 in., inside

Daniel B. Lyons photo

The racy 280-hp V-8 Thunderbird engine.

Daniel B. Lyons photo

The T-Bird interior included power seats, front and side airbags, leather seats, and six-disc CD stereo.

rotor diameter 7.83 in., total swept area 211.1 sq. in. Fuel tank capacity: 18 gal. Transmission: Special close-ratio five-speed automatic with overdrive. Wheels: 17 x 7.5-in. alloy rims. Tires: P235/50VR17. Fuel tank: 18 gal.

OPTIONS

17-in. chrome wheels. Removable top with heated glass rear window, storage cart and cover. 68B Black Ink interior accent package ($295). 68C full color interior accent package ($800). 68D partial interior color accent package ($595). 68E partial interior color accent package ($695). Heated driver and passenger seats. 53S SelectShift five-speed automatic transmission ($130). 51P supplementary parking lights (no cost).

HISTORICAL FOOTNOTES

On April 22, 2003, Ford Division President Steve Lyons announced that the company was planning to stop production of the retro T-Bird convertible after the 2005 or 2006 model year. "We have always planned to build it for four model years and that's what we are going to do," Lyons said. "It would be wrong to keep building it and erode its value. It's a collectors vehicle."

Ford initially planned to sell 25,000 Thunderbirds a year, but never reached those levels. In model year 2002, the company built 31,121 T-Birds, but calendar-year U.S. sales were only 19,085. From January to the end of March 2003, only 4,065 were sold. That was a 21-percent drop from the same period a year earlier. "We could bring it back," Lyons said. "But there is no set timetable. We will have to have the right design."

Ford attempted to promote 2003 T-Bird sales with its coral-colored 007 Edition model. It was patterned after the car driven by Halle Berry in the latest James Bond movie, "Die Another Day." In honor of the secret agent's 007 code name, only 700 of these cars were scheduled for production. The decline in sales was related to the late introduction of an upgraded V-8 for 2003. Because of this delay, Ford kept making the 2002 model T-Bird through November, instead of stopping in July. Demand for the less-powerful 2002 models dropped off, creating inventory problems for dealers. Lyons admitted the problem. "If I could do it again, I would have just stopped building the Thunderbird for a month or two," he said. "We had people coming to dealerships saying, 'Why do I want a year-old Thunderbird?'"

The newest Thundebird has few rivals when it came to looking good and grabbing attention.

Ford photo

The 2004 Thunderbird

2004

Thunderbird

The 2004 Thunderbird continued to deliver a unique combination of classic American sportiness, offering balanced performance with touring comfort. The retro-styled car helped attract a new generation of buyers to Ford showrooms and provided a powerful link with loyal Ford customers.

The 2004 model again echoed the relaxed look of the original "Classic T-Bird" in a distinctly modern interpretation. Key design elements included the classic egg-crate grille found on the 1955-1957 Thunderbirds and a hood scoop reminiscent of the 1961 model. At 6.9 cubic feet, the Thunderbird's fully lined trunk was spacious enough for two sets of golf clubs. A soft vinyl boot was provided to cover the black, woven soft-top when it was lowered.

Inside, the "roadster" (really a convertible) provided a comfortable environment for its occupants. The black instrument panel was highlighted with bright accent colors and brushed aluminum appliqués. The center stack flowed out of the instrument panel with a sculpted line that created a waterfall effect leading to the console. The standard interior had black leather surfaces. An interior with body-colored accents is optional for those who want to match the interior and exterior colors.

A new Light Sand interior appearance package was added for 2004. It included a Light Sand color applied to the convertible top, full seats, steering wheel, shift knob and optional soft boot. This package also featured bronze metallic tinted appliqués on the instrument panel, door trim, center stack, shifter bezel and scuff plates. Light Sand was also applied to the floor mat edging complemented by cream-colored instrument cluster gauges. Other new-for-2004 features included a universal three-button garage door

BODY COLOR INFORMATION

Color Name	Code	Color Name	Code
Evening Black	UA	Torch Red	D3
Platinum Silver	JP	Vintage Mint Green	EI
Merlot	FX		

THUNDERBIRD PRODUCTION

Model Number	Body Type & Seating	Factory Price	Shipping Weight	Production Total
DELUXE THUNDERBIRD - (V-8)				
60	2d Convertible-2P	$36,925	3,775 lbs.	—
PREMIUM THUNDERBIRD - (V-8)				
60	2d Convertible-2P	$37,970	3,863 lbs.	—
NOTE: The removable hardtop was optional				

inch chrome wheels.

The car came standard as a convertible and offered an optional removable top with classic porthole windows. The removable top weighed 83 lbs., making it easy to remove or install. A secure pin-and-bolt system at the two front attachment points and two clamps at the rear connected the removable top to the car.

The T-Bird's ride and handling were specially tuned and structural braces under the car enhanced the chassis rigidity, giving the roadster world-class driving dynamics.

STANDARD EQUIPMENT

Deluxe: 17-inch, painted cast-aluminum wheels, or seven-spoke, 17-inch chrome wheels, universal three-button garage door opener, chrome chevron with integrated V-8 badge on the front fenders, improved map lighting, newly styled seats with leather seating surfaces, dual exhausts with bright tips, dual power outside rearview mirrors,

opener, a chrome chevron with integrated V-8 badge on the front fenders, improved map lighting, newly styled seats with leather seating surfaces and a choice of 16-spoke, 17-inch, painted cast-aluminum wheels, or seven-spoke, 17-

The 2004 Thunderbird interior.

Ford photo

perimeter alarm system, power retractable convertible top with black boot, two-speed variable-intermittent windshield wipers, air conditioning with dual-zone automatic temperature control, AM/FM stereo with 6-disc in-dash changer, clock and Audiophile sound system, analog instrument cluster with tachometer, auto headlamps with on/off delay, center console with storage and leather-wrapped armrest, delayed accessory power shutoff, dual vanity mirrors, illuminated entry with theater-dimming feature, leather-wrapped steering wheel with audio and speed controls, power 6-way driver's seat, power two-way passenger seat, power tilt/telescoping steering column, power windows, power door locks, premium leather-trimmed seats with recliners, rear window defroster, remote keyless entry, 3.9-liter 32-valve aluminum DOHC V-8 with 280-hp, four-wheel anti-lock braking system, five-speed automatic transmission with overdrive, all-speed traction control, power four-wheel ventilated disc brakes, Belt-Minder safety belt reminder, front and side airbags for driver and passenger with passenger side deactivation switch, lower and top anchors for child safety seat, SecuriLock passive anti-theft system, and side intrusion door beams. **Premium:** In addition to or instead of deluxe equipment, the Premium model includes chrome alloy wheel rims and traction control.

I.D. NUMBERS

VIN stamped on aluminum tab riveted to dashboard on passenger side and observable through the windshield from outside the car. First symbol 1 denotes built in the United States. Second symbol F denotes Ford. Third symbol A denotes Ford passenger vehicle. Fourth symbol denotes type of restraint system: F=Driver and passenger airbags and side airbags and active belts and H=Driver and passenger airbags and side airbags, curtains or canopies and active belts. Fifth symbol P denotes passenger-type vehicle. Sixth and seventh symbols denote body style: 60=Thunderbird base convertible. Eighth symbol denotes engine: A=3.9-liter EFI double-overhead cam V-8. Ninth symbol is the check digit. Tenth symbol 4=2004 model year. Eleventh symbol denotes assembly plant: Y=Wixom, Michigan. Twelfth through 17th symbols denote sequential production number of specific vehicle starting at 100001.

ENGINE

THUNDERBIRD V-8: Double-overhead-cam V-8. 32 valve. Variable-cam timing. Aluminum block and heads. Displacement: 240 cid (3.9 liters). Bore and stroke: 3.39 x 3.35 in. Compression ratio: 10.75:1. Brake hp: 280 at 6000 rpm. Torque: 286 lbs.-ft. at 4000 rpm. Sequential multiport electronic fuel injection. Coil-on-plug ignition with platinum-tipped spark plugs. Lightweight, low-friction pistons. Dual exhaust. VIN code A.

CHASSIS

Wheelbase: 107.2-in. Overall length: 186.3. Overall width: 72. Overall height: 52.1 in. Front headroom: 37.2 in. Front legroom: 42.7 in. Front hip room: 53.7. Front shoulder room: 57.3 in. Luggage capacity: 8.5 cu. ft. Front tread: 60.5 in. Rear tread: 60.2 in. Front suspension: Independent, short-and-long control arms made of aircraft-grade forged or cast aluminum, dual taper coil springs, twin tube-type shock absorbers with integral rebound springs and 1.22-in. tubular steel stabilizer bar. Rear suspension: Independent, short-and-long control arms with anti-lift coil springs over shock absorbers design, dual taper coil springs, twin tube-type shock absorbers and 0.73-in. solid steel rear stabilizer bar. Steering: Power, speed-sensitive, variable-assist rack-and-pinion with 18.0:1 overall ratio and 35.2-ft. curb-to-curb turn circle. Turns lock-to-lock: 3. Frame: Cross-car beam and three bolted-on X-braces. Front brakes: Power disc with ABS, outside rotor diameter 11.8 in., inside rotor diameter 7.17 in., total swept area 277 sq. in. Rear brakes: Power disc with ABS, outside rotor diameter 11.3 in., inside rotor diameter 7.83 in., total swept area 211.1 sq. in. Fuel tank capacity: 18 gal. Transmission: Special close-ratio five-speed automatic with overdrive. Wheels: 17 x 7.5-in. alloy rims. Tires: P235/50VR17. Fuel tank: 18 gal.

OPTIONS

Light Sand appearance package ($1,000). 17-in. chrome wheels (N/A). Removable top with heated glass rear window, storage cart and cover ($2,500). 68B Black Ink interior accent package ($295). 68C full color interior accent package ($800). 68D partial interior color accent package ($595). 53S SelectShift five-speed automatic transmission ($130). 51P supplementary parking lights (no cost). Soft top boot ($125).

THUNDERBIRD
Price Guide

Vehicle Condition Scale

1: **Excellent:** Restored to current maximum professional standards of quality in every area, or perfect original with components operating and apearing as new. A 95-plus point show car that is not driven.

2: **Fine:** Well-restored or a combination of superior restoration and excellent original parts. Also, extremely well-maintained original vehicle showing minimal wear.

3. **Very Good:** Complete operable original or older restoration. Also, a very good amateur restoration, all presentable and serviceable inside and out. Plus, a combination of well-done restoration and good operable components or a partially restored car with all parts necessary to compete and/or valuable NOS parts.

4: **Good:** A driveable vehicle needing no or only minor work to be functional. Also, a deteriorated restoration or a very poor amateur restoration. All components may need restoration to be "excellent," but the car is mostly useable "as is."

5. **Restorable:** Needs complete restoration of body, chassis and interior. May or may not be running, but isn't weathered, wrecked or stripped to the point of being useful only for parts.

6. **Parts car:** May or may not be running, but is weathered, wrecked and/or stripped to the point of being useful primarily for parts.

	6	5	4	3	2	1
1955 102" wb						
Conv	2,560	7,680	12,800	25,600	44,800	64,000
NOTE: Add $1,800 for hardtop.						
1956 102" wb						
Conv	2,480	7,440	12,400	24,800	43,400	62,000
NOTE: Add $1,800 for hardtop. Add 10 percent for 312 engine.						
1957 102" wb						
Conv	2,520	7,560	12,600	25,200	44,100	63,000
NOTE: Add $1,800 for hardtop. Add 60 percent for supercharged V-8 (Code F). Add 20 percent for "T-Bird Special" V-8 (Code E).						
1958 113" wb						
2d HT	1,200	3,600	6,000	12,000	21,000	30,000
Conv	1,600	4,800	8,000	16,000	28,000	40,000
1959 113" wb						
2d HT	1,160	3,480	5,800	11,600	20,300	29,000
Conv	1,560	4,680	7,800	15,600	27,300	39,000
NOTE: Add 30 percent for 430 engine option.						
1960 113" wb						
SR HT	1,320	3,960	6,600	13,200	23,100	33,000
2d HT	1,160	3,480	5,800	11,600	20,300	29,000
Conv	1,560	4,680	7,800	15,600	27,300	39,000
NOTE: Add 30 percent for 430 engine option Code J.						
1961 113" wb						
2d HT	960	2,880	4,800	9,600	16,800	24,000
Conv	1,400	4,200	7,000	14,000	24,500	35,000
NOTE: Add 20 percent for 390-375 hp engine. Add 25 percent for Indy Pace Car.						
1962 113" wb						
2d HT	960	2,880	4,800	9,600	16,800	24,000
2d Lan HT	1,000	3,000	5,000	10,000	17,500	25,000
Conv	1,360	4,080	6,800	13,600	23,800	34,000
Spt Rds	1,600	4,800	8,000	16,000	28,000	40,000
NOTE: Add 20 percent for 390-340 hp engine. Add 40 percent for M Series option.						
1963 113" wb						
2d HT	960	2,880	4,800	9,600	16,800	24,000
2d Lan HT	1,000	3,000	5,000	10,000	17,500	25,000
Conv	1,360	4,080	6,800	13,600	23,800	34,000
Spt Rds	1,600	4,800	8,000	16,000	28,000	40,000
NOTE: Add 12 percent for Monaco option. Add 20 percent for 390-340 hp engine. Add 40 percent for M Series option. Add 10 percent for 390-330 hp engine.						

	6	5	4	3	2	1
1964 113" wb						
2d HT	800	2,400	4,000	8,000	14,000	20,000
2d Lan HT	840	2,520	4,200	8,400	14,700	21,000
Conv	1,280	3,840	6,400	12,800	22,400	32,000
NOTE: Add 10 percent for Tonneau convertible option. Add 30 percent for tonneau option and wire wheels.						
1965 113" wb						
2d HT	800	2,400	4,000	8,000	14,000	20,000
2d Lan HT	840	2,520	4,200	8,400	14,700	21,000
Conv	1,300	3,950	6,600	13,200	23,100	33,000
NOTE: Add 5 percent for Special Landau option.						
1966 113" wb						
2d HT Cpe	840	2,520	4,200	8,400	14,700	21,000
2d Twn Lan	920	2,760	4,600	9,200	16,100	23,000
2d HT Twn	880	2,640	4,400	8,800	15,400	22,000
Conv	1,350	4,100	6,800	13,600	23,800	34,000
NOTE: Add 20 percent for 428 engine.						
1967 117" wb						
4d Lan	560	1,680	2,800	5,600	9,800	14,000
1967 115" wb						
2d Lan	600	1,800	3,000	6,000	10,500	15,000
2d HT	608	1,824	3,040	6,080	10,640	15,200
NOTE: Add 30 percent for 428 engine option.						
1968 117" wb						
4d Lan Sed	560	1,680	2,800	5,600	9,800	14,000
1968 115" wb						
4d Lan Sed	580	1,740	2,900	5,800	10,150	14,500
2d Lan HT	588	1,764	2,940	5,880	10,290	14,700
NOTE: Add 30 percent for 429 engine option, Code K or 428 engine.						
1969 117" wb						
4d Lan	560	1,680	2,800	5,600	9,800	14,000
1969 115" wb						
2d Lan HT	588	1,764	2,940	5,880	10,290	14,700
4d Lan	580	1,740	2,900	5,800	10,150	14,500
1970 117" wb						
4d Lan	560	1,680	2,800	5,600	9,800	14,000
1970 115" wb						
2d Lan HT	588	1,764	2,940	5,880	10,290	14,700
4d Lan	580	1,740	2,900	5,800	10,150	14,500

	6	5	4	3	2	1
1971 117" wb						
4d HT	560	1,680	2,800	5,600	9,800	14,000
1971 115" wb						
2d HT	580	1,740	2,900	5,800	10,150	14,500
2d Lan HT	588	1,764	2,940	5,880	10,290	14,700
1972 120" wb						
2d HT	540	1,620	2,700	5,400	9,450	13,500
NOTE: Add 20 percent for 460 engine option.						
1973 120" wb						
2d HT	520	1,560	2,600	5,200	9,100	13,000
1974 120" wb						
2d HT	520	1,560	2,600	5,200	9,100	13,000
1975 120" wb						
2d HT	432	1,296	2,160	4,320	7,560	10,800
1976 120" wb						
2d HT	412	1,236	2,060	4,120	7,210	10,300
1977 114" wb						
2d HT	364	1,092	1,820	3,640	6,370	9,100
2d Lan	368	1,104	1,840	3,680	6,440	9,200
1978 114" wb						
2d HT	380	1,140	1,900	3,800	6,650	9,500
2d Twn Lan	420	1,260	2,100	4,200	7,350	10,500
2d Diamond Jubilee	520	1,560	2,600	5,200	9,100	13,000
NOTE: Add 5 percent for T-tops.						
1979 V-8, 114" wb						
2d HT	360	1,080	1,800	3,600	6,300	9,000
2d HT Lan	380	1,140	1,900	3,800	6,650	9,500
2d HT Heritage	400	1,200	2,000	4,000	7,000	10,000
NOTE: Add 5 percent for T-tops.						
1980 V-8, 108" wb						
2d Cpe	240	720	1,200	2,400	4,200	6,000
2d Twn Lan Cpe	252	756	1,260	2,520	4,410	6,300
2d Silver Anniv. Cpe	260	780	1,300	2,600	4,550	6,500
1981 V-8, 108" wb						
2d Cpe	224	672	1,120	2,240	3,920	5,600
2d Twn Lan Cpe	232	696	1,160	2,320	4,060	5,800
2d Heritage Cpe	236	708	1,180	2,360	4,130	5,900
NOTE: Deduct 15 percent for 6-cyl.						

	6	5	4	3	2	1
1982 V-8, 108" wb						
2d Cpe	232	696	1,160	2,320	4,060	5,800
2d Twn Lan Cpe	240	720	1,200	2,400	4,200	6,000
2d Heritage Cpe	248	744	1,240	2,480	4,340	6,200
NOTE: Deduct 15 percent for V-6.						
1983 V-6						
2d Cpe	364	1,092	1,820	3,640	6,370	9,100
2d Cpe Heritage	376	1,128	1,880	3,760	6,580	9,400
1983 V-8						
2d Cpe	376	1,128	1,880	3,760	6,580	9,400
2d Cpe Heritage	392	1,176	1,960	3,920	6,860	9,800
1983 4-cyl.						
2d Cpe Turbo	380	1,140	1,900	3,800	6,650	9,500
1984 V-6						
2d Cpe	276	828	1,380	2,760	4,830	6,900
2d Cpe Elan	368	1,104	1,840	3,680	6,440	9,200
2d Cpe Fila	372	1,116	1,860	3,720	6,510	9,300
1984 V-8						
2d Cpe	376	1,128	1,880	3,760	6,580	9,400
2d Cpe Elan	384	1,152	1,920	3,840	6,720	9,600
2d Cpe Fila	388	1,164	1,940	3,880	6,790	9,700
NOTE: Deduct 10 percent for V-6 non turbo.						
1984 4-cyl.						
2d Cpe Turbo	376	1,128	1,880	3,760	6,580	9,400
1985 V-8, 104" wb						
2d Cpe	256	768	1,280	2,560	4,480	6,400
2d Elan Cpe	272	816	1,360	2,720	4,760	6,800
2d Fila Cpe	276	828	1,380	2,760	4,830	6,900
1985 4-cyl. Turbo						
2d Cpe	360	1,080	1,800	3,600	6,300	9,000
NOTE: Deduct 10 percent for V-6 non turbo.						
1986 104" wb						
2d Cpe	256	768	1,280	2,560	4,480	6,400
2d Elan Cpe	264	792	1,320	2,640	4,620	6,600
2d Turbo Cpe	368	1,104	1,840	3,680	6,440	9,200
1987 V-6, 104" wb						
2d Cpe	260	780	1,300	2,600	4,550	6,500
2d LX Cpe	264	792	1,320	2,640	4,620	6,600

1955 Thunderbird

	6	5	4	3	2	1
1987 V-8, 104" wb						
2d Cpe	360	1,080	1,800	3,600	6,300	9,000
2d Spt Cpe	368	1,104	1,840	3,680	6,440	9,200
2d LX Cpe	372	1,116	1,860	3,720	6,510	9,300
1987 4-cyl. Turbo						
2d Cpe	368	1,104	1,840	3,680	6,440	9,200
1988 V-6						
2d Cpe	180	540	900	1,800	3,150	4,500
2d LX Cpe	200	600	1,000	2,000	3,500	5,000
1988 V-8						
2d Spt Cpe	220	660	1,100	2,200	3,850	5,500
1988 4-cyl. Turbo						
2d Cpe	350	1,100	1,850	3,700	6,450	9,200

NOTE: Add 20 percent for V-8 where available.

	6	5	4	3	2	1
1989 V-6						
2d Cpe	272	816	1,360	2,720	4,760	6,800
2d LX Cpe	360	1,080	1,800	3,600	6,300	9,000
2d Sup Cpe	520	1,560	2,600	5,200	9,100	13,000
1990 V-6						
2d Cpe	260	780	1,300	2,600	4,550	6,500
2d LX Cpe	360	1,080	1,800	3,600	6,300	9,000
2d Sup Cpe	520	1,560	2,600	5,200	9,100	13,000

NOTE: Add 10 percent for Anniversary model.

	6	5	4	3	2	1
1991 V-6						
2d Cpe	240	720	1,200	2,400	4,200	6,000
2d LX Cpe	260	780	1,300	2,600	4,550	6,500
2d Sup Cpe	340	1,020	1,700	3,400	5,950	8,500
1991 V-8						
2d Cpe	360	1,080	1,800	3,600	6,300	9,000
2d LX Cpe	380	1,140	1,900	3,800	6,650	9,500

	6	5	4	3	2	1
1992 V-6						
2d Cpe	360	1,080	1,800	3,600	6,300	9,000
2d LX Cpe	368	1,104	1,840	3,680	6,440	9,200
2d Sup Cpe	380	1,140	1,900	3,800	6,650	9,500
1992 V-8						
2d Cpe	364	1,092	1,820	3,640	6,370	9,100
2d Spt Cpe	392	1,176	1,960	3,920	6,860	9,800
2d LX Cpe	380	1,140	1,900	3,800	6,650	9,500
1993 V-6						
2d LX Cpe	372	1,116	1,860	3,720	6,510	9,300
2d Sup Cpe	380	1,140	1,900	3,800	6,650	9,500
1993 V-8						
2d LX Cpe	404	1,212	2,020	4,040	7,070	10,100
1994 V-6						
2d LX Cpe	300	900	1,500	3,000	5,250	7,500
2d Sup Cpe	360	1,080	1,800	3,600	6,300	9,000
1994 V-8						
2d LX Cpe	320	960	1,600	3,200	5,600	8,000
1995 V-6						
2d LX Cpe	300	900	1,500	3,000	5,250	7,500
2d Sup Cpe	350	1,100	1,800	3,600	6,300	9,000
1995 V-8						
2d LX Cpe	300	950	1,600	3,200	5,600	8,000
1996 V-6						
2d LX Cpe	300	900	1,500	3,000	5,250	7,500

NOTE: Add 10 percent for V-8.

1960 Thunderbird

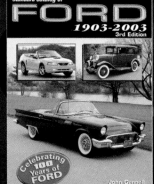

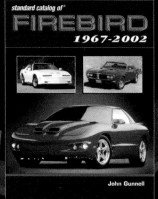